# WHEN JESUS COMES AGAIN

Great Christian Books
Lindenhurst, New York

# WHEN JESUS COMES AGAIN

## EVERETT I. CARVER

A GREAT CHRISTIAN BOOKS publication
Great Christian Books is a division of Rotolo Media
160 37th Street Lindenhurst, New York 11757 (631) 956-0998
www.GreatChristianBooks.com
email: mail@greatchristianbooks.com

When Jesus Comes Again ISBN 978-1-61010-135-6

©2013 Rotolo Media & Great Christian Books

All rights reserved under International and Pan-American Copyright Conventions. No part of this book maybe reproduced in any form, or by any means, electronic or mechanical, including photocopying, and informational storage and retrieval systems without the expressed written permission from the publisher, except in the case of brief quotations embodied in articles or reviews or promotional/advertising/catalog materials. For additional information or permissions, address all inquiries to the publisher.

Carver, Everett I., 1906-1989
When Jesus Comes Again / by Everett I. Carver, M.A., M. Div.
p. cm.
A "A Great Christian Book" book
GREAT CHRISTIAN BOOKS a division of Rotolo Media
ISBN 978-1-61010-135-6
Recommended Dewey Decimal Classifications: 228, 236.
1. Religion—Christian literature—Eschatology
2. Christianity—The Bible—Revelation
I. Title

The book and cover design for this title are by Michael Rotolo. It is typeset in the Minion and Myriad typefaces by Adobe Inc. and is quality manufactured in the United States on acid-free paper stock. To discuss the publication of your Christian manuscript or out-of-print book, please contact Great Christian Books.

MANUFACTURED IN THE GREAT UNITED STATES OF AMERICA

*Dedicated to those students who received a portion of their training under my instruction at Gulf-Coast Bible College.*

*It is hoped that this volume will add to the effectiveness of their ministries, and to the ministries of others whom I did not teach.*

This book is intended to be a comprehensive study of the last things (eschatology). It is designed for all earnest Bible students, but especially for young ministers, seminary students, Bible college students, and others who are developing their theological concepts. Present conditions "within the veil" receive some consideration, but the major thrust is about the second coming of Christ and events that are closely connected with it. Read the book for a fresh insight into those events, soundly based on biblical exegesis, quite foreign to the sensational type of reading that presently floods the market.

# CONTENTS

| | |
|---|---|
| **PREFACE** | 9 |
| **PART ONE - ESCHATOLOGICAL FOUNDATIONS** | 13 |
| THE KINGDOM OF GOD | 15 |
| THE KINGDOM OF GOD (continued) | 27 |
| HERMENEUTICS | 45 |
| HERMENEUTICS (continued) | 63 |
| ESCHATOLOGICAL SYSTEMS, TERMS, & HISTORICAL DATA | 81 |
| **PART TWO - THE ESCHATOLOGY OF THE OLD TESTAMENT** | 95 |
| THE ESCHATOLOGY OF THE PENTATEUCH | 97 |
| THE ESCHATOLOGY OF THE HISTORICAL & POETIC BOOKS | 115 |
| THE ESCHATOLOGY OF ISAIAH | 127 |
| THE ESCHATOLOGY OF JEREMIAH | 141 |
| THE ESCHATOLOGY OF EZEKIEL | 151 |
| THE ESCHATOLOGY OF DANIEL | 169 |
| THE ESCHATOLOGY OF THE MINOR PROPHETS | 197 |
| **PART THREE - THE ESCHATOLOGY OF THE NEW TESTAMENT** | 217 |
| THE SECOND COMING OF JESUS CHRIST | 219 |
| THE OLIVET DISCOURSE | 237 |
| THE OLIVET DISCOURSE (continued) | 257 |
| THE ESCHATOLOGY OF CHAPTERS 9-11 OF ROMANS | 279 |
| THE ESCHATOLOGY OF THE CORINTHIAN LETTERS | 299 |
| THE ESCHATOLOGY OF I & II THESSALONIANS | 313 |
| THE ESCHATOLOGY OF THE REVELATION | 339 |
| **PART FOUR - BEFORE AND AFTER THE SECOND COMING** | 367 |
| THE EVENTS PRECEDING THE RAPTURE | 369 |
| THE RAPTURE | 383 |
| ANTICHRIST & THE GREAT TRIBULATION | 399 |
| THE BATTLE OF ARMAGEDDON | 415 |
| THE MILLENNIUM | 429 |
| THE RESURRECTION OR RESURRECTIONS | 451 |
| A FINAL JUDGMENT OR A SERIES OF JUDGMENTS | 463 |

# PREFACE

Prior to the preparation of the manuscript for this book, several questions were seriously considered. Should the style be for popular consumption with an appeal that was strongly emotional, or should it be written for serious minded students of the Bible? Was there to be any effort at erudition and scholarship which so often results in vagueness or dullness, or was clarity of expression to be of prime importance? Was the proof-text method to be used, or must the approach be exegetically sound with proper attention being given to hermeneutical principles? And what about motivation? Just why write a book on the millennium and related events? And lastly, is there a need for such a book as *When Jesus Comes Again*.

Most of the answers came easily. My temperament, training, and teaching experience all militated against the popular, emotional approach. Having taught logic and hermeneutics as well as Bible and theology, a logical and rational approach properly balanced by a dependence on the Spirit of God and the word which He inspired, plus adequate consideration for proper exegesis and hermeneutics was the only style suitable to my orientation. I have no desire to appear erudite, nor am I interested in proving my scholarship to anyone; hence clarity of expression and incisiveness of thought are given high priority. Accordingly, foreign words will be spelled with English letters rather than with the original characters, because many who will read this book will not be familiar with the Greek and Hebrew alphabets.

I am strongly opposed to the proof-text method when used to link unrelated texts from several books of the Bible into a crazy quilt pattern or a hodgepodge picture that suits the writer's fancy. Only when the context adds little or nothing to the meaning, or when giving supportive evidence to teachings already validated on more solid exegesis, is this method acceptable. Any departures from this position are oversights, or are made necessary by space limitations.

A time of serious introspection during which the many reasons that others have for writing books, and which might be making some contribution to my motivation, has failed to reveal any motive other than that

God might be glorified, and that His *truth* might prevail in the hearts and minds of men. The reader is encouraged to study this volume as having been written by one who is an earnest Christian who feels he is obeying the admonition to "earnestly contend for the faith which was once delivered unto the saints" (Jude 3).

The need for this book will not be apparent to many. As a professor who has taught courses in eschatology, the need is apparent. Of course, my theological persuasion is part of the picture. But many books lack breadth. Even though these may be theologically acceptable to me, they elaborate more fully on specific areas while giving little or no attention to other related areas. In this volume some depth must be sacrificed in order to attain the breadth desired, but every effort has been made to confine these sacrifices to the less important subject material. I am chiefly concerned to make this book more exegetically and hermeneutically sound than most are.

Most readers desire to know something of the author's beliefs and presuppositions. It is semantically dangerous to make an effort to satisfy this very natural desire; however, you do have a right to know these things. I hold the Bible to be authoritative for all men whether or not they recognize it. The inspiration of the Bible is accepted without the least reservation. The Bible claims it, and I believe the Bible. This inspiration extends to the words as well as the ideas expressed. Though not dictated, I hold that God so closely supervised the writing of the books of the Bible that the original autographs expressed exactly what God wanted written, so that each book was completely free of error.

I further hold that properly transmitted and translated, and properly interpreted, no portion of the Bible will contradict any other portion of the Bible. The Bible not only contains the word of God; *it is the word of God!*

I accept the predictive elements of the Bible as from God and certain of fulfillment unless conditional in one or more aspects. It must be recognized that conditional elements may not be explicitly stated, and yet God has placed them there. The story of Jonah preaching to Nineveh is an example. Jonah intuitively knew it was there, but he was not permitted to verbally express it. When his prediction failed of fulfillment, he considered himself disgraced. Paul's prediction of safety for all on the boat also had a conditional element not stated at first (Acts 27:21-32). It is not held that any specific prophecies concerning Israel had unexpressed conditions which nullify them. It is only asserted that such is a possibility. But this is one of the several reasons why it is dangerous to set forth a dogmatic interpretation of prophecies relating to a specific nation.

The Old Testament is fully accepted as *the word of God* for that dispensation which preceded the first coming of Christ. The New Testament, however, is accepted as a fuller revelation from God, and it is the covenant under which we live today. The New Testament cannot be properly understood independent of the Old. On the other hand, the New Testament furnishes much light on aspects of the Old Testament. Therefore, I hold that the Old Testament should be interpreted in the light of New Testament teachings, rather than force the New Testament to teach what may have been gathered from the Old Testament independent of the New.

It is firmly believed that the unconditional promises of the Old Testament either have been fulfilled or will be fulfilled in the future. Commentators are in general agreement that many of the Old Testament prophecies have been fulfilled, but for many others there are differences of opinion. My tendency is to accept a spiritual fulfillment in many places that others are strongly convinced require a physical type of fulfillment.

My reason for taking this position is that the New Testament, as I understand it, supports this view. It is recognized that those who hold to a future fulfillment that is physical in nature are as set in the defense of the Bible as I am, but it is my opinion that they are misinterpreting the word of God. Reasons for this view will appear from time to time in the body of this book. The following paragraph will serve for the present in this connection.

In Exodus 3:8 God promised Israel "a land flowing with milk and honey." In Jeremiah 32:22 and elsewhere it is claimed that Israel was given a land which "flowed with milk and honey." I have yet to find a literalist who claims that there were literal streams of milk and of honey in the land of Canaan. I see no more reason for holding that many of the Old Testament prophecies which the New Testament says were fulfilled in a spiritual sense are yet to be fulfilled in a literal sense, than to hold that God must yet give Israel literal streams of milk and of honey in Palestine. Bear this in mind as we study Ezekiel, Isaiah, Joel, Matthew chapter 24 and Revelation.

The reader is invited to peruse the pages of this book for answers regarding my belief about the millennium, the rapture, the tribulation, the judgment or judgments, the resurrection or resurrections, the second coming or comings, and other eschatological events. It is hoped that each reader will consider the teachings of this book prayerfully and thoughtfully as befits any Bible student. My prayer is that God will guide you in your final acceptance or rejection of any or all views which are set forth in this volume. I am equally earnest in praying that, if I am in error at any point, the Holy Spirit will reveal this unto me.

Bible college teachers are urged to study this volume, regardless of their particular eschatological persuasions. It is hoped that it will be recommended for collateral reading, even by professors who disagree with many of its teachings. After all, students need to be exposed to more than one view of what awaits mankind in the consummation. For those who are in general agreement with what is contained in this book, consideration of its adoption as a textbook will be appreciated.

Should you feel a disproportionate amount of this book is taken up in refuting the positions of others, please bear in mind that a flood of material of the sensational type is being marketed today. A positive position without a serious effort to prove contrary teachings are false will not adequately meet the need that exists. This is particularly true of students who are in the process of forming their own theology. Attacks made on the teachings of others are made in Christian love, though the approach is positive and firm. I do not permit differences in theology to separate me from those who hold opposing views, unless the doctrines involve the essential nature of Christ and the plan of redemption. On the other hand, I cannot be loyal to God, to His word, and to my own conscience without standing firm for what I believe to be the truth on the subjects discussed in this book.

To my wife I wish to express my appreciation for her understanding and sacrificial release of time which normally have been spent with her. My gratitude is extended to those laymen and ministers who have encouraged me in my writings, especially through the way they have received my previous works. My colleagues at Gulf-Coast Bible College have also been a source of very real encouragement. For the many students who have assisted me by their expressions of appreciation, I am deeply indebted. To students who have challenged my positions from time to time, I say, Thank you. This has stimulated further research and reevaluation. To those ministers, teachers, and writers who have helped me formulate my own views, I acknowledge my debt. For that which is profitable in this volume, I give credit to the Holy Spirit. For that which is chaff, I assume the responsibility.

A firm believer in the "blessed hope,"
Everett I. Carver

## — PART ONE —

# ESCHATOLOGICAL FOUNDATIONS

Essential material for understanding the several systems of eschatology (last things), as well as the bases upon which the views expressed in this volume are built, and specific interpretations are made.

CHAPTER 1

# THE KINGDOM OF GOD

Some books on eschatology omit any discussion of the kingdom of God, but inasmuch as this book is designed to be comprehensive, this subject demands attention. Certain systems of eschatology claim the kingdom was established at Christ's first advent and exists at this present time. Others contend it is yet future. The former generally hold that the Church is an expression of the kingdom, whereas the latter believe a future civil rule is yet to be established with Christ reigning as a literal monarch, for no such rule of Christ has been established thus far. These questions are necessarily involved in any interpretation placed upon eschatological events. Chapters 1 and 2 set forth the author's views regarding the nature of the kingdom of God and whether or not it was established at Christ's first coming or is to be established later.

There is a sense in which the entire cosmos constitutes the kingdom of God. One Old Testament text uses the term "kingdom" in this sense. It reads in part, "All that is in the heaven and in the earth is thine; thine is the kingdom, O Lord, and thou art exalted as head above all" (I Chron. 29:11). The term "kingdom" is frequently applied to the Israelitish nation, and there is ample evidence that this was a kingdom that enjoyed a special relationship to God, but the specific expressions "kingdom of God" and "kingdom of heaven" are not used of the kingdom of Israel. In fact, Jesus clearly distinguishes between the two. Following the centurion's expression of implicit faith in Jesus' power over sickness and disease, Jesus said,—

> And I say unto you, That many shall come from the east and west, and shall sit down with Abraham, and Isaac, and Jacob, in the kingdom of heaven. But the children of the kingdom shall be cast out into outer darkness: there shall be weeping and gnashing of teeth (Matt. 8:11-12).

In this passage it can hardly be questioned that "children of the kingdom" refers to the Jews and to that political division of the Roman empire which they occupied. In other words the reference was to the kingdom of Israel according to the flesh. But in the preceding verse, Jesus had spoken of the "kingdom of heaven," and He sharply contrasts these two kingdoms. The inference is that Gentiles will enter the kingdom of heaven in place of Jews, and that in the final consummation Jews would be condemned to "outer darkness." This distinction and eschatological meaning should be kept in mind as the meaning of the kingdom of God is explored more fully. It is also vital to understanding Paul's statement, "And so all Israel shall be saved" (Rom. 11:26). Jews can be lost according to Jesus' teaching.

Another possible meaning of the term "kingdom of God" could be the moral rule God exercises over all mankind, evil as well as good. But this kind of kingdom, like that of the cosmos, has been in existence throughout human history, hence could hardly be considered a "future" development, nor a "new" addition to kingdoms already established. Most of the prophecies of the kingdom of God came during the existence of Israel as a kingdom, hence could not apply to that kingdom as something new or something yet future. In fact, both John the Baptist and Christ announced the coming of the kingdom of God as something previously nonexistent. Though its rootages goes back at least as far as Abraham, it was indeed a new dimension in God's redemptive plan. Jesus Himself said, "The time is fulfilled" (the time established by the prophecies of the Old Testament) "and the kingdom of God is at hand" (Mark 1:15).

## Jewish Expectations

To set forth the totality of Jewish expectations in relation to the coming kingdom would extend the limits of this chapter division into a volume of its own, therefore only a brief summary is attempted. We know the Jews expected the advent of a king, a savior or deliverer, for Matthew records, "There came wise men from the east to Jerusalem saying, Where is he that is born king of the Jews?" Later, Herod "demanded of them where Christ should be born. And they said unto him, In Bethlehem of Judaea" (Matt. 2:2-5). It should be noted that two designations are found in this passage. One is "king"; the other is "Christ."

The Hebrew term for Christ most familiar to Americans is Messiah. It comes from the Hebrew *mashiach* or *mashach*. It means to anoint, and when used of Christ it means "the anointed One." The Greek *messias* is a form of these words, whereas the specific Greek term that has the same meaning is *christos* or Christ. The Jewish elders correctly interpreted Micah 5:2 as referring to the future king, and to His title of Christ, the anointed One. However, very little of the remaining expectations they had are supported by the Scripture.

One of the mistakes of the Jews was in literalizing Old Testament prophecies to an extent that their true meaning was not only obscured, but actually distorted into a meaning foreign to the intent of the Scripture. A second error was to misapply the "Suffering Servant" passages to themselves instead of to the Christ. They failed to discern that these two lines of prophecy portrayed two distinct aspects of the coming King and Messiah. Even His disciples did not fully understand this truth until after Pentecost.

They also misinterpreted the kingly prophecies. They anticipated a king who would deliver them from Roman rule and establish the Jewish nation as sovereign over many of the other nations of the world. The disciples apparently were unable to disabuse their minds of this same error until after Pentecost, even though Christ had explained this on several occasions. Christ tried to get the idea to them, but preconceived notions are often difficult to remove. This is just as true today as it was in the time of Christ's incarnation.

Included in the Jewish expectations were one thousand years of carnal pleasures. The Zealots tended to anticipate a political state to be instituted by the Messiah. No doubt many others who were not Zealots did likewise. The apocalyptists expected this to be accomplished miraculously. A reading of the *Apocalypse of Baruch,* especially chapters 29, 72 and 73, and the *Book of Enoch,* chapters 10 and 11, reveals preposterous claims of what will occur during this golden age of the Jewish hegemony. It is unfortunate that some of these Jewish errors are being propagated in the Church today.

## What Kind of Kingdom Did Jesus Come to Establish?

I sincerely regret the necessity of this chapter division. The New Testament so vigorously supports the idea that Christ, from the very first, came to establish a moral and ethical kingdom that it would seem that any other view is completely ruled out. However, such men as Scofield, Walvoord, Blackstone and others have developed a system of interpretation that denies this. The main support for their approach is the claim that Old

Testament prophecies were not fulfilled at Christ's first coming, hence must be fulfilled at a later coming. This requires that constructions be placed on New Testament material for which there is no exegetical or hermeneutical justification. I refer specifically and pointedly to the claim that Jesus came to offer, and did indeed offer, to the Jews a civil type kingdom such as they envisioned, and that because the Jews rejected this offer, He changed His plan from establishing a kingdom to that of dying on the cross, and establishing a fellowship called the Church. This makes the Church an afterthought; a substitute measure to at least temporarily cover over His inability to accomplish the mission He had originally intended to accomplish. Dispensational writers, and others who have accepted this view, often refer to this as "The Great Parenthesis."

The implications of this doctrine are tremendous. Some of these will be considered near the close of this section. But right now, the basis on which this teaching rests must receive consideration. Scofield's note on Matthew 11:20 makes this text the point where the Jews "morally rejected" the offer of a civil kingdom though he recognizes that the official rejection was the crucifixion. Then in his note on Matthew 11:28, he indicates that Christ was presenting an entirely new message of rest to those who would seek it. He adds, "It is a pivotal point in the ministry of Jesus."[1]

Walvoord places Matthew 16:17-18 as the point of changed emphasis. He writes, "Of major significance is the declaration 'I will build my church.' What is here contemplated is *obviously* not a continuation of that which had begun in the Old Testament....He proclaims a *new* divine purpose, namely the formation of a new assembly to be delineated on spiritual rather than racial lines and without territorial or political characteristics" (emphasis added).[2] What appears so "obvious" to Dr. Walvoord is not all that obvious to many biblical scholars.

A study of the writings of various authors who support the view briefly outlined above reveals little contextual analysis upon which they base their claims. In most cases the reader is expected to accept it on the basis of the writer's word. Does Matthew say that his 11th chapter is "pivotal"? Not at all. It is Dr. Scofield who says it is. Does Matthew indicate that what Jesus

---

1 C. I. Scofield, *The Scofield Reference Bible.* Quoted material is from the original work rather than the revised volume. Locations will be given in the body of this volume rather than in footnotes.
2 John F. Walvoord, *The Church In Prophecy*, p. 21

said about the Church in chapter 16 is something new? By no means. It is Walvoord who says so. We might go so far as to ask why Walvoord did not add verse 19 to his statement? In this verse, Jesus speaks of giving the "keys of the kingdom of heaven" as if the Church of verse 18 were closely related to, if not identical to, the kingdom of heaven. Matthew's use of two different terms does not require that he is speaking of two separate institutions. In fact, Matthew employs the two terms as synonyms.

Dr. Walvoord trips himself by claiming a change in Christ's plans. He claims that Christ came to do two things that cannot be reconciled. He asserts, "Christ was come to reveal God, to present Himself to Israel as their king, to die on the cross as our Redeemer…but undergirding the whole was the divine purpose to found the church as the supreme example of the grace of God in time and eternity."[3] Now if Christ came to establish a political kingdom such as Walvoord envisions, He did not come to die on the cross, nor did He come to establish the Church. However, if He came to establish a spiritual kingdom which is but a synonym for the Church, then these two purposes are not only compatible, but they are complementary. Seemingly, Walvoord does not recognize his inconsistency. Most writers of the Dispensational persuasion frankly avoid this inconsistency by making the Church an afterthought or a parenthesis.

Did Christ come to die for our sins and to establish the Church? The answer is definitely, Yes. God planned this before the creation of man. The Revelator pictures Christ as "the Lamb slain from the foundation of the world" (Rev. 13:8). That critical problems exist regarding this text is admitted. But Alford states it very cogently, "The difficulty however is but apparent: I Peter 1:19-20 says more fully the same thing. That the death of Christ which was foreordained from the foundation of the world, is said to have *taken place* in the counsel of Him with whom the end and the beginning are one."[4]

Many texts agree with this concept. Matthew says the use of the thirty pieces of silver given to Judas for the purchase of a potter's field (Matt. 27:9-10) was a fulfillment of an Old Testament prophecy (Zech. 11:12-13). The Psalmist wrote, "They gave me also gall for my meat; and in my thirst they gave me vinegar to drink" (Ps. 69:21). This was fulfilled during

---

[3] Walvoord, *op. cit.*, p. 1 of Preface.
[4] Henry Alford, *The Greek Testament*, vol. 4, p. 677.

Christ's crucifixion (Matt. 27:34). In like manner the gambling for His clothing was a fulfillment of prophecy (Ps. 22:18; Matt. 27:35; John 19:24). The piercing of Christ's side was foreseen by the prophet (Zech. 12:10; John 19:34, 37). But why multiply texts? Just read Isaiah 53 and see God's redemptive plan set forth.

Jesus testifies to the same truth. To the two on the road to Emmaus He said, "Ought not Christ to have suffered these things?" (John 24:26). Then later He said, "Thus is it written, and thus it behooved Christ to suffer, and to rise from the dead the third day: And that repentance and remission of sins should be preached in his name among all nations, beginning at Jerusalem" (Luke 24:46-47). What is Jesus saying? He is saying that those who deny His major purpose was to come to suffer for sin and to establish a fellowship of believers (the Church), have somehow misinterpreted His mission into the world.

Assuming that Christ did indeed offer a political kingdom to the Jews, what would have happened had they accepted it? Dispensationalists usually say that God would have found some other way. But not one text of Scripture do they offer to support this assumption. On the contrary, Jesus prayed three times for the Father to relieve Him of the cross if such could be done without breaking the will of the Father. Surely God would have answered this most pitiful cry of His Son had there been any other way! But there was no other way. Jesus had to die to fulfill Old Testament prophecy, and His death was prophesied for it was the only way man could be redeemed.

There is general agreement that Christ came to establish a kingdom. The lack of agreement is over the kind of kingdom He came to establish. Having looked at some of the background of His coming, and reasons why we know He came to establish a spiritual kingdom rather than a civil one, His actual appearance is considered. Matthew tells us His name was to be called Jesus, "for he shall save his people from their sins" (Matt. 1:21). Thus the announcement of Christ's advent included the idea of His death for our sins. This is contrary to the teaching that He came to establish a political kingdom. Simeon's testimony to Mary to the effect that she would suffer because of Christ (Luke 2:35) apparently has reference to her anguish over the torture Jesus had to endure. This does not sound as if He was to set up a political kingdom.

John the Baptist recognized Jesus as "The Lamb of God" (John 1:36). In verse 29 it is this Lamb of God "which taketh away the sin of the world." Thus even before Jesus began to preach, the redemptive nature of His coming was fully recognized. John also recognized Jesus as the bridegroom (John 3:29) very early in the ministry of Jesus. Likewise Jesus understood He was the bridegroom (Matt. 9:15; Mark 2:19; Luke 5:34-35). Now for Christ to be the bridegroom, there must have been a bride. It is recognized that Israel is spoken of as married to God in the Old Testament, but in New Testament symbolism, the bride is always the Church ( Matt. 22:1-14; II Cor. 11:2; Rev. 19:7; 21:2, 9, 10; 22:17; Eph. 5:22-32). Thus the word *ekklesia* is not found very early in Jesus' ministry, but the idea is.

John the Baptist also recognized Jesus as the one who would send the Holy Spirit upon the Church. He declared, "I indeed baptize you with water unto repentance: but he…shall baptize you with the Holy Ghost and with fire" (Matt. 3:11). This was fulfilled on the day of Pentecost, and on other occasions (Acts 2). What was this that John foresaw, but the Church being empowered for her task and functioning as propagators of the gospel of Jesus Christ? With this array of evidence that the Church was envisioned from the very start of Jesus' ministry and even before, it is amazing that learned men who are at the same time godly men, can be so blind as to contend that the Church does not come into focus until Matthew 11 or 16.

Mark tells us that Jesus preached, "The time is fulfilled, and the kingdom of God is at hand: repent and believe the gospel" (Mark 1:15). This was probably at the beginning of Jesus' second year of preaching the gospel. Several things require attention here. Did Jesus preach two gospels? Did he begin preaching a civil kingdom for the Jews and call this a gospel, and later preach deliverance from sin as another gospel? Hardly. What was the time that was fulfilled? Nothing more nor less than that the kingdom which was promised in the Old Testament was now about to become a reality. Was Jesus mistaken in this? Paul tells us it is preferable to consider "every man a liar" (Rom. 3:4), rather than that God be untrue. It is tragic that men fail to recognize the impossible situation they put Christ into by contending He was mistaken on the one hand, or that He taught two gospels on the other. Neither of these should be acceptable to one who believes in the deity of Jesus Christ.

Scofield goes so far as to classify the "Sermon on the Mount" as "pure law" (note on Matt. 5:2). Jesus is thus accused of preaching law rather than gospel. In this same notation he adds. "The Sermon on the Mount in its primary application gives neither the privilege nor the duty of the Church.

These are found in the epistles." He means that these teachings of Christ are not for us today. But Jesus commissioned us to include these duties: "Teaching them to observe all things whatsoever I have commanded you" (Matt. 28:20). And that includes the Sermon on the Mount. Jesus was "preaching the gospel" (Matt. 4:23) in chapter 4, and Matthew doesn't say he switched to preaching law in chapters 5-7. It is Scofield who says that He did. The Bible knows nothing of Christ teaching law.

Not only does the repentance that both John and Christ demanded in their proclamation of the coming of the kingdom prove the ethical and moral nature of the kingdom, as opposed to a political kingdom, but the baptism they required is part of the gospel the Church is charged to proclaim. It is impossible to distinguish between the repentance and baptism that Christ taught in his proclamation of the kingdom, and the repentance (Luke 24:47) and baptism (Matt. 28:19) the Church is enjoined to preach and to practice. This indicates that the gospel of the kingdom is the same as the gospel the Church preaches. It follows that what Christ offered the Jews is the same thing the Church now offers to all men. Christ did offer the Jews a kingdom, but it was a spiritual kingdom which finds its fulfillment in the Church, rather than a political kingdom such as is taught by Dispensationalists and most Premillennialists of today.

Jesus' refusal to permit Himself to be made king clearly establishes the nature of the kingdom He offered the Jews. Following the feeding of the five thousand some wanted to take Him "by force to make him a king" (John 6:15), but He would not permit it. Had Jesus planned to establish a political kingdom among the Jews with Himself as king, that was His chance. Christ's refusal to jump at this opportunity is strong evidence that the kingdom He came to establish was not a political one. Advocates of a future political kingdom of the Jews usually lay great stress on the refusals of the Jews to accept Christ, but strangely enough this particular incident is ignored by such advocates. Had Christ offered the Jews a political kingdom, they would have accepted Him and it. The Jews were well aware that Christ offered them a spiritual kingdom, rather than a political one, and this is the very reason they rejected His offer.

Christ taught that His kingdom was spiritual in nature. The Pharisees very pointedly asked Jesus when the kingdom of God would come (Luke 17:20). Since they looked for a political kingdom, Jesus knew they would not be satisfied with a statement to the effect that it was already established.

# The Kingdom of God

He had given them such a statement in Matthew 12:28 and they had not received it. Therefore, He attempted to explain to them the spiritual nature of the kingdom He came to establish. He said, "The kingdom of God cometh not with observation." The NEB translates, "You cannot tell by observation when the kingdom of God comes. There will be no saying, 'Look here it is!' or 'There it is!' " Then, regardless of whether the translation is "within" or "among you," Jesus affirmed that the kingdom He came to establish was at that time a reality.

Scofield admits a "spiritual aspect" to the kingdom (see his insertion between Luke 17:19 and 20), but he contends for a deferred, political aspect (see reference given above and reference inserted between Luke 19:10 and 11). If this is true, then Christ is guilty of double talk. The Pharisees definitely asked about the establishment of a Jewish political kingdom. If Jesus meant the spiritual aspect of His kingdom was then operative, but the political aspect would come centuries later, He is guilty of deceit. But we know that no "guile" (*dolos*—baiting, deceitfulness) was ever "found in his mouth" (I Pet. 2:22). One is wise to accept Christ's words at face value, rather than to follow Scofield's devious reasoning. Those who follow Scofield's specious reasoning have real trouble harmonizing the saying of Jesus regarding the invisibility of His kingdom (Luke 17:20-21) with their later claims of all Jews being converted in a single day (try to imagine the headlines and news releases that would incite) and Jesus reigning visibly from Jerusalem.

If the kingdom were deferred, as many claim, then Christ's kingship must also be deferred. But Jesus asserted His kingship right to the very end. The week of His passion is just as definite as the time of His birth. Christ's triumphal entry into Jerusalem just before His trial and crucifixion was a declaration of His kingship. Those who contend this was a final offer of a political kingdom to Israel obtain this from a fruitful imagination and not from exegesis. The prophecy is given as a proclamation of the kingship of the Messiah (Zech. 9:9), not an offer to become king. The same is true of the Gospel accounts which record the fulfillment of this prophecy. Jesus accepted the role of King in this instance just as surely as he accepted it from the wise men following His birth.

Jesus again affirmed His kingship during His questioning by Pilate. Surely if the kingdom were deferred until later, and if the kingship of Jesus were likewise deferred, some inkling of it would be given here. The absence of such is significant. To Pilate's question regarding His kingship, "Art thou the king of the Jews?" Jesus replied, "My kingdom is not of this world: if my kingdom were of this world, then would my servants fight, that I should not be delivered to the Jews, but now is my kingdom not from hence" (John 18:33-36). In the next verse Pilate again asked, "Art thou a king then?" In answer Jesus said, "Thou sayest that I am a king." Most commentators agree that this constitutes an affirmation. It is somewhat equivalent to our statement, "You have said it." He then adds, "To this end was I born, and for this cause I came into the world, that I shall bear witness unto the truth." His kingship was certainly one aspect of this truth to which He witnessed.

Jesus stood accused before Pilate. The charge before the Jewish Sanhedrin had been blasphemy, but before Pilate He was accused of treason. Now if Jesus had come to establish a political kingdom of the Jews, as most Premillennialists affirm, according to Roman law He would have been guilty, and, according to law, worthy of death. If Christ had defended Himself by denying that He had intended to overthrow the Roman rule over the Jews, when in fact He had intended to do just that, He would have been guilty of falsification as well as treason. This doctrine of the postponement of the kingdom thus implies that Christ was guilty of sin as well as guilty of treason against Rome. The facts are that He was not guilty of either. While He continued to assert His kingship, Christ again emphatically testified that His kingdom was not of this world. In other words He had never intended to establish a political kingdom. The peacefulness of His followers and their refusal to fight in His defense is added as supportive evidence that the testimony He had just given was true and correct.

Now Pilate was astute enough to recognize the validity of the defense Christ made. It is not claimed that Pilate fully perceived the spiritual nature of Christ's kingdom and His kingship, but he was convinced it posed no threat to Roman rule. To those who had attempted to trap Him into outright opposition to Roman rule, Jesus had said, "Render therefore unto Caesar the things which are Caesar's; and unto God the things that are God's" (Matt. 22:21). Throughout the ministry of Christ, He proclaimed a kingdom that was spiritual in nature. Those who contend otherwise do disservice to our Lord.

The nonviolent nature of the kingdom is supported by Old Testament prophecy as well as by the testimony of the New Testament. Two words depict Christ's rule. These are "love" and "peace." These must ever remain paramount in the kingdom Christ came to establish. However, it is a sad commentary that many Premillennial writers envision a complete reversal of this program sometime in the future. Any teaching that has the followers of Jesus taking up physical weapons of warfare should be suspect because it is contrary to the whole tenor of the Scripture. It should further be noted that those who contend the followers of Christ will engage in such warfare are usually of the persuasion that Christ came to set up a political kingdom which they say was deferred, but that it will be set up some time yet future.

Dispensationalists and the majority of Premillennialists hold with Scofield that the future Messianic kingdom will "be established by power, not persuasion" (Scofield's note 2 on Zech. 12:8). Many envision this as being accomplished by a war of unparalleled carnage. Such an alleged reversal in the very nature of Christ our Lord is contrary to the evidence. The idea that the kingdom would be established by force is so foreign to the tenor of the New Testament that it is almost inconceivable that such a teaching could be accepted.

The Church has rejected this strange teaching with a fair degree of consistency prior to the present century. Yet, a multitude of followers of the Prince of Peace now envision the possibility of their taking up arms to force Christ's rule on others and to kill those who resist. To change from spiritual weapons and a spiritual warfare to carnal weapons and carnal warfare is not the message of Christ and the New Testament. This teaching cannot be harmonized with Christ's statement, "My kingdom is not of this world: if my kingdom were of this world, then would my servants fight, that I should not be delivered to the Jews: but now is my kingdom not from hence" (John 18:36). And I hasten to add, it never will be! Praise God, His kingdom is spiritual in nature, and it will always be spiritual in nature.

If Jesus must eventually establish His kingdom by force, why did not He do so at His first coming? He claimed twelve legions of angels were at His disposal (Matt. 26:53), and that all power in heaven and earth were His (Matt. 28:18). Had Christ come to establish an earthly kingdom, He could have utilized this unlimited power to accomplish His objective. He could have forced submission just as easily then as at His second coming.

CHAPTER 2

# THE KINGDOM OF GOD
## (CONTINUED)

### Did Christ Establish a Kingdom?

The New Testament repeatedly affirms, often in the words of Jesus Himself, that Christ did establish a kingdom at His first coming. It has been pointed out already that Jesus declared His kingdom was at hand (Matt. 3:2). Later He proclaimed that the kingdom "Is come unto you" (Matt. 12:28). He even established a time limit for the fully established kingdom to become a functional reality. This time limit was the life span of individuals then living. All three Synoptic writers declare that some then living would not die until after the power of His kingdom was fully operative.

Matthew records Jesus as saying, "There be some standing here, which shall not taste of death, till they see the Son of man coming in his kingdom" (Matt. 16:28). This is capable of being translated "King" instead of kingdom (see TEV). Mark phrases it as, "There be some of them that stand here, which shall not taste of death, till they have seen the kingdom of God come with power" (Mark 9:11). Luke states it more simply, "There be some standing here, which shall not taste of death, till they see the kingdom of God" (Luke 9:27). These three witnesses have Jesus boldly proclaiming that the kingdom He came to institute would become a reality during the lifetime of persons present. Mark adds the idea of "power" and Matthew may mean the establishment of Christ as King.

Now Jesus either did establish His kingdom within the time limit He Himself set, or He is convicted of being a false prophet. Those who accept the deity of Christ and the inspiration of the Bible must believe that Christ spoke the truth and nothing but the truth. That being the case, we must believe that Christ did establish His kingdom during the first Christian century. Thus Christ's kingship is presently being exercised from His mediatorial throne in heaven; the coming with power probably refers to Pentecost and the enduement of power which accompanied it (Acts 1:8); and the tremendous impact of the Church during that first Christian century gave visible evidence of the spiritual power being exercised.

For those who insist that the kingdom must be political in nature, we refer such back to chapter one and that portion that deals with the kind of kingdom Christ came to establish. It is not to come in a manner that is ostentatious. Those who contend that the kingdom will become a reality in the future through the conversion of the total Jewish population of that time in a single day fail to take Jesus seriously at this point. I can envision the headlines and telecasts of that event should it become a reality. But Jesus said His kingdom would work gradually like leaven, or like a plant growing. His kingdom would not begin by any such spectacular events as the conversion of the entire Jewish population of that day, plus the return of Christ and the Church from a seven year marriage festival.

Those who insist that Christ will establish His government in Jerusalem also fail to give adequate credence to Jesus' statement that the kingdom of God was not the kind of kingdom which could be said to be "Lo here!" or "Lo there!" as could be said if Christ ruled from Jerusalem. He insisted that His kingdom was "within" people or "among" people. But we must consider several facts as well as these general statements.

Jesus makes John the Baptist the connecting link between the law and the kingdom of God. His words are, "The law and the prophets were until John: since that time the kingdom of God is preached, and every man presseth into it" (Luke 16:16). John is not placed in the kingdom for he was the one sent to prepare the way for Christ, but Jesus claimed that since the time of John people were truly entering the *kingdom of God*. What kingdom were these people entering? Jesus said they were entering the kingdom of God. If he means something other than that they were entering the kingdom He had announced as being at hand, the least that can be said is that He is guilty of what logicians call the fallacy of equivocation. This involves a verbal shift of meaning for a term which is not explained.

The credibility of Christ is the issue we face. Did Jesus use a verbal shift of meaning, a semantical dodge to cover up His inability to establish a Jewish political unit with Himself as king? Those who explain plain statements of Christ in this fashion are guilty of importing preconceived notions into the text, as well as utilizing some fancy hermeneutical gymnastics and logical acrobatics. Jesus said folks were entering the "kingdom of God."

# The Kingdom of God - continued

John the Baptist is made the connecting link between the law of Moses and the kingdom of God (Luke 16:16). If the kingdom is yet future, as Premillennialists contend, then John is the most elongated person in all history, for nearly 2,000 years have elapsed since Jesus spoke these words. If the kingdom is yet future, and if the Church is a parenthesis, then the Church is the connecting link between the law and the kingdom. This would require that Jesus be in error in saying that John was the connecting link.

In Christ's high priestly prayer He said, "I have finished the work which thou gavest me to do" (John 17:4). Now if Christ came to establish a Jewish political kingdom, He failed miserably. Yet, this is what many writers and preachers are telling the Church. Now it was prophesied that Christ would not fail. "Behold my servant, whom I uphold: mine elect, in whom my soul delighteth....He shall not fail" (Isa. 42:1-4). Even Scofield admits this relates to His "first advent" (note on Isaiah 42:1). Jesus testified, "The works that I do" are "the works which the Father hath given me to finish" (John 5:36). Hence if He attempted to establish a kingdom, He did establish that kingdom, else His claim to have "finished the work" He was given to do (John 17:4) is utterly false.

All are agreed that Christ did not establish a Jewish political state. If Christ came to do that, then Christ failed, utterly and completely. Could our beloved Son of God fail to accomplish a mission He was given to perform? What a ghastly thought! But Jesus does not admit failure. Instead He testifies triumphantly, "I have finished the work which thou gavest me to do" (John 17:4). Was this statement false like Saul's who earlier had said, "I have performed the commandment of the Lord" (I Sam. 15:13)? God forbid. It was not Christ who failed. It is those who misinterpret the intents and actions of Jesus that are at fault. Christ came to set up a spiritual kingdom, and He did just that. Christ did not fail.

Did the early Church understand the spiritual nature of the kingdom? The evidence indicates they did not until after Pentecost. During the forty days between Christ's resurrection and ascension He taught the disciples many things "pertaining to the kingdom of God" (Acts 1:3). The context (vv. 4 and 5) indicates that the focal point of these discussions was the coming of the Holy Spirit in a baptism of spiritual empowerment. It should be evident that this referred to the activities of the new fellowship, the Church if you please, and not to some distant political coup that some have conjured up. Much has been made of the fact that the question was asked, "Lord, wilt thou at this time restore again the kingdom to Israel?" (Acts 1:6), and the fact that Jesus did not plainly tell them that the kingdom was now available to the Jews, and that their idea of a political ascendancy coming to the Jews was a misconception. But these give little consideration to the testimony found in the Acts of the Apostles which shows the truth was understood after Pentecost.

Toward the close of Jesus' ministry, He said, "I have yet many things to say unto you, but ye cannot bear them now. Howbeit when he, the Spirit of truth, is come, he will guide you into all truth" (John 16:12-13). Previously He had said that the Comforter would "bring all things to your remembrance, whatsoever I have said unto you" (John 14:26). The Jewish expectation of a political kingdom for the Jews was so strong in the disciples that Christ's efforts to show them the error of their anticipations had been fruitless. For Him to have dashed their hopes to the ground just when He was about to leave them would have been cruel and disheartening. Instead, Christ simply left it to the Holy Spirit to bring to their minds the truths He had taught them, but which they did not grasp.

That the Holy Spirit did instruct them is evident from later recordings in the Acts. Philip traveled to Samaria and "preached Christ unto them" (Acts 8:5). Then Luke records, "But when they believed Philip preaching the things concerning the kingdom of God, and the name of Jesus Christ, they were baptized, both men and women" (Acts 8:12). Unquestionably, the Church is functioning at this point. But note that Philip's message was "concerning the kingdom of God" as well as about Christ. In fact one cannot preach Christ without preaching the biblical kingdom of God.

That the last statement above is true can be seen from the text itself. The result of this preaching of the "kingdom of God" was that these people believed on Jesus Christ and were baptized. Preaching against sin, and showing the need for repentance is to preach the kingdom of God. This is what Christ Himself came preaching. Would people have accepted Christ and been born again had Philip been preaching about a supposed future political triumph of the Jewish nation? Not at all, for the Jews and Samaritans had strong antipathies toward each other. Will the Arabs of today get saved on that message? Hardly. I doubt if anyone would. It would never have moved me to repent.

Paul was permitted to speak for three months in the Jewish synagogue at Ephesus. His message focused on "the things concerning the kingdom

# The Kingdom of God - continued

of God" (Acts 19:8). In the next verse we are informed that strong opposition arose which made it necessary for Paul to move to "the school of one Tyrannus" (Acts 19:9). The question naturally arises, Why did the Jews reject Paul? For no other reason than that his message conflicted with their expectations. And what were their expectations? The same as Dispensationalism and Premillennialism are preaching today: the political ascendancy of the Jewish nation. The strong Jewish opposition Paul faced throughout his ministry is evidence that his message of the "kingdom of God" was not in accord with these views.

Several years later, after a number of churches had been established in the vicinity of Ephesus, Paul met with the elders of the Ephesian church. What had Paul been preaching among them? Here, near the close of his missionary journeys, he testified, "I know that ye all, among whom I have gone preaching the kingdom of God, shall see my face no more" (Acts 20:25). What had produced the cluster of congregations around Ephesus? Simply preaching the kingdom of God. But preaching a future ascendancy of the Jews will not produce Christian churches. Therefore, Paul was evidently preaching the same ethical and moral message that Christ proclaimed.

Twice in the closing chapter of Acts, Luke emphasizes that the message Paul preached was about the "kingdom of God." First, "He expounded and testified the kingdom of God, persuading them concerning Jesus, both out of the law of Moses, and out of the prophets" (Acts 28:23). Thus the message of Paul regarding the reality of the kingdom of God in that day was taken from the law and the prophets or the Old Testament. In other words, the Old Testament record is being interpreted contrary to the way Paul interpreted it, if it is made to teach a future Jewish state, rather than the present gospel and Holy Spirit age. Luke's account of Peter's second sermon is even more pointed. After proclaiming the necessity of Christ's suffering, and calling on his hearers to repent (Acts 3:18-19), he declares that "all the prophets from Samuel and those that follow after, so many as have spoken, have likewise told of these days" (Acts 3:24).

Thus both Peter and Paul stress the idea that the message of the Old Testament is of the gospel age, the Church age, if you please. Regardless of how sincere men are who proclaim that the prophets did not see the Church age, they are mistaken. Either they are mistaken or Peter and Paul were mistaken, or I have incorrectly exegeted these passages. That Peter and Paul were mistaken is rejected outright. And I challenge anyone to fully exegete these passages and obtain any meaning other than that which I have given them. Only through eisegesis, the importing of foreign ideas into the text thus reading something "into" the text, rather than drawing out of it that which it contains, can any other meaning be obtained. The "these days" of Acts 3:24 is a "road block" very difficult to get around by those who make the message of the Old Testament one that refers to a future age.

The second affirmation of Paul in the last chapter of Acts is found in the last verses. "And Paul dwelt two whole years in his own hired house… preaching the kingdom of God" (Acts 28:30-31). That this had reference to the present age hardly needs defending, however a statement of Paul's is added for confirmation. He wrote, "Giving thanks unto the Father…Who hath delivered us [aorist tense—completed action in past time] from the power of darkness, and hath translated us [aorist tense—completed action in past time] into the kingdom of his dear Son: In whom we have redemption through his blood, even the forgiveness of sins" (Col. 1:12-14). To deny that Paul taught that the kingdom was established at Christ's first coming, and that we enter it through Christ's redemptive sacrifice, is utter folly. Christians are not "just in a sense" in the kingdom. We are in it lock, stock, and barrel, as the old saying has it.

Now if Christ established a kingdom, if His reign was not postponed, contrary to those who claim otherwise, then He must be reigning as King at this time. The Bible fully confirms that Jesus is King right now. He will never be King any more so than is true at this time. The Revelator depicts Christ as the "prince of the kings of this earth" (Rev. 1:5), not at some future time, but at the time of John's banishment to the isle of Patmos. The later designations of "Lord of lords and King of kings" (Rev. 17:14, and "KING OF KINGS AND LORD OF LORDS" (Rev. 19:16) may well involve future events, but apparently they were appropriate designations for Christ during the first Christian century. John saw Christ in this fashion then.

This is not the place to fully exegete I Timothy 6:13-16, except to say that the expression "King of kings, and Lord of lords" in verse 15 does refer to Christ and that it also refers to the fact that He is presently a King. This is not the only legitimate interpretation of this passage, but it is an acceptable one. It is in agreement with Paul's contention that Christ must reign until His "coming" (*parousia*, I Cor. 15:28). According to this passage, "Christ [is] the firstfruits; afterwards they that are Christ's at this coming" (*parousia*). That this refers to the resurrection of the righteous should be evident. Following

# The Kingdom of God - Continued

this He delivers "up the kingdom to God, even the Father" (vv. 23-24). "For he must reign, till he hath put all enemies under his feet" (v. 25). This places the reign of Christ as currently in effect. He is to reign until the *parousia* at which time He ceases to reign, rather than as the time He begins to reign as some would say. Others defer the beginning of Christ's reign an additional seven years, and others half that long.

The exaltation of Christ following His resurrection is a final proof Christ now reigns as King. Even Dr. Scofield admits that Christ did begin to reign after His resurrection. (See his insertion between verses 24 and 25 of Acts 2.) But Premillennialists generally contend that the reign set forth in Acts 2:25-36 is the cosmic reign He exercised prior to the incarnation. Not so. Verse 33 speaks of His sharing the throne with the Father as an exaltation. This could hardly be true if it was simply a restoration to a position previously held but temporarily dropped during the incarnation. Elsewhere Paul declares that God "highly exalted him," and gave "him a name which is above every name" (Phil. 2:9). This reign is not simply over nature. It is Christ exercising a spiritual rule over His subjects here upon earth.

The "throne of David" will receive full consideration later, but in passing let it be said that in Acts 2:29-33, Peter is saying that Christ is now ruling from heaven, and that this is the fulfillment of the promises made to David. In other words, Christ is now on David's throne. Most will admit that Christ is now ruling in a sense, but many deny that He is on the throne of David, and that the rule He exercises from heaven indicates that the kingdom of God is fully established. The major objection to this interpretation is based on the contention that David's throne was on earth, hence only an earthly rule can fulfill the promise. We cannot bind God in this way.

We have no right to force God to follow our lines of reasoning. God could make a promise such as this and He could fulfill it from heaven. The question is, Did He do it that way? In support of the spiritualizing of David's throne, consider Psalms 89:2. "For I have said, Mercy shall be built up for ever: thy faithfulness shalt thou establish in the very heavens." Verses 3 and 4 make it clear that the establishment of the throne of David is the "faithfulness" involved. Most commentators link verses 2-4 with verse 37 in such a manner that the sun and moon become the evidences of God's faithfulness. But this is not the only possible construction that can be given to verse 2. The statement, "Thy faithfulness shalt thou establish in the very heavens" may mean that the throne of David would be established in heaven rather than on earth.

At least God's faithfulness is established there, rather than here on earth.

Paul's remarks regarding Isaiah 55:3 should be conclusive. Isaiah wrote, "I will make an everlasting covenant with you, even the sure mercies of David." Scofield tacitly admits that this refers to the Davidic covenant and the throne of David by placing II Samuel 7:8 in his center column references as one of the points of reference for this verse. However, Scofield's remarks on II Samuel 7:8-17 make this refer to a future kingdom, yet to be established. This assertion is contradictory to Paul who referred "the sure mercies of David" to the exaltation of Christ, rather than a future civil or political kingdom such as Scofield has in mind. In the following rather lengthy quotation, note how Paul's sermon agrees perfectly with the interpretation we gave of Peter's sermon in Acts 2.

And we declare unto you glad tidings, how that the promise which was made unto the fathers, God hath fulfilled the same unto us their children, in that he hath raised up Jesus again;…and as concerning that he raised him up from the dead, now no more to return to corruption, he said on this wise, I will give you the sure mercies of David. Wherefore he saith also in another psalm, Thou shalt not suffer thine Holy One to see corruption. For David, after he had served his own generation by the will of God, fell on sleep, and was laid unto his fathers, and saw corruption: But he, whom God raised again, saw no corruption (Acts 13:32-36).

What was "the promise which was made unto the fathers referred to in verse 32 above? The context shows it was the Davidic promise for that is what Paul discusses. The Greek term Paul uses to say the promise had been fulfilled is not used elsewhere in the New Testament. It means to accomplish, to complete, to fill up or fulfill in a complete manner so that nothing remains to be fulfilled about it. It was not a partial fulfillment. It was a complete fulfillment. The tense used is the perfect tense. This involves completed action in past time with present significance. In other words, the fulfillment came prior to the time Paul was speaking, but the benefits of that fulfillment were available at the time he was speaking.

And how had these "sure mercies of David" been completely fulfilled in past time but whose benefits were presently available? He testifies that it was through the resurrection of Christ. Even verse 33 which was omitted in the above quotation refers to the resurrection rather than the begetting of Jesus, as Alford and others have pointed out. Thus the New Testament contends that the promises to David and Israel were fulfilled in Christ's resurrection—completely fulfilled. Those who contend for a future fulfillment are denying the New Testament teaching that we are now enjoying the fulfillment, and those who say this fulfillment will be a future millennium of civil and political ascendancy of the Jews are rejecting the spiritual nature of the kingdom. This is nothing less than a perpetuation of the Jewish interpretation of prophecy which led to their rejection of Christ as their Messiah.

## The Kingdom of God Versus the Kingdom of Heaven

In spite of being illogical and devoid of any positive biblical support, many make a distinction between the kingdom of God and the kingdom of heaven. Scofield lists five ways they differ (see his note on Matt. 6:33). In this note he admits that parallel passages in Mark and Luke use "kingdom of God" which have "kingdom of heaven" in Matthew. Then he adds, "It is the omissions which are significant." This is an admission that he has no positive evidence.

Walvoord is less dogmatic than Scofield. He makes no positive claims; only that there "seems" to be a difference. He says, "In some instances, however, there seems to be a contrast between the kingdom of heaven as it is portrayed in Matthew's gospel and the kingdom of God as it is unfolded in the other gospels and the rest of the New Testament."[5] The array of scholarship against this supposed difference is so great that one would not expect a seminary president to defend it. But what are the "seeming" differences Scofield and others claim they have found?

Scofield contends that the kingdom of God includes all intelligent creatures of all ages who voluntarily submit to God's will. Humans enter it through the new birth. On the other hand, the kingdom of heaven is institutional in nature and includes all professors regardless of their true nature. The two have much in common during the present age, and will merge at the final consummation. All of this may seem innocent enough, but it is the eschatological significance that makes this distinction important. The separation of these enables Dispensationalists to allow for people being born into the kingdom of God during this age (John 3:3), and at the same time hold that a kingdom of an entirely different nature will he established later (note on Matt. 6:33).

Scofield allows that the kingdom of heaven now exists through professed followers of Christ, but that in the future it "is to be manifested in glory

---

5 Walvoord, *op. cit.*, p. 25.

upon the earth" (same note as above). The reader is then referred to his note on Zechariah 12:8. Section e of that note reads, "The kingdom is to be established by power, not persuasion." This is a most serious attack on the personality of Christ. Shall the loving Christ force Himself upon recalcitrant humanity? Never! Christ will punish unbelievers, it is true, but He will never establish His kingdom by force. Had force been acceptable to Him, He would have used it at His first coming. The texts Scofield gives are subject to other interpretations, and the time element he assigns them cannot be verified from the texts themselves.

Now let us apply Scofield's definition of the kingdom of heaven to specific texts. Jesus said, "Except your righteousness shall exceed the righteousness of the scribes and Pharisees, ye shall in no case enter into the kingdom of heaven" (Matt. 5:20). Thus the kingdom of heaven is a moral and ethical kingdom, as we have contended from the first, but Scofield says it contains professors of Christ but who have not had their lives changed. Even stronger are Jesus' later words, "Except ye be converted, and become as little children, ye shall not enter the kingdom of heaven" (Matt. 18:3). This has the identical meaning as John 3:3 which reads, "Except a man be born again, he cannot see the kingdom of God."

Again we find that entry into the kingdom of heaven demands obedience. "Not every one that saith Lord, Lord [professes to be a disciple] shall enter into the kingdom of heaven; but he that doeth the will of my Father which is in heaven" (Matt. 7:21). How then can Scofield's statement be justified, "The kingdom of God is entered only by the new birth (John 3:3, 5-7); the kingdom of heaven, during this age, is the sphere of a profession which may be real or false" (note on Matt. 6:33) Scofield's distinctions between the kingdom of God and of heaven cannot be applied to what Jesus said about John the Baptist. "He that is least in the kingdom of heaven is greater than he [John the Baptist]" (Matt. 11:11). Scofield attempts to cover his unjustified distinction between the kingdom of God and the kingdom of heaven by holding the greatness is positional rather than moral. Forced exegesis is again evident.

Parallel passages are always recognized as having the same meaning though different terms are used. Unless this is done in regard to these two expressions for the kingdom, we have Matthew saying Jesus meant one thing on a given occasion and Mark and Luke saying He meant something else. Among these instances would be: Matthew 4:17 and Mark 1:15; Matthew

11:11 and Luke 7:28; Matthew 13:31 and Mark 4:30: Matthew 13:33 and Luke 13:20-21; Matthew 19:14 and Luke 18:16-17. It should be noted that the expression "kingdom of heaven" is peculiar to Matthew. Matthew uses both "the kingdom of God" and the "kingdom of heaven," which could mean that he uses them selectively or with different meanings; but when elsewhere in the New Testament the expression "kingdom of heaven" is conspicuous by its absence, especially in parallel passages, the conclusion is unavoidable that those who make a distinction between these terms are propagating error rather than truth.

## Relating the Kingdom to the Church

Three important truths have been set forth about the kingdom: (1) Jesus came to establish a spiritual kingdom, rather than a carnal, political kingdom. (2) Jesus did establish the kingdom He came to establish. (3) That kingdom is called the kingdom of heaven or the kingdom of God. However, it is quite evident that He also established a Church. The problem we now consider involves the relationship that exits between these two institutions Christ established at His first coming. Are they identical, completely separated, or somewhere in between these two extremes. The position we take is that, though they undoubtedly are synonymous terms that can be used interchangeably, they are not absolutely identical. A review of some of the things which were said earlier in this connection should be helpful.

Christ was the Jewish Messiah, and He did come to establish a Messianic kingdom; but the kingdom He came to establish was spiritual in nature which did not meet the expectations of the Jews who considered Jesus an imposter because of this. At no time did Christ offer the Jews a political kingdom. Jesus claimed He was King right up to the end. His kingdom is a peaceful kingdom. The claim that He will later establish His kingdom through force is a reflection on the person of Christ. The preaching of the kingdom of God established congregations of believers which were called churches. This establishes a very close relationship between the kingdom and the Church. A few additional thoughts are now considered.

Three institutions trace their origin back to Abraham and promises God made to him. These are the Jewish nation, the kingdom of God, and the Church. It has been shown that the Israelitish nation was spoken of as a kingdom, especially where the Jews were called "the children of the kingdom." But Jesus contrasted that kingdom with His kingdom, as has already been shown, hence the Jewish nation cannot be equated with the kingdom of God. That any recognition from God depended on faith rather than descent is evidenced by the fact that Ishmael, the six sons of Abraham by Keturah, Esau and many others had no part in the promises in spite of the fact they were direct descendants of Abraham. Jesus very pointedly told the Jews who rejected Him that even though they were lineal descendants of Abraham (John 8:37), "Ye are of your father the devil" (John 8:44).

Paul contends that Jewish credentials are not outward (physical circumcision and lineal descent) but are inward in the spirit (Rom. 2:28-29). He teaches the same thing further in this same book, "For they are not all Israel, which are of Israel" (Rom. 9:6). Paul's argument is that lineal descent is not the important factor, for one may be a lineal descendant and still not be one of "the children of promise" (Rom. 9:8). A final and conclusive statement which makes forever indefensible the contention that racial lines or lineal descent have any place in the kingdom of God reads in part, "For he is our peace, who hath made both one, and hath broken down the middle wall of partition between us...for to make in himself of twain one new man, so making peace" (Eph. 2:14-15).

Those who would again erect that middle wall of partition, that wall of Herod's temple that marked the limits of the court of the Gentiles beyond which Gentiles were forbidden to enter, are opposing the work of Christ. Though the sincerity of these teachers is recognized, their position tends to deny an important element of what Christ accomplished through His sacrifice on Calvary. It is inconceivable that Christ would restore a division which He had previously eliminated by the shedding of His own blood.

Thus the kingdom of Israel, in spite of its descent from Abraham, is ruled out as having any important connection with the kingdom of God either now or later. Jews have the same access to Christ and the kingdom as Gentiles, but they have no special privileges now, nor will they have any at a later time. Christ removed that "middle wall of partition" thus making Jews and Gentiles one in Him, and that old barrier is gone forever, thanks be to God.

In tracing the Church back to Abraham, the intimate connection between it and the kingdom becomes evident. The Scriptural term *ekklesia* literally means "the called out ones." It is a New Testament term, though the Hebrew *qahal* was translated by it in the Septuagint translation of the Old Testament. Inasmuch as Abraham was a called out person from Ur of Chaldee (Gen. 11:31), it is fitting that he should be the "father" of a called

# The Kingdom of God - continued

out people. The New Testament proclaims Abraham to be "the father of us all" (Rom. 4:16). Paul's argument in this chapter is that the inheritance does not come by the "law" or lineal descent, but that it comes by "faith." This places Jew and Gentile on the same ground or level at the foot of the cross.

The close connection between the kingdom and the Church is further demonstrated by the fact that the covenant God made with Abraham included the gospel. Paul states, "And the scripture foreseeing that God would justify the heathen through faith, preached the gospel unto Abraham saying, In these shall all nations be blessed" (Gal. 3:8). Admittedly, the covenant (*berith*) that God made with Abraham is the beginning of God's efforts to establish His kingdom, but the intimate connection between the gospel and the Church make it evident that the Abrahamic covenant is also the fountainhead from which the Church emanated.

Paul is very plain if not emphatic in this connection. He says, "Know ye therefore that they which are of faith, the same are the children of Abraham" (Gal. 3:7). That the promise made to Abraham finds its fulfillment in the Church rather than in the lineal descendants of Abraham could hardly be stated any more succinctly. In verse 18 of this chapter Paul contends that our inheritance is not "of the law" or the Sinaitic covenant which is purely Jewish, but rather it comes through the Abrahamic covenant. It is futile for persons to argue that the Abrahamic covenant includes special promises to a portion of Abraham's descendants who are presently classified as Jews.

Paul completely annihilates the claim that the physical descendants of Abraham are the inheritors of the blessings promised him and his seed. In Paul's exposition regarding the Abrahamic covenant, he adds, "Now to Abraham and his seed were the promises made. He saith not, And to seeds, as of many; but as of one, And to thy seed, which is Christ" (Gal. 3:16). The promise given Abraham pointed directly and unequivocally to Christ. The "seed" of Abraham does not refer to the Israelites at all. It refers to that One who was to come. The lineal descendants of Abraham are effectually eliminated as the heirs. Christ is the heir, according to Paul.

It is admitted that a reading of the various promises in Genesis that God gave Abraham leaves the impression that some of them do refer to at least a certain portion of his physical posterity, but it is my firm conviction that the Holy Spirit which gave the initial details through Moses has used Paul to give us the proper interpretation of those details. It is generally held that the New Testament is the interpreter of the Old Testament.

The Bible interprets itself in many cases, and the New Testament sheds much light on the Old. Inasmuch as the New Testament is the ultimate in special revelation of God to man, it holds a higher place in hermeneutics than does the Old Testament.

For these reasons, if there seems to be a conflict between the Testaments, the interpretations of the New take precedence over those of the Old. In the passage from Galatians, Paul excludes literal or racial Israel as heir to the promises made to Abraham, and substitutes Christ. To reverse this process is not logically or hermeneutically sound. It invites chaos. The confusion this doctrine has created should be recognized as a detrimental influence.

But does not this exclude the Church, as well? No, for the Church is the body of Christ (Col. 1:18; Eph. 1:22-23; 4:15-16). Repeatedly we are said to be "in Christ" or baptized "into Christ." Thus if Christ is the recipient of the promises, and we are in Christ, it follows that we are partakers of those blessings through our relationship to or with Christ. This is borne out by Paul's affirmation that Abraham "is the father of all them that believe" (Rom. 4:11). This makes Abraham the father of the Church, or at least of those who composed the Church. Thus we conclude that the body of believers, the Church, is the body that has reason to hope through the *berith* God made with Abraham. It is further held that physical Israel has no hope other than that which comes through union with Christ which will always come through persuasion and never by force. Thus in Abraham, the kingdom and the Church become blended into one, at least in the main.

Additional evidence that the kingdom and the Church are basically one includes the spiritual nature of both. One gets into the kingdom through the new birth, a spiritual operation, (John 3:3, 5), and we are spiritually inducted into the Church (I Cor. 12:13). It is also evident that Christ occupies a place of comparable authority in both. He is King over the kingdom (John 18:37), and He is head of the Church (Col. 1:18). Jesus refers to the kingdom (Matt. 16:19), immediately after saying He would build His Church (Matt. 16:18). He evidently considered them at least somewhat comparable to each other. Paul does the same in Colossians 1:13-14. In the first of these verses he speaks of being "translated into the kingdom," and in the next verse he speaks of redemption and forgiveness of sins through the blood. Without question this last refers to the Church.

Though basically identical, certain differences may exist. The evidence is not sufficient to justify insistence at this point. It is certain that Christ included children in the kingdom (Luke 18:16), but there is no text that places them in the Church. Whatever is true of children is probably also true of idiots and others who never attain the necessary mental and spiritual maturity to become accountable to God. The Church is conceived of as those who have been born again, and only those. The kingdom is slightly larger, according to this concept, in that it includes all who are eligible for heaven.

Possibly an analogy will make this clearer. Analogies prove nothing, but they can assist in clarification. Within most nations there is a body called the electorate who are qualified to vote. This group is analogous to the Church. The nation, however, includes many who are too young to vote or who are otherwise disqualified to vote, even though they are classified as citizens. I conceive this to be analogous to the kingdom. Thus one may be in the kingdom without being in the Church, but it is impossible to be in the Church without being in the kingdom. The Church is used here as being the total body of born again believers rather than the institutionalized church which may contain professors who are not born again.

## Phases of the Kingdom

The kingdom of God is considered as having existed in two phases in the past with a future phase yet to come. These are: (1) the germinal or incipient stage; (2) the present phase; and (3) the future phase. There should be no question that God set in motion spiritual forces when He made a covenant with Abraham that were to eventuate in the kingdom of God. Even those who anticipate an earthly, political type kingdom, yet future, should not find this concept objectionable. During the ministry of John the Baptist and the early ministry of Jesus, it was not fully established. Both of these began their ministry with the declaration that the kingdom was "at hand" rather than that it is fully established.

Somewhat later, Jesus said, "And from the days of John the Baptist until now the kingdom of heaven suffereth violence, and the violent take it by force" (Matt. 11:12). I, along with many others, take this to mean that the kingdom was sufficiently completed for people to enter by climbing in, but before the intended means of access was installed. The illustration suggests a building that has walls and roof but the door is boarded up pending the hanging of the doors. Access is gained by climbing in through a window.

This germinal or incipient stage was definitely over at Pentecost. Jesus had said, "I will give unto thee the keys of the kingdom of heaven" (Matt.

16:19). At that time the kingdom could not be considered what is sometimes called a "lock and key" job. Jesus meant that the fullness of the kingdom was yet future. Additional changes were required before He could turn the keys over to the Church. No doubt Christ's death, burial, and resurrection were essential to making the kingdom a "lock and key" job. Whether the baptism of the Holy Spirit was also necessary is not clear. Peter did use the keys on the day of Pentecost, hence we know that by that time the germinal stage was past, and the fullness of the kingdom was evident by the use of the keys.

The present age is the period of growth and development of the Church and of the kingdom. This period began at Pentecost and will continue to the consummation. We understand that Christ is now reigning from His throne in heaven, and that He will continue to reign until the consummation, at which time He will turn the present kingdom over to the Father ( I Cor. 15:23-26). There is no time nor place nor need for an earthly, political type reign of Christ here on earth. This is made as an arbitrary statement at this point, but it will be fully supported in subsequent chapters.

The future phase of the kingdom is nothing less than our final reward in heaven. All references to a future kingdom consist of allusions to the future phase of the present kingdom. It will be recalled that eternal life or everlasting life is said to be a present possession (John 6:54; 3:36), but they are also spoken of as a future attainment or blessing (Matt. 19:29; Mark 10:30). This was explained as meaning that salvation does impart to one that quality of life called by these names, but that the conditional aspect continues to exist until death. The final reward is different because the conditional aspect will no longer exist.

Being in the kingdom now and inheriting it later have a similar explanation. While on earth, Jesus said that people were pressing into the kingdom of God (Luke 16:16), and Paul indicated that Christians were then translated into the kingdom (Col. 1:13). On the other hand, Jesus stated that at the judgment He would say to the righteous, "Inherit the kingdom prepared for you from the foundation of the world" (Matt. 25:34). It is the same kingdom we are now in, but that which we inherit will be the heavenly phase of the present kingdom.

## Concluding Observations

The fact that the kingdom of God was established at Christ's first coming is crucial. Premillennialism stands or falls on the issue of the kingdom. If

# The Kingdom of God - Continued

Christ did establish His kingdom at His first advent, no place can be found for the establishment of a millennial kingdom. A recent work which has the blessing of Dispensational leaders has the following note: "The postponement of the kingdom is an important link in literal hermeneutics. If the kingdom offered by Jesus were not postponed but actually realized, then Old Testament kingdom prophecies must be spiritualized and seen as 'fulfilled' at the first advent of Christ."[6] This admission should not be taken lightly. It is the Achilles heel of Premillennialism. If one has a correct understanding of the kingdom, other problems will be solved more readily.

The distinction Dispensationalists make between the kingdom of God and the kingdom of heaven is almost as important to their system of interpretation. Scofield makes seven insertions or captions about the mysteries of the kingdom of heaven in Matthew 13 and adds 13 notes on these mysteries. These contain a strange doctrine.

The first mystery is the parable of the sower or of the soils. Mark and Luke give the same parable, and they speak of it as a mystery or mysteries "of the kingdom of God" (Mark 4:11; Luke 8:10), rather than of the "kingdom of heaven." These are parallel passages that cannot be interpreted differently without violating the rules of hermeneutics. The distinctions that Scofield and others make at this point cannot be justified exegetically or any other way.

In Christ's explanation of the parable of the tares among the wheat, He clearly states that the "field is the world" (Matt. 13:38). Scofield contradicts this by claiming it is the professed church. The "kingdom" (Matt. 13:41) must also mean the world or Christ's cosmic rule to avoid any contradiction in Christ's own explanation. The drag-net is interpreted the same as the tares and the wheat.

Much is made of the fact that the two last parables of Matthew 13 are not found in any of the other Gospels. But why make something over these two? Two other parables of Matthew 13 are not recorded elsewhere. If two are important, why not the other two? A study of the parables reveals that Matthew has a total of eleven parables that are peculiar to his Gospel. Omissions prove nothing, and if some omissions are important, then all are.

The interpretation Scofield gives of the parable of the leaven (Matt. 13:33-35) is even more tortuous, devious, and forced. Jesus indicated the

---

6 Paul Lee Tan, *The Interpretation of Prophecy*, p. 306.

gradual permeation of society by Christianity in this parable. But since Premillennialism holds that the expected future kingdom is to come suddenly, climactically, and even by force, he is forced to interpret this parable in a strange way to protect the other error of interpretation.

In his note on Matthew 13:33 he contends that the meaning of "leaven" is always bad. He goes farther by claiming that "the Lord Himself" fixed this meaning. His references are Matthew 16:6-12. I checked those references and found that Jesus there spoke of "the leaven of the Pharisees and of the Sadducees" (Matt. 16:6, 12). There is no justification for Scofield's claim that this sets a standard by which all other uses of leaven must be measured. Christianity's leaven is a good leaven; that of the scribes and Pharisees was a bad leaven.

And it must not be forgotten that Jesus said, "There be some of them that stand here, which shall not taste of death, till they have seen the kingdom of God come with power" (Mark 9:1). If the kingdom was deferred or if it was not established at Christ's first advent, then Christ spoke an untruth here. The idea of a deferred kingdom cannot be harmonized with Christ's words and the rest of Scripture.

CHAPTER 3

# HERMENEUTICS[7]

Hermeneutics refers to the principles of Biblical interpretation and their application. Because persons holding different views of eschatology usually have hermeneutical differences. Walvoord has gone so far as to say, "The hermeneutic rather than the individual argument determines the outcome of the discussion."[8] The task of reducing this very large subject to reasonable proportions requires that many aspects be omitted, and many others touched on very lightly. Every effort will be made to elaborate on those principles that affect eschatological views, and to omit or briefly consider those that have less significance for prophetic and eschatological interpretations.

Anyone who interprets the Bible should be spiritually and morally qualified. He should be sympathetic toward the Bible and its message. The Bible claims to be inspired, and there is a supernatural element running through the Bible from beginning to end; hence one who rejects the supernatural cannot be fully sympathetic with its message, and, therefore, is not qualified as an interpreter of it.

Ordinarily, the Bible should be interpreted much like any other book. The historical setting must receive due consideration, and the grammatical significance of its contents should form the basis for the theological views which are drawn from it. Figures of speech, poetry, parables, figurative language, and different writing styles should receive the same consideration they receive when secular writings are being interpreted. However, full recognition of the activity of the Holy Spirit as the true author of each book of the Bible makes biblical interpretation somewhat different from the interpretation of strictly human productions.

Inasmuch as prophecy is, in the main, peculiar to the Bible, it requires

---

7  I am indebted to Clinton Lockhart (*Principles Of Interpretation*), Bernard Ramm (*Protestant Biblical Interpretation*), L. Berkhof (*Principles Of Biblical Interpretation*), Milton S. Terry (*Biblical Hermeneutics*), and F. G. Smith (*The Revelation Explained*) for most of the rules set forth in this chapter.

8  Walvoord, *op. cit.*, p. 116.

special attention; but even prophecy must depend on the grammatico-historical meaning as the basis for whatever interpretation one gives it. Much is made of the fact that some prophecy is interpreted literally by some interpreters, whereas others interpret the same prophecies figuratively. Hence some are said to be "literalists," whereas others who hold to figurative interpretations are called "spiritualizers" or some other name of similar meaning. This question is considered in detail later in this section, but for the present I must say that no one follows these approaches absolutely. All fall somewhere between the two extremes. The difference is the tendency one has to favor one over the other.

Though all the Bible is fully inspired, progress is evident in that revelation. The message of the prophets is of a higher order in certain ways than the law. Christ is declared to be the full revelation of God (Heb. 1:1-3), and His revelation is superior to previous revelations. The New Testament is generally conceded a higher position in revelation than the Old Testament. In this sense progressive revelation is recognized and accepted. However, the claim of liberal theologians that revelation progressed from error to truth is rejected.

The Bible is accepted as its own interpreter. Not only must the interpreter allow each author to interpret his own meaning, but since all of the Bible is inspired, no portion should be interpreted in a way that contradicts any other portion. Bible scholars have agreed on many basic rules of interpretation. Those who ignore these rules can usually be placed in one of two categories. Some have not studied biblical exegesis enough to know, understand, and appreciate the value and necessity of these rules. Others ignore such rules because they get in the way of their preconceived system of interpretation.

One of the basic rules of hermeneutics is that passages that are plain and clear, free of ambiguity and vagueness, should carry more weight in establishing a doctrine than obscure passages. Passages that are highly figurative are frequently capable of being interpreted in more than one way, hence are notoriously unsafe as a foundation for any doctrinal emphasis. Yet, Premillennialism rests on this kind of a foundation. There is but one book in all the Bible that mentions a reign of 1,000 years, and that is the most figurative book in all the Bible. Except for this one obscure passage (Rev. 20:1-7), it is doubtful if millennialism would have become a theological issue.

Now, a single passage that is plain and clear, that is free from ambiguity and vagueness and figures of speech, is sufficient to establish a doctrine if it does not contradict other portions of the Bible. But the Apocalypse is full of symbols and figures of speech, and only a misguided fanatic will claim certitude for the interpretations he gives to the book. But since this is the only text that mentions a reign of 1,000 years, Premillennialists must interpret this text as though their interpretation were the only valid interpretation, and that it is well nigh infallible. This has the appearance of demagoguery whether or not the term is appropriate.

Another important rule is that the New Testament be recognized as the fuller, higher revelation that it actually is. Most Protestants are comfortable worshiping on Sunday, even though the Old Testament is quite rigid regarding Saturday as the Sabbath. The reason for this is the recognition that the New Testament interprets the Sabbath in a spiritual sense, making the day of worship a matter of minor significance. An Old Testament theology, however, cannot accept this interpretation by the New Testament, for which reason some groups worship on Saturday.

It is our contention that Premillennialism is an Old Testament hermeneutic, and that the New Testament is disregarded by those who teach this doctrine, just as Sabbatarians disregard it in relation to certain other aspects of the Old Testament. A later section of this volume will discuss this more adequately.

Simplicity is a rule of hermeneutics just as it is in logic. In science this is called parsimony. Problems arise in many areas of life. To explain certain phenomena, scientists suggest hypotheses. Theories, such as these, are then tested to determine if any one is the correct one. The general rule is to start with the simplest one. It is considered more likely to be the correct one, than a complicated theory. The same is true in hermeneutics. The extremely complicated system of eschatology of present day Premillennialism is suspect because of its complexity.

It is not contended that complexity alone proves it to be erroneous; only that it makes it suspect. But as the complexity increases, problems have a way of increasing. For this reason Premillennialists are hard put to explain certain things relative to their system of interpretation. Examples include the two-phase second coming, the restoration of Jewish sacrifices and circumcision, the restoration of the "middle wall of partition," the stopping of the prophetic clock, the several resurrections that are necessary, and the several judgments that are usually included in the system. Against this is the simple one time second coming, one resurrection, one judgment, and the distribution of awards and the assessment of penalties which ushers in the eternal state. The hermeneutic rule of simplicity means the latter should be accepted until it has been disproved. To date, disproof is lacking.

Another rule is that parallel passages should be interpreted harmoniously. Dispensationalists violate this rule by making a distinction between the kingdom of God and the kingdom of heaven. This distinction can be maintained only by interpreting parallel passages with different meanings. Most Premillennialists are guilty of this same violation in their interpretation of the Olivet discourse. Portions of Luke 21 are accepted as referring to the destruction of Jerusalem by the Roman legions in A.D. 70, but almost identical wording in Matthew and Mark is made to refer to a future battle. This disregard for hermeneutical rules is regrettable.

The importance of the context can hardly be over emphasized. No one expects a writer to fully exegete every passage he uses, but the common practice of Premillennial writers of selecting isolated passages of Scripture and linking them together according to a preconceived pattern is without justification. This is frequently done from contexts that contain elements which disprove their allegations, and from others that make their interpretation impossible. Texts from the Psalms, Ezekiel, Zechariah, Revelation, and Matthew 24 are most often handled this way.

Possibly the most difficult rule of hermeneutics for the exegete to follow is that each passage be approached without any preconceived opinion of what it should say. The purpose of this rule is to enable one to accept what the text says, rather than reading one's own ideas into it. The expression "forced exegesis" is but a way of saying that this rule has been violated. Many examples of forced exegesis by Premillennialists and Dispensationalists have already been cited, and many others are cited in the succeeding pages of this volume.

## Presuppositions Determine the Hermeneutic

Each person brings presuppositions into his Bible study. These presuppositions often determine the hermeneutic one accepts. A person who rejects the supernatural element in the Bible does so because of his presuppositions. He does not reject the inspiration of the Bible and the miracles it tells about because of his hermeneutics; he does so because of his presuppositions. His presuppositions determine his hermeneutic, rather than his hermeneutic determining his doctrinal stance.

Similarly, anyone who believes that prophecy must be interpreted literally and futuristically cannot study a prophecy free of these presuppositions. Before they study a prophecy, something of what it must say has been determined by their presuppositions. Sandeen has shown that millennialism is a product of the literalism of Fundamentalism.[9] This is not intended as a slam, for I am sufficiently conservative to be comfortable under the Fundamentalist designation, although I do reject their literalism and its by-product, Premillennialism.

This presupposition of extreme literalism is held to be the basis of much of the eschatological teaching of today. Thus the presuppositions determine their hermeneutics. This should not be the case. Some of the strongest attacks on Dispensationalism have come from such men as Floyd E. Hamilton, Phillip Mauro, and Robert Strong who after being steeped in Dispensational doctrine came to realize the weaknesses of this approach. Once these men began to allow the Bible to serve as its own interpreter, they quickly recognized the fallacies of their former interpretations and cast them aside.

I do not claim to be without presuppositions in my study of the Bible and eschatology in particular, but I have made every effort to keep my heart and mind open to new ideas, and carefully evaluate the writings of others. I am convinced that my hermeneutics and eschatological beliefs have been shaped by the Bible rather than by any presuppositions I may have brought into my study. As I see it, the Bible contains both literal *and* figurative prophecies and fulfillments. Thus, specific prophecies fall into whichever category a full exegesis would indicate. A great deal of forced exegesis is avoided by this means.

However, the important question is not stated fully in the above. The important question is, Does the Bible support my position or any other? First, the figurative or nonliteral aspect of prophecy is considered.

The very first prophecy of Christ is found in Genesis 3:15. It reads, "And I will put enmity between thee and the woman, and between thy seed and her seed; it shall bruise thy head, and thou shalt bruise his heel." A literal fulfillment would have a literal descendant of Eve using his heel to damage the head of a literal snake, and the snake in turn striking the heel of his

---

9 Ernest Sandeen, *The Roots of Fundamentalism*.

attacker. Even Scofield's note on this verse recognizes the reference is to Christ and His redemptive work. This single example is sufficient to prove some symbolic fulfillment, but let us consider further.

Four times Moses declared that God had promised the Israelites a land flowing with milk and honey (Ex. 3:8, 17; 13:5; 33:2-3), and Jeremiah and Ezekiel each declare twice that God gave them such a land (Jer. 11:5; 32:22; Ezek. 20:6, 15), but if any literalist has contended that there were literal streams of milk and honey in Palestine, I haven't read where. Yet if this was not literally fulfilled, then the literalist position requires that Moses be considered a false prophet and Jeremiah and Ezekiel liars, or else that this be fulfilled at some future time. But even this would make Jeremiah and Ezekiel liars for they said God had fulfilled this in the past, when according to this interpretation, He had not done so.

I have carried this method to a ridiculous extreme in order to make a point. The interpretations many literalists give to prophecy place Christ and the New Testament writers in the same position as Jeremiah and Ezekiel in the above illustration. Repeatedly, the New Testament writers indicate fulfillment of Old Testament prophecies, but these are cast aside as meaningless, reinterpreted, held to be more than a partial fulfillment, or by forced exegesis, their evident meaning twisted so that it conforms to their system of hermeneutics. I see no more reason for contending that Zechariah's fig tree and vine (Zech. 3:10), or Isaiah's "streams in the desert" (Isa. 35:6), and lions eating "straw like the ox" (Isa. 11:7) must have a future literal fulfillment, than to hold that literal streams of milk and honey will one day flow across the Palestine countryside.

On the other hand, many Old Testament prophecies were literally fulfilled. In the prophecy of milk and honey, there was also that which was literal. The tribes that had previously occupied Palestine were very literal and real. They had to be conquered. But in that same prophecy there is the figurative which was not intended to be literally fulfilled, and which was not literally fulfilled. The Amorites and the Hittites were very real, but the milk and honey was a figurative expression for abundance.

It should be clear that not only may prophecy be fulfilled either literally or figuratively, but that the same prophecy may contain elements of both. It is important that it be understood that the so-called "dual hermeneutic" we employ is not something invented by man to support his preconceived notions, but is indeed the hermeneutic of the Bible itself.[10] If this is not clear, when passages such as Isaiah 35 are considered, the force of our interpretation will be lost, for in that chapter we have a vivid example of the literal with the figurative or spiritual.

## Old Testament Prophecies Interpreted by the New Testament

Earlier in this chapter the superiority of the New Testament over the Old Testament was mentioned—not superior in regard to inspiration, but superior in that it gave insights and truths which had not been revealed during the Old Testament period. I doubt if there is a Dispensationalist or other Premillennialist who would deny this. The conclusion seems unavoidable, however, that their hermeneutic is of the Old Testament rather than the New. The eschatological message of the New Testament is not allowed to alter their previously developed system of Old Testament interpretation. This, in effect, nullifies a portion of New Testament truth. It is similar to the Adventists inability to see that the law of Moses is no longer operative in the gospel age. New Testament interpretations are forced to conform to a hermeneutic that is built on the Old Testament. We need to get our priorities in proper order.

It has already been shown how this Old Testament hermeneutic and the literalism it employs places Jesus in a most embarrassing predicament. It is claimed He came to establish a political kingdom and failed to do so. This brings the deity of Christ into question. This could well be expected from His enemies, but that it should come from His friends is beyond comprehension. Ample arguments were given to prove that the New Testament writers, and Christ Himself, hold that the kingdom He came to establish was established. If you could not accept the views on the kingdom which were given in chapters 1-2, you are urged to reread those chapters and note how New Testament applications of Old Testament prophecies are rejected by literalists.

A very important illustration of this rejection of New Testament interpretations is found in what is said of John the Baptist. John himself said he constituted the fulfillment of Isaiah 40:3-4 (John 1:23). Now a literal

---

10 The "single hermeneutic" seeks to interpret all Scripture either literally or figuratively, while the "dual hermeneutic" accepts either the literal or the figurative as may seem appropriate.

interpretation of the Isaiah passage requires that John be a modern highway builder for the road he was to build leveled mountains and filled valleys to construct a highway that avoided the steep grades of the roads of that day. John the Baptist did not fulfill this prophecy in a literal manner, but his preaching did pave the way for Christ in a figurative way.

Jesus also spoke of the work of John the Baptist. He testified that John was the "Elias, which was for to come" (Matt. 11:14). The prophetic utterance to which Christ referred is Malachi 4:5-6. But according to the Old Testament hermeneutic used by Dispensationalists, this passage must apply to a future kingdom; therefore it cannot apply to Christ's first coming, even though Christ said it did. His words are, "Elias truly shall first come, and restore all things. But I say unto you, That Elias is come already, and they knew him not" (Matt. 17:11-12). Matthew adds in the next verse that the disciples then "understood that he spake unto them of John the Baptist."

Is the evident meaning of Christ accepted by Dispensationalists and others who contend for a future earthly kingdom? No, it is not. Scofield contends that the words, "Elias truly shall first come, and restore all things" refers to a future literal return of Elijah and not to John the Baptist. To him, the words "Elias is come already" is but "adumbrative and typical" of the future ministry of the literal Elijah (note on Matt. 17:10). Other writers make much of the future tense in Christ's words that Elias "shall first come," but this is because Christ was practically quoting from Malachi, and for this reason He uses the same tense as the prophetic utterance. Only forced exegesis can make this refer to a time yet future.

This same pattern of interpretation is apparent in relation to Pentecost. Two instances of this stem from Peter's sermon. The instance where Peter announces that Christ is now King, and He is now reigning on the throne of David, has been discussed already. The other involves Peter's interpretation of Joel 2:28-32. Peter affirms that the infilling of the Holy Spirit which had just occurred was the fulfillment of these verses from Joel. His words are, "This is that which was spoken by the prophet Joel" (Acts 2:16). He goes on to quote the verses listed above (Acts 2:17-21). Nothing could be plainer than the words, "This is that." But Dispensationalists are unable to accept this plain statement. They contend that Peter did not really mean "this is that" but rather that he meant this was somewhat like and distantly related to what Joel really prophesied.

This disregard for the dependability and veracity of the written word is not in keeping with the claim of being the "chief defenders of the word," nor is it in harmony with their claim of adhering to the "literal interpretation of the Bible." This again illustrates the way the New Testament interpretation is rudely pushed to one side if not denied outright. Preconceived ideas based on Old Testament hermeneutics are not congenial to New Testament interpretations.

Now consideration centers on the Jerusalem conference in Acts 15. Peter, Paul, and Barnabas all gave witness to the conversion of Gentiles under their ministry. James, functioning as chairman, drew together the conflicting points of view by saying "the words of the prophets" (Acts 15:15) are in agreement with Peter's testimony. He then quotes Amos 9:11-12 as proof of the correctness of his conclusion. It reads as follows:

After this I will return, and will build again the tabernacle of David, which is fallen down; and I will build again the ruins thereof, and I will set it up: That the residue of men might seek after the Lord, and all the Gentiles, upon whom my name is called, saith the Lord, who doeth all these things (Acts 15:16-17).

Scofield says, "Dispensationally, this is the most important passage in the N.T." (note on Acts 15:13). Then, instead of exegeting the quotation from Amos, he uses the introductory statement of James as a springboard to project the prophecy of Amos to a future age. This is forced exegesis. No lawyer, grammarian, logician, or junior high school student could possibly arrive at this conclusion unless he had first been steeped in the old Jewish expectations, or those of modern Premillennialism or Dispensationalism. The views of the latter two largely coincide with the Jewish expectations, the major difference being that the anticipated political kingdom has been projected to the second coming rather than the first coming of Christ.

In verses 13 and 14 James simply recounts the facts as Peter had given them. God had indeed visited "the Gentiles to take out of them a people for his name." The contrast between "Gentiles" and "a people for his name" is the heart of what James is saying. Only Jews were thought of as the people of God in Jewish thought. All other people were Gentiles. But now God has blessed Gentiles with salvation, and these are accepted as the people of God on an equal basis with the Jews.

Verse 15 simply states that the prophets, that is all of the prophets who had spoken of the conversion of the Gentiles, were in agreement with what has now become a fact. He could have used Isaiah, or another of the Twelve, but he was led to select this passage from Amos. Much has been made of James's statement "after this" of verse 16. The quotation is from the Septuagint or the LXX, although some feel that Luke substituted this rendering for the Hebrew which these feel James probably used. The argument is far from convincing, but it is not vital to the meaning of the passage. The problem is in determining what James meant by "After this" which does not appear in either the Hebrew or the LXX.

Scofield makes the "after this" refer to after Christ had called out a group of Gentiles into the Christian Church; or after the Church age, He would return to again build the tabernacle of David. But this is to do violence to James's use of this passage as referring to the salvation work accomplished among the Gentiles through the preaching of the gospel. Lenski holds that the "after this" or the "after these things" as he translates, "refers to the afflictions of which Amos had spoken," and not to after God had called out a people.[11] This is the only legitimate approach, since James substitutes these words for the "in that day" of both the Hebrew and the LXX. Thus the "after this" refers to the context in Amos rather than the context in Acts as Scofield and others erroneously apply it.

Walvoord takes honor and credit for something which is truly a most shameful thing. He is proud to be counted as one of those who "distinguish the program of Israel from the program of the church."[12] Before and after the above statement, he contends this distinction is the correct one, and only those who maintain it are in the mainstream of prophetic truth. But that is not the New Testament position, and it cannot be maintained without creating tremendous and irreconcilable contradictions with basic New Testament teachings.

Ephesians 2 constitutes a devastating refutation of separate programs for Israel and the Church. Space precludes a full exegesis of this chapter, but something less than that should be sufficient. These Ephesians had been "in time past Gentiles" (v. 11). The inference of this statement is that they are no longer Gentiles, but Jews. This is made plainer further on. While they "were without Christ" they were "aliens from the commonwealth of Israel, and strangers from the covenants of promise" (v. 12). The meaning here is that when they accepted Christ, they became citizens

---

11  R. C. H. Lenski, *The Interpretation of the Acts of the Apostles*, p. 609.
12  Walvoord, *loc. cit.*

of the "commonwealth of Israel" and also became recipients of the "covenants of promise." This is so plain, I hesitate to comment on it. It means nothing less than that one becomes a Jew and an heir to the Jewish promises and covenants through accepting Christ, rather than through lineal descent or circumcision of the flesh.

Paul contends that through Christ's sacrifice (v. 13) He "hath made both one" through the breaking down of "the middle wall of partition between us" (v. 14). Is this "oneness" a temporary relationship? Is the middle wall again to be raised? Shall the work of Christ on the cross be nullified by such a restoration? God forbid! Paul adds, "Having abolished in his flesh the enmity" (v. 15) between Jew and Gentile based on Old Testament distinctions, "for to make in himself of twain one new man, so making peace." Though the passage quoted next has no bearing on the subject under discussion, it is a most fitting statement at this point: "What therefore God hath joined together, let not man put asunder" (Matt. 19:6).

Jews and Gentiles now constitute one body, according to verse 16, because the conditions that made for two separate bodies have been "slain" through Christ's death on the cross. As a result of this we Gentiles "are no more strangers and foreigners" (v. 19). Strangers and foreigners where and to whom? We are no longer strangers and foreigners to the commonwealth of Israel as set forth in verse 12. We Gentiles are actually Jews in the sight of God. Whatever blessings God has for the Jews, He has the same for Gentile Christians, for the distinction between Jew and Gentile has been broken down. This is the New Testament teaching.

Premillennialists are strangely silent on this chapter except for verse 7. Verse 7 does speak of an age to come, but it is something the Ephesian Gentiles would enjoy. Their resurrection from a dead state of sin (vv. 1 and 5-6) is what makes them eligible for that future reward. And this is the important element by which the constituency of this "one body" is determined. If it included all Jews and all Gentiles, it would include the total population of the earth. Rather it is the Jewish believers plus the Gentile believers which constitute this "new man" the "commonwealth of Israel." It is not the lineal descendants of Abraham, nor the more selective descendants of Israel that make up this new man. Nor does it refer to the even more selective group from Judah which went into the Babylonian captivity whose descendants, as New Testament Jews, have a better right to the term "Jew" than either of the larger groups.

The believers in Christ, Jew and Gentile, constitute the New Testament Israel. God has selected some from Gentile stock, and He has selected some from Israelitish stock to make "one man" where two had previously existed. This "new man" is the Church, and the Church is the only group upon which the blessings of God can rest. In the Church there is neither Jew nor Gentile (Col. 3:11), and we are spiritually inducted into this "one body" whether we be racially of Jewish descent, or whether we be Gentiles by descent. Those who accent the racial distinctions and try to restore the distinction that Christ abolished (Eph. 2:15) have completely misunderstood certain aspects of the redemptive work of Christ. Romans 9-11 is the stronghold of the opposing view. In a later section these chapters will be shown to be in full agreement with Ephesians 2 as given above.

## The Myth of a Single Hermeneutic

There was a time when the Church was plagued with a great deal of allegorizing. There was a tendency to look for hidden meanings in historical events which were interpreted as the deeper meaning of such passages. This gave way in the course of time to recognizing that the grammatico-historical meaning of passages must be accepted as the basic meaning. Anything beyond this was a lesson or application, rather than a hidden meaning.

Even in nonprophetical statements conflicts arise over whether they are factual or figures of speech. A famous discussion between Luther and Zwingli centered around Jesus' assertion, "This is my body" (*Hoc est corpus meum*). Luther insisted on a literal interpretation. Zwingli correctly said it was a figure of speech. This being true of matters having a historical base, it is no surprise that prophecy which has no historical base as yet should produce controversy.

Some fulfilled prophecies have been shown to be figurative. The very first one in the Bible (Gen. 3:15) regarding Christ was of this kind. Others were mixed literal and figurative. The literal Canaanites along with the figurative streams of milk and honey were of this kind. And no one questions that many prophecies regarding Christ were fulfilled literally. This being true of fulfilled prophecy, it is not unreasonable to expect the same of all prophecy.

But some insist that all future prophecy be interpreted literally. They contend further that they do interpret future prophecy according to the single rule of literalness. I have already shown the first of these claims to be unreasonable, and I shall now show that the second is untrue.

## HERMENEUTICS

Walvoord says that Augustine interpreted most of the Bible "normally, historically, and grammatically," but that prophecy required "a nonliteral interpretation."[13] Walvoord contends that Amillennialists follow Augustine's dual hermeneutic, whereas "premillenarians generally have adopted a single hermeneutic."[14] The purpose of this section is to prove the last statement to be inaccurate. The fact is that all theologians have a dual hermeneutic. The question is not of kind but of degree. Premillennialists do tend to interpret more prophecies by the single rule than is true of Amillennialists, but their claim of interpreting all prophecy literalistically is inaccurate. Many spiritualized interpretations could be cited.

Walvoord does recognize that some Premillennialists, "especially those who are not Dispensational, have used to some extent the dual hermeneutics of Augustine." Although Walvoord leaves the impression that any spiritualizing of prophecy is to be rejected regardless of who does it, he is not caustic about it as some are. DeHaan uses some very strong words in this connection. He says, "Let me say here that the miserable invention of Satan is this spiritualizing of Scripture. The curse of Christendom today is the failure to distinguish between the Church and the kingdom....Instead of spiritualizing, it is a 'demonizing' of the Scriptures."[15] He adds elsewhere,

Let me mention a simple rule of interpretation which applies not only to the book of Revelation but to the entire Bible. Always interpret every statement in the Word of God literally as meaning exactly what it says, unless it is definitely stated otherwise or the structure and context are such that you can plainly see that the passage concerns a figure and a symbol.[16]

Does Dr. DeHaan follow the rules he has established for others? He does not. In the same book from which the above quotation is taken, he contends that the seven churches of Asia represent seven periods in the life of the Church. He takes this position about the letters to these churches found in chapters 2 and 3 of the Revelation. One may search these chapters of the Revelation or the remainder of the Revelation as well, and he will not find one vestige of evidence that John intended the letters written to these churches to constitute prophecies of seven future periods. DeHaan goes even further and gives the years covered by each Church.

---

13 *Ibid.*
14 *Ibid.*
15 M. R. DeHaan, *The Second Coming of Jesus*, pp. 81 and 83.
16 M. R. DeHaan, *Revelation*, p. 143.

The Church of Ephesus is a picture of the early Apostolic Church. The Church of Smyrna represents the Church of the second and third centuries, the persecuted Church. The Church of Pergamos typifies the worldly Church, beginning with the so-called conversion of Constantine the Great in 312 and extending to about 500 A.D.[17]

He continues in this vein through the other four churches. And all of this without solid exegetical grounds on which to base such amazing disclosures. It is true that John indicated the book in general was a prophetic book (Rev. 1:3), but that statement is no justification for the extended spiritualizing DeHaan engages in. These are no more than letters of warning or of commendation to churches of that day. DeHaan's position has no more warrant than other views which contend that these represent seven great denominations of our day, or seven national and international churches, such as the Coptic, Armenian, Greek Orthodox, Roman Catholic, and Russian Orthodox.

In another book he says, "In the previous chapter we pointed out that the very first sentence in the Bible is a picture of Jesus Christ." After quoting Genesis 1:1 he adds, "This is a picture of the Lord Jesus, but we would never recognize it as such until we look at it through the magic lantern of the New Testament."[18] He then quotes John 1:1-3 to prove that Genesis 1:1 is a "clear" picture of Christ. This is spiritualizing running wild! It is amazing that he can see a picture of Christ in Genesis 1:1 because of John's prologue, but cannot see that the Israel of the Old Testament finds its fulfillment in the Church, even though the picture is painted ever so clearly in Romans 2:28-29; Galatians 3; and Ephesians 2. Examples of this from DeHaan could easily be multiplied. But instead, let us consider Dr. Scofield who is a most eminent Dispensationalist.

The whole system known as Dispensationalism is built on a spiritualization of the Scripture. That is a big order regarding those who claim to hold to a single hermeneutic, but it is true. Scofield writes,

The Scriptures divide time...into seven unequal periods, usually called "Dispensations" (Eph. 3:2)...These periods are marked off in Scripture by some change in God's method of dealing with mankind....Five of these dispensations, or periods of time, have been fulfilled; we are living in the sixth, probably towards its close, and have before us the seventh.[19]

---

17  *Ibid.*, pp. 38-39.
18  M. R. DeHaan, *Portraits of Christ in Genesis*, p. 30.
19  C. I. Scofield, *Rightly Dividing The Word of Truth*, p. 12.

## HERMENEUTICS

Scofield goes on to list these seven dispensations and certain passages of Scripture on which he bases his views. Space does not permit elaboration of these so-called dispensations, but the second one will receive some attention. It is entitled "Man under Conscience." It is said to cover the period from the expulsion from Eden to the flood. The texts given are Genesis 3:7, 22; 6:5, 11, 12; 7:11, 12, 23. It is interesting to note that these verses say absolutely nothing about the conscience. These texts say nothing about a dispensation. Scofield says that "The Scriptures divide time" after this fashion. But it is Scofield who is responsible for these divisions.[20]

This is a most rank sort of spiritualizing. It is a gross attempt to force the Scripture to teach what the writer believes. Scofield is quite emphatic about the close of this period. He contends, "God closed the second testing of the natural man with judgment—the Flood."[21] What Scofield is saying is that the second of his so-called dispensations, the dispensation of "Man under Conscience" came to an end. That this marked an epoch in God's dealings with man, no one will question, but it is denied that this ended the dispensation that Scofield has superimposed upon the Scripture. The New Testament denies Dr. Scofield's claims. If there ever was a dispensation of "Man under Conscience" it continued to exist in Paul's day. It did not end with the flood.

For when the Gentiles, which have not the law, do by nature the things contained in the law, these, having not the law, are a law unto themselves: which show the work of the law written in their hearts, their conscience also bearing witness, and their thoughts the mean while accusing or else excusing one another (Rom. 2:14-15).

This rather lengthy quotation shows that God still judges those who have not the law, on the basis of their conscience. Paul uses the word "conscience" in this passage. The word is not found in the portions of Scripture Scofield claims teach a special dispensation of the conscience. His booklet *Rightly Dividing the Word of Truth* contains some fancy twisting of the Scriptures, inasmuch as the age of conscience as well as the other divisions of Dispensationalism cannot be proved by sound exegesis.

Another case of "spiritualizing" or allegorizing which is hermeneutically invalid is the position taken on the Sermon on the Mount. Scofield says, "It

---

20   Ibid., p. 13. See also notes in the *Scofield Reference Bible,* Genesis 1-12 plus Exodus 19:8; John 1:17; Ephesians 1:10.
21   Ibid.

gives the divine constitution for the righteous government of the earth," the establishment of which he considers yet future, and has only a "beautiful moral application to the Christian."[22] Does he offer any exegetical support for this nonliteral interpretation of the Scripture? None whatsoever. It is clearly a case of a dual hermeneutic.

DeHaan is also guilty at this point. He encourages his readers, saying "Read your Bible as you would any other book of history or fact."[23] This sounds great and perfectly in line with the claim of a single hermeneutic, but in his discussion of Matthew 5-7 he says,

We are now come to three chapters (Matthew 5, 6, 7) which you all know as the Sermon on the Mount, probably the most misunderstood and misrepresented chapters of the Bible. In these three chapters Jesus gives the constitution and by-laws of the kingdom He had come to offer. It is a rule of the kingdom and contains the laws which will govern the subjects of the King during His reign on earth.[24]

Now, if one reads Matthew as one "would read any other book of history or fact," the meaning Scofield and DeHaan give this passage is not at all apparent. The reader is invited to read the entire book of Matthew to see the context, and by this means determine for himself whether the interpretation given is the one you get from reading it like any other book. In reality Scofield and DeHaan are guilty of a dual hermeneutic and of allegorizing far beyond that followed by conservative Amillennialists. Their claim of a single hermeneutic is incorrect, to say the least.

One other example of the inconsistency under consideration should suffice. H. A. Ironside, in discussing the opening of the sixth seal (Rev. 6:12) remarks, "We are not to take this as a literal earthquake....It is therefore not a world-wide, literal earthquake that the sixth seal introduces, but rather the destruction of the present order political, social, and ecclesiastical—reduced to chaos."[25] Now my interpretation of this passage is very similar to that of Dr. Ironside, but I resent being castigated for doing what the most eminent Dispensationalists do whenever it suits their purposes.

Loraine Boettner addresses this problem:

---

22  *Scofield Bible* (note on Matt. 5:2).
23  DeHaan, *The Second Coming of Jesus*, p. 83.
24  *Ibid.*, p. 96.
25  H. A. Ironside, *Lectures on the Revelation*, p. 114.

## HERMENEUTICS

It is inconsistent for Premillennialists to pick and choose in deciding what statements they will take symbolically and what ones they will take figuratively while at the same time criticizing Post- and Amillennialists for accepting figurative or symbolical interpretations when those seem preferable. If figurative or symbolical interpretation is wrong in principle, it should not be resorted to at all. Otherwise Premillennialists do exactly what they accuse Post- and Amillennialists of doing,—take Scripture literally where that seems preferable, and spiritualize where that seems preferable.[26]

Oswald Allis observes the same tendency in Premillennialism: "In dealing with Old Testament history its treatment is highly figurative."[27] DeHaan's Portraits of Christ in Genesis is a shining example of this fact. Allis then observes that especially in prophecy their "treatment is marked by a literalism which refuses to recognize types and figures. Israel must mean Israel; it does not and cannot signify the Church."[28] He then poses a question that points out the unfairness of the attack.

Why is the method of interpretation which is regarded as so suitable to the Pentateuch, so utterly unsuited to Ezekiel? If Ruth can give a "foreview of the Church," if "the larger interpretation" of the Song of Solomon concerns the Church, why must the Church be absent from the glorious visions of Isaiah?[29]

This question Allis raises is not directly concerned with the question of a dual hermeneutic, but it does point up an inconsistency in the way Dispensationalists interpret the Bible. Viewed in this light, the matter is related to the question under consideration. Allis's question requires an answer, but no satisfactory answer has been given. They are literalists when they find it convenient, and they are spiritualizers when they find that better suits their interests.

Sandeen gives us an accurate statement of the situation. He quotes another's opinion: "Critics like James Grant concluded that the millenarians simply applied the literalistic interpretation whenever it suited their fancy."[30] And, of course, when it does not suit their fancy, they feel free to allegorize and spiritualize. The moral is that those who make rules should obey them.

---

26 Loraine Boettner, *The Millennium*, p. 105.
27 Oswald T. Allis, *Prophecy and the Church*, p. 23.
28 *Ibid.*
29 *Ibid.*, p. 24.
30 Sandeen, *op. cit.*, pp. 109-110.

CHAPTER 4

# HERMENEUTICS
## (CONTINUED)

### Justification for a Dual Hermeneutic

Exploding the "myth of a single hermeneutic" does not of itself justify a dual hermeneutic. A dual hermeneutic requires adequate biblical support, and it should meet the demands of logic and reason. Starting with the latter, we all recognize that certain modes of expression lend themselves more readily to the use of figures of speech than do others. Poetry is often rich in metaphors and similes, as well as other figures of speech. This is recognized in biblical hermeneutics, just as it is in literature. When poetry is studied in the Bible, it is interpreted according to this rule. For this reason, a different hermeneutic is used for poetry than for prose. Thus there is no logical reason for rejecting the idea of a hermeneutic for prophecy different from that for history. The answer lies in showing that some prophecy is highly figurative.

No one in his right mind would contend that all poetry must be interpreted as figures of speech. Much poetry is just as true to facts as any prose writing. It is just that poetry contains more figures of speech, hence we should watch for them with greater diligence than when studying Bible portions which are written in prose. Therefore, if prophecy is found to contain more figures of speech than the rest of the Bible, it would not require that all prophecy be interpreted as symbolic, any more than all poetry be so interpreted. Each prophecy would have to be interpreted on its own merits.

It is generally recognized that prophecy has at least two distinct forms. The prophecies that are clothed in ordinary terms are less likely to be figurative than a specialized type of prophecy usually designated as apocalyptic. Many of the figures used in regular or ordinary forms of prophecy are often recognized as figurative by all expositors. Most of the difficulty, though certainly not all of it, will be in understanding the several apocalyptic prophecies of both Testaments. I hold that in some cases it is impossible to determine whether the prophecy is entirely literal in meaning, or if it is entirely figurative, or if it contains elements of both. In pressing for a dual hermeneutic, our purpose is to make room for a figurative interpretation rather than becoming dogmatic to the extent of insisting that all prophecy be interpreted figuratively.

Cox states, "An axiom of Bible Study is that most sections demand literal interpretation unless the context or other known scripture passages demand figurative or spiritual interpretation."[31] I am in full accord with that statement. Hamilton says,

> Literal interpretation of the prophecy is to be accepted unless (a) the passages contain obviously figurative language, or (b) unless the New Testament gives authority for interpreting them in other than a literal sense, or (c) unless a literal interpretation would produce a contradiction with truths, principles, or factual statements contained in non-symbolic books of the New Testament.[32]

I am in agreement with the above, but I also concur with Hamilton's further statement regarding an interpretation that violates rule (c) above. It reads:

> For Christians to look forward to a literal temple in Jerusalem, with the restoration of the whole sacrificial system, seems to dishonor the sacrifice of Christ on the cross....The very heart of evangelical truth is the once-for-all character of the sacrifice of Christ on the cross of Calvary.[33]

In the above quotation Hamilton refers to an apocalyptic prophecy. It is found in Ezekiel, and will be exegeted later. At this point it serves as an introduction to this special classification of prophetic utterances. It is assumed that adequate evidence has been given in the foregoing to prove that certain aspects of general prophecy are correctly interpreted figuratively, and that even those who contend for a single hermeneutic so interpret them. But the evidence for figurative interpretation is much stronger for apocalyptic prophecy than is true for general prophecy. Most of the present flood of Premillennial literature is based on apocalyptic passages, and it is here that their extreme literalism is most patently in error.

Apocalyptic literature is a term reserved for a distinctive type of prophecy. It freely uses symbols, and, like poetry, is given to superlative

---

31  Wm. E. Cox, *The Millennium*, p. 22.
32  Floyd E. Hamilton, *The Basis of Millennial Faith*, p. 53.
33  *Ibid.*, p. 40.

imagery. The heavenly bodies, sun, moon, and stars, are often referred to; animals of various kinds are mentioned frequently, disasters on the one side and triumphs on the other are woven into these prophecies in a manner that is often confusing to the average reader, and from the host of interpretations given these passages, at least some of the authorities are confused about them. It is altogether possible that those who are most certain of the interpretations are the ones who are most confused.

It is generally recognized that apocalyptic passages are found in most, if not all, of the prophets; but certain prophets are noted for their use of this kind of language, hence they are called apocalyptic writers or prophets. Joel is considered the oldest apocalyptist by the majority of scholars. Isaiah has some passages that are definitely apocalyptic, but he has so much that is of a different nature that he is not generally considered an apocalyptic prophet. Daniel, Ezekiel and Zechariah are the ones that are most definitely apocalyptic of the Old Testament. The title of *Apocalypse* indicates that the last book of the Bible is apocalyptic in nature, and its contents certainly bear out this conclusion. The Olivet discourse of Christ (Matt. 24; Mark 13; Luke 21) is also a short apocalyptic.

Isaiah chapter 13 is an interesting apocalyptic prophecy. In verse 1 Isaiah informs us that he is speaking against Babylon. In his pronouncement of doom upon this wicked city, he waxes eloquent declaring, "For the stars of heaven and the constellations thereof shall not give their light: the sun shall be darkened in his going forth, and the moon shall not cause her light to shine." To take that literally would be folly. That this is said of literal Babylon seems evident from verse 17 which indicates the Medes would conquer Babylon, which they did in the course of years. And that this refers to a literal overthrow is found in verses 20-22 which indicate utter desolation and abandonment to the wild beasts. This gives an accurate picture of the site of Babylon as it is today.

The point we wish to make here is that we accept a literal fulfillment as it is set forth in verses 17-22, but we must consider as figurative verse 10 which was quoted in the preceding paragraph. But we must rely on the plain verses for this explanation. The reference to the sun, moon, and stars is figurative of that destruction which is spelled out in the plain portion of the chapter. This use of the sun, moon, and stars is frequently utilized by the apocalyptists in their prophecies of doom. This should be kept in mind as consideration is given to Matthew 24 and Acts 2. It should be noted in passing that

Scofield spiritualizes this far more than I have done. He contends that literal Babylon is not involved. He projects this into the future as the destruction of "the Gentile world-system." (See note on Isa. 13:1.) This is spiritualizing with a vengeance, and shows the extremes to which the so-called literalistic concept takes one. This business of the sun, moon, and stars must be fulfilled literally, regardless of how it distorts other portions of Scripture.

Isaiah 34 is another apocalyptic chapter. It forecasts the destruction of Idumea which is but another name for Edom and that of Bozrah, one of the principal cities of Edom. Note the extravagant language that is used in this apocalyptic passage.

Their slain also shall be cast out, and their stink shall come up out of their carcasses, and the mountains shall be melted with their blood. And all the host of heaven shall be dissolved, and the heavens shall be rolled together as a scroll: and all their host shall fall down, as the leaf falleth off from the vine, and as the falling fig from the fig tree. For my sword shall be bathed in heaven: behold, it shall come down on Idumea, and upon the people of my curse, to judgment. The sword of the Lord is filled with blood…for the Lord hath a sacrifice in Bozrah, and a great slaughter in the land of Idumea (Isa. 34:3-6).

Note such statements as mountains being "melted with their blood," the host of heaven (stars and planets) being "dissolved," and the heavens being "rolled together as a scroll." Now Isaiah says these words against Idumea and Bozrah. She also has become literally desolate, and abandoned to owls and wild beasts, nettles and brambles as verses 13-15 state. As in chapter 13 the literal fulfillment of the literal portion also constitutes a fulfillment of the apocalyptic expressions which are but figurative descriptions of the literal desolation which came upon Idumea and Bozrah. Jeremiah evidently made reference to this earlier prophecy of Isaiah's when he wrote, "For I have sworn by myself, saith the Lord, that Bozrah shall become a desolation, a reproach, a waste, and a curse" (Jer. 49:13). This prophecy plainly referred to the destruction of Edom and Bozrah as evidenced by both Jeremiah and Isaiah, but Scofield says it refers to the battle of Armageddon. (Heading inserted at the beginning of Isaiah 34 by Scofield.)

Ezekiel is counted as one of the apocalyptic prophets because a great deal of his prophecy is of that nature. Ezekiel 32:1-32 is a lament over Pharaoh and Egypt for the destruction which is to come to them. One reason for selecting this portion is because even Scofield admits that it refers to what it says it does rather than to some distant fulfillment yet future. Part of this lament reads,

And when I shall put thee out, I will cover the heaven, and make the stars thereof dark; I will cover the sun with a cloud, and the moon shall not give her light. All the bright lights of heaven will I make dark over thee, and set darkness upon thy land, saith the Lord God (Ezek. 32:7-8).

Scofield really slipped on this last one. Nothing like the above has happened, therefore according to the literalistic mode of interpretation, it must be literally fulfilled sometime in the future. If the two passages from Isaiah refer to a time yet future, this one from Ezekiel must also be future. On the other hand, I have interpreted all three of them as apocalyptic, and as figures of speech. They are not to be interpreted literally as events in the future when the heavenly bodies will become dark. Instead they depict the punishment and destruction that God has already meted out to these nations. It is worthy of note that Scofield interprets the apocalyptic portions of the two passages from Isaiah as literal and future, and he spiritualizes the literal fulfillment of the plain portions found in the latter verses of each section. This reverses hermeneutic principles endorsed by the literalists.

Literalists admit that passages that plainly involve figures of speech should be interpreted accordingly, and that others should be interpreted literally. But apocalyptic passages are patently figures of speech, so much so that Cox holds that they demand figurative interpretation unless other elements require a literal interpretation.

An axiom of Bible study is that most sections demand literal interpretation unless the context or other known scripture passages demand figurative or spiritual interpretation. In apocalyptic literature the very opposite is true; here one must interpret figuratively, unless literal interpretation is absolutely demanded. The nature of such books as Ezekiel, Daniel, and the Revelation makes understanding impossible apart from an appreciation of the tools of the artist who painted the picture.[34]

Terry writes in a similar vein. After discussing Isaiah 13:2-13, he adds:

Such highly emotional and figurative passages are common to all the prophetic writers, but in the so-called apocalyptic prophets we note a peculiar prominence of symbolism. In its earlier and yet undeveloped form it first strikes our attention in the book of Joel, which may be the oldest apocalypse. But its fuller development appears among the later prophets,

---

34  Cox, *op. cit.*, pp. 22-23.

Daniel, Ezekiel, and Zechariah, and its perfected structure in the New Testament Apocalypse of John.[35]

Snowden remarks that it is "little less than stupidity" to take such passages as Amos 9:13 "literally and mechanically."[36] Now few, if any, of these men are stupid. Most of them interpret Amos 9:13 as figurative. I know of none that contend that the "mountains shall [literally] drop sweet wine," or that literally "the hills shall melt"; but they do hold that this symbolism must refer to literal Israel, and that it does not find its fulfillment in the Church. And thus it is with all prophecy. Where it suits their thesis of a restored Israel, they insist on a literal interpretation; but where it does not, they are free to interpret figuratively just as others do. But in passages such as Amos 9:13 they combine the figurative and the literal, but castigate others if they interpret Isaiah 35 as being part figurative and part literal. Dozens of instances where apocalyptic passages are interpreted figuratively could be cited from their writings, but beware of spiritualizing those passages they use to support a future literal reign of Christ on earth with the Jews in the driver's seat.

When apocalyptic writings are interpreted literally, it can produce various anomalies. Animal sacrifices must be restored. Circumcision will again be a religious requirement. The division that Christ broke down between Jew and Gentile will be erected again. The old Mosaic system is to be restored, and the temple and Jerusalem rebuilt, even though these things involve conditions that are impossible. Then, according to Ezekiel interpreted literally, Gog will be destroyed in a battle fought with bows and arrows (Ezek. 39:3) just prior to the period they interpret as the millennium.

But if Revelation 20 is also interpreted literally, Gog will be destroyed at the close of the millennium, rather than before the millennium. If these passages be interpreted as symbolic or figurative, no difficulty occurs; but when they are interpreted literally, Ezekiel and the Revelation contradict each other. But truth does not contradict truth. And the Bible, being truth, does not contradict itself. It is essential that it be understood that apocalyptic prophecies are given in figurative or symbolic language if other contradictions are to be avoided.

---

35  Milton S. Terry, *Biblical Hermeneutics*, p. 415.
36  James H. Snowden, *The Comning Of The Lord*, p. 257.

## The Hermeneutics of Symbolic Language

Probably the first form of written communication was picture writing. We are so dependent on our system of an alphabet from which words have been constructed, which words have been assigned an arbitrary signification, that picture language seems strange and very enigmatic. Symbolic language is likewise unwieldly and imprecise, but it does follow certain general rules, else it would not be true communication. The Bible gives us several inspired interpretations by which we understand many word pictures. Logic supplies others that are helpful.

Symbolic language follows the principle of analogy just as hieroglyphics or picture writing does. The analogical relationship may be real or acquired. When one person calls another a "skunk," or "a hog," he is inferring that a certain attribute of the animal is shared in common by the individual thus categorized. On the other hand if we read of the Atlanta Braves clobbering the Pittsburgh Pirates, the designations are acquired. The Atlanta team is not necessarily any braver than the Pittsburgh team, nor are they any more likely to have a large number of Indians on their team. And we cannot be certain that the Pirates are better base stealers than the Braves.

Thus a lion-like creature could represent the cruel and despotic rule of Nebuchadnezzar and Babylon (Dan. 7:4, 17), and at the same time it could represent the tribe of Judah which had adopted that animal as the figure to go on their banner or ensign which was no doubt based on Jacob's words (Gen. 49:8-10; Rev. 4:7). The former is based on analogy or similitude; the latter may have been so originally, but for the tribe, it must be thought of as an acquired relationship. A sheep is a symbol of a Christian (John 10:1-18) by analogy, but a sheep is a symbol of Christ by both analogy (Isa. 53:7 and Matt. 26:62-63) and also by acquirement (Rev. 14:1-4).

In a number of places the writer explains some of the symbols used, just as Jesus explained some of His parables. We can be sure of the meanings in these instances, but we cannot know that every other apocalyptist uses them in exactly the same way. Just as a "run" in a stocking is quite different to a "run" by the Atlanta Braves, in Daniel 7 certain wild beasts are said to represent kings or kingdoms, but in Luke 10:3 other wild animals, wolves in this instance, are symbols of opponents the disciples were to face: men with a wolf nature. Even today, the "wolf whistle" speaks of one's nature. Thus a lion-like creature in Daniel 7 refers to an oppressive government, whereas in Isaiah 35 it refers to men who have a ferocious nature.

Horns have been a symbol for power among many people. Thus, ten horns of Daniel 7 represent ten kings or kingdoms, whereas the seven horns of the "Lamb slain" refer to Jesus' omnipotence. In this figure the Lamb is symbolic of the redemptive work of Jesus Christ. Seven is a symbol for perfection or completeness, and a horn is a symbol of power, therefore the total symbol is of Christ and His omnipotence. Stars are symbols of leaders. In Isaiah 14:12 Nebuchadnezzar is referred to as a star.[37] Then in Revelation 1:20 religious leaders, possibly pastors, are symbolized by stars.[38] Thus, when apocalyptic prophecies refer to the darkening of these heavenly bodies, we understand that political or ecclesiastical leaders, or both, are suffering a loss of their former power and in some cases even death.

All recognize that whenever the temple is a symbol, it is a symbol of religious conditions. The problem is determining when it is a symbol and when it is to be taken literally. Other symbols from the temple and temple worship, such as the altar and sacrifices, are also symbols of religious conditions or events. Likewise human beings are usually symbols of ecclesiastical matters. Women, marriage, giving birth and similar symbols are used of the Church in both apocalyptic and nonapocalyptic writings. For example, the Church is the bride (John 3:29 and Rev. 21:9). All agree that the woman and the manchild of Revelation 12 is to be interpreted religiously, but agreement is lacking as to the significance of these symbols.

Certain symbols in Daniel and the Revelation involve a strange mixture of human and beastly characteristics. In Daniel 7:7-8, a beast is pictured that is fierce and terrible. It, according to the rules we have set down as guides to interpretation, represents a tyrannical government. The horns also represent kings or governments. But the eleventh horn had human characteristics, for its eyes and mouth were those of a man, and the mouth "spoke great things." It is held that this combination of human characteristics with those of a wild beast is a way of saying this symbol is dual in nature, partaking of both political and religious elements.

The same mixture of characteristics is attributed to the 10 horned beast, the two-horned beast, and the image to the beast in Revelation 13. Again we

---

37  This refers to the king of Babylon (v. 4). When this is made to refer to Satan, it is another case of spiritualizing prophecy and further evidence of a dual hermeneutic by Premillennialists.

38  The Greek term for angel means "messenger." These were Church leaders, possibly pastors or other representatives.

would interpret as a dual politico-religious institution. The "great whore" (apostate human) refers to an apostate religious institution that supports her, but which she controls (Rev. 17). This particular feature is peculiar to Daniel and the Revelation. Wild beasts in other apocalyptic writings are more apt to refer to the beastly nature of individual human beings. This interpretation cannot be proved, but it is reasonable, and it gives a logical explanation to a symbolism that is either ignored or for which no answer is attempted by most commentators.

Domesticated animals do not necessarily refer to governments in any prophecies or other figures of speech. The sheep is a common symbol for one rightly related to Christ. Destruction of cattle probably refers to the judgments of God, either spiritual or temporal. The four horses of Revelation 6 are probably additions partly to complete the picture, and partly to inject a color symbol. It would appear that the four colors represented in these successive scenes are far more important than the horses themselves.

The time element of prophecy is often not stated in the context. Apocalyptic prophecy is especially difficult at this point. And inasmuch as all prophecy contains elements of uncertainty until the fulfillment occurs, every one needs to maintain an element of reserve in forecasting future events. The practice of most Premillennial writers of linking a bunch of the "timeless" prophecies of "doubtful" meaning into a pattern of future events shows a shameful disregard for hermeneutical rules and solid exegesis. Even Dr. Graham in his book *World Aflame* is guilty of this very questionable practice.

Premillennialists tend to muddy the waters, even where a time factor is stated in the context. I refer to the expression, "In the last days." One can be certain that this does not refer to a future millennium, for the New Testament repeatedly informs us that the gospel age constitutes the "last days" (Heb. 1:2), or the last times, seasons or hours (I Pet. 1:20; I John 2:18). Scofield's efforts to establish two sets of "last days" (note on Acts 2:17) is completely unwarranted. It is forced exegesis if it can be termed exegesis at all. The distinction he makes is arbitrary and without scriptural support.

## The Year-Day Theory of Prophetic Time

The period of time covered by a prophecy is often not stated. Even when it is stated, questions do arise regarding whether the time given is literal or figurative. Daniel did not jump to conclusions regarding the seventy years of Jeremiah 25:11-12 (Dan. 9:2). Apparently it was revealed to him that these were seventy literal years. In other instances it seems that days are used as symbols of years, and that years are used as symbols of 360 years—each day representing a year. There is some scriptural support for this theory, but it is not sufficient to require that all prophecies be so interpreted. Each prophecy must await its fulfillment for one to be sure of just how to interpret the time element. It is unwise to apply the year-day rule to prophecies yet to be fulfilled, for the rule may not be applicable. Terry has an excellent statement concerning the year-day theory.

The year-day theory is thought to have some support in Daniel's prophecy of the seventy weeks (Dan. ix, 24-27). But the prophecy says not a word about days or years, but seventy heptads, or sevens. The position and gender of the word indicate its peculiar significance. It nowhere else occurs in the masculine except in Dan. x, 2-3, where it is expressly defined as denoting heptads of days. Unaccompanied by any such limiting word, and standing in such an emphatic position at the beginning of ver. 24, we have reason to infer at once that it involves some mystical import. When, now, we observe that it is a Messianic oracle, granted to Daniel when his mind was full of meditations upon Jeremiah's prophecy of the seventy years of Jewish exile (ver. 2), and in answer to his ardent supplications, we must naturally understand the seventy heptads as heptads of years. But this admission furnishes slender support to such a sweeping theory as would logically bring all prophetic designations of time to the principle that days mean years.[39]

The year-day theory has many advocates. It appears applicable to certain prophecies of the past, for history appears to furnish sufficient evidence to justify its application in specific cases. But there are too many uncertainties about unfulfilled prophecies, especially apocalyptic prophecies, to justify its use as a rule for future date setting. Possibly the 2,300 days found in Daniel 8:14 (literally evenings and mornings) has not been equaled as a source of problems relative to setting future dates. Wm. Miller forecast the end of the world from it. He counted from 457 B. C. forward for 2,300 years and got 1843 from it. The Seventh Day Adventists claim their movement was foretold prophetically from these same dates (except it is 1844 instead of 1843).[40]

The year-day theory depends a great deal on Daniel 7:25. In this passage the 11th horn was to continue for a time, considered as one year; times, the

---

39  Terry, *op. cit.*, p. 388.
40  Uriah Smith, *The Prophecies of Daniel and Revelation*, p. 145.

simple plural or two years; and the dividing of time, or half a year. Three and one-half years of 360 days each equals 1260 days which is said to mean 1260 years. This verse has been applied to the Roman Catholic Church with considerable cogency, though the period involved may have a date from late in the 3rd century A.D. to a date well into the 6th century A.D. as the beginning date. The ending date, of course, is set 1260 years from the beginning date. That this is a possible meaning cannot be denied, but it is short of absolute proof. If it be true, it still does not prove that days always mean years even in apocalyptic prophecy.

Herbert Armstrong makes a rather unusual use of the term "times." From Leviticus 26, it is found that God promised to punish Israel seven times under certain conditions. Armstrong admits that the word "times" or its equivalent is not found in the Hebrew text, but even so he applies the year-day theory to it. Seven times equals seven years which in turn equals 2,520 years. This is said to cover the period from the Assyrian captivity (c. 721 B.C.) to A.D. 1800. No justification can be found for this use of the year-day theory. Strange as this example is, it was not original with Armstrong. Years before, Russell had used this method to set A.D. 1914 as the year of Christ's return. The only difference was that Russell used 606 B.C. as the starting date. This was the beginning of the Babylonian captivity of Judah which he used as his starting point. Armstrong used the earlier date of the Assyrian captivity of Israel as his initial date. Apparently, Oswald J. Smith used this method to set the battle of Armageddon prior to 1933.[41] He used the destruction of Jerusalem as his starting date.

## Other Types of Symbolism

Color symbolism has been mentioned already, but it needs some discussion. When white is used symbolically, it always refers to purity. The soul that is cleansed is said to be white (Isa. 1:18; Dan. 12:10) or these are said to have white clothing (Rev. 3:5; 4:4; 7:9, 13, 14; 15:6). The Ancient of Days (Dan. 7:9) had garments of white. Angels appeared in white (Matt. 28:3; Mark 16:5; Acts 1:10). When Jesus was transfigured, His raiment became

---

[41] Walter K. Price, *The Coming Antichrist*, p. 39. Chapter 1 of this book lists many efforts to identify the Antichrist with some ruler such as Nero or Napoleon. In spite of the fact that all of these have been proved false by subsequent events, Mr. Price falls into the same error by attempting to establish time limits for his eschatological views.

white (Matt. 17:2); and He is seen by the Revelator riding a white horse (Rev. 19:11). God's throne is seen as being white (Rev. 20:11).

Since Christ is pictured riding a white horse (Rev. 19:11), it is natural to expect the Church to be in a similar fashion. The first horseman of Revelation 6 rides a white horse. Since Dispensationalists claim that the Church is raptured to heaven at the beginning of Revelation 4, they are forced to make an unnatural interpretation of this symbol.

In our day red may refer to courage, war, bloodshed, Russia, communism, or a house of prostitution. In the Bible it refers to sin (Isa. 1:18), and war (Rev. 12:3, 7). In the latter instance, the "great red dragon" not only signifies war or persecution, but it also refers to the institution which waged that war. Revelation 12 pictures the battle between the Church and the paganism of the Roman empire. It is our opinion, therefore, that in the Revelation, red is a symbol of paganism. Thus when the second horseman of Revelation 6 appears riding a red horse, this is taken to refer to paganism, the major opponent of the early Church after A.D. 70. This warfare is again indicated in Revelation 12, the major difference being that the Church is depicted as a woman, and paganism is symbolized by the great red dragon. That this dragon symbolizes paganism, rather than the prince of demons is important in interpreting Revelation 20.

The black horse (Rev. 6:5) is the opposite of white, hence it is a symbol of apostasy. It refers to the development of Roman Catholicism and other apostate churches that developed out of the early Church. The fourth horseman of Revelation 6 was colored a yellowish-green (like chlorine from *chloros*). It refers to the fully developed papacy.

There is also a symbolism of numbers which is almost universally recognized. In both the Old Testament and the New certain numbers appear repeatedly. The numbers are 1, 2, 3, 4, 7, 10, and 12. Without a great deal of elaboration, the symbolic meanings of these numbers are given. The number "1" represents unity, oneness, and independence. The number "2" symbolizes strength and courage. The number "3" is a perfect number. It may refer to the Trinity of God as well as certain trinities in things of this world. The triangle is a geometric figure of three sides which represents perfection because of its rigidity. The number "4" refers to the cosmos: four winds, four compass points, four corners. Seven unites God and man or the sacred and the worldly. The number "3" symbolizes the Trinity of God, and the number "4" symbolizes the cosmos or world God created. These, added

# Hermeneutics - Continued

together, give us the important number "7". Six may refer to man who was created on the sixth day, or it may be an evil number because it falls short of the perfect number which is seven.

The number "10" came to mean human perfection. The man who is perfect has ten toes and ten fingers. God listed the duties of man in ten words or commands. Apparently the number "12" has a special religious signification for there were twelve tribes of Israel, and Christ chose twelve apostles for the Church. As the sacred number "7" is obtained by adding the divine number "3" to the cosmic number "4" in a similar manner multiplying these two numbers results in the number "12."

Jesus' use of "seventy times seven" (Matt. 18:22) is an expression for an infinite number. The number 1,000 employs two numbers of special importance: ten and three. This would be expressed as ten to the third power. The number 144,000 is twelve times twelve times ten to the third power.

The time, times, and half a time (Dan. 12:7; Rev. 12:14) is a broken seven or half a seven. This could mean something important, or it could be of little consequence. However, in the Revelation this is not only expressed as a broken seven, it is also expressed as forty-two months or 1260 days. This evidently refers to a period of time, but it is not clear whether it is literal days that are intended, or whether the year-day theory applies. I apply the year-day theory to these periods in the Revelation, but in Daniel 12:7 I take them as literal. My reason for this is the way I interpret historical events. Others reverse this. Exegesis alone is not determinative. Dogmatism at this point, especially regarding the future, is nothing more nor less than egotism and should be recognized as such.

Number symbolism would not be complete without discussing the number 666 (Rev. 13:17-18). The number "6" is an ill-omened number that was considered ominous or sinister. It falls short of the sacred number "7," hence indicates failure or defeat. A single "6" thus is an omen of evil, but three of them linked together could be thought of as referring to complete or perfect evil. Two terms are frequently offered as the designations symbolized. These are *lateinos* and *Vicarius Filii Dei*. Both yield 666 when the numerical value of each letter is applied. The first simply refers to the Latin or Roman Church; the latter being one of the official designations of the Pope.

It is impossible to prove that either of these terms was intended or if they were not intended. Such applications do not rest on exegesis but upon a variety of interrelated matters. That these terms add up to 666 may be purely coincidental. However, for those who see the Roman Church portrayed in such passages as II Thessalonians 2 and Revelation 13, it is supportive evidence. It does not prove anything, but it is an additional segment of a chain of interpretations, none of which constitutes proof standing alone. Thus, the latter of these terms which declares that the Pope is the official representative of Jesus Christ, I find particularly appealing to me as the fulfillment of this prophecy. Others have an equal right to react differently.

## Further Considerations

Every serious Bible student is encouraged to obtain some knowledge of logic if he does not possess it already. This can be especially helpful in avoiding serious mistakes in biblical interpretation. A persuasive writer can present his material in such a manner that the unwary are fooled into accepting arguments that are not worthy of acceptance. Premillennial writers are often adept at using the proof-text method. Passages are lifted out of context and linked together in such a way as to impress the unwary, whereas those with a good background in logic are able to detect the weaknesses in the presentation.

Hanson speaks to this point. After referring to such books as *The Late Great Planet Earth*, *Bible Prophecy Reexamined*, and *Guide To Survival*, he adds, "These books attempt to show us the future by quoting predictions right out of the Bible…They take pieces out of the Bible and put them together in fantastic constructions." He concludes from this that "the writers are using the Bible rather than letting it speak for itself."[42] This is particularly evident in the use of prophecies which are contextually timeless, but to which they assign a time that fits the author's eschatological scheme. Often it is necessary to read the context to enable one to detect the element that has been injected into the passage.

A single example of this will suffice. Walvoord and others repeatedly refer to John 14:1-3 as referring to the rapture of the Church. This is done in such a way as to lend support to the eschatological scheme of the writer, when the fact is this text says nothing about a particular scheme of last things. John 14:1-3 is just as friendly to the Amillennial and Postmillennial views as it is to the Premillennial view. One does not have to believe in a

---

42  Richard S. Hanson, *The Future Of The Late Great Planet Earth*, p. 12

# HERMENEUTICS - CONTINUED

pretribulation rapture or a posttribulation rapture because of this verse. The fact that Christ is speaking of coming for the Church does not prove that the Church will be raptured before the consummation. Nothing is said in this passage of any relation to any other eschatological event.

Beware of any writer who speaks with the "voice of authority" on unfulfilled prophecy. This denies the general rule of hermeneutics that prophecy is enigmatic and obscure prior to fulfillment. The certitude with which many Premillennialists set forth their theory of eschatology gives the reader the impression the writer considers his interpretations to be infallible. Lindsey outlines the progress of a future war, the alignment of nations, strategies that will be used, and even a mistaken attack. Fairbairn quotes Bishop Butler as saying, "Prophecy is nothing but the history of events before they come to pass."[43] This is unacceptable to most interpreters. Past mistakes should make interpreters more cautious.

During the early stages of World War II, I listened to a radio program entitled *History Prewritten*. This prophet's thesis was that Italy, Germany, Russia, and Japan would be allies and that the battle of Armageddon would soon be fought. At that time Russia was not in the war, and she did have a nonaggression pact with Germany. News reports of Germany massing troops on her eastern border did not affect this man's confidence in the least. The infallibility of the Bible made his predictions an absolute certainty, in his mind, but the morning Germany attacked Russia his program was taken off the air.

Dr. D. Shelby Corlett was editor of the *Herald of Holiness* at this particular time. Had Hitler's attack been delayed by twenty-four hours, that paper would have been in the mails with a similar article. He was saved from disaster by this narrow margin. Past misconceptions regarding Napoleon Bonaparte, Mussolini, Stalin, et al, should make people quit attempting to tie current events in with prophecy in this manner, but some people are unable to profit by the mistakes of others. Lindsey's date setting is even more presumptuous. There is even lack of unanimity regarding a number of fulfilled prophecies, so there is no solid basis for knowing that a certain political or social development will result in the fulfillment of any prophecy. All such efforts are but guesses. God has not intended for us to fully understand prophecies sufficiently to forecast

---

43 Patrick Fairbairn, *The Interpretation of Prophecy*, p. 85.

their fulfillment in time, or how to relate current developments to prophecy which may be in the process of fulfillment.

An examination of Lindsey's book *The Late Great Planet Earth* brings this section to a close. Chapter 14 is appropriately entitled *Polishing the Crystal Ball*. Those who read this book should consider it just that or as pure fiction. It has no place in serious Bible study or biblical literature. Only its major deficiencies can receive attention:

1. Only forced exegesis can make "this generation" (Matt. 24:34) apply to the present generation. Even those who apply it to the Jews as a race are not accepting the apparent meaning, but to apply it to the generation living in 1948 does violence to the Bible. This smacks of biblical quackery. The tenuousness of his position is so evident that he sounds more like a charlatan than a biblical scholar.

2. Most of the texts he uses are from apocalyptic passages in Ezekiel, Daniel, Zechariah, Revelation, and Matthew 24. These passages are so figurative that a literal interpretation is quite dangerous. Date setting is always dangerous and as uncertain as all guesses are.

3. Exegesis does not establish a time factor in Ezekiel, and Matthew 24:34 lends itself more readily to the destruction of Jerusalem in A.D. 70 than it does to the consummation. The building of the temple Ezekiel describes could be symbolic, and even if literal, the time element cannot be proved to coincide with the time of Matthew 24:34. Thus Lindsey's time schedule does not depend on exegesis, but it relies on his particular interpretation of an apocalyptic passage.

4. Beyond the fact that Lindsey's date setting depends on his interpretation of apocalyptic passages, the basis for starting his generation in 1948 depends on a parable within an apocalyptic passage. This makes for double uncertainty. To whom does the parable of the fig tree refer? Jesus does not say. It is not explained in the context. Upon what authority, then, does Lindsey start his generation in 1948, this year that the nation of Israel was formed? He does so only on his own authority. So Lindsey has built an air castle out of the imaginations of his head. The sad thing is that this book is making a tremendous impact on the American people. But as with Miller and other date setters, the final result is likely to be damaging.

The more likely explanation of the parable of the fig tree is that Christ had reference to the Church, the kingdom of God if you please. It was then in its infancy. Its shoots were tender and could easily be broken. But the tender shoot did presage something more substantial. Before that generation passed or people who were then living should all die, the Church would be more substantial. History bears out that this did occur. It can be checked on. But Lindsey cannot be proved wrong prior to 1988 or shortly thereafter.

Several times Lindsey uses the expression, "If my interpretation is correct," and he denies any claim to infallibility; yet he leaves no room for his timetable to be in error. The events he looks for at the end of this age must come while some of those living in 1948 are still living. He sets forty years as a general limit for a generation, but allows enough time beyond that to make sure he is dead before it can be said with absolute certainty that he was wrong. He expects the rapture about 1988, but admits it might be some years later.

He takes an equally adamant stand on the rebuilding of Ezekiel's temple. In spite of the apocalyptic nature of the latter chapters of Ezekiel; and though physical impossibilities are involved in the temple plans, the reapportionment of the land, and the rebuilding of Jerusalem; and in the face of irreconcilable conflicts with New Testament teachings which grow out of a literal interpretation of Ezekiel, Lindsey pompously declares, "Obstacle or no obstacle, it is certain that the temple will be rebuilt. Prophecy demands it."[44] Even if it occurs as Lindsey has prophesied, it will not be because prophecy demands it. Prophecy does not demand it. Rather Lindsey's interpretation of prophecy demands it. And the two are by no means identical.

The extreme literalism of Dispensationalism and much Premillennialism is but another link with ancient Judaism. The Jews took the command of Moses to bind his words to their arms and foreheads (Deut. 6:8) very literally. Their amulets and phylacteries were a product of this rigid literalism. This is closely akin to the literal interpretation of Mark 16:18 which produced groups of "snake handlers." A similar literalism causes some Jehovah's Witnesses to refuse blood transfusions, medicines, and participation in the salute to the flag.

If the same approach is taken towards Jesus' words in Matthew 18:8-9, we would be required to instruct certain people to maim themselves physically by cutting off their hands or feet or plucking out an eye. I am thankful that few have gone so far. However, Allis cites Dr. L. S. Chafer as one who claims this does refer to self mutilation, but that it will take place

---

44 Hal Lindsey, *The Late Great Planet Earth*, p. 56.

during the millennium.[45] Dr. Chafer, as president of the Dallas Theological Seminary, was the spokesman for Dispensationalists during his tenure as president of that institution. I am not aware of whether this teaching is still being advocated by that school and other Dispensationalists or not, but this does show the dangers of such extreme literalism in regard to exhortations within the Scriptures which have nothing to do with prophecy. But since it is dangerous at that level, it is even more dangerous when applied to prophetic utterances.

---

45   Allis, *op. cit.*, pp. 264ff.

CHAPTER 5

# ESCHATOLOGICAL SYSTEMS, TERMS, & HISTORICAL DATA

The Greek term *eschatos* appears more than 50 times in the Greek New Testament. Its basic meaning is "last" and is so translated 46 times. This word is combined with the Greek *logos* as in psychology or sociology to give us the term "eschatology." It refers to what the Bible teaches regarding the end of time or of the age, or what a denomination or theologian teaches about the consummation. This is a very important aspect of biblical truth that was not emphasized like it should have been, but which is now being emphasized unduly. Too many are so preoccupied with the future that they are not as effective in soul winning as they should be.

From its inception the Church has had to fight heresy. At times the line between orthodoxy and heresy has been obliterated. Other theological concepts have been allowed to develop side by side, with neither being defined as heretical. It appears that the doctrine of an earthly reign of Christ is handled in this manner. As has been observed already, this teaching was prominent in Jewish traditions before and after Christ; hence there was a likelihood that some converts would bring this teaching into the Church. It has been shown that some of the disciples expected this prior to Pentecost, but its presence in the New Testament is denied.

One of the early advocates of an earthly reign was a heretic named Cerinthus. Irenaeus, Hippolytus, and Dionysius all classify him as a heretic. Polycarp is said to have affirmed that John the apostle once fled from a building because Cerinthus was seen in it.[46] Eusebius even classifies him as the *heresiarch* or chief heretic. But it is not certain that the mere fact that he taught a future earthly reign of Christ had very much to do with him being so classified. It was his teaching of fleshly gratification and sensual pleasures during the millennium plus various other heresies that earned him this title.

---

46 Eusebius Pamphilus, *The Ecclesiastical History*, bk. 3, chap. 28.

It is generally agreed that after Augustine strongly endorsed the Amillennial approach Premillennialism quickly died out, but there is considerable disagreement about the extent of Premillennialism prior to the time of Augustine. Dispensationalists, of which Walvoord and Tan are but examples, contend that the ante-Nicene fathers are permeated with Premillennialism.[47] This is not true and it is false that Amillennialists generally accept the above claim. Several writers can be quoted to discredit this claim. Albertus Pieters in his study of the "Apostolic Period" found that "references...to a millennium" were "rare." Of the nine authors of that period, he found "only two of them voicing such an expectation."[48]

A study by Murray indicated that one of these two, Barnabas, gave "evidence of acquaintance with chiliastic strains of thinking," but that these references did not prove "that he was a chiliast."[49] Kromminga's study verified Murray's findings. Thus he concluded, "This reduces the number of chiliasts which I recognize among the Apostolic Fathers to just one."[50] That one was Papias whose claims of personal knowledge direct from the apostles themselves is discounted by Eusebius. It is recognized that Papias was a millennialist, but it is denied that Christ and the apostles are the true source of his teaching. In regard to Barnabas, I must dissent with Murray and Kromminga to side with Pieters. Papias was the only Premillennial writer up to A.D. 150, but Barnabas was a millennialist. Barnabas denied anyone would be resurrected prior to the millennium. Thus he is a Postmillennialist. The book of Barnabas is a strongly worded polemic against Jewish expectations, hence his millennialism brings no comfort to those who teach a Judaistic restoration during the millennium.

For the remainder of the ante-Nicene period (A.D. 150 to A.D. 325) Kromminga recognizes only six millennialists but out of a great host of writers. These are Justin Martyr, Irenaeus, Tertullian, Commodianus, Victorinus, and Lactantius.[51] This list closely parallels that of Jerome.[52]

---

47 Tan, *op. cit.*, p. 68. He quotes from *The Millennial Kingdom* by Walvoord, p. 123.
48 Quoted by D. H. Kromminga, *The Millennium In The Church*, p. 41.
49 *Ibid.*, p. 42.
50 *Ibid.*
51 *Ibid.*, p. 53.
52 Jerome, *Nicene and Post-Nicene Fathers*, vol. III, p. 367.

# Eschatological Systems, Terms, & Historical Data

My own research is in full agreement with Kromminga's findings for this period, except that Tertullian changed his views.

Of the later ante-Nicene fathers who are most frequently said to be millenarians, Justin Martyr and Tertullian both held that the Jewish promises were fulfilled in the Church. Lactantius and Victorinus both held that the first resurrection was a spiritual resurrection. Apparently, Tertullian was an Amillennialist prior to his defection to the Montanist sect. Irenaeus was one of the few who made reference to the Abrahamic covenant, but he repeatedly affirms that the promise is fulfilled in the Church—not the Jews. He contends of Abraham, "together with his seed, that is those who fear God and believe in Him, he shall receive it at the resurrection of the just. For his seed is the Church which receives the adoption to God through the Lord."[53]

Hippolytus is claimed by most millenarians. Kromminga refutes this claim.[54] Hippolytus had a great deal to say about the Antichrist and his anticipated reign.[55] But he said nothing about a millennial reign. Later he will be quoted as believing that eternity is the condition which immediately follows the persecution of the Antichrist. This proves that expecting an Antichrist and a future persecution does not of itself prove the writer to be a millennialist.

## Eschatological Terms Defined

This section is largely definitive, but certain comments will be added whenever it seems appropriate. Technical terms such as the *parousia* will be considered later. Only the larger, more comprehensive terms are considered in this section.

1. **Chiliasm.** A Greek term from *chiliad* which means 1,000. It refers to a 1,000 year period. It is the older term for what is now most frequently called "millennialism" or "millenarianism." The time of the *chiliad* and the nature of the age to which it refers vary according to three major schools of thought with additional differences sometimes evident within these three schools.

2. **Millennialism.** This term derived from the Latin is identical in meaning to *chiliasm*. In earlier literature, the Greek term was universally used. The Latin term has now superseded the older term almost to the point of excluding it from writings of this age.

---

53  Irenaeus, *Ante-Nicene Fathers,* vol. I, p. 561. See pp. 558-561.
54  Kromminga, *op. cit.,* p. 60.
55  Hippolytus, *Ante-Nicene Fathers,* vol. V, pp. 204ff.

**3. Premillennialism.** The prefix is designed to relate the time of Christ's second coming to the millennium. This term means that the second coming of Christ is pre, i.e., before, the millennium. It is contended by Premillennialists that the true kingdom of God was not established at Christ's first coming, or that a fuller expression of the kingdom awaits the millennium. The second coming of Christ is held to be the event that will initiate the kingdom and that it will continue for 1,000 years or for whatever time this 1,000 years represents if it be symbolic. This future kingdom, or fuller expression of the present kingdom, will involve an earthly reign of Christ over a civil or political body that will be world-wide. It will be a time of universal peace and prosperity. Many hold that drastic changes in nature and animal life will accompany this millennium.

**4. Postmillennialism.** Those of this persuasion believe that the second coming of Christ will be post (after) the millennium. They believe that the kingdom was fully established at the first coming, and that the Church is an expression of the kingdom. According to this school of interpretation, the gospel will eventually win the world to Christ; then after this, there will be 1,000 years of peace and prosperity to be followed by the second coming of Christ. No earthly reign of Christ is anticipated, nor is there to be a political kingdom yet future. Christians are now in the kingdom of God.

**5. Amillennialism.** This designation is anomalous in two different ways. First, a Greek prefix, the *alpha* privative, which has the force of "no" or "non" is joined to a Latin term. This is not exactly consistent. Second, it does not accurately describe the belief of most of those who accept this designation. Cox says, "This is an unfortunate term, however, since the great majority of amillennialists definitely do believe in a millennium based on Revelation 20:1-10."[56] He goes on to add that term is applied to them because the passage from the Revelation is taken to be "figurative language describing the spiritual reign of Christ in the hearts of his people which is already going on."

Augustine held that the millennium of Revelation 20 was coextensive with the gospel age, and that both will close with the second coming of Christ. Other Amillennialists believe it will be but a portion of the gospel age. But this does make the term Postmillennialism applicable to Amillenialists for they do place the second coming of Christ post (after) their spiritualized millennium. This has caused Kromminga to say,

---

56 Cox, *op. cit.*, pp. 15-16.

"Therefore Postmillennialism is the generic term and Amillennialism is a variety of it."[57]

Amillennialists are in agreement with Postmillennialists regarding the kingdom being established at Christ's first coming, and that his second coming will usher in a general resurrection, the final judgment, and the beginning of our eternal state. However, Amillennialists are in agreement with Premillennialists that good and evil will continue to function in opposition to one another until the second coming. It is evident that Amillennialism has fewer points of difference from Postmillennialism than is true of Premillennialism. Thus, if Postmillennialism is abandoned by anyone as no longer tenable, he is more likely to turn to Amillennialism than to Premillennialism.

6. **Dispensationalism.** Just as Amillennialism is a specialized form of Postmillennialism, so Dispensationalism is a specialized form of Premillennialism. It is a "Johnny-come-lately" in the field of eschatology, but it has made a tremendous impression on eschatological thought, especially among those who were already Premillennialists. Although Dispensationalism is not especially strong *per se,* so much of their teaching has become standard among Premillennialists in general that special attention must be given to its rise and the innovative doctrines which it stresses.

In the first section of this chapter, it was stated that Augustine laid millennialism to rest during his life time. Some Postmillennialism did develop during medieval times, and it became the leading eschatological view in the 18th and 19th centuries. Then it faded into less prominence, and there was a resurgence of Premillennialism. Because of its radical distinctions from the old *chiliasm* which has sometimes been designated as Historic Premillennialism, and because of its impact on present day eschatology, special attention is given to it.

In the early days of Protestantism, many writers identified the first beast of Revelation 13 with Romanism, tending to make the Pope the Antichrist. In an effort to divert attention away from Romanism, a Spanish Jesuit named Francisco Ribera presented a futuristic interpretation of the Revelation.[58] This was about 1585 or 1590. It was done to confuse the Protestants

---

57  Kromminga, *op. cit.,* p. 299.
58  Boettner, *op. cit.,* p. 367; also J. Barton Payne, *The Immiment Appearing of Christ,* p. 30.

of that day. It was not accorded a great deal of attention in those days, but it has arisen as a plague here in the 20th century.

Later, when Napoleon became such a scourge, Protestantism often named him the Antichrist, but in the course of time this became untenable. It was in 1826 that Samuel R. Maitland introduced the futurism of Ribera to Protestantism.[59] In 1828 a number of persons interested in prophecy came together to form the Catholic Apostolic Church. These came to be called Irvingians or Irvingites from their main leader, Edward Irving.[60] Irving set the date of "Christ's return for 1864."[61] The Irvingites were criticized because of their "speaking in tongues" and the excesses which accompanied this manifestation.

From 1830 onward the torch was picked up by the Plymouth Brethren. J. N. Darby was so forceful in his presentation of this futurism that the movement came to be called Darbyism. Ironside, an early leader and writer of the movement, cites Darby as the person most responsible for the development and propagation of what developed into present day Dispensationalism. The fact that it was a new teaching is emphasized in this same quotation: "In fact, until brought to the fore through the writings and preaching of a distinguished ex-clergyman, Mr. J. N. Darby, in the early part of last century, it is scarcely to be found in a single book or sermon throughout a period of 1600 years!"[62] Of course, Ironside attempts to locate this new teaching as being part of the revelation given to Paul, but this cannot be done by legitimate methods of biblical interpretation.

So Dispensationalism received its approach to the Revelation, futurism, from the Roman Catholic Church. Its approach to Old Testament prophecy is identical to that of the Rabbis, except for this futurism they have injected into it. The date fixing of Irving gives Lindsey an excellent example to follow. The excesses, visions, and alleged revelations which accompanied its beginnings are just the kind of conditions one would expect a heresy to utilize. The newness of their doctrines is an added indication that it is heretical.

---

59 Sandeen, *op. cit.*, p. 37, and J. Barton Payne, *The Imminent Appearing of Christ*, p. 30.
60 Kromminga, *op. cit.*, pp. 250-251, and Sandeen, *op. cit.*, pp. 26-28.
61 James P. Martin, *The Last Judgment*, p. 191.
62 Geo. L. Murray, *Millennial Studies*, p. 132; quoted from H. A. Ironside, *Mysteries of God*, p. 50.

The Plymouth Brethren brought this strange new teaching to the United States. Seiss is probably the best known of these early propagators of this new eschatology in this country. W. E. Blackstone, who usually signs himself as W. E. B., wrote a book entitled *Jesus is Coming* which has been acclaimed as the most forceful presentation of Premillennialism ever written. Although it has been castigated by scholars as unscholarly, it did make a very real impact on Protestantism in America. My review of this work indicates it is not only unscholarly, but devious and questionable methods of convincing the reader are evident within its pages.

For example, on two different occasions he quotes, "and the dead in Christ shall rise first": and abruptly stops at that point. The unwary reader, especially those with little biblical knowledge, would naturally jump to the conclusion that this means to infer that those who are not "in Christ" will rise later. Of course, this is exactly what W. E. B. wanted them to believe. But this is not the thought of the apostle. The next verse gives the event that follows the first as referring to the living righteous, rather than to the wicked dead. This type of trickery and subterfuge, if not outright deceit, is not worthy of a professed follower of Christ, much less one who holds forth as a defender of biblical truth.

An even more important book which may be equally influential, and possibly of even greater influence than the book by W. E. B., is the *Scofield Reference Bible*. This Bible carries the King James Version plus copious footnotes and many explanatory insertions as chapter headings and headings of even smaller divisions. This book carries the name of Rev. C. I. Scofield as the editor of this volume, and the names of several prominent churchmen of that day. Among them is that of Dr. James M. Gray who was president of Moody Bible Institute at that time. The sincerity of these men is not questioned, but the doctrine they have inserted within a book classified as a Bible is subject to considerable question; and even more questionable is this means of propagating their heresy.

I accept the Bible as the word of God, but I resent and deplore the printing of a Bible that contains any additions designed to influence the reader toward any particular interpretation of the Bible. Many naive Bible students will accept Scofield's notes and interpolations as gospel truth, simply because they read them out of a Bible. I am hesitant to judge the motives of men, but it does make one wonder if this is not exactly what these men desired. I have sufficient notes of criticism of the Scofield Bible to fill several pages, but refrain from doing so. I do recommend that every one read the short treatise by Albertus Pieters entitled *The Scofield Bible*.

One illustration of how interpolations are used in this Bible must suffice. In John 5:25 Jesus speaks of a spiritual resurrection which was at that time available to those who would heed the call. Then in verses 28-29 he speaks of the future resurrection of the dead, both of the good and also of the evil. Now the average reader who reads this book like any other book would take Jesus to mean all would be raised at one time. But Dr. Scofield is unwilling for anyone to draw that conclusion, so he inserts between verses 27 and 28 the heading *The Two Resurrections*. This is an apparent effort to make the Bible and Jesus say what he feels is the meaning, rather than allowing the Bible to speak for itself. The word of God is too sacred for any man to treat it in this manner. It is an effort to substitute the traditions of men for the divinely inspired Bible.

Dr. Scofield was "chiefly responsible for the founding of Dallas Seminary in 1924, where his reputation and teachings are still upheld."[63] Dr. Walvoord, the current President of that institution, is probably the most influential writer of the Dispensationalists at this time. Some slight changes, such as admitting that the rapture, so-called, will not be secret, have been made in compliance with the arguments of biblical exegetes; but some tenaciously hold to the older teaching despite its indefensibility. But on the whole, Scofield's seven dispensations and his other basic teachings are still accepted by Dispensationalists in general.

Dispensationalism has had a far greater effect on eschatological emphases than their numbers would indicate. This is because a major segment of Christian leaders, especially those who were already Premillennial in their convictions, have accepted the Dispensational approach, hook and line, and possibly even the sinker as well. Sandeen expresses it this way: "Although unwilling to admit their affiliation with his denominational views, Americans raided Darby's treasuries and carried off his teachings as their own."[64] What Sandeen means is that the futurism of Darby, as well as his Old Testament hermeneutic of a restored Israel, and his two-phase second coming or pretribulation rapture of the Church are accepted by a

---

63 Sandeen, *op. cit.*, p. 223.
64 *Ibid.*, p. 102.

large number of Premillennialists of today. These are possibly in agreement with 90 percent of Dispensationalism, but prefer not to be classified as such.

7. *Historic Premillennialism.* Premillennialism and *Chiliasm* prior to the rise of Dispensationalism did not involve a complicated series of events such as is now commonly taught. These anticipated an earthly reign of Christ, but the connection was to the Church rather than to a revived Judaism. If a time of great tribulation was taught, the Church had to endure it. The rapture was a simple rising to meet Christ only to immediately return with Him to be in the 1,000 year reign. The two-phase second coming was not involved, being unheard of, and the so-called judgment of nations had not even been thought of. God's prophetic clock had not stopped, and a seven year marriage feast had not been found in the New Testament.

Historic Premillennialism, then, is the Premillennialism that existed before Dispensationalism entered the scene. It must be distinguished from modern Premillennialism which is often almost identical in content with Dispensationalism. It is doubtful if conditions could admit of there being anyone today who could be classed as a Historic Premillennialist, but George E. Ladd probably comes as near to it as anyone. He does accept the Church as the kingdom, although he holds that the millennium will see it in a fuller measure.

8. *The Great Tribulation.* Certain passages of Scripture are interpreted as pointing to a time of intense suffering which is yet future. It involves the last half of a seven year period. Some say it pertains mainly to the Jews, whereas others say all men will be involved. Some say the Church will have to endure this period of suffering, but others deny this. Premillennialists teach the "great tribulation." Amillennialists and Postmillennialists say the prophesies involved were fulfilled when the Roman army destroyed Jerusalem in A.D. 70.

9. *The Rapture.* This is another term peculiar to Premillennialists and Dispensationalists. It is their belief that there will be at least two resurrections. Some extend this to several. But it is held that only the righteous will he resurrected when Christ comes and that the wicked will be resurrected 1,000 years to 1,007 years later. The claim is that the Church will he caught up to meet the Lord in the air. The righteous dead will be resurrected with their immortal bodies, and the living righteous will be changed so that their mortal bodies also become immortal. This snatching away of the Church is called the "rapture."

Historic Premillennialism placed the rapture in very close proximity to the establishment of the millennial reign. It was analogous to some of the Christians going to The Three Taverns to meet Paul who was on his way to Rome. According to this view, if there was a great tribulation, the Church would suffer through it. This view is held by Ladd and a few others. It is the posttribulation belief. So many present day Premillennialists have accepted the Dispensational teaching that Ladd feels he and other posttribulation advocates are almost shoved out of the fellowship of other Premillennialists. Posttribulationists are considered about as bad as Amillennialists and Postmillennialists by those who insist that pretribulation rapture is the orthodox belief. Yet, the Church existed for almost eighteen centuries before this view was taught by anyone.

Dispensationalists and most modern Premillennialists contend that the Church will be raptured to heaven for a seven year marriage feast immediately prior to the seven year reign of the Antichrist. After seven years, Christ will return to set up His millennial kingdom. This involves two second comings of Christ. Although the Bible knows nothing of two second comings, or the two-phase second coming, it is confidently affirmed that certain texts require it. Although Jesus spoke of but one return, it is contended that these texts are sufficiently different to demand two returns. Others are able to reconcile the differences that do exist, but most Premillennialists are not able to do so. Presuppositions may blind them to a harmony of these texts within the framework of a single return.

Dispensationalists argue against those who hold that the rapture will be posttribulation in a similar vein. If the Church endures the tribulation, they can count seven years from the beginning, or three and one-half years according to the midtribulationists, and thus know that Christ would come within that period of time. But this assumes that His coming is imminent only for the Church. Such an assumption is completely unjustified. Paul taught that the "day of the Lord" and the judgments it would bring on sinful men would come as "a thief in the night" and "as travail cometh upon a woman with child" (1 Thess. 5:2-3).

Jesus spoke of His second coming as "at an hour when ye think not" (Luke 12:40). In the next verse Peter asked if the parable was to them only, "or even unto all?." Verse 48 indicates it was to all. Peter's statement in II Peter 3:10 is very much akin to Paul's statement quoted earlier in this paragraph. But this cannot be according to either pre- or posttribulation rapture. For

# Eschatological Systems, Terms, & Historical Data 91

the wicked, the only difference in the two is the time when the Church is supposed to be raptured. Both start a chain of events with the beginning of the great tribulation. Then follows the millennium according to both. After this comes the resurrection, the final judgment, and other connected events. Sinners can start counting at the time of the great tribulation just as well as Christians.

What I am trying to say is that every eschatological scheme other than Amillennialism, establishes a series of events that controls an aspect of the second coming of the Lord—that coming in judgment on sinful people. But since Amillennialism spiritualizes the millennium, its time limits are vague or unknown; therefore no time schedule is established. According to Amillennialism, a single coming brings judgment on the evil and rewards to the faithful, and it can come at any time. Not only can it come now, but it can be delayed as long as God sees fit. Premillennialsits and Dispensationalists as well as Postmillennialists deny the imminency of Christ's return for the wicked. All of these claim a period of time, usually 1,000 years or more, must elapse between a given event and the judgment of the wicked individuals.

The relationship of the rapture to the great tribulation is the thing that makes Historical Premillennialism nonexistent today. The early Church writers felt that they had endured the great tribu[la]tion or were enduring it. For this reason they were posttribulationists. But all Premillennialists have pushed the great tribulation out into the future. This dislocation of the so-called "Great Tribulation" from the experiences of the early centuries to some future time has made the question of pretribulation and posttribulation of today altogether different to the posttribulation Premillennialism of the early Christian centuries. For this reason none of the Premillennialism of today can identify itself with Historic Premillennialism. Dispensationalism has brought in more innovations than posttribulation Premillennialism has, but even the latter is somewhat different to Historic Premillennialism.

The importance of the pretribulation rapture to Dispensationalism and most modern Premillennialism can hardly be overemphasized. It makes a break between the Church and Israel that is fairly distinct. The Church is raptured away to enjoy the festivities connected with her marriage to Christ for seven years. This leaves Israel here on earth to suffer through the tribulation experience. When Christ comes seven years later to set up His kingdom, as Dispensationalism teaches, He will bring the Church back to earth. For the Jews to be reestablished as a separate people while the Church was still on earth would require that Jewish Christians separate themselves from the Church and become a part of the Jewish community. This disruption of the Church is evaded by their two-phase coming.

However, several problems appear out of this strange doctrine. It is taught that the Holy Spirit will be withdrawn at the rapture. It is also taught that Jewish Christians will be raptured with the Church. But in spite of these two doctrines, it is also held that a "remnant" of some sort will appear from among the Jews, and this group will do a great deal of gospel preaching so that a group called "tribulation saints" will be on earth when Christ comes to set up His kingdom.

First of all no remnant is involved. A remnant is a small residue from a larger quantity or category. This implies a connection between the remnant and the larger object or body. But since those who teach about a remnant during the great tribulation also teach that the Church will be raptured away at Christ's first second coming, then no remnant is left behind. Only if Jewish Christians do not participate in the rapture would a true remnant remain. But this is usually rejected because it would deny that Jews and Gentiles are truly one body in Christ.

An even greater problem is the question of how this remnant is to come into existence. With the Holy Spirit no longer in the world to convict people of sin, and with the Church not here to preach the gospel, no agency for evangelization is indicated. In spiritual affairs as in the sciences, every result must have an adequate cause. But Dispensationalists claim the only forces capable of evangelism are removed with the rapture. This leaves the "remnant" without an adequate cause for its existence, and also for its successes. Until Dispensationalists correct this deficiency, the entire plan must be rejected as having no foundation.

The Dispensational system is exceedingly complicated. Few can understand it apart from a systematic study of its teachings. It often fools the naive and the unwary because it is usually presented in a very persuasive manner and with what appears to be the voice of authority. It is only by checking each passage and its context, determining whether a time element is given in each passage, ascertaining whether the way they link passages together is legitimate, checking the original language whenever possible, and finding the places where the rules of logic and hermeneutics are violated that the weakness of the entire structure becomes apparent. As long as one allows himself to be carried along by their presentation without seriously checking for fallacies, conclusions that do not follow from the material presented, forced exegesis, improper use of proof-texts, and eisegesis, the likelihood of being fooled is great; but when a thorough check is made, the weaknesses of the system become apparent.

And since present day Premillennialism has adopted the pretribulation rapture, the two-phase second coming, and the Judaistic millennium of Dispensationalism as the orthodox position, we find most of the weaknesses of Dispensationalism evident in the very warp and woof of the Premillennialism of our day. Concerned persons should be much in prayer that the Holy Spirit will work in the hearts of those who are entangled in the meshes of this heresy of a restored Judaism to reveal to them the error which they are propagating.

— PART TWO —

# THE ESCHATOLOGY OF THE OLD TESTAMENT

In this section on Old Testament eschatology, and to some extent in the following section on New Testament eschatology, the biblical verses being considered are not printed to conserve space. For this reason, the reader is urged to study this section with an open Bible handy for reference purposes. Unless this is done, the reader will not be able to follow the reasoning of the author.

CHAPTER 6

# THE ESCHATOLOGY OF THE PENTATEUCH

I have before me a volume entitled *The Thousand Years in Both Testaments*.[65] This book is above average size, containing almost 500 pages. One might assume that hundreds of passages that speak of a thousand year period must be involved to justify a book of this size. But not so. In all of the Bible, only one text can be found that speaks of such a period of time, and it is written in apocalyptic style which makes it subject to being interpreted symbolically, rather than literally. In all of the Old Testament, not a single passage can be found positing such a period. As we study the Pentateuch and the other Old Testament books, keep in mind that not a single prophecy in it mentions a thousand year reign.

Then how can so much be said about so little? It is because many texts are interpreted as applying to such a period, even though they say nothing of a thousand years. This might be termed as secondary evidence, for no direct or positive evidence of such a period is found in the Old Testament, and the interpretation these give of the one New Testament text is rejected on several grounds which will be discussed when the Revelation is considered.

Two of the divisions into which Premillennialists may be separated are: (1) those who depend on Revelation 20 for their foundation, weak though it is, and (2) those who frankly admit to having an Old Testament hermeneutic. Most Dispensationalists fit into this latter category. Walvoord, as the spokesman for this group, says,

> It is not too much to say that the exegesis of the Abrahamic covenant and its resulting interpretation is the foundation for the study of prophecy as a whole, not only as relating to Israel, but also for the Gentiles and the church. It is here that the true basis for premillennial interpretation of the Scriptures is found.[66]

---

65 Nathaniel West, *The Thousand Years in Both Testaments*
66 Walvoord, *Israel in Prophecy*, pp. 44-45.

This espousal of an Old Testament hermeneutic might be compared to a doctor who continues to make his diagnoses on older, less precise methods after newer precise methods have been developed. It is comparable to an artist insisting on using an old blurred photograph for his model, when the person whose picture he is painting is available for sittings. And it cannot depend on exegesis alone, for not a single Old Testament text speaks of a thousand year Jewish ascendancy. Hence, "the resulting interpretation" is really the foundation of this hermeneutic.

## The Abrahamic Covenant: Conditional or Unconditional?

Scholars of all persuasions recognize the importance of God's covenant with Abraham, but several questions must be answered. Was it conditional, unconditional, or did it contain conditional aspects as well as unconditional aspects? Has it been fulfilled in the past, or is it to be fulfilled in the future? Has any portion of it been abrogated? Will it be fulfilled through the physical seed of Abraham (the Jews), or is it being fulfilled through the spiritual seed of Abraham (the Church)? The promise of a land area is considered first.

The first land promise was for "all the land which thou seest" (Gen. 13:15). Later its boundaries are given as extending "from the river of Egypt unto the great river, the river Euphrates" (Gen. 15:18). The time element was "forever" (Gen. 13:15). Although no conditions are stated in these prophecies in Genesis, the same inspired writer, Moses, does place conditional elements in his fifth book, Deuteronomy. One of the rules of hermeneutics given in Part One was that the Bible must serve as its own interpreter, and that an author must have the right to interpret his own statements.

Moses, in his closing address to the people he had led for forty years, places very definite provisions and conditions regarding this land inheritance. Moses speaks of the blessings God will give them if they are obedient (Deut. 28:1-14). He then lists the terrible curses God will send upon them if they are disobedient (Deut. 28:15-68). Deuteronomy 29 continues in somewhat the same vein. In chapter 30 it is specifically stated, "But if thine heart turn away...I denounce unto you this day, that ye shall surely perish, and that ye shall not prolong your days upon the land, whither thou passest over Jordan to possess it" (Deut. 30:17-18).

This should be sufficiently plain to convince those who are willing to let the Bible speak for itself, but it fails to convince some. Walvoord, for example, contends that "Only by indiscriminate spiritualization of all the terms and promises relating to the land can these prophecies be nullified."[67] But I have spiritualized nothing thus far. All I have done is let the inspired writer, Moses, interpret his previous inspired promises. The land promises of the Abrahamic covenant were conditional. My authority is none other than Moses who recorded the Abrahamic covenant in the first place.

Walvoord tacitly admits the conditionality of the land promise as originally given to Abraham by admitting it was subject to revision. He admits that "through Esau, it is clear that the particular promises of God to the seed are narrowed first to Isaac and then to Jacob and through Jacob to the twelve tribes of Israel."[68] Having admitted this much, he should go all the way and accept the limitations Moses sets in Deuteronomy 28-30, and the ultimate designation of Christ as the seed in Galatians 3:16.

Walvoord further admits,

"Second, the expression 'the seed of Abraham' is used in special reference to the spiritual lineage coming from Abraham, that is, those in Israel who trusted in God, who kept the law, and qualified for many of the blessings of the covenant."[69]

Now since Walvoord admits that God cut out Ishmael, Esau, Abraham's six sons by Keturah, and all the unbelieving descendants of Jacob, he has admitted the conditionality of the original promise made to Abraham, or at least that it was subject to review and revision.

We hold that he has no grounds upon which to deny the further exclusions that Moses makes in Deuteronomy. And when the New Testament further narrows this down to Christ (Gal. 3:16), he should be willing to accept this narrowing, just as he did the earlier narrowing. The New Testament further indicates that it is the spiritual seed of Abraham through Christ, both Jews and Gentiles, who are the true inheritors of the promises made to Abraham. If this be classified as "spiritualizing," so let it be. Nonetheless, it is the teaching of the New Testament hermeneutic; and I prefer to take the teaching of the better Testament, rather than one built on the shadow.

---

67  *Ibid.*, p. 72.
68  *Ibid.*, p. 36.
69  *Ibid.*

## National Israel and the Land Promises

One of the bases for a future fulfillment of the land promises is the claim that they have had no fulfillment in the past. This claim is of small value after the conditionality of those promises has been thoroughly established, but it is considered anyway. A superficial examination of this argument indicates a degree of validity, but if the Bible is allowed to be its own interpreter, the argument is found to be without adequate support.

Two lines of proof are used in refuting the claim that the promise has not been fulfilled in past time. First, the same Bible through which the promise is recorded, also says those promises were fulfilled. A second line of evidence is the fact that the prophecy that is said to point to a future fulfillment is even more restricted in area than that originally occupied under Moses and Joshua. These will be considered in the above order.

The inspired writer of the book of Joshua says Israel did possess the land. "And the Lord gave unto Israel all the land which he sware to give unto their fathers; and they possessed it and dwelt therein" (Josh. 21:43). The two verses which follow further emphasize this fulfillment. Now this statement is either true or untrue. If it is true, as I regard it to be, then we must accept it as meaning the promise was fulfilled, even though technical arguments against the fulfillment are available. Walvoord denies the statement is true. But the Bible is the true interpreter of the Bible; hence, the statement is true even though all the land to the Euphrates was not occupied. Our interpretation is that the land of Canaan was the central core that was promised them, but that certain other lands might be included.

Later expansions lend validity to this interpretation. At the peak of Israel's expansion, Solomon did reign over or control all the area from the Euphrates to the border of Egypt (I Kings 4:21). Hence, even if it is denied that the promise was fulfilled through Joshua, it cannot be denied that it reached fulfillment under Solomon. The claim that this was not a fulfillment because some of these lands were not incorporated into the Jewish nation is not worthy of much consideration. It is but a subterfuge.

Having once possessed the land, the promise does not leave any room for being dispossessed, if the promise was unconditional. The expression "forever" means just that. But having possessed the land, Israel was expelled from that land. This being true, the only solution is to recognize that the promise was conditional. So when Israel was dispossessed, the conditionality of the promise was verified. Walvoord recognizes three major dispossessions. He lists these as the sojourn in Egypt, the Assyrian captivity of Israel and the Babylonian captivity of Judah, and the one that followed the destruction of Jerusalem in A.D. 70.[70]

## Ezekiel and the Jewish Restoration

Ezekiel's prophecies will be considered fully in a later chapter, but for the present it is necessary to consider the land area only. The reason for considering Ezekiel at this point is that the last twelve chapters of Ezekiel are interpreted eschatologically by Dispensationalists and many other Premillennialists. These chapters are stressed as telling of a revived Israel, the rebuilding of the temple, the restoration of animal sacrifices, the Levitical priesthood, and the law of Moses, as well as many other things supposedly connected with the millennial kingdom they envision.

The reader should bear in mind that the claim is made that the Abrahamic covenant insures the land from the Euphrates to Egypt to the physical descendants of Jacob. It is also affirmed that these last chapters of Ezekiel describe conditions as they will exist in the millennium. With these two thoughts in mind, let us compare the Israel of the Pentateuch with the Israel of Ezekiel.

The boundaries Moses gave in Numbers 34 and those of Ezekiel 48 are similar but not identical. Ezekiel's boundaries extend farther north and farther south by a few miles than the boundaries set by Moses. On the other hand, Ezekiel's boundary is the Jordan river to the east, whereas Moses gave the tribes of Gad, Reuben, and half the tribe of Manasseh their inheritance on the east side of the Jordan. Now if Ezekiel is interpreted as a prophecy of the millennium, it should make the river Euphrates the eastern boundary of a restored Israel, if the Abrahamic covenant's land promises are to be fulfilled to the Jews at that time. It is impossible to piece all of this together in such a manner as to fit the expectations of Premillennialists.

No doubt Dispensationalists will deny or ignore the fact that this places them on the horns of a dilemma, but it should be apparent that they are. Since Ezekiel places the eastern boundary of Israel at the Jordan, rather than the Euphrates, it is evident that his Israel is not a fulfillment of the Abrahamic covenant as they claim. Hence, they must either drop their teaching regarding a fulfillment of the Abrahamic covenant during the millennium, or else they must drop their millennial concepts based on Ezekiel. If they do neither, they will be advocating conflicting interpretations.

---

70  *Ibid.*, p. 72.

## The New Testament on the Abrahamic Covenant

Extensive arguments from the New Testament will be reserved for a later time, but since it does have something to say about Israel and the Abrahamic covenant, this chapter would not be complete without some general references. Walvoord maintains, "The N. T. declares the Abrahamic covenant immutable (Heb. 6:13-18)."[71] It is admitted that that portion of the Abrahamic covenant which referred to the person and work of Jesus Christ is indeed immutable; but it is denied that the physical and racial aspects are. This has been proved true already from Old Testament texts.

Hebrews 6 does not contradict the above, for it has reference to Christ and His redemptive work. In fact, the book of Hebrews is a contrast between the Mosaic system and what Christ has accomplished. A review of the first five chapters of Hebrews reveals that the work of Christ is shown to be an improvement over that of the Mosaic dispensation. Thus, the writer is emphasizing the fact that believers in Christ, the spiritual seed of Abraham if you please, have distinct advantages over the Jews who continued to follow the Mosaic system of worship. Verses 19-20 of chapter 6 bring this out very clearly, verses which for some reason Walvoord did not include in his statement. These verses read: "Which hope we have as an anchor of the soul, both sure and stedfast, and which entereth into that within the veil; whither the forerunner is for us entered, even Jesus, made an high priest for ever after the order of Melchisedec."

Instead of teaching a hope for a revived Israel inhabiting Palestine for 1,000 years, the hope set forth here is the Christian hope of the resurrection from the dead. Paul agrees with this in Acts 26:6-8. He says in part that "the promise made of God unto our fathers" (v. 6) i.e., to Abraham, Isaac, and Jacob, was that "God should raise the dead" (v. 8). Paul contends further that the "seed" of the Abrahamic covenant refers to Christ, rather than to the physical descendants of Abraham (Gal. 3:7-9, 14, 16-18). In verses 28-29 of this same chapter, he indicates that Jews and Gentiles share alike and equally in the promises to Abraham through faith in Christ. Genetic descent is obliterated.

Paul contends further that Christ has "broken down the middle wall of partition" that formerly existed (Eph. 2:14). Verse 12 indicates that the

---

71 *Ibid.*, p. 43.

# The Eschatology of the Pentateuch

Gentiles had formerly been "aliens from the commonwealth of Israel." The plain intent of that which follows is to assert that these Gentiles are now, through faith, a part of "the commonwealth of Israel." These saved Gentiles had been "strangers from the covenants of promise" with the equally plain inference that they are now equal participants with the Jews in those "covenants of promise." Note the plural "covenants." It is futile to contend, as Walvoord and others do, that the "new man" (v. 15) God made out of these two still leaves room for the two old men, Jews and Gentiles, to continue with separate promises for each.

Any effort to re-establish the distinction between Jew and Gentile, or to tear them apart, is to tear down some of the work which Christ accomplished through His death. Such teaching is essentially destructive to the gospel message. It needs to be exposed as heresy. It involves retrogression back to the shadows of the Old Testament with its deficiencies, rather than being an expression of the glorious light of the gospel.

## The Remnant Concept

The basic idea of the Jewish remnant is that within national Israel or Jewry in general there is a smaller group of true believers who are considered the remnant. Paul wrote, "Even so then at this present time also there is a remnant according to the election of grace" (Rom. 11:5). In verse 4 he had mentioned the 7,000 in the time of Elijah who had not bowed their knees to Baal. It is apparent that this 7,000 constitutes a remnant, according to Pauline theology. Even Dispensationalists recognize the remnant concept.

Walvoord has written,

> ...the expression "the seed of Abraham" is used in special reference to the spiritual lineage coming from Abraham, that is, those in Israel who trusted in God, who kept the law, and qualified for many of the blessings of the covenant. It is evident, for instance, that all of the Israelites do not actually inherit the land and that only spiritual Israel will enter the future millennial kingdom and fulfill the promise.[72]

Scofield's summary of the remnant concept (note on Rom. 11:5) indicates the remnant was very small in the time of Isaiah. During the Babylonian captivity, Ezekiel, Daniel, the three Hebrews, Esther, and Mordecai are said to be representative. Those who returned with Ezra and Nehemiah

---

72 *Ibid.*, p. 36.

were the remnant of that time. And then he adds, "During the church-age the remnant is composed of believing Jews (Rom. 11:4-5)."

These admissions by Scofield and Walvoord show that national Israel has no part in the Abrahamic covenant. Yet, both of these men hold out a hope for national Israel. In our later study of Jeremiah, it will be shown that Israel has been permanently divorced by Jehovah God. The hope these men hold out to the Jews as a body or race is not the true concept. The remnant concept cannot be extended to cover the Jews as a race or national Israel. National Israel has been divorced, and God's own laws prohibit Him from remarrying her, as will be shown in our study of Jeremiah.

As Scofield and Walvoord have admitted that the present remnant is composed of believers in Christ, they have admitted that the remnant is part of the New Testament Church. Since there are no Jews or Gentiles in the Church (Col. 3:11), only Christians, it is folly to extend hope to any, Jews or Gentiles, who are outside of Christ and His Church. For one to be a part of this remnant which alone is to inherit the promises of the Abrahamic covenant, even according to Scofield and Walvoord, he must accept Christ as his Saviour. Jews outside of Christ have no hope.

## The Constituency of National Israel Versus the Remnant

When a Gentile lived among the Israelites, he became a Jew or a member of national Israel by circumcision. According to the Talmud, he was given a special bath or baptism and required to keep the law of Moses if he were to be accepted as a full-fledged Jew. This made him eligible to partake of the passover, and he became as a native born Jew (Ex. 12:48). By this means one could become a part of national Israel, and just as much a partaker of the promises made to Abraham as any who depended on genetic descent from Jacob. But this did not necessarily make him a part of the remnant.

One may take a similar route to becoming a Jew today, but he could not do so and remain a true believer. Christians must depend on Christ—not on racial connections. Paul renounced any confidence in the flesh and indicated all Christians should do likewise. Although he was a circumcised Jew, he wrote, "For we are the circumcision, which worship God in the spirit, and rejoice in Christ Jesus, and have no confidence in the flesh" (Phil. 3:3). Any Jew who places his racial descent as part of his hope is not a part of the remnant. The remnant places its hope in Christ alone.

The Hebrew epistle indicates it is fatal to turn back to the Jewish rites, therefore we must rely on spiritual processes to become true Jews. Paul contends that physical circumcision does not make one a true Jew (a member of the remnant), "But he is a Jew, which is one inwardly" (Rom. 2:27-29). This truth is pressed home with even more force in the Galatian letter. "They which are of faith, the same are the children of Abraham" (i.e., part of the remnant and inheritors of the promises to Abraham. Gal. 3:7). Also, "If ye be Christ's, then are ye Abraham's seed, and heirs according to the promise" (i.e., according to the promises to Abraham. Gal. 3:9).

Verse 28, which comes between the two verses just quoted from Romans 2, nullifies the efforts of those who claim there is a distinction between the Jewish believer and the Gentile believer. That the verses just quoted do refer to the remnant, i.e., true believers in Christ, cannot be denied. But verse 28, immediately preceding the last verse quoted, reads, "There is neither Jew nor Greek, there is neither bond nor free, there is neither male nor female: for ye are all [i.e., Jews, Gentiles, slaves, freemen, men, women] one in Christ Jesus." Hence a believing Gentile is just as much a part of the remnant as the believing Jew to the exclusion of all unbelievers be they Jew or Gentile.

Walvoord attempts to maintain a distinction between believers who are racially Jews and those who are racially Gentiles.[73] But this is indefensible in the light of Paul's repeated declarations that all are one in Christ, that the middle wall of partition is broken down, that Gentile believers are inheritors of the Abrahamic promises, and that racial barriers no longer exist. All are one in Christ, hence it would constitute a rending of the body of Christ to separate them into the old categories.

In spite of accepting the remnant idea, Dispensationalists tend to hold to the conversion of national Israel at the second coming of Christ. Scofield calls the Jews "the people of God" even while living in unbelief (note on Rev. 7:14). Jesus said unbelieving Jews were of their "father the devil" (John 8:44). An unbeliever, be he Jew or Gentile, is not one of God's people regardless of what men may say. When Christ comes again, He will come, "In flaming fire taking vengeance on them that know not God, and that obey not the gospel of our Lord Jesus Christ" (II Thess. 1:8), whether they be Jews or Gentiles. Contrary to this, Scofield says that at Christ's second coming the generation of Jews then living will be converted (note on Acts 1:11).

---

73  *Ibid.*, pp. 37ff.

## A Summary on the Abrahamic Covenant

1. The Abrahamic covenant was amended to leave out various descendants of Abraham and Isaac, according to the account by Moses.

2. These changes prove that insofar as the descendants of Abraham are concerned, it was conditional and subject to alteration, amendment, and limitation, even though the original covenant did not say it was conditional or subject to revision.

3. This leaves room for revision under the New Testament or New Covenant.

4. The New Testament does, in fact, limit the beneficiaries of the Abrahamic covenant to Christ and those who are believers in Christ.

5. Moses pointed out that the covenant was conditional by informing the Israelites that God would bless them if they were obedient, but that he would punish them severely if they were disobedient. This punishment included their removal from the promised land.

6. The promised land was possessed under Joshua, and under Solomon this possession included the land eastward to the Euphrates. The fact that the Israelites were dispossessed after having possessed it, is further proof of the conditionality of the covenant, at least as far as the people to be benefited is concerned.

7. The remnant concept is further proof that the covenant has certain conditional aspects.

8. The remnant concept makes the covenant applicable only to those who were obedient under the old dispensation, and applicable only to believers in Christ in the gospel dispensation.

9. This effectively rules out national Israel as a beneficiary of the Abrahamic covenant.

10. The immutable aspects of the Abrahamic covenant were fulfilled in the person and work of Jesus Christ.

11. He is the "seed" of which the covenant speaks.

12. Believers in Christ are said to be the true descendants of Abraham, hence are the beneficiaries of the Abrahamic covenant.

13. Since the body of believers constitute the Church, the provisions of the Abrahamic covenant are now being fulfilled through the Church and its work.

14. The conditional aspects of the Abrahamic covenant were either fulfilled during the Old Testament dispensation, or they were set aside because of the disobedience of the people.

15. National Israel was permanently divorced because of her disobedience.
16. This destroyed the preference she had previously enjoyed.
17. Under the gospel dispensation, Jews and Gentiles have equal access to Christ.
18. Jews and Gentiles are one in Christ.
19. They share alike in the benefits of the Abrahamic covenant.
20. Efforts to re-establish the old middle wall of partition which was broken down through the work of Christ is a repudiation of the work of Christ. It is heresy and should be recognized for what it is.
21. A literal fulfillment at some future time of the land provisions of the covenant to the Jews is rejected for the following reasons: (a) Israel was so disobedient that she was dispossessed of the land after having possessed it. Thus, the promise of perpetual possession has been broken already. Possession at a later date would still not constitute a fulfillment of the original promise. The conditionality of the promise is thus proved by history. (b) A tenure of 1,000 years, as proposed by Premillennialists, would still fail to be forever. Only eternal possession could meet the strict terms of the original prophecy. (c) The main support for a future fulfillment is from the last chapters of Ezekiel. But this prophecy does not meet the land boundaries set by the Abrahamic covenant. The Abrahamic covenant sets the eastern boundary at the Euphrates; the prophecy in Ezekiel sets it at the Jordan.

## The Church Fathers on the Abrahamic Covenant

In Part One of this volume, it was admitted that an element of millennialism was evident during the early centuries of Christianity. The problem of the extent and number has not been settled to the satisfaction of all concerned, for different authors quote figures which cannot be reconciled. My main source of information has been *The Ante-Nicene Fathers, The Nicene Fathers,* and *The Post-Nicene Fathers.* The Ante-Nicene Fathers received the closest scrutiny for two reasons. First, they were closer to the apostles than the latter writers. Second, even Premillennialists admit that millennialism went into eclipse from the time of Augustine onward.

I used the index of subjects as one approach to this study. It is reasonably complete. But to be thorough, I decided to check all references to texts which are used by modern Dispensationalists and other Premillennialists. This index is exhaustive. It includes allusions as well as quotations. The results of this research were very enlightening.

First, the index had the words "chiliasm" and "millennialism" only now and then. A check of these passages revealed that not one of them referred to a Jewish millennium. I am confident that not one of the early writers taught a Jewish restoration and millennium such as is being advocated today.

Second, an index check of such words as "Abraham," "Abrahamic Covenant," "Covenant," and "Covenants," revealed very little. Each reference was closely checked for content. I failed to find a single instance where the covenants—the Abrahamic covenant in particular—were used as a basis for teaching a millennium. Millennial writers of the first Christian centuries simply did not base their belief in a millennium on the Abrahamic covenant.

But to make sure, I went the third mile and checked all references to Genesis 15, Deuteronomy 4, 29, and 30. Again I looked in vain for a single writer who taught a Jewish millennium based on either the Abrahamic covenant or the Palestinian covenant. I found numbers of writers who indicated that the Abrahamic covenant was fulfilled in Christ and the Church, but I did not find even one who based a millennial reign upon it. There was some millennialism in the early Church, but it was not Judaistic, and it was not based on either the Abrahamic covenant or the Palestinian covenant.

This means that Walvoord's doctrine of a restored Israel based on the Abrahamic covenant is without support during the early Christian centuries. And since he admits that from the time of Augustine, millennialism went into an eclipse to the point of vanishing, we conclude that a Judaistic millennium is without support for the major portion of the Christian era. Regardless of the number of men who were millennialists in the early centuries, they taught a kind of millennium different from that being taught today; and they based their views on things other than the Abrahamic covenant.

Four sources of early millennialism were found, but only two of them were canonical. Papias made some outlandish claims about an expected millennium.[74] He improperly attributed these sayings to Jesus, whereas they are actually from noncanonical Jewish apocalyptists. A second source was the Jewish idea of 6,000 years of ordinary conditions with each 1,000 years analogous to one of the days of creation, to be followed by 1,000 years of peace and prosperity analogous to the seventh day in which God rested. Analogy proves nothing, as has been said before. Neither of these sources is

---

74 Papias, *Ante-Nicene Fathers,* vol. l. pp. 153-154.

# The Eschatology of the Pentateuch

considered important today, except by a few who cling to the first of these.

Of the two canonical texts used to support the millennial doctrine, one was from the Old Testament and one from the New. In the citation listed above, Papias did contend that wild beasts would become tame and that they would become vegetarians, so that wolves and sheep would dwell together in peace and eat the same food. This involves a literal interpretation of Isaiah 11:6-9 much as many Premillennialists interpret it today. Irenaeus accepted the claims of Papias without question, but even so, he recognized that this applied to changed natures in men. He held that these verses spoke of changed natures in men during this dispensation, but that they involved changes in animals during the millennium. Tertullian altered his interpretation from figurative to literal (men to animals) when he became a Montanist. Jerome left an obscure statement which cannot be evaluated.

Writing in favor of the figurative interpretation were such men as Origen, Theodoret, Athanasius, Chrysostom, Augustine, and Cyril of Jerusalem, and as given above, Tertullian before he became a Montanist. These will be given further consideration in the study of the eschatology of Isaiah. Footnotes will be given there.

The other canonical text that was used to support the teaching of a millennium was Revelation 20. Lactantius held to two bodily resurrections with a millennium between based on this passage. Commodianus held similar views, but we know he did not believe in a pretribulation rapture, for he taught that those who suffered under Antichrist would participate in the first resurrection. Tertullian allowed for two bodily resurrections with a millennium between in his later writings, but his millennium was for the Church—not the Jews.

Justin Martyr believed in a millennium, but he did not support his ideas from Revelation 20. He held to a single bodily resurrection after the millennium. He must be classified as a Postmillennialist. Prior to his defection to the Montanists, Tertullian interpreted this passage much as Amillennialists now interpret it. Hippolytus held to a single bodily resurrection thus denying the millennial doctrine. Augustine, Eusebius, and Gregory of Nisa all interpreted this passage in such a manner as to omit any reference to a millennium here on earth. Footnotes will be given when these matters are considered in our later study on the Revelation.

Of the half-dozen or so early churchmen who taught a millennium, not one was in agreement with much that is being taught today. They did not teach a restoration of the Jews as a nation, nor did they teach a future occupation of Palestine by the Jews. They did not teach a restoration of the Jewish temple, the Jewish priesthood, the Mosaic law, the animal sacrifices, and Sabbath keeping. They did not teach a restoration of the middle wall of partition between Jews and Gentiles. They did not teach the pretribulation rapture of the Church, nor did they teach the two-phase second coming of Christ. There is very little support for two bodily resurrections and more than one judgment.

Now let us consider the evidence regarding the Abrahamic covenant. I did not find a single defender of Walvoord's position that the Abrahamic covenant is the basis for interpreting prophecy. Of the millennialists in the early Church, Irenaeus probably wrote most extensively. He considered the Abrahamic covenant fulfilled in Christ and the Church. He wrote, "The Patriarchs and prophets sowed the word concerning Christ, but the church reaped, that is, received the fruit."[75] Cyprian contended that the Jews had been rejected because of their evil ways.[76]

Justin Martyr contended that "faithless and disobedient" Jews will never inherit the promises. Their only hope was in believing the gospel.[77] Barnabas held that God had disinherited the Jews, and that one purpose of Christ's first advent was that "He might bring to a head the sum of their sins who had persecuted His prophets to the death."[78] Clementina held that the prophets themselves taught that the Jews had been rejected.[79] No doubt Jeremiah was his principal reference, for he definitely taught that the Jews had been permanently divorced, as will be shown when that prophet is studied. Lactantius declared: "That the Jews were disinherited because they rejected Christ, and that we, who are Gentiles, were adopted in their place is proved by the Scriptures."[80]

Of the later writers, the opinions expressed were just as forceful and unanimous. Chrysostom argued that the Jews did not profit or gain any more advantage by their racial descent than an evil son does who had a believing

---

75  Irenaeus, *Ante-Nicene Fathers,* vol. I, pp. 495-496.
76  Cyprian, *Ante-Nicene Fathers,* vol. V, p. 510.
77  Justin Martyr, *Ante-Nicene Fathers,* vol. I, p. 269.
78  Barnabas, *Ante-Nicene Fathers,* vol. I, p. 140.
79  Clementina, *Ante-Nicene Fathers,* vol. VIII, p. 90.
80  Lactantius, *Ante-Nicene Fathers,* vol. VII, p. 242.

father.[81] He also was certain that the rejection of the Jews as a nation was permanent. He wrote, "They will never lift up their heads again."[82]

Augustine repeatedly wrote that the fulfillment of the Abrahamic covenant is through the Church. He wrote, "In this world hath God fulfilled His promise concerning the seed of Abraham." He means the Church is the fulfillment of the Abrahamic covenant, especially through the Gentile converts. He quoted Galatians 3:29 in support of his position.[83] Elsewhere he adds that the Jews have "been deservedly overthrown," and that these who are "the enemy of our faith" bear witness to "our prophecies" which they take with them.[84] In this he agrees with Lactantius that the Old Testament prophets told of the permanent rejection of the Jews.

If it appears that I have belabored the matter of the rejection of the Jews, it is because Premillennialists are so insistent that the Jews still have a major role to play in the end of the age. I am equally insistent that such is not the case. It certainly is true that the early Church gave no hope to the Jews other than that of accepting the gospel message now being proclaimed by the Church.

## Texts from Leviticus and Numbers

The day of atonement is recorded in Leviticus 16. One goat was to be sacrificed for the sins of the people, and a second goat termed the "scape goat" symbolically carried the sins outside the camp. Both goats are typical of the work of Christ as our sin-bearer. Hebrews 9 should make this clear. However, Scofield's note on Leviticus 16:18 reads, "Dispensationally, for Israel, this is yet future; the High Priest is still in the holiest. When He comes out to His ancient people they will be converted and restored." To the contrary, when Christ comes again, He will come taking vengeance on all who know Him not, be they Jews or Gentiles. The only hope for the Jew is that of accepting Christ and the gospel—*now!*

Scofield lists texts from Zechariah, Romans, and the Revelation in support of his claim. The note from the Revelation is not germane to the subject, and those from the other sources will be fully considered as those books are studied.

---

81 Chrysostom, *Nicene and Post-Nicene Fathers*, (set l), vol. X, p. 59.
82 *Ibid.,* vol. XIII, pp. 333-334.
83 Augustine, *Nicene and Post-Nicene Fathers*, (set I), vol. VI, p. 500.
84 *Ibid.,* vol. II, p. 571.

Balaam's fourth prophecy (Num. 24:14) is often interpreted eschatologically without adequate justification. It reads, "Come therefore, and I will advertise thee what this people [the Israelites] shall do to thy people in the latter days." No necessity exists for interpreting "latter days" eschatologically. This prophecy was fulfilled under David. The Jews admitted a partial fulfillment through David, but they expected the Messiah to do more. The Jews wanted revenge, not the love and mercy Jesus advocated. Had Christ offered to fulfill their expectations, they might have accepted Him. Judaistic Premillennialism now offers the Jews that which Christ refused to give them. Since Christ is ever the same (Heb. 13:8), He will never offer this to the Jews. Reasons for rejecting the eschatological interpretation are overwhelming.

Such an interpretation requires that Judah's old enemies be reconstituted as nations. The text says nothing of such a restoration, hence those who claim a future fulfillment of this have no exegetical basis for doing so. The Prince of Peace taught us to forgive and love our enemies. Does He teach the Jews to hate and expect revenge? No; they are taught the same as we are.

The time of fulfillment is "the latter days," but this is too indefinite to be of much value. That Saul, David, and Solomon did conquer the people involved cannot be disputed. The text does not demand that this be a partial fulfillment. It is final.

Four interpretations of the "Star out of Jacob" and his conquests (Num. 24:17-20) are considered. The purely literal interpretation is that Saul's destruction of the Amalekites, and David's conquering of the other nations involved is the fulfillment. David is the "Star" according to this view. Few hold to this interpretation. A second view is that the "Star" refers to the Messiah and His first advent. The conquest of certain nations is understood to refer to the nonviolent conquests of Christ and the Church during the gospel dispensation. A third view is that it refers to Christ, but the picture is of the millennium age, rather than the gospel age. Scofield takes this position.

The fourth view is the one I regard most acceptable. This interpretation considers the primary fulfillment to be David and his conquests which in turn are symbols of Christ and His nonviolent conquests. The nations are viewed as symbols of the forces of evil which Christ and the Church conquer. The eschatological view of Scofield is rejected because it requires the restoration of Israel's old enemy nations, something the text says nothing about. It also indicates a renewal of these old wars under the blessing and leadership of the Prince of Peace. It is unthinkable that the Christ of love should become the Christ of hate, and that He would tell us Gentiles to love our enemies, whereas He would tell the Jews to kill theirs.

## Texts from Deuteronomy

The average Bible student will find little in Deuteronomy that is definitely eschatological, but Judaistic Premillennialists say it contains much that is very significant. On very technical and tenuous grounds, it is held that this book tells of the scattering after A. D. 70, and also of the migration that has produced the modern nation of Israel. An adequate examination of Deuteronomy proves this claim is invalid.

Moses mentioned a scattering and a conditional return (Deut. 4:27-29). It is generally conceded, even by Premillennialists, that this return was accomplished in Old Testament times. A scattering is again mentioned in chapters 28-30. This is the scattering that is said to have occurred following the destruction of Jerusalem in A.D. 70. There is nothing in the text to establish this as a different scattering from that in chapter 4, but it is still insisted that it is different. A great deal is made of the use of the word "all" as applied to the nations where they were scattered.

However, a study of the Hebrew words *amim* and *goim* shows that these words need not apply to nations in the sense of governing bodies with specific geographical boundaries. They are also applied to Gentiles, people, and heathen. Thus the meaning need not be to a plurality of nations. The meaning is such that the Assyrian and Babylonian captivities are not ruled out. Three reasons are offered in refutation of the teaching that modern Israel is the subject of either of these returns spoken of by Moses.

Both returns are conditional. A return was promised, "If thou seek me with all thy heart" (Deut. 4:29); and God would "return and gather thee from all the nations [peoples], whither the Lord thy God hath scattered thee" (Deut. 30:3), provided they returned "unto the Lord thy God, and shalt obey his voice...with all thine heart" (Deut. 30:2). The Jews have not returned unto God with all their hearts. Scofield holds that the Jews will return "to Palestine in unbelief" (note on Rev. 7:14). Tan admits that this is true of those who have recently returned to Israel. He quotes from a survey by Louis Harris to the effect "that only 13% of the Jews in Israel today would describe themselves as having even an interest in God."[85] Since the condi-

---

85 Tan, *op. cit.*, p. 232.

tions that Moses established for a return have not been met, it is certain that the present return is not a subject of prophecy in Deuteronomy.

Second, the return was to be from captivity (Deut. 30:3). A few Jews may be considered captives in Russia, but the major number who have returned, or who desire to return, are perfectly free to do so. And of those leaving Russia, less than half of those with Israel visas really go to Israel. Dial Torgerson reports that in November of 1976, "Only 719 of some 1,500 Jews leaving the Soviet Union reached here" (i.e., Israel).[86] With 1,500 Jews leaving Russia in a single month, it is difficult to think of them as fully captive, although it is recognized that severe restrictions are in effect concerning the emigration of Jews from Russia.

Both of the captivities involved the worship of idols (Deut. 4:28 and 30:17). Now it is generally recognized that the Jews did not worship idols after their return from the Babylonian captivity. They went so far as to make the valley of Tophet the place where the people of Jerusalem burned their refuse. Therefore these captivities came before the one in A.D. 70, and certainly the returns had to be those earlier returns, rather than any present day population.

## Concluding Remarks

Moses had little or nothing to say about last things. Those passages which are used to support a future restoration of the Mosaic order have been shown to be erroneously interpreted. The Abrahamic covenant is now being fulfilled through the Church. Jews have no special place in God's economy. The Church fathers held that the Abrahamic covenant is fulfilled through the Church, and that the only hope for the Jews is through accepting the gospel of Jesus Christ as it is now being presented, and as it has been presented for nearly 2,000 years.

---

86 *Houston Chronicle,* issue of Dec. 13, 1976.

CHAPTER 7

# THE ESCHATOLOGY OF THE HISTORICAL & POETIC BOOKS

## II Samuel

Two passages (II Sam. 7:8-29; I Chron. 17:7-27) are so similar that only the first one will be considered. A detailed analysis of this passage will not be necessary inasmuch as there is general agreement regarding its contents. The problem centers on the fulfillment, rather than the prophecy itself. The question involves whether Christ now rules from the throne of David, or whether this will have a future fulfillment in an earthly reign of Christ from Jerusalem. The passage itself does not speak of the fulfillment. Therefore if it is given eschatological significance it is largely based on faulty interpretation and not on sound exegesis.

Of David's posterity it is said, "I will establish his kingdom" (v. 12), and "I will establish the throne of his kingdom forever" (v. 13). "My mercy shall not depart away from him, as I took it from Saul" (v. 15), and "Thine house and thy kingdom shall be established for ever" (v. 16). Although verses 14 and 15 seem to have specific reference to Solomon, even the literalists are in general agreement that it finds, or will find, its ultimate fulfillment in Christ. Of course, this constitutes a breach of the "single hermeneutic" and the "literal interpretation" approach, but that is their problem. Our investigation must determine the time and nature of the fulfillment.

God promises to establish the kingdom of David's son (v. 12). This son, according to verse 13, would build a house (temple) for Jehovah. The literal interpretation of this demands that this refer to Solomon who constructed the temple that was the pride of the Jews until its destruction by Nebuchadnezzar in 586 B.C. Verse 13 further states that God would "stablish the throne of his kingdom forever." Although God did prolong the regnancy of David's posterity through the tribe of Judah, the Bible and secular history agree that the Davidic line came to an end when king Zedekiah was deposed and taken captive by Nebuchadnezzar in 586 B.C. Thus a literal fulfillment is impossible. Once the dynasty of David was broken, the expression "for ever" cannot apply. It simply did not continue forever.

Literalists are faced with a dilemma. They must accept the idea of a spiritualized fulfillment, or admit that the promise was conditional in spite of the seemingly unconditional language of the promise. They have chosen to forsake their basic tenet that no prophecy is to be spiritualized, rather than accept the idea of a conditional promise. They could hardly do otherwise for the New Testament indicates a spiritual fulfillment. In their effort to cover this departure from their own rule of interpretation, they have retained a literal interpretation for part of the text, but have accepted a spiritualized interpretation for another part.

What they have done is admit that the fulfillment will come to pass through Christ, rather than through Solomon and his descendants, but that this reign of Christ must be literal. But the ruse is easily detected. Verses 14-15 make it impossible to apply this section to Christ if the grammatico-historical concept is accepted. Verse 14 states, "If he commit iniquity, I will chasten him with the rod of men." For even a suggestion that Christ might have to be chastened for sin is unthinkable. Verse 15 indicates that God would not take the kingdom away from Solomon as he did from Saul, even though Solomon did sin grievously in his later years. The fact remains that he took it away from his posterity, however; hence the promise must have had certain conditional aspects, even though they are not stated.

But why not go all the way and recognize that the kingdom over which Christ would rule must also be spiritualized? It is not logical to spiritualize one aspect of an equation and not do the same for the other portion. Such a procedure produces imbalance. Just as Solomon is a type of Christ in this prophecy, so the house or temple he was to build, and did build, is a type of the New Testament Church. And as Israel over which Solomon ruled was a type of the spiritual Israel, the Church, so the literal kingdom over which he ruled is a type of the spiritual kingdom over which Christ now rules. Let us note how the New Testament supports these conclusions.

First, we shall consider the literal temple as a type of the Church. Paul declared to the Athenians on his second missionary journey while the temple of Herod still stood in all of its magnificent beauty, "God… dwelleth not in temples made with hands" (Acts 17:24). God had permanently forsaken the Jewish temple for the fleshly temple of the hearts of his children. God will never again go back to conditions of the Mosaic covenant, Dispensationalists and Premillennialists to the contrary. Paul voices this same sentiment in his letter to the church at Corinth. "Know ye not that ye are the temple of God …? the temple of God is holy which temple ye are" (1 Cor. 3:16-17). Again he says, "Know ye not that your body is the temple of the Holy Ghost which is in you …?" (I Cor. 6:19).

Peter agrees with this where he wrote, "Ye also, as lively stones, are built up a spiritual house, an holy priesthood, to offer up spiritual sacrifices, acceptable to God by Jesus Christ" (I Pet. 2:5). From these passages it should be clear that the house or temple Christ constructed is a spiritual house composed of born again believers. This can be shown to conform to the other aspects of the total picture in contrast to the picture Dispensationalists paint of what is to take place at some future time. Specific reference is made to the relationship of the builder to the house or temple that was built.

Jesus did say. "I will build my church" (Matt. 16:18). Thus, if Solomon is a type of Christ, as most commentators believe, then the spiritual house or temple, the Church, which Christ began to build at His first advent must be the fulfillment or antitype of the temple Solomon built. This maintains the proper relationship between builder and building. Solomon as a type of Christ built a literal temple. Christ, the spiritualized fulfillment of the Old Testament type, builds a spiritual building or temple which is the Church.

This relationship is not maintained by those who give an eschatological import to II Samuel 7. These admit that Christ is the fulfillment of the passage, and that the passage must be spiritualized to that extent, but they insist that the Jews will build the temple which they envision as a future construction on the site of the old temple where the Dome of the Rock mosque now stands. But if Christ is indeed the fulfillment of this passage, then He must build the temple, just as Solomon constructed the earlier temple. This is an additional reason for rejecting any eschatological import to this text.

Even Scofield's note on II Samuel 7:16 leaves room for a spiritual fulfillment. He defines David's throne as possessing "royal authority." To make it necessary for the literal, physical throne on which David sat to be restored was a little too much even for him. And the kingdom is defined as a "sphere of rule." Both of these terms are quite acceptable as applying to Christ's present rule over the Church. Since New Testament passages will be considered fully in a subsequent section of this volume, only limited New Testament support for this is given at this point.

Peter affirms that Christ (Greek, *Christos*) is a title God had given Jesus through His glorification (Acts 2:36). Now this is the Greek equivalent of *Messiah*. Hence, Jesus was not only "called the Christ": He was the Christ or Messiah. This indicates that the Messianic kingdom was operative on the day of Pentecost (Acts 2:36). The title of "Lord" is also given Him, according to Peter. Now *kurios* has meanings other than that of authority, but the idea of authority is inherent in this context.

Luke makes this even clearer in connection with charges made against Paul, Silas, and Jason by certain Jews of Thessalonica. The accusation was that there was another king besides Caesar, one named Jesus. The term used here is *basilea* (accusative of *basileus*) and definitely means king when applied to a person. The accusation is not that some day Jesus will become king. Rather it is that He is *now King*. The verb, participle, and infinitive are all in the present tense. These men were repeatedly guilty of declaring that Jesus was King—not that some day He would become king. Since Christ is now reigning as King, it follows that He is now seated on the throne of David. Thus we must reject the doctrine that declares that II Samuel chapter 7 has any eschatological import. It refers to the gospel age, according to the New Testament, not to a future millennial reign.

The early Church fathers were searched just as carefully for all references to the throne of David as was done on the Abrahamic covenant. Each item under the heading of "David" was checked as well as "throne of David." Then each reference to II Samuel 7:8-29 and I Chronicles 22:6-16 was checked. Out of the thousands of pages of printed matter covered by this investigation, only four men were found who wrote on this subject or on these verses. It is interesting to note that not one of these literalized this passage. All four spiritualized it. Even Lactantius who held some millennial concepts contended that Solomon's house was not firmly established, whereas the house Christ built was firmly established. This house he calls "the Church which is the temple of God."[87]

Justin Martyr also held that this passage was fulfilled in Christ and the gospel age.[88] Tertullian who anticipated a millennium for the Church, urged the Jews to recognize that "you cannot contend that is future which you see taking place."[89] Augustine contended that promises were not fulfilled in

---

87 Lactantius, *op. cit.*, vol. VII, p. 113.
88 Justin Martyr, *op. cit.*, vol. I, p. 258.
89 Tertullian, *Ante-Nicene Fathers*, vol. III, pt. I, p. 173.

Solomon, rather they were "most fully fulfilled in Christ."[90] He elaborated in another place, "Things are said of Solomon, for example, the scope of which reaches far beyond him, and which are only properly understood when applied to Christ and His Church."[91] Thus, the early Church fathers who did write on this passage or this subject are unanimous in applying it spiritually to Christ and His rule over the Church. Not one of the early fathers, be he a millennialist or not, held that Christ would rule over the Jews during a millennium.

## Psalms

### Psalm Two

This Psalm is generally recognized as Messianic. But in it we find little to guide us insofar as time is concerned. Much depends on interpretations of it, and these depend on presuppositions and other considerations, rather than on exegesis alone. That some of it applies to Christ's incarnation, crucifixion, and resurrection even Scofield admits (note on Ps. 2:6). However, we must reject as completely fanciful the six point program he sets up. The basis of this six point program lies more in his fertile, overactive imagination than it does on legitimate exegesis. This chapter simply does not set forth the eschatological schedule he claims he finds in it.

This Psalm is attributed to David (Acts 4:25) and the first three verses are quoted as applicable to the events of their time. The vexing in verse 5 is basically timeless. It could refer to any judgment which God visited on the Israelites after David's time. However, it is not unreasonable to assume that the vexing comes after verses 1-3 in time as well as in the Psalm, hence we see as a possibility, the destruction of Jerusalem in A.D. 70. Scofield admits as much. He wrote, "(3) The vexation (v. 5) fulfilled, first in the destruction of Jerusalem, A.D. 70;...and to be fulfilled more completely in the tribulation" (note on Ps. 2:6).

Now one of the most controversial subjects in eschatology is this so-called tribulation. The Bible is not sufficiently clear to know such a time will come, and if it comes whether it will be on all men then living, or mainly on the Jews. Yet, Scofield confidently asserts such an event, as do most Premillennial writers. He does not get this out of the second Psalm, however. Nothing

---

90 Augustine, *op. cit.*, vol. II, p. 348.
91 *Ibid.*, p. 570.

beyond the destruction of Jerusalem in A.D. 70 can be drawn from this passage. If the Bible does teach a future time of great tribulation, it must be derived from other passages.

Scofield's fourth point is the establishment of the King (Christ) upon Zion (v. 6), the fifth being the "subjugation of the earth to the King's rule." He refers points four and five to the so-called millennium yet future. We have already proved that the New Testament teaches that Christ came as a King and that He now reigns as King. Now we wish to show that the second Psalm is interpreted by the New Testament in accordance with this view, bearing in mind that the word "begotten" as used in the second Psalm is generally recognized to mean "declared" or "manifested." It does not refer to the virgin birth.

The Psalm has the word *yalidti* from *yalad,* the basic meaning of which is "to bear" rather than to beget. But as used in this Psalm, it means to bear witness to His sonship. Calvin, Clarke, Lange, and many others agree that this is the meaning. The question raised by Scofield and others is, Has God declared Christ's sonship in fulfillment of the passage in question, or does it involve a future fulfillment at the *parousia* or second coming? The Bible gives several occasions when God declared Jesus to be His Son. These include the announcement to Mary, the testimony to Joseph, the angelic choir which sang to the shepherds, and the voice from heaven at Christ's baptism as well as on the mount of transfiguration. However, there is no indication that these are to be taken as the fulfillment of Psalms 2:7.

Paul affirms that the resurrection of Jesus, and possibly the exaltation which accompanied His ascension, constitute the fulfillment of the second Psalm. In Paul's message to the people of Antioch in Pisidia as recorded in Acts 13, he says, "But God raised him from the dead" (v. 30). He then relates this miracle to the promised blessings of the Old Testament in general, and to Psalm 2 in particular:

> And we declare unto you glad tidings, how that the promise which was made unto the fathers, God has fulfilled the same unto us their children, in that he hath raised up Jesus again; as it is also written in the second Psalm, Thou art my Son, this day have I begotten thee. And as concerning that he raised him from the dead...he said on this wise, I will give you the sure mercies of David (Acts 13:32-34).

Now what was the "promise" which was made unto the fathers? And what are the "sure mercies of David"? Unquestionably, the promise to the fathers refers to the Abrahamic covenant. Christ was the "seed" to which that covenant referred (Gal. 3:16), and it was through the resurrection of Christ that Paul declares the fulfillment. Now Paul leaves no room for a future fulfillment. The verb form translated "fulfilled" is the Greek *ekpleroo* which means to accomplish or perform in full. Not only so, but he uses the perfect tense to indicate completed action in past time, but with continuing results. This means that the resurrection as a completed act is the basic fulfillment of the promise of Psalm two, but the effects that stem from that completed act are continuing to function on a durative basis. Thus, each time a person is converted, he participates in the promise made to the fathers which was authenticated by the resurrection of Christ.

Therefore we conclude that the second Psalm has reference to the exaltation of Christ which took place in past time. It does not refer to eschatological events. Paul quotes this Psalm and pinpoints its fulfillment in the resurrection of Christ and the gospel age. Dispensationalists and Judaistic Premillennialists must tear the Bible apart to make this Psalm teach a future Davidic kingdom and an earthly reign of Christ. The "sure mercies of David" are nothing less than the spiritual blessings we enjoy as a result of Christ's resurrection. Christ is now reigning from the throne of David which is His mediatorial throne in heaven. A future literal kingdom is not found in the second Psalm. Luke's recounting of Paul's message in Acts chapter 13 should lay that teaching quietly to rest.

### Psalm 16

Peter quoted verses 8-10 of this Psalm in his sermon on the day of Pentecost. The important portion reads, "For thou wilt not leave my soul in hell; neither wilt thou suffer thine Holy One to see corruption." It is impossible to draw out of this a promise of a future kingdom. Even Scofield admits it "is a prediction of the resurrection of the King" (note on Ps. 16:9). But an added statement has no biblical support whatsoever. This statement reads, "As a prophet David understood that, not at His first advent, but at some time subsequent to His death and resurrection Messiah would assume the Davidic throne." This is completely foreign to the 16th Psalm, and only by twisting New Testament teachings can it be supported from that portion of the Bible.

### Psalm 72

It is suggested that you "read this Psalm as you would any book of history or fact," before reading Scofield's notes. In reading his note on the first verse of this Psalm, compare his findings with yours. If you throw out every thing you did not find in it, you will probably discard all that he has written. What king is meant in verse 1? David probably meant himself, if he is the author as many believe. The "king's son" of verse 1 would be Solomon or he and his descendants who became kings. For those who say that Solomon wrote it, the difficulties are even greater.

The primary significance of this Psalm is temporal. Verse 1 does not primarily refer to Christ. If Christ is the king's son, then we have God imparting *righteousness* to His Son. But Christ is God, and righteousness cannot be imparted or given to Him, for in His very being and nature He is essentially righteous. Thus to hold that this Psalm is essentially Messianic is to reflect on the deity of Christ. Scofield's note on verse 1 reads in part, "Verse 1 refers to the investiture of the King's Son with the kingdom." The capital "S" in "Son," as well as other comments in this note indicate that he means a future reign of Christ on earth. That this Psalm has Messianic overtones is not questioned. It is the effort to make it pure prophecy that is objectionable.

In this same note Scofield writes of Psalm 72, "The Psalm as a whole forms a complete vision of Messiah's kingdom as far as the Old Testament revelation extended." This is an unsubstantiated claim that no impartial writer would make. It leads back to the question of a single hermeneutic. Verse 16 reads in part, "There shall be an handful of corn in the earth upon the top of the mountains." Note the unwarranted spiritualizing of this passage by Scofield: "Converted Israel will be the 'handful of corn'....It is through restored Israel that the kingdom is to be extended over the earth." The texts given in support of wild claims such as these are completely inadequate. The Messianic overtones of this chapter cannot be used legitimately for supporting the Premillennial or Dispensational scheme of eschatology.

### Psalm 89

Probably no other portion of the Old Testament is utilized by Premillennialists to support a future Davidic reign as much as this one. However, a close study of this Psalm annihilates the entire superstructure they have built on a sandy foundation. The first 37 verses recount God's promises to David. Premillennialists press these for all they are worth. Verses 3 and 4 plus verses 28-37 set forth the Davidic covenant in very strong terms. David's seed and his throne are to endure forever. Even if they forsake the way of the Lord (vv. 30-31), He promises not to utterly forsake them, nor will he break the covenant made to David (vv. 32-37). Reading these verses leaves the impression that the Judaistic Premillennialists have made their point. But as many other instances, the full text is not considered.

The same inspired writer who prophesied of the continuation of the Davidic kingdom (Ps. 89:3-37), quickly reverses himself to keep one from drawing a false conclusion from these statements. Note his words:

But thou hast cast off and abhorred, thou hast been wroth with thine anointed. Thou hast made void the covenant of thy servant: thou hast profaned his crown by casting it to the ground...Thou hast made his glory to cease, and cast his throne to the ground (Ps. 89:38, 39, 44).

Whatever this passage may mean, it pulls the rug out from under the claim that the earlier portion of this Psalm must be literally fulfilled at some future date. The certainty of the covenant *not* being broken in the earlier portion is completely counteracted by the equally positive statement the covenant was "made void" or abrogated. Just as God divorced Israel, He also nullified the literal covenant made to David. Any effort to harmonize these conflicting statements of the 89th Psalm is a matter of interpretation. The seeming absolute certainty which many Premillennialists give to the early verses of this Psalm is not warranted. Fairness also demands that they explain the seeming contradiction found in verses 38, 39, and 44. This they do not do.

The second portion affirms that the literal aspects of the covenant has been abrogated. The first portion affirms that in Christ and the Church it is given a spiritual fulfillment. It has previously been shown that the New Testament supports the view that Christ is now reigning on the throne of David. It has also been shown that the Church constitutes spiritual Israel. In this way the Church, as spiritual Israel, is married to Christ, even though literal Israel was permanently divorced: also, that the spiritual aspect of the Davidic covenant is being fulfilled through Christ's reign in the hearts of Christians, although the literal aspects have been permanently abolished.

Not one of the early Church writers interpreted this Psalm as referring to the millennium. Even Tertullian who was tainted with millennialism said it referred to Christ's present reign over the Church. His words will bear repeating where he urged the Jews to recognize that "you cannot contend that is future which you see taking place."[92] Augustine interprets this Psalm in this same manner. He spiritualized such verses as 34-37, making them refer to Christ and the Church. Verses 38-45 are said to refer to the literal

---

92 Tertullian, *op. cit.*, Pt. 1, p. 173.

descendants of David and are to be interpreted literally in that the literal throne of David has been cast down, just as these verses state.[93]

Elsewhere Augustine contends that the seed of David refers to Jesus Christ, just as Paul made the seed of Abraham refer to Christ. In this passage he has Christ reigning on the throne of the hearts of His followers rather than from His throne in heaven.[94] Cyril of Jerusalem interpreted the earlier verses of this Psalm after this fashion: "Thou seest that the discourse is of Christ, not of Solomon. For Solomon's throne endured not as the sun. But if any deny this because Christ sat not on David's throne of wood, we will bring forward the saying, *The Scribes and the Pharisees sit in Moses' seat:* for it signifies not His wooden seat, but the authority of His teaching."[95] What he means it that Christ is now reigning on the throne of David. Eusebius[96] and Theodoret[97] also interpreted this Psalm in reference to the gospel age.

### Psalm 102

Verses 25-27 of this Psalm are quoted in Hebrews 1:10-12. These verses compare the immutability of Christ with the changing conditions of the earth. Although the expressions of these verses are in poetic form, and although the possibility of apocalypticism cannot be ruled out, it does appear that these verses point to a time when the earth will be destroyed or will perish. It is to be cast aside as a worn out garment is discarded for newer attire. This agrees with other New Testament texts which declare that this earth will be destroyed by fire. These verses will be considered in due course.

Premillennialists attempt to make verses 15-18 apply to a future period of time; but the people who shall be created, according to verse 18, are none other than the Church. This is proved by verses 19-20 which indicate that God had heard "the groaning of the prisoner; to loose those that are appointed unto death." Similar words are in Isaiah 61:1-2. Jesus read these verses in Nazareth (Luke 4:16-19), and then declared, "This day is this scripture fulfilled in your ears" (Luke 4:21). The only eschatological teaching

---

93 Augustine, *op. cit.*, vol. II, pp. 349ff.
94 Augustine, *op. cit.*, vol. VIII, p. 430.
95 Cyril of Jerusalem, *Nicene and Post-Nicene Fathers*, second series, vol. VII. pp. 78-79.
96 Eusebius, vol. I, p. 324 of the same set as No. 10.
97 Theodoret, vol. III, pp. 169ff, of the same set as above.

# The Eschatology of the Historical & Poetic Books

that can be drawn from this Psalm is the eventual dissolution of the earth.

A summary of the teaching of the historical and poetic books includes life after death, the ultimate dissolution of the earth, and possibly a final judgment. However, absolutely nothing is mentioned about a millennial reign, separate resurrections, two second comings, nor about the other aspects of Dispensationalism and Premillennialism. Apart from other texts which Dispensationalists use to bolster their system of last things, they fail to find support for their teachings in this portion of God's word. The texts which they cite from this portion simply do not apply. One is reminded of the small town mill operator who blew a whistle at 12 noon. He depended on calling the telephone operator to obtain the correct time, only to find out later that the operator depended on his whistle for her correct time.

CHAPTER 8

# THE ESCHATOLOGY OF ISAIAH

Many consider Isaiah the greatest of the Old Testament prophets. In spite of the claim of Dispensationalists that the Old Testament prophets did not envision the Church age, many commentators hold that Isaiah pictured the gospel age so clearly that his prophecy has been termed "The Gospel According To Isaiah." However, several of his prophecies of the gospel age have been applied to an anticipated millennium. Much of the content of this chapter constitutes an effort to place the prophecies of Isaiah in their proper prospective.

*Isaiah 2:1-4*

Most civilized people recognize war as an evil. Christians are especially concerned about eliminating war. Thus the prophecy of Isaiah regarding a time when nations shall no longer "learn war any more" (Isa. 2:4) holds a tremendous appeal to large numbers of people. But we should not jump to hasty conclusions. Jesus indicated that wars would continue to plague humanity (Matt. 24:6-7), for which reason we must carefully consider every aspect of this prophecy before we can know how to interpret it.

Our first consideration should be the time of the fulfillment. The time of fulfillment, according to Isaiah, is "the last days" (v. 2). Just what Isaiah meant by "the last days" cannot be determined by exegesis alone. The term is sufficiently general to be capable of several interpretations. Since we must depend on interpretation, only a degree of probability can be derived from the sources upon which we must depend. However, the most frequent explanation of this expression in the New Testament, and therefore the most likely answer in this instance, is that it has reference to the gospel age. Peter used it in connection with the giving of the Spirit on the day of Pentecost (Acts 2:17), and the Hebrew epistle speaks of Christ having spoken "in these last days" (Heb. 1:2). Peter writes of his day being "these last times" (1 Pet. 1:20).

Scofield attempts to prove that the term is used in two distinct references. He admits that it is used of the Church age which "began with the advent of Christ" (note on Acts 2:17), but he claims it is also used in a separate sense regarding Israel. The two passages he lists are this one from Isaiah, and a similar one from Micah 4. Now neither of these passages says when these last days are to be. And he gives not one New Testament reference to substantiate his contention. Thus his claim is without biblical support. Therefore, we hold that Scofield's assertion must be discarded as the teachings of men. No second set of "last days" beyond the Church age can be substantiated by legitimate exegesis.

Our next consideration is the literary style of the passage. It is poetic in form, and probably apocalyptic as well. Much of that portion of the chapter which follows is definitely apocalyptic. Thus the literary style points to the probability of figurative language beyond that found in ordinary prose writings. In fact there is almost unanimous agreement that Isaiah does use figurative or symbolic speech in this section. Contrary to the claim of a single hermeneutic by Dispensationalists, they freely admit this. The point of difference is not whether or not figurative language is used: rather it is the question of how much is symbolic or figurative.

Scofield's note on Isaiah 2:2 admits that the expression "the mountain of the Lord's house" is symbolic. He says "A mountain, in Scripture symbolism, means a kingdom." Paul Lee Tan, a radical literalist, recognizes that Isaiah uses figurative language in the text being considered.[98] Of course, he applies it to the millennium he expects some time in the future. However, in keeping with his extreme literalism, he cannot allow the figure to constitute a symbol. So he insists, "The temple area will be...upon a very high mountain supernaturally raised for this purpose."[99]

This expected time of universal peace, according to Isaiah 2:4, is to be ushered in by people heating "their swords into plowshares and their spears into pruning hooks." Now in all fairness, let us consider how many people have swords and spears? Another question worth asking is what earthly use would our urban population have for plowshares and pruning hooks, if we had swords and spears to make them out of? To honestly face these questions is to recognize the fallacy of interpreting this passage literally.

---

98 Tan, *op. cit.*, p. 164.
99 *Ibid.*, p. 320.

Further evidence of the figurative nature of Isaiah 2:1-4 is obtained by comparing it with Micah 4:1-5. Now Micah says very much the same things as Isaiah. However, he adds a most interesting verse not found in the Isaiah passage. Verse 4 reads, "But they shall sit every man under his vine and under his fig tree; and none shall make them afraid: for the mouth of the Lord of hosts hath spoken it." Now if nations learning war no more is taken literally, we can hardly evade the necessity of taking this verse literally. But how can it be that every man will have a vine and a fig tree to sit under? Are our apartment complexes to be abandoned? Will there be a massive return to the rural areas? Or will dwellers in high-rise apartments raise their vines and fig trees on roofs and in window boxes?

The questions above are not intended to be taken seriously. My purpose in placing them there is to show how illogical it is to interpret this literally. Just as corn and wine constitute a symbol of plenty, so resting under vines and fig trees is a symbol for safety and security. Micah's statement, "and none shall make them afraid" should be conclusive at this point. There still remains the knotty problem of how much of this prophecy is symbolic, and how much, if any, is literal. Most commentators tend to take verses 2 and 3 as symbolic of the Church, then they switch to a literal interpretation of verse 4 as referring to a future time of universal peace. But this need not be. Verse 4 of Isaiah 2, and verse 3 of Micah 4 can be interpreted symbolically. This is the smoothest way of handling them, for even these verses contain figures of speech as has already been shown.

There yet remains the matter of interpretation. It is not enough to show that a passage contains figures of speech as these do. These figures of speech require the interpreter to attach meanings to them that are reasonable and that have some biblical support. If we accept the biblical texts from the New Testament already given as definitive of the "last days," then the entire prophecy refers to the gospel or Church age. "The mountain of the Lord's house" is the Church. Paul pointedly and specifically declares that the Christian community constitutes the "temple of God" (I Cor. 3:16; 6:19).

What Paul was saying was that under the old dispensation, God had dwelt in the tabernacle and temples of the Israelites, but under the gospel dispensation, He dwelt in people. This is reinforced by his sermon at Athens. In this message he said, "God...dwelleth not in temples made with hands" (Acts 17:24). When the veil of the temple was rent in twain, God forsook that human structure to take up His abode in the hearts of His people. And, praise be to God, He will never return to the old pattern again. Even if a new temple is constructed in Palestine or Jerusalem, God will not grace it with His presence as He did in former days. The only temple He now recognizes, or will ever recognize, is that "spiritual house" Peter wrote about (I Pet. 2:5).

This mountain of the Lord's house, the Church, "shall be established in the top of the mountains, and shall be exalted above the hills" (Isa. 2:2). This simply refers to the exaltation of the Church. Isaiah uses poetic terms and figures of speech to depict the glory of the Church. The expression in the same verse, "and all nations shall flow into it," refers to the conversion of people of all cultures and races. This cannot refer to a Judaistic millennium that most Premillenarians anticipate, for the temple they picture is a Jewish temple. The old wall of partition will be reestablished, they say. Hence Gentiles cannot fully participate in the temple worship they expect. Only the Church complies with the symbolism that is set forth in this passage.

Then in verse 4 the Prince of Peace reigning in the hearts of His people is figuratively expressed by the figure of men beating their swords into plowshares and their spears into pruning hooks. The judgment that is mentioned in this verse is now in progress through the condemnation that rests upon all individuals who reject the plan of redemption which is presently offered unto them. The "walk in his paths" (v. 3) refers to the Christian way of life. It is to "walk in the light, as he is in the light" (I John 1:7). The teaching and going forth of the law in verse 3 refers to the teaching and preaching of the gospel in the present age.

The interpretation given here is not some wild, implausible concoction of a disordered imagination. The laws of analogy have been adhered to. A sound basis for a nonliteral, figurative or symbolic interpretation was established. It was shown that even Dispensationalists recognize that figures of speech are involved. These things weaken the foundation of any millennial doctrine based on this passage, if they do not in fact eliminate it. Therefore, we reject as false the eschatological concepts that are built on this passage and the similar passage in Micah 4. We affirm that these portions of the prophets refer to the gospel age. There is no necessity that they be interpreted eschatologically, and valid reasons have been given for not doing so.

The early Church fathers who discussed this passage consistently interpreted it as applicable to the gospel age, even by those who held certain millennial concepts. Justin Martyr commenting on the fulfillment of this passage and of verse 4 in particular states, "And that it did so come to pass, we can convince you. For from Jerusalem there went out into the world, men, twelve in number" who proclaimed peace.[100] Tertullian held that the mountain of the Lord had already been exalted in his day. He spiritualized the farm implements as well as those of war.[101] In another place he explains exactly what he means: "In other words, they shall change into pursuits of moderation and peace the disposition of injurious minds, and hostile tongues."[102] He then contends that these things have been accomplished "in Him of whom they were predicted."[103]

Origen applies it to the gospel age: "For the law came forth from the dwellers in Sion, and settled among us as a spiritual law." He spiritualizes the implements by adding, "We no longer take up 'sword against nation,' nor do we 'learn war any more' having become children of peace."[104] A number of quotations from Augustine, Chrysostom, Athanasius, and Cyril of Jerusalem could he given, for all of these interpreted the passage under consideration in the same manner as those we have quoted. Only two citations will be given to conserve space. Athanasius interpreted verse 4 as the change Christ makes in people,[105] and Cyril of Jerusalem interprets the mountain as the Church. The latter reads, "Of this the blessed Esaias prophesying of old time said, *And on this mountain*—(Now he calls the Church a mountain elsewhere also, as when he says, In the last days the mountain of the Lord's house shall be manifest)."[106]

## Isaiah 9:1-7

All agree that most of this portion of Scripture applies to the first advent. Jesus Himself interpreted verses 1-2 in reference to His earthly ministry (Matt. 4:15-16). All accept the birth of the child (v. 6) as referring to the birth of Jesus. However, Premillennialists tend to interpret part of verse 6 and all of verse 7 eschatologically. Since we have proved that the kingdom of God has been established already, and that Christ is now reigning on the throne of David (chaps. 6 and 11), our remarks will be brief.

---

100 Justin, *op. cit.*, vol. I, p. 175.
101 Tertullian, *op. cit.*, pt. I, p. 154.
102 *Ibid.*, (Part Second), p. 340.
103 *Ibid.*
104 Origen, *Ante-Nicene Fathers*, vol. IV, p. 558.
105 Athanasius, *Nicene and Post-Nicene Fathers*, second series, vol. IV, p. 64.
106 Cyril, *op. cit.*, p. 142.

The expression "throne of David" is a figure of speech. The elevated seat from which David issued his decrees has long since ceased to exist. If this passage is to be taken literally without any spiritualizing whatsoever, then God must restore that literal seat for Christ to sit on. I know of no one who carries literalism that far. But if that chair, seat, or throne is not to be restored, we move immediately into the figurative or symbolic method of interpretation.

Nearly all commentators agree that the throne of David does not refer to the government Christ exercises, or will exercise at some time in the future. But since it will not be from the literal, physical, material throne from which David ruled, the time and place of the ruling is a matter of interpretation—not of exegesis. Those who interpret the reign to be future and from Jerusalem do so by spiritualizing the throne but literalizing other aspects of the prophecy. I have interpreted the totality of the prophecy as figurative or symbolic. According to this view, Christ is now ruling from David's throne. His rule is over the Church, the new Israel, if you please.

Jesus Himself said, "All power is given unto me in heaven and in earth" (Matt. 28:18). From this we say that Christ is now exercising all the power on earth He will ever exercise. The government is at this time "upon his shoulder." Peter, commenting on David's prophecy, on the day of Pentecost, speaks of Christ now on the throne of David:

Therefore being a prophet, and knowing that God had sworn with an oath to him, that of the fruit of his loins, according to the flesh, he would raise up Christ to sit on his throne; He seeing this before spake of the resurrection of Christ…Therefore let all the house of Israel know assuredly, that God hath made that same Jesus whom ye have crucified, both Lord and Christ (Acts 2:30, 31, 36).

Now Peter affirms that the fulfillment of Christ on the throne of David came through the resurrection. Note Peter's words. He says that David "spake of the resurrection of Christ" when he spoke of One to sit on his throne. Then Peter adds that God has already made Jesus both Christ and Lord. Therefore, we reiterate that Christ is now reigning on the throne of David. Thus, this passage from Isaiah finds its fulfillment in the present age, rather than some future millennium. There is no sound basis for interpreting this passage eschatologically.

The early Church fathers are in agreement with this view. Justin held that verse 6 referred to the power of the cross.[107] Tertullian made the resurrection the time His reign began. He wrote of "Christ, who has reigned from that time onward when he overcame the death which ensued from His passion 'on the tree.' " He goes on to interpret the government as being on His shoulder as referring to the present age.[108] *The Constitutions of the Holy Apostles* contends this passage was fulfilled at the first advent and castigates the Jews for not accepting it as fulfilled.[109] Cyril of Jerusalem applied it to Christ's reign over the Church.[110]

The only writer of the early Church whose interpretation of this passage could contain any eschatological or millennial import is Athanasius. He indicated that Christ was the "Father of the coming age."[111] The problem is in determining whether he meant to use this from the time situation of the prophet or if Athanasius anticipated a future age beyond the gospel age. Since we have no evidence that Athanasius was a millennialist, I believe that he spoke from the standpoint of the prophet Isaiah and that the "coming age" was the gospel age.

### Isaiah 11:1-16

To deal adequately with this passage would require at least a full chapter and possibly more. However, because of space limitations a portion of a chapter must suffice. Many Premillennialists interpret this entire chapter eschatologically. Others confine this view to verses 6-9. Amillennialists contend it refers to the gospel age and that verses 6-9 are figurative expressions for human personalities couched in terms of animal dispositions.

The Bible is replete with instances where dispositions of animals are used to refer to people whose natures were like those of the animals mentioned. Jesus used sheep and goats to indicate the saved and the unsaved (Matt. 25:33). He called Herod a fox (Luke 13:32). He called the scribes and Pharisees serpents and a generation of vipers (Matt. 23:33). Jesus also told the seventy that He was sending them out as "lambs among wolves" (Luke 10:3). This is so nearly identical to Isaiah's reference to the wolf and the lamb

---

107 Justin, *op. cit.*, p. 174.
108 Tertullian, *op. cit.*, p. 166, pt. I.
109 Constitutions, *Ante-Nicene Fathers*, vol. VII, p. 446.
110 Cyril, *op. cit.*, p. 79.
111 Athanasius, *op. cit.*, pp. 89, 400, 415, and 428.

(Isa. 11:6) that Jesus may have had the prophecy of Isaiah in mind when He said these words.

You should keep in mind that not one Old Testament passage speaks of a millennial reign, hence no Old Testament passage can be proved to refer to a millennium on the basis of exegesis alone. In spite of these limitations many millennial writers confidently affirm that the Old Testament prophets do indeed speak of a millennium. This is one of the passages most often used to support this theory. Let us examine these verses to determine their meaning and the time of fulfillment.

In verse 1 the Branch out of the stem of Jesse definitely refers to Christ. All are in agreement at this point. We contend that it must refer to His first advent. Coming out of the stem of Jesse refers to the humanity of Christ. If there is to be a millennium, it must refer to the deity of Christ and His glorification. Therefore, verse one has no reference to a millennium. Verse 2 begins very much like Isaiah 61:1 which Christ read at Nazareth (Luke 4:18), and which He declared was being fulfilled at that time. On this basis we contend that verse 2 of this chapter was likewise fulfilled at the first advent. It follows that verses 3-5 also refer to the first advent.

But what of verses 6-9? These verses had no literal fulfillment at the first advent, therefore they must be interpreted symbolically or considered yet future. I interpret them symbolically. Millennialists hold to a literal future fulfillment. Both are matters of interpretation—not of exegesis. H. C. Heffren lists 14 passages where the term "lion(s)" is used figuratively or symbolically.[112] Wolves, dogs, sheep, snakes, gnats, and camels are all used figuratively. Instead of taking it for granted that the animal references in verses 6-9 are to be taken literally, millennialists should spend some time proving they are not to be taken symbolically.

A literal interpretation demands tremendous changes in the way animals react as well as in the way they eat. Without adequate support from science or the Bible, millennialists often contend that no animals were carnivorous prior to the fall. It is claimed that Isaiah both here and in 65:25 is pointing to a restoration of that condition. But there is nothing in the Bible to indicate that lions have not always fed on smaller animals, nor that large fish have not fed on smaller fish. This is no more than a theory they have developed.

---

112  H. C. Heffren, *There's A Great Day Coming*, pp. 5-6.

And to base such tremendous changes as this theory claims on a passage as subject to other interpretations as this one is, cannot be considered logical.

Admittedly, God is all powerful. He could make vegetarians out of both man and beast, but it requires more support than I've had presented to me to accept such a fantastic alteration of life as we know it. If all animal life becomes vegetarian, small fish, rats, and sundry wild animals will become so populous that the amount of vegetable food available will be totally inadequate. The sea would become overstocked with fish until the algae and other vegetable sources of food were exhausted. Then they would die. With birds no longer eating worms and insects, these would increase to the point of destroying the plant life upon which all life would then be dependent. The picture is too illogical for acceptance while clear proof is lacking.

A more likely explanation is that the animals mentioned in verses 6-9 are illustrative of men's natures which are changed through the power of God. The lion natured man loses his aggressiveness and become docile as a Christian. The wolf-like man becomes gentle. Even in our day the expression "wolf-whistle" refers to a man of lustful disposition who seeks to attract women through the medium of sound. But if that man gets truly converted, you could trust him with your daughter. Therefore, these verses have reference to the gospel age as do the earlier verses of this chapter.

Again in verse 10 we find a reference to "a root of Jesse." As in verse 1, this refers to the incarnation, not to the exaltation of Christ. Hence, we take the remainder of chapter 11 as apocalyptic to be treated symbolically, rather than literally. The first effort to recover the "remnant of his people" (v. 11) was the literal return from the Babylonian captivity. The second effort is the gospel being preached to all the peoples of the world, so that even persons of pagan religions and cultures find acceptance with the Lord.

The early Church fathers are generally in agreement with the interpretation I have given. Irenaeus quotes Papias to the effect that in a future millennium the earth will become exceedingly productive and that the natures of ferocious animals will be changed. The latter is based on a literal interpretation of this passage. It is quite frequently interpreted after this fashion today. However, this was not true during the early years of Christianity. In fact, I found only two other authors who even intimated such a change.

These were Tertullian and Jerome. Tertullian wrote in favor of a literal interpretation in one place,[113] and a spiritualized interpretation[114] in another place. Jerome's statement is indecisive.[115] The change from a symbolic interpretation to a literal one by Tertullian can be associated with his affiliation with the Montanist sect which did teach a millennial reign. I did not find where he gave any explanation for this changed attitude toward these verses or a millennium.

Opposed to Papias and Irenaeus and two questionable sources, nine authors were found who spiritualized Isaiah 11:6-8. Origen said the Jews' literalism caused them to reject Christ when real wolves were not changed so they could "feed with the lamb" and lions did not "eat straw like the ox."[116] Yet, a similar literalism is strongly advocated today. Chrysostom compared the animal changes to the change God would make in people. A king might threaten like a lion, but through prayer God will calm him down.[117] Cyril of Jerusalem wrote that in the "church the calf, and the lion, and the ox feed in the same pasture."[118] Athanasius wrote that of old the law went just from "Dan to Beersheba," but now that the "disciples have made disciples of all nations, and now is fulfilled what is written, 'they shall be all taught of God.' "[119]

### Isaiah 13, 14, 34

These chapters contain apocalyptic passages which describe the downfall of a king and nations in highly figurative terms. Babylon, a king of Babylon (Nebuchadnezzar?), and Idumea are intended in that regard.

*Isaiah 35 and related material in chapters 41-44.* As previously indicated, Scofield and Dispensationalists in general misapply the extravagant language of Isaiah 34:3, 4, 9, 10 to the battle of Armageddon and the time of the consummation, instead of to the destruction of Idumea as verses 5 and 6 declare. Then, since chapters 34 and 35 are closely related, it almost compels them to apply chapter 35 to the consummation although

---

113 Tertullian, *op. cit.*, p. 483.
114 *Ibid.*, pp. 388-389.
115 Jerome, *op. cit.*, vol. VI, pp. 265-266
116 Origen, *op. cit.*, p. 356.
117 Chrysostom, *op. cit.*, vol. IX, p. 356.
118 Cyril, *op. cit.*, vol. VII, p. 126.
119 Athanasius, *op. cit.*, vol. IV, p. 341.

the evidence against this is monumental. But as is so often the case, one error leads to another.

Most of verses 5 and 6 were literally fulfilled during Jesus' earthly ministry. He opened the eyes of the blind and unstopped the deaf ears. The dumb were enabled to speak, and the lame had the use of their limbs restored to them. But as has been shown before, some prophecies mix the figurative or symbolic with the literal. The Canaanites were very real or literal, but the streams of milk and honey were figurative and symbolic. The streams that Isaiah prophesies in verse 6 are just as figurative and symbolic as the streams of milk and honey. The only difference is that the streams of milk and honey referred to temporal abundance, whereas the streams of Isaiah 35:6 refer to the spiritual blessings God would shower upon the Church.

During His incarnation, Jesus claimed to be the water of life (John 4:10-14; 7:37). He said further of anyone who received the Holy Spirit, "Out of his belly shall flow rivers of living water" (John 7:38). Thus during the gospel age, all the water is available that is needed to mark the fulfillment of the waters Isaiah prophesies of in chapter 35 and those chapters which follow. In fact Isaiah 44:3 is probably the Old Testament text Christ had in mind when He spoke of "rivers of living waters." Isaiah 43:19-20 has a similar meaning.

It is also interesting to note the defense Christ made of His messiahship to the disciples of John the Baptist. Jesus could hardly have meant anything other than that He was the fulfillment of Isaiah 35:5-6 when He said, "The blind receive their sight, and the lame walk" (Matt. 11:5). Also, His reference to the fact that "the poor have the gospel preached to them" is nothing short of a claim that His ministry is a fulfillment of Isaiah 41:17-18. In this passage verse 17 mentions the poor and needy, then in verse 18 the promise to open rivers and fountains to them is fulfilled through the preaching of the gospel. In this passage as in many others rivers and fountains refer to the blessings of the gospel, rather than to literal rivers and fountains.

The highway of holiness (v. 8) is nothing less than the strait and narrow way of the Gospels. Our future destiny will be with the demons in hell unless we travel this road, for the Hebrew epistle clearly states that without this quality of life we cannot see God (Heb. 12:14). Those who interpret Isaiah 11 and 35 as yet future really have a problem with the lions of these chapters. According to their interpretation the lions will be tame in chapter 11, but chapter 35 says no lions will be there. The literalism they insist upon drives them into a corner when these two chapters are considered together. But if chapter 11 is made to refer to people whose nature has been changed, and chapter 35 is made to refer to the exclusion of persons whose nature has not been changed, a beautiful harmony is evident.

A careful search of the early writers of the Church did not reveal a single instance of Isaiah 35 being used in reference to a millennium. Ignatius, Justin, Irenaeus, Origen, Novatian, Lactantius, Constitutions of the Holy Apostles, Augustine, Eusebius, and Gregory of Nyssa all apply it to Christ and the gospel age. Chrysostom does apply verse 10 to heaven in a couple of places, but not to a millennium.

## Isaiah 50-66

Various portions of these chapters are interpreted eschatologically by Premillennialists, especially those verses which speak of Israel and Zion. But instead of taking these to mean a restored Israel, we should understand these words as referring to spiritual Zion or the Church. The return unto Zion in 51:11 refers to the salvation work now in progress. Chapter 52 does not refer to a future kingdom age, but to the Church age. Paul quotes Isaiah 52:7 and indicates that the preaching of the gospel to the lost is the meaning of this prophecy (Rom. 10:15). Isaiah 52:13-53:12 refers to Christ's trial and crucifixion.

Scofield interprets chapter 54 as a restoration of Israel as the wife of Jehovah, but it has been shown already that Israel was permanently divorced. Jeremiah makes this very clear.

A lengthy discourse begins with Isaiah 59:20. Dispensationalists strongly assert that much of this refers to a restored Israel. This is denied with equal vigor. The "Redeemer" (Isa. 59:20) is none other than Christ our Saviour, and the "covenant" (v. 21) is nothing less than the new covenant Christ established at His first advent. Jesus placed this interpretation on this portion by applying Isaiah 61:1-2 to His earthly ministry. Scofield inserts the heading "The two advents in view" at the beginning of Isaiah 61, but Jesus makes but a single application (Luke 4:16-22). Instead of the "day of vengeance" referring to the consummation, it refers to the defeat of the forces of Satan as a result of Jesus' life and sacrifice on Calvary.

The key to understanding that which follows is to recognize that Isaiah uses the terms Zion and Jerusalem as symbols of the Church. It is pure folly to apply these chapters to a restored Judaism, as Dispensationalists do. The idea of a restored Judaism is repugnant to the New Testament emphasis which is that Jews and Gentiles are one in Jesus Christ.

Premillennialists make much of the latter part of Isaiah 65. The idea of heaven—not a millennium here on earth—is paramount in the closing verses of Isaiah. Peter places the new heavens and the new earth (Isa. 65:17) as being beyond the existence of the planet earth (II Pet. 3:10-13). After this earth has been dissolved, the new heavens and earth are to appear. This makes heaven the point of reference. Only heavenly beings could be entirely free of tears and crying (Isa. 65:19). A child of 100 years (Isa. 65:20) does not depict a millennial reign: it speaks of continuing existence in a heavenly abode.

## A Summarizing Statement

Most of the passages in Isaiah that some interpret eschatologically are figurative or symbolic expressions about the gospel age. Another part are apocalyptic accounts of the destructions of nations before the gospel era. The only portion of Isaiah that is definitely eschatological is from Isaiah 65:17 to the end of the book, and this refers to *heaven—not to an earthly millennium.*

CHAPTER 9

# THE ESCHATOLOGY OF JEREMIAH

A comparison of the books of Isaiah and Jeremiah reveals many striking similarities, but it also reveals some differences. Both men were great prophets who fearlessly spoke God's word to kings. Isaiah prophesied before and after the fall of Israel, whereas Jeremiah prophesied before and after the fall of Judah. Both men frequented the palace area and advised the kings of their time. Their advice was not accepted at times. Both men prophesied of captivity and return. Both pronounced dire judgments of God on those who refused to do that which was right. Both prophesied of the new covenant which Christ was to institute at His first advent, though futurists of our day deny it.

The personalities of these two men were quite different. Jeremiah was more emotional and less optimistic than Isaiah. This difference is reflected in their writings. Eschatological problems are scattered throughout the book of Isaiah, whereas they are concentrated in chapters 30-33 of Jeremiah.

Jeremiah gives a very graphic description of the new covenant in chapter 31. Chapter 30 considers "the time of Jacob's trouble." The siege of Jerusalem in 586 B.C. or that in A.D. 70 is intended. Premillennialists often interpret this as a future time of persecution of the Jews by the Antichrist during the last three and one-half years of his reign. Although some of Isaiah's prophecies are interpreted similarly, the basis for such an application is much weaker than that of Jeremiah 30.

However, Premillennialists who believe the Church will endure the "great tribulation" (Posttribulation rapturists) tend to agree with Amillennialists and Postmillennialists that Jeremiah's "time of Jacob's trouble" refers to the destruction of Jerusalem in A.D. 70. The "great tribulation" is conceived of by Premillennialists as coming during the reign of an anticipated man who is designated as *the* Antichrist who rules the world for the seven years prior to the establishment of the millennial kingdom. This particular aspect of Premillennial teaching will receive fuller consideration in the New Testament portion of this volume.

### Jeremiah 3

This chapter has already received some attention. The fuller discussion promised there is now given. Premillennialists make much of the return (v. 14), and of Israel and Judah being together (v. 18), but they tend to ignore the earlier portions of the chapter. Jeremiah points out that Moses clearly taught that a woman divorced from her first husband could not be remarried to him after having been married to another man. He indicates this is the situation between God and Israel (v. 1). The divorcement of Israel is again stated in verse 8. In verse 9 Judah is said to be even more unrighteous than Israel. Since God is just in His dealings, we must recognize that the destruction of Jerusalem in 586 B.C. points to her divorcement as well.

But someone asks, "What about the call to return in verse 14?" In the *Amplified Bible* this verse reads,

> Return, O faithless children [of the whole twelve tribes], says the Lord, for I am Lord and Master and Husband to you, and I will take you [not as a nation, but individually] one from a city and two from a tribal family, and I will bring you to Zion.

It is my opinion that the above reading gives the proper meaning of this verse. National Israel was completely rejected forever. For her to again be married to God would cause the land to be "greatly polluted" (v. 1). Since only a very few, "one from a city and two from a tribal family," would answer the call, it indicates the remnant would be small indeed. The fact that very few Jews do accept Christ proves the accuracy of this observation.

Now I am aware that Premillennialists interpret verse 14 as yet future. They also teach that the total Jewish population will return to God. But that is not the intent of Jeremiah 3:14. This refers to those Jews who have accepted Christ as their personal Saviour during the present gospel age. The union of Israel and Judah refers to the present unity that Jews and Gentiles have in Christ. Israel had become the wife of a Gentile nation, hence had lost her Jewish heritage. She represents the Gentiles. Judah represents the Jews. The joining of these two constitutes a symbol of Jewish and Gentile oneness that Jesus referred to in John 10:16, and which Paul expresses so forcefully in Ephesians 2:11-22. Thus Jeremiah 3:18 depicts the gospel age—not a future millennium.

### Jeremiah 12:14-17

*Jeremiah 12:14-17.* This speaks of a return. A return of "every man to his heritage" is indicated (v. 15). This sounds as if a future return must occur, for all Jews did not return in the previous returns. But we must read further to get the full import of this promise. It is definitely a conditional promise for verse 17 reads, "But if they will not obey, I will utterly pluck up and destroy that nation, saith the Lord." Once again we stress the necessity of considering each text within its own context. To stress verses 14-16 as an unfulfilled promise, and to claim it must be fulfilled in a future millennium which is not once mentioned in the Old Testament, without due consideration of verse 17 simply is not ethical. The prooftext method employed by many Premillennial writers enables them to present a case that seemingly is quite strong and valid. The unwary are fooled by it, for only those who search out these texts fully uncover the basic weaknesses of their position.

### *Jeremiah 23:1-8*

This passage speaks of a return, but it refers to the gospel age, not to a future millennium. The shepherds (v. 1) that scattered the flock, probably mean the last of the wicked kings of Judah prior to the destruction of Jerusalem by Nebuchadnezzar. The gathering of the flock (v. 3) refers to the salvation work done by Christians preaching the gospel. The good shepherds who would feed the children of God are faithful ministers of the gospel. Verses 5-8 indicate that the interpretation given is the correct one, for Christ, the righteous Branch, is the one who will direct this operation. As before noted, the title Branch is applicable to the incarnation. What the Branch does refers to the gospel age. The designation of Branch would be inappropriate of the glorified Christ at the *parousia*.

### *Jeremiah 30-31*

These two chapters form a unit. They were probably written during the siege of Jerusalem just prior to its destruction and the final deportation to Babylon. It has been characterized as a book of consolation and a hymn of triumph. It was designed to give the people hope in spite of the tragic circumstances they were enduring at that particular time. They should not be considered as any less truly prophetic simply because they were historically given to provide encouragement and hope to a distressed people. However, no time is given for the fulfillment, and much of the material is of such a nature that about all that can be determined by exegesis is that hope for the future is the theme. No system of eschatology should lean on these chapters.

The "time of Jacob's trouble" (v. 7) is the first portion of importance. Most Premillennialists interpret this as referring to a future time of severe persecution which the Jews are expected to have to endure. The usual approach is eschatological. It is contended that the Antichrist will initiate it. The time usually set for it is immediately prior to the establishment of the millennial kingdom. Some hold that the Church will be raptured away prior to this time of persecution, but others say the Church will also endure the tribulations of that time also.

Now there is not a single text that sets forth the picture given in the above paragraph. It is arrived at by linking various interpretations of various passages into a chain that doesn't really prove anything. Since each link in this chain involves interpretation which goes beyond exegesis, every link is as weak as the human interpretation given it. Keep in mind, Jeremiah does not say when the time of Jacob's trouble would come. I believe, along with many other commentators, that it refers to the time of the destruction of Jerusalem by Titus in A.D. 70. This is an opinion, but it appeals to me as involving fewer difficulties than that given by Premillennialists.

The Olivet discourse of Jesus which will be considered later mentions a future time of distress (Matt. 24:21-22) of unparalleled intensity. Now Jeremiah 30:7 also points to a time of great trouble. It is altogether possible, therefore, that they refer to the same event. It is my opinion that they do. But I deny that either one of them refers to a time yet future. The reader is asked to reserve judgment on this matter until the New Testament division is read that considers the Olivet discourse. Instead of this passage in Jeremiah pointing to an eschatological event, it was fulfilled in A.D. 70.

The portion of this verse (Jer. 30:7) that is usually appealed to as making this interpretation unacceptable is the phrase in it, "But he" (i.e., Jacob) "shall be saved out of it." Premillennialists persistently contend that Jacob or Israel was not saved out of this destruction under Titus. Their objections are refuted from two different angles. First, it is quite evident that the literal Jews did survive the troubles of A.D. 70. Had they not done so, there would be no country of Israel today. It is true that many Jews did die during that terrible ordeal, but a remnant were saved. Reading the account in Josephus will impress the most callous, but even so, some did come out of it alive.

A second approach takes Jacob as a symbol of the true Israel of God, the Church. Combining information found in the works of Flavius Josephus and Eusebius Pamphilus, the encircling of Jerusalem began weeks before it was finally sufficiently complete to stop all entry and exit. The preliminary features occurred under Vespasian. He was at Caesarea ready to attack, when he heard of Nero's death. He was eventually crowned as the new emperor, after a period of rival claimants. He entrusted the campaign to his son, Titus, who was the military leader who directed the campaign of attrition which eventuated in the capture and destruction of Jerusalem. But the Church did not suffer the agonies of that siege.

The reason for this is that the Church took Christ's words seriously. When the encirclement began, they evidently watched for an opportune time and fled the city. Eusebius gives this account: "The whole body, however, of the church at Jerusalem, having been commanded by a divine revelation, given to men of approved piety there before the war, removed from the city, and dwelt at a certain town beyond the Jordan called Pella."[120]

Now the church at Jerusalem was largely composed of Jews. Hence most of those who escaped were descendants of Abraham, genetically, as well as spiritually. The term Israel or Jacob is therefore appropriately applied to them. They constitute the true remnant to whom the promises were given. They were the believing Jews. It was the unbelieving Jews such as those who crucified our Lord who suffered the terrible ordeal of the destruction of Jerusalem. Therefore, there is no legitimate reason for insisting that the time of Jacob's trouble is yet future.

The king that they were to serve (v. 9) is called David, but only extreme literalists take this to be the successor of Saul as king of Israel. Most apply this to Christ either presently or at some future time. The expression "whom I will raise up" probably points to the resurrection of Christ as similar passages are interpreted by Peter in Acts 2. Those who withdrew to Pella were indeed serving the risen Lord and King who was promised. The time element of this prophecy is not stated in this chapter, hence it is a matter of fitting events in with the conditions set forth in the prophecy. As shown above, the conditions existing at the time of Nero's death and shortly afterwards do fit the conditions set forth in Jeremiah 30:7-9. The return mentioned in chapter 30 is either a drop back to the return under Cyrus or it finds its fulfillment spiritually in the Church.

The return of Jeremiah 31:4-10 should not be taken literally for at least some of it is definitely symbolic. It is a well known fact that rivers wind

---

120 Eusebius, *op. cit.*, bk. III, sec. 5, p. 86.

around and meander towards their ultimate point of dispatch into a larger body of water. Therefore the statement in verse 9, "I will cause them to walk by rivers of waters in a straight way, wherein they shall not stumble," must be taken as a figure of speech. The walking in a straight way refers to spiritually obeying God. The expression "they shall not stumble" has the same meaning. It would be ridiculous to apply these statements to the literal land of Palestine and a straight walkway by a crooked river.

That it refers to the gospel age is indicated by the way Matthew applies verse 15. Matthew quotes this passage in 2:18 of his gospel and says it fulfills this passage from Jeremiah. Those who attempt to make chapters 30-31 refer to a future time have real difficulty in defending their position when this passage is seriously considered.

Verses 27-30 also apply to the gospel age. Under the Old Testament order, there was a certain corporate responsibility or guilt. It was not unusual for a prophet to make confession for the totality of his people—not simply for his own sins. Job made sacrifices for his children on the basis of some failure on their part. However, in the gospel age no such corporate guilt is indicated. Each person is directly responsible to God. The setting of teeth on edge is an idiomatic expression for guilt. The statement that only those who eat sour grapes have their teeth set on edge is explained as meaning that each person is individually and personally responsible to God for his sinful acts. That this is applicable to the gospel dispensation can hardly be denied.

The reason it is applicable to the gospel age is that God has no special nation. Men of every nation become one in Christ. On the other hand, should the Jews again be restored to a place of special favor, as Dispensationalists and many Premillennialists teach, it is not unreasonable to assume that national guilt would also be restored. It follows that this is a prophecy that is confined to the gospel age. It does not refer to a Judaistic millennium.

Immediately following the above reference to the gospel age, the new covenant is brought into focus. Early Christian writers such as Justin Martyr, Irenaeus, Clement of Alexandria, Tertullian, and Cyprian uniformly applied this to the gospel age. For centuries this was the standard interpretation. Then with the rise of Dispensationalism, an entirely new dimension was added to the long accepted understanding of Jeremiah's prophecy. The key aspects of the prophecy read:

> Behold the days come, saith the Lord, that I will make a new covenant with the house of Israel, and with the house of Judah...But this shall be the

covenant that I will make with the house of Israel; After those days, saith the Lord, I will put my law in their inward parts, and write it in their hearts; and will be their God, and they shall be my people. And they shall teach no more every man his neighbor, saying, Know the Lord: for they shall all know me, from the least of them unto the greatest of them, saith the Lord; for I will forgive their iniquity, and will remember their sin no more (Jer. 31:31-34).

Scofield's heading to chapter 31 reads, "Summary: Israel in the last days." About all this implies is that the new covenant was not established at the first advent, hence is to be established at some future time. It is in his reference to Hebrews 8:8 that his full meaning is given. In his first note he lists the superiority of the second covenant over the first. All can accept this. In his second note he lists eight covenants. The seventh of these covenants is the Davidic covenant. Then completely skipping the gospel age he posits the New covenant as a future covenant which "rests upon the sacrifice of Christ," but which was not instituted at that time. According to this plan, we do not now live under any covenant with the Lord. It raises a serious question as to the validity of calling the last 27 books of the Bible the New Testament or Covenant, at least if his interpretation and plan are accepted.

But they are not accepted by many Premillennialists or any Postmillennialists and Amillennialists. Only Dispensationalists are able to swallow this strange teaching. Walvoord defends this teaching[121] as does Paul L. Tan[122] and other Dispensational writers. Possibly Walvoord's defense is the stronger and more direct of the two specifically mentioned, hence we shall consider his view on this text. He begins his argument with verses which follow the ones quoted above. In these verses there is a promise made to Israel. He states, "It is most significant that this strongest prophecy in the Old Testament for the continuance of Israel is given in a setting when Israel is manifestly in apostasy and about to be carried off into captivity."

Walvoord, however, depends entirely too much on an English translation. The Hebrew *goi*, as previously explained, does not always refer to nations in the sense of a body of people within a geographically defined area and with a single government. It is just as appropriately applied to a subject people and even to a scattered people who are bound together by race, practices, or purpose. Thus the Jews were still a *goi* (people) even during their captivity

---

121 Walvoord, *Israel in Prophecy*, pp. 49ff.
122 Tan, *op. cit.*, pp. 240ff.

and following the destruction of Jerusalem in A.D. 70. However, the promise of continuance as a nation (people) is greatly modified by verse 37 which reads in part, "If heaven above can be measured...I will cast off all the seed of Israel." Note that not all the seed of Israel are to be cut off.

Most commentators accept the idea of a remnant of the literal Jews retaining their faith and allegiance to God. Paul argues this in the Roman letter. If God had cut off all the Jews, he, Paul, would have also been cut off. Some limbs of the tame olive remained. He, and the other Jews who accepted Christ, constituted the remnant. The point of debate is over national Israel—not the believing remnant. Thus, Paul and Jeremiah are in accord. Jeremiah prophesied that God would not cut off *all* of the Israelites after the flesh. He does not say that *none* will be cut off. Paul argues in the same vein from the fulfillment, not all of the Jews were cut off—just some of them were cut off.

Four passages of Scripture indicate the gospel and the new covenant are one and the same. At the Last Supper, Jesus said of the fruit of the vine, "This cup is the new testament in my blood" (Luke 22:20). The Greek word translated "testament" is *diatheke* which is usually translated "covenant." Paul also uses *diatheke* in I Corinthians 11:25 in an expression almost identical to that from Luke. Then twice in the Hebrew epistle strong support for the new covenant being then in operation is found. Even though Hebrews 8 is patently referring to the gospel age, Walvoord declares it must be future for the new covenant of Jeremiah 31:31-34 and which is quoted in Hebrews 8:8 is one with Israel and Judah, whereas the present covenant, if indeed we have a covenant at all, was not with Judah and Israel.

The last verse of Hebrews 8 proves Walvoord to be twisting the intent of the writer. It reads, "In that he saith, A new covenant, he hath made the first old. Now that which decayeth and waxeth old is ready to vanish away." The time the old covenant was discarded is declared to be the time the new covenant superseded the old. That the old has been cast aside cannot be denied. It follows that the new is now in effect. A future covenant with the physical Israelites and Jews has no place in the book of Hebrews.

Walvoord does not admit that Hebrews 10:15-23 has reference to the same covenant, but a careful reading should enable anyone to recognize that chapters 8 and 10 are saying exactly the same thing; namely, that the new covenant Jeremiah prophesied was established with Christ's passion, resurrection, and ascension. Those who place the new covenant in the future to fit it with their Judaistic millennium do so without adequate justification of any sort. Not only is modern scholarship opposed to it, but the early Church writers are unanimous in applying the new covenant of Jeremiah to the gospel age. Above all, the New Testament itself refutes the Dispensational approach.

### Jeremiah 32

The early portion of this chapter deals with a return which is generally accepted as beginning under Cyrus in 536 B.C. Verse 40 speaks of an everlasting covenant which, of course, is the new covenant as in chapter 31.

### Jeremiah 33

Verses 7 and 8 speak of a return and a cleansing. The cleansing indicates the gospel era is the subject of this prophecy. This is substantiated by the "Branch of righteousness" (v. 15). This must refer to Christ's incarnation. It cannot refer to an earthly reign of the glorified Christ, for the term "Branch" can refer only to His physical descent from the line of David. The latter portion of the chapter considers the Davidic covenant and the throne of David. As in other passages that have been discussed already, these verses apply to Christ's present reign over the Church. He now sits on the throne of David. It is not a reference to a future millennium, but a reference to the gospel era.

If verse 18 is interpreted literally, and if the time of fulfillment is accepted as in a future millennium, then the Aaronic priesthood which Jesus set aside is to be reestablished. Also, the animal sacrifices of the Mosaic period are to be restored. Dispensationalists accept this without batting an eye. Tan even says that this passage is the strongest passage in the Old Testament for this renewal, because it is connected with the Davidic covenant.[123] But such a reversal of what Jesus did is unthinkable. The old covenant has passed away. The new covenant is now in operation. It is apostasy to go back to the former things. Regardless of how conscientious the propagators of this teaching are, it is rank heresy.

## A Summary Statement

Jeremiah says nothing of a millennium, but certain passages of his book are interpreted as applying to it or to events immediately preceding it. The principal errors of interpretation are in relation to "the time of Jacob's

---

123 *Ibid.*, p. 294.

trouble" and the new covenant. The time of Jacob's trouble was fulfilled in A.D. 70. It is not a reference to some future persecution by the Antichrist. The new covenant was universally recognized as referring to the gospel age until recent times. This innovation is completely unacceptable. Jeremiah made no prophecies that reach beyond the gospel age.

CHAPTER 10

# THE ESCHATOLOGY OF EZEKIEL

Possibly Erich von Daniken's book *The Chariots of the Gods* has contributed more to a revival of interest in the book of Ezekiel than any other single factor. This book tells of many mysterious facts which he interprets as evidences of space ships, landing fields for space ships, and the utilization of a type of power beyond anything known today. (See also his later book *Gods From Outer Space*.) Among other things, he contends that the wheels of Ezekiel (chapters 1, 3, 10, 11) are nothing more nor less than a space ship which literally transported Ezekiel from one place to another. The evidences he mentions have received considerable TV coverage, and some former skeptics have come to the point of accepting his conclusions.

The other element that has revived interest in Ezekiel is the tremendous volume of printed matter and sermonic material by Premillennialists which teaches that Ezekiel gives definite information regarding a new temple in Jerusalem, the battle of Armageddon, and a regathered Israel and a rigidly enforced law of Moses. Now Ezekiel's wheels may have been a space ship, but it was not a human invention, nor was it powered by physical energy. It was of God—not of man. I must also reject the popular interpretation of Ezekiel 37-48, because it cannot be harmonized with the work of Christ and New Testament principles. Reasons for this will be given in the studies which follow.

### Ezekiel 11

Scofield inserts the following caption between verses 16-17: "Israel to be restored to the land and converted." Tan applies verses 16-21 to the Palestinian covenant.[124] It is admitted that verses 16-17 do speak of a return, but it is denied that this should be interpreted eschatologically. The reason for this is that verses 18-20 can be appropriately applied to the conversion experience and the reception of the Holy Spirit of the gospel age, and was consistently

---

124 Tan, *op. cit.*, footnote p. 191.

so applied until the rise of Dispensationalism. Verse 19, the key verse reads, "And I will give them one heart, and I will put a new spirit within you; and I will take the stony heart out of their flesh."

This is one of three different Old Testament references to God giving His people "one heart." This passage includes the idea of God injecting a "new spirit" within them. That both of these aspects were fulfilled through the reception of the Holy Spirit is proved by Acts 4:31-32. In verse 31 it is recorded that "they were all filled with the Holy Ghost" or Holy Spirit. This is the new Spirit God placed in believers. The next verse adds, "And the multitude of them that believed were of one heart and one soul." It is not necessary that one wait for a millennial mirage for this text's fulfillment. Praise God, this is accomplished now through the gospel!

It is true that the New Testament does not say that the stony heart is replaced by a heart of flesh. However, it does not say it will be accomplished at some future time, either, and besides this it has passages that are easily construed as the equivalent of Ezekiel's statement. "New creatures" (II Cor. 5:17), "should walk in newness of life" (Rom. 6:4), "serve in newness of spirit" (Rom. 7:6), and speak "with new tongues." Such expressions convey the same idea. The fathers of the early Church consistently applied this passage to the gospel age. Barnabas, Origen, Augustine, and Cassian all gave positive testimony to this view. Only one inconclusive statement was found which could be interpreted as referring to a future situation such as Dispensationalism now teaches. In fact the Church has almost unanimously interpreted this passage as fulfilled in the gospel age until the rise of this new doctrine.

### *Ezekiel 20:33-44*

Verse 34 indicates a return, and verse 37 refers to some covenant; but just which one is uncertain. Dispensationalists and sundry Premillennialists hold that no such gathering has occurred in the past, nor is it now going on, they say; hence they project this into the future as applicable to the millennium which they expect. I see no solid basis for denying this to be a prophecy of the gospel age. Only two early writers were found who discussed this matter, and both of them interpreted it as applying to the present gospel age. Aphrahat contended that the Jews held for such a regathering as is now part of Premillennialism, but that the Church held a different position. In concluding his remarks he says, "All this argument have I written to thee, because the Jews pride themselves, [saying] 'It has been covenanted to us, that we shall be gathered.' "[125] Thus his testimony places this doctrine where it properly should be placed as a revival of the Judaizing influences that plagued the early Church.

### Ezekiel 28:25-26

These verses do speak of a return, but the time of fulfillment depends on interpretation for Ezekiel fails to indicate when this will occur. Some have held that this was fulfilled in the Jewish returns of the past. Others have applied it to the gospel age. Still others apply it to a future millennium. I see no reason to reject the literal fulfillment as having been accomplished in the recorded returns of the Old Testament, although there may be overtones of the gospel age included in the intent of the passage.

It is interesting to note the fact that the writers of the early Church tended to ignore this passage. Certainly, they did not posit a future millennium from it. The only early writer that interpreted this passage was Irenaeus. Now Irenaeus did have some millennialistic concepts, but they are not based on this passage. He based his ideas mainly on the analogy of the six days of creation, and a seventh day of rest. Irenaeus applied this to the present resurrection from death in sin, and to the future general resurrection. After quoting these two verses he adds, "Now I have shown a short time ago that the Church is the seed of Abraham; and for this reason, that we may know that He who in the New Testament 'raises up from stones children unto Abraham,' is He who will gather, according to the Old Testament those who shall be saved from all nations."[126] This is a far cry from the Judaistic millennium that is being taught today. He contends that the Old Testament taught that the Church was the seed of Abraham.

### Ezekiel 34:11-31

Scofield has the following caption for this section, "Israel restored: the Davidic kingdom to be set up." What he expects the reader to infer is that this refers to the future millennium of Jewish ascendancy which he advocates. But this text refers to the gospel era. The shepherd God planned to send is none other than Jesus Christ (v. 23), and the covenant is none other than the new covenant that Christ established at His first coming. Jesus Himself said, "I am the good shepherd" (John 10:11). He did not say I will become the good shepherd during a millennium. His testimony was that He was even

---

125 Aphrahat, *Nicene and Post-Nicene Fathers,* second series, vol. XIII, p. 394.
126 Irenaeus, *op. cit.,* vol. I, pp. 563-564.

then the good shepherd. In like manner He indicated He was establishing the new covenant at that time. His words are, "This cup is the new testament in my blood" (Luke 22:20). The Greek has *diatheke* for testament, and it is more properly translated "covenant." We live under the new covenant. It is not something yet future.

The writers for the early Church are unanimous in interpreting this passage in this manner. Not a single one applies it to a millennium. Cyprian declares that the old temple and the old pastors were removed so that a new temple, the Church, could be established with new pastors.[127] An anonymous writer applies this to Christ and the Church. The parables of Christ after the lost sheep and the woman after the lost coin are utilized to explain just what he meant.[128] Augustine, Chrysostom, Gregory Nazianzen, and Gregory the Great complete the list of early writers who discussed this passage, and all of them applied it to the gospel age. Writers of today who project this into the future do so without sufficient justification from any source.

### Ezekiel 36:8, 24-38

This passage is very similar to that from chapter 11 which was discussed in the earlier part of this chapter. The removal of the stony heart and the gift of a new heart and a new spirit are prominent in both. The arguments for applying this to the gospel age need not to be repeated. We simply add a list of the early Church writers who discussed this passage. These were Barnabas, Cyprian, Irenaeus, Augustine, Gregory of Nyssa, Jerome, and Cyril of Jerusalem. Among the early Church fathers there is not a dissenting voice raised against applying this to the gospel age and the covenant of peace to the present covenant under which the Church functions.

### Ezekiel 37

This chapter is one of the more controversial portions of the Old Testament. It is definitely figurative in that it is a truth clothed in terms of a parable or allegory. For this reason no one should be dogmatic in his interpretation. Verses 1-10 tell of a vision given to Ezekiel. He saw a valley of dry bones—skeletons of human beings which were no longer linked together at the joints. However, after he prophesied unto them, the bones drew together

---

127 Cyprian, *op. cit.*, p. 511; see also p. 338.
128 Unknown author, *Ante-Nicene Fathers*, vol. V. p. 662.

into proper relations with one another. Later, flesh and sinews were given, and finally they breathed and stood erect as an army. The fact that it was a mighty force or army is important to properly understand this figure. As an army it must be interpreted as a symbol. But is it a symbol of literal Israel or spiritual Israel, the Church? I prefer the latter.

Verses 11-14 tell us that this is "the whole house of Israel" and that God will open their graves and bring them forth into their own land. This section includes the statement that God would put His spirit in them as was stated in 11:19 and 36:27. This is presumptive evidence that the subject considered is the same in all three places. Now, it was shown that chapters 11 and 36 referred to the gospel age. Hence, we are inclined to interpret this chapter in the same fashion. The giving of the Holy Spirit in the gospel dispensation may well be the major thrust of the passage. This requires that "the whole house of Israel" be interpreted as a symbol of the Church, but the validity for doing this has been established in chapters which precede this one.

Much is made of the joining of the stick of Judah with that of Israel (vv. 16-19), but as explained in a similar statement in Jeremiah 3:18, Israel, Joseph, and Ephraim refer to the Gentiles with whom the northern kingdom had already become identified. Thus the union of the two refers to the union of Jews and Gentiles. Then verse 22 informs us that "neither shall they be divided into two kingdoms any more at all." This means that those who advocate a Jewish millennium with a real distinction between the Jews and the Gentiles are misreading prophecy.

David is declared to be the king or prince who will rule over the united kingdom. Now if I be accused of spiritualizing, my defense is that those who judge me are guilty of the same thing. Although some Premillennialists hold that David will be resurrected to assist Christ in His rule, all commentators recognize that David is a type of Christ. Now if David is a type of Christ, it cannot be considered illogical to make the nations of Israel and Judah types of the fusion of Jews and Gentiles through which the Church was produced. And the covenant of peace which God was to make with them (v. 26) is readily recognized as the new covenant which Christ established at His first advent rather than a supposed future covenant such as many Premillennialists posit.

The writers of the early Church uniformly interpreted this chapter eschatologically but not premillennially. The statements that God would "open your graves," and cause them "to come up out of your graves," and "when

I have opened your graves...and brought you up out of your graves" (vv. 12-13) were consistently interpreted as referring to the future resurrection of the body. Justin, Irenaeus, Tertullian, Methodius, Cyprian, Augustine, Rufinus, Gregory of Nyssa, Cyril of Jerusalem, John of Damascus, Ambrose and others interpreted these verses in this manner. In all the passages investigated no evidence was found to indicate that these views were in any way related to a millennial reign. Because the doctrine of a future resurrection was under constant attack, it was quite natural for the writers of that day to interpret this chapter as they did. Although it is generally interpret as a parable in our day, the idea of a resurrection is involved.

## Ezekiel 38-39

These chapters are also very controversial. Premillennialists often equate this with the battle of Armageddon of the Revelation. The difficulty with this approach is that according to Ezekiel's prophecy, Gog and Magog are destroyed prior to that portion of Ezekiel that is interpreted as comprehending the millennium whereas the Revelation places the destruction of Gog and Magog as being after the millennium (Rev. 20:8-9). Scofield, with his usual versatility as a juggler of the Scriptures, stretches it out to include battles before and after the millennium. However, it should be kept in mind that Ezekiel says nothing about a millennium, hence connecting the battles of these chapters is a matter of interpretation, not of exegesis.

Scofield in his note on Ezekiel 38:2 mentioned above contends that Gog is the prince and Magog is the land with the primary reference being to Russia. The Hebrew *Rosh* which does not appear in the AV is taken to refer to Russia, and *Mesheck* and *Tubal* to Moscow and Tobolsk, modern cities of Russia. But this is pure conjecture. Dr. Bert H. Hall observes that *Rosh* "is never used in the Old Testament for a country or people."[129] He quotes Hengstenberg in support of this statement in which the Byzantine and Arabic word which came to be applied to a people is, historically, some 1,000 years later than Ezekiel's time. Similarity of spelling constitutes no valid basis for identification. If it did, we would do better to identify Mesheck with the Babylonian god, Meshack, for whom Mishael was renamed (Dan. 1:7), than with Moscow. The difference in spelling is certainly less. But this kind of evidence is so tenuous that it is absolutely worthless.

---

129  Bert H. Hall, *The Wesleyan Bible Commentary*, vol. III, p. 470.

## The Eschatology of Ezekiel 157

Several reasons may be found for rejecting chapters 38-39 as eschatological. The phrase "latter years" is simply too vague to prove that it means the time of the consummation. As previously shown, terms such as this are used of the gospel dispensation. The hodgepodge assortment of texts from such books as Daniel and the Revelation which are utilized in support of a certain eschatological scheme carry little or no weight, logically. Each of these texts depends on specific interpretations which many commentators reject. Taken alone, these two chapters are extremely difficult to place in the future.

It is true that a restoration is promised (Ezek. 39:25-29), but it is impossible to prove that this refers to a millennium. Ezekiel fails to say it does. In fact the verses which precede these seem to say that all of this that happens to Israel is for the information of the heathen (39:23) as well as for that of Israel (39:22). But Babylon is much more wicked than Israel, hence she too must suffer for her wickedness. This makes Gog and Magog refer to Babylon and her rulers, and the fulfillment is long since past. Part of chapter 39 is figurative. Even extreme literalists are forced to admit this.[130] Let us examine some statements that show figurative meanings are intended.

A great shaking is to occur in Israel (38:19-20). Even fish are to shake, and "the mountains shall be thrown down." Now this could be accepted as literal if it referred to the consummation or destruction of the earth at the end of time, but those who are extreme literalists cannot so interpret it, for their contention is that chapters 38-39 are prior to the millennium which is to take place on this earth according to their teaching. This expression appears to be apocalyptic and figurative in nature. It is not taken to refer to the end of time. Instead it is taken to refer to God's judgment on whatever nations are included in the expression "Gog and Magog." Verses 4-6 seem to indicate that Persia, which was the world power succeeding Babylon, was the main power considered, since it comes first in the listing of nations in verse 5.

In chapter 39 even greater evidence of apocalyptic or figurative language is found. Verse 3 has the battle being fought with bows and arrows. Walvoord, Tan, and others defend the literal interpretation of this, but their defense is too weak to be taken seriously. It is a strain on the imagination to conceive of a future war being fought with bows and arrows. This verse must refer to

---

130 Tan, *op. cit.*, p. 138.

an event of the past or it must be accepted as figurative. Taken literally or figuratively, there is no solid basis for interpreting it eschatologically.

Verses 9-10 are even more difficult to accept as literal. In these verses the abandoned weapons of war are made of wood. Such tremendous quantities of these wooden weapons remain that there was no need for the inhabitants to cut firewood for a period of seven years. In this day of metals, alloys, plastics, synthetics, and noncombustible compositions, it is hardly conceivable that at some future time war will be waged with weapons that are almost exclusively wood. Nor is it easy to conjure up a situation in which wood burning becomes the principal source of energy. Even more difficult is the envisioning of a seven years wood supply for such an economy from abandoned war implements.

Another difficulty with a literal interpretation is verses 12-14. These verses say that it will take a period of seven months to bury the dead from this war fought with wooden machines of war and with bows and arrows. This could hardly be literal without bringing on an epidemic of diseases that would annihilate the population. Yet, this chapter says nothing about such an epidemic. Instead of interpreting this literally and eschatologically, it should be remembered that it was stated in the symbolism of numbers that seven was a symbol of perfection or completeness. Therefore, it is best to hold that the seven years of burning (v. 9), and the seven months of burying (v. 12), are symbols rather than literal periods of seven months or years.

The difficulty of interpreting this passage should be apparent to every one. This may be the reason Ambrose is the only early writer to venture an interpretation. He applied Gog to the Goths, and predicted a victory for Gratian in his battles with them.[131] This interpretation is hardly acceptable today, but it has just as much merit as that which applies it to nations of today. There simply is no way of determining the time element of this prophecy, and without the time, any effort to identify the nations is an exercise in futility.

Besides this there is the question of whether or not it is to be taken literally or figuratively. I have attempted to refute the more common futuristic-literalistic interpretation. If it is largely literalistic, then it has been fulfilled in the past. It could have reference to the attack of Nebuchadnezzar against Jerusalem which was then in progress according to some authorities. This

---

131 Ambrose, *Nicene and Post-Nicene Fathers*, second series, vol. X, p. 241.

was to be followed by a judgment against the attacking nations. Verse 17 of chapter 38 seems to imply this. However, there are problems with this interpretation which are difficult to resolve. Possibly the best solution is to apply it to no single or specific event or time but that it is a figurative depiction of the battle between good and evil or God and the devil. Thus it could have reference to what happened in 586 B.C. or 168 B.C. It might also have reference to A.D. 70 or to the battle between the Church and evil. However, if it has eschatological implications, it is impossible to know just how this prophecy fits into the picture.

### Ezekiel 40-48

These chapters are also the subject of controversy. Two basic interpretations are given. The Judaistic-Literalistic-Futuristic school holds that Ezekiel is prophesying of a future era in which the Jews will build another great temple. It calls for a restoration of the Levitical priesthood, a return to the Jews keeping the Mosaic law including Saturday observance and animal sacrifices. It envisions Christ ruling from a material throne in Jerusalem for one thousand years. According to this teaching, the Jews will be restored to their land and also to their special place in God's favor. The length of this reign is imported from the Revelation, and other anticipated changes are based on interpretations of other passages.

The other school holds that this prophecy is symbolic and idealistic, rather than literal. The temple refers to the Church. The Israel of these chapters is not based on genetic descent but on faith. The reestablishment of the Mosaic law and the Aaronic priesthood, the restoration of the Sabbath and animal sacrifices, as well as the raising again of the middle wall of partition constitute a repudiation of the work of Christ. Such an interpretation as given above is considered antichristian because it restores things Jesus did away with by His atoning sacrifice. Hence, these chapters must be interpreted as symbolic or they constitute a return to things which make for apostasy. As a defender of the inspired word, I must accept the symbolic method.

Space will not permit a verse by verse analysis of these chapters. Only the broad outlines can be considered. The time the prophecy was given was "the five and twentieth year of our captivity" (40:1). This was possibly ten or twelve years later than the giving of chapters 38 and 39. However, the time of its fulfillment is not stated. Thus one must depend on secondary considerations for the establishment of the period of fulfillment. Those who claim a future fulfillment do so on the basis of no past literal fulfillment. However, these must reject a spiritualized fulfillment for this argument to have much weight; and it has previously been shown that extreme literalism is dangerous.

The man who conveys this prophecy to Ezekiel is considered a theophany or preincarnate appearance of Christ, for in 44:2 and 5 He is called Jehovah. (When "Lord" is printed with upper case or capital letters throughout, the Hebrew is *Yahweh* or Jehovah.) The measuring rod he used was six cubits in length (40:5) which is approximately 11 feet. Some of the measurements are given in terms of the measuring rod or reed of approximately 11 feet according to the Talmudic standard, whereas other measurements are given in cubits or approximately 22 inches. (The Roman equivalents are somewhat shorter, but the Talmudic standard is no doubt the one Ezekiel used.) There is some disagreement over certain texts as to whether cubits or reeds are intended, but in every instance the reed appears to be the measurement intended unless cubits are specifically stated in the Hebrew text.

The problem of distance is acute in two areas. In 42:16-20 the temple area is said to be 500 units square. If these units are cubits, the size is reasonable; but if they are reeds, the temple area would be about one mile square or approximately the size of the city of Jerusalem in the days of Josephus.[132] The older commentaries favored the reed or longer measurement, whereas more recent writers have tended to use the shorter cubit as the unit. This change does not appear to be justified. Ezekiel seems to make the temple complex of buildings about one mile square.

Another problem is the location of the temple. A study of chapters 45 and 48 seem to place the new temple well above the present city of Jerusalem. It is to be in the center of a section which is 25,000 reeds square or slightly more than 47 miles on each side. The totality of this sacred area appears to be above or north of the city of Jerusalem both ancient and modern. However, it is hardly conceivable that a new temple would be built on any site other than the ancient site. The loss such a change would produce would be enormous. The Jewish expectations would almost demand that it be on the old temple site. But if placed there, the Dome of the Rock Mosque would

---

[132] Flavius Josephus, *Wars of the Jews*, bk. V, chap. IV, p. 781, and *Against Apion*, bk. I, p. 871.

have to be removed which is most unlikely, and complex architectural problems for such a large structure would make the project most difficult. Literalists must face these problems and give reasonable explanations.

The most acute problem, however, is whether or not the sacred area of some 47 statute miles each way can be placed between the Mediterranean Sea and the Jordan River which constitute the western and eastern boundaries of the Israel Ezekiel depicts. The substitution of the shorter cubit in place of the longer reed is considered an effort to resolve this problem. However, I find the argument for the shorter unit of measurement to be shallow and based on inadequate textual analysis. Keil gives the best exegesis of these passages that I have found, and he presents arguments for reeds over cubits which appear to be irrefutable.[133] And since I am bound by the word, I must accept the larger dimensions, even though the land area is inadequate. The simplest method of resolving the problem is to hold that Ezekiel's description was not intended to be taken literally, and that the impossible dimensions is proof of the idealistic nature of the chapters involved.

In order that the reader may get the proper perspective of this matter, an effort will be made to describe distances involved. The northern extremity of the square area with sides of 47 miles would run east and west from about the ancient city of Dor or the lower end of the Mt. Carmel range. However, the distance from the Mediterranean Sea to the Jordan is only about 40 miles at this point. This would require several miles of territory on the east side of the Jordan to complete the distance Ezekiel's figures demand. But the Jordan is given as the eastern limits of Israel's territory in Ezekiel's prophecy, hence we have no basis for extending the line beyond the Jordan.

Then in addition to the square itself, areas east of the square and also west of the square are given for the prince or ruler. On the west a triangular portion would be formed by a line running due south from Dor, because the coast line gradually veers to the west. But on the east, any portion for the prince would extend still further beyond the Jordan which is the eastern boundary established by Ezekiel. Thus the division of land which Ezekiel describes is larger than the land area it is supposed to fit into. This is a very forceful argument for the figurative or idealistic interpretation. Surely Ezekiel is giving a clue that this should not be taken literally.

---

133   Carl Friedrich Keil, *Keil and Delitzsch Bible Commentary: Ezekiel,* vol. II. pp. 268ff. and 370ff.

However, literalists have their answer. They claim that Palestine will be enlarged so that the conflict will be resolved. Tan contends this is necessary because Jerusalem will be the center of worship for the world,[134] as well as because it is necessary in order that Ezekiel's dimensions may become reality. But this ignores all the rules of hermeneutics. This is not exegesis, and it hardly deserves being called interpretation. Ezekiel says nothing of an expanded Palestine. No text from either Testament even hints at an enlarged Palestine. Literalists are guilty of positing a millennium of which the Old Testament says not one word, then compounding the error by positing conditions in that millennium about which not a single word is given. This is utter chaos as far as interpreting God's word is concerned.

The portion on the east and the portion on the west of the central square which are reserved for the "prince" are of special concern for another reason. Just who is this prince? Just why are two portions reserved for him? Now interpreters of all persuasions accept the idea that the Old Testament prophecies about David and the throne of David do find, or will find, their fulfillment in Christ. However, literalists have a tough time locating Christ in this prophecy by Ezekiel. Jesus would not need these portions of land. Besides, 45:8 implies that this is reserved for Him so He will not oppress the people, having sufficient for Himself, thus eliminating any need for oppression. But Jesus is a spiritual being and will have no such physical needs as mortal men have.

Even David is rejected as the "prince" of chapters 45-48 by literalists. This prince is considered mortal, and David will also be a resurrected person, according to the Dispensational approach. Christ is scheduled to rule with an iron hand, they say. No insubordination will be permitted, they say. Then what need is there for a special area for the prince, whoever he is, in order to keep him from oppressing the people.

That this "prince" is indeed "The Prince of Peace" should be evident from 45:17. In this verse several offerings the Prince is to make are "to make reconciliation for the house of Israel." The Hebrew for "reconciliation" is *kaphar* which is repeatedly translated "atonement" in the Old Testament. By spiritualizing this prophecy we have Ezekiel foretelling of the coming sacrifice of Christ on Calvary which constituted our atonement, but a literal interpretation can be maintained only by injecting explanations that have no legitimate place in interpretation much less in exegesis.

---

134 Tan, *op. cit.*, p. 321.

Before leaving the land area aspect of this prophecy and its various ramifications, permit me to drive home once again the fact that if this is a literal picture of the millennial age, then it does not fulfill or meet the requirements necessary for this to be a literal fulfillment of the land area set forth in the Abrahamic covenant. In chapter 6 we considered Walvoord's claim that Israel must one day literally occupy and govern the entire land area from Egypt to the Euphrates. He contended it had not been fulfilled in the past, hence must be fulfilled in the future, which, as far as he was concerned, would be in the millennium.

But if this is the picture of the land area occupied by the Jews during the millennium, it fails to reach the Euphrates by a much greater distance than even the original land settlement did. Moses settled two and one-half tribes on the east side of the Jordan. But Ezekiel's division has all tribes west of the Jordan. The full length of the Jordan forms the eastern boundary in these chapters of Ezekiel. Will the land expansion Tan theorizes will take place include moving the Jordan River eastward to or beyond the Euphrates? To most people this is inconceivable. Yet, only by positing such a miracle as this can it be maintained that Ezekiel tells of the fulfillment of the Abrahamic covenant to the literal descendants of Abraham.

It should be kept in mind that Ezekiel says nothing about a millennium, a rapture of the Church, a return of Christ and the Church, nor of resurrected beings living with mortal beings. Ezekiel does not even mention Christ ruling in the new temple or from the restored throne of David. All of these are superimposed upon Ezekiel's prophecy by Premillennialists. On the other hand, the fact that all tribes are placed west of the Jordan or in the land of Canaan proper, and that each tribe receives a portion of equal width regardless of its size, indicates that these chapters are idealistic rather than literal.

Another miracle must be posited by literalists in this connection. I refer to the fact that Jewish genealogical records were destroyed in A.D. 70. It is impossible to prove tribal descent, humanly speaking. If Ezekiel is taken literally, then God must reveal each one's lineage to some one. But Ezekiel says nothing about such a miracle or even the need of such a miracle.

And if literalists are indeed taking Ezekiel seriously, they should pay very close attention to 47:22-23. These verses speak of "strangers" or non-Jews which "sojourn among you, which shall beget children among you: and they shall be unto you as born in the country among the children of Israel; they shall have inheritance with you among the tribes of Israel…in what tribe the stranger sojourneth, there shall ye give him his inheritance." Failure to advocate a migration of Christians to Palestine seems to indicate this is not taken seriously by the literalists, or else it has been overlooked. What these verses really signify is the present union of Jews and Gentiles in the Church through Christ who broke down the middle wall of partition. It is presently being fulfilled rather than having reference to a future millennium about which Ezekiel says not one word.

Another problem faces the literalists in connection with the flow of waters described in the first 12 verses of chapter 47. This has been consistently interpreted of the gospel age until recent years. Not a single writer of the early Church interpreted it eschatologically. The present emphasis grows out of an extreme literalism—not from a rootage in the past. Many advocates of the premillennial concept of today, even some who believe in a Jewish literal restoration, are unable to accept the Dispensational claim that this is to be fulfilled literally.

The first problem that is considered involves the way water flows. Water tends to seek a lower level and flows downward through the pull of gravity. Now the waters in this chapter are said to flow eastward toward the Jordan and the Dead Sea, but to do so they must flow upward. Admittedly, God could interpose His spiritual power into the situation and cause the water to flow other than in accordance with the laws of nature, but Ezekiel gives no indication that a miracle of this nature is involved.

The second problem is the rapid increase in the quantity of water in the stream without any tributaries flowing into it. At least none is mentioned. This requires the injection of a second miracle about which Ezekiel says nothing. Then, how does this stream sweeten the waters of the Dead Sea? By a third miracle? But this is not exegesis. This is adding to the word of God through assumptions that have no basis in Scripture. It is an effort to bend the Scripture to a preconceived pattern. The foundation for this explanation is in the mind—not the Bible. I know it is said that miracles will be common place in the millennium, but I have yet to find a writing which supports such a statement with a good solid text of Scripture.

Now let us consider how the waters would be sweetened if no miracle is involved. This would require that this new stream of water be great enough to raise the level of the water in the Jordan valley hundreds of feet until it began to empty into the ocean. This would probably be over the southern end of the rift into the Gulf of Aqaba, or into the Mediterranean Sea via the Kishon River. This would flood the entire Jordan valley. The Dead Sea and the Sea (lake) of Galilee would be joined together to form an immense inland lake. The Jordan River would no longer exist. Instead, there would be a large lake for the length of the Jordan valley and extending several miles on either side of the Jordan, as well as far below or south of the Dead Sea and north of Capernaum. The only river would be a new stream into the Sea—a stream that does not even exist at this time if it flowed into the Gulf of Aqaba.

But bear in mind that Ezekiel specifically makes the Jordan the eastern boundary of the Israel he depicts in these chapters. But if the Jordan became a lake instead of a river, the appropriateness of Ezekiel's description would be called into question. And it would make the problem of the land area even more acute. The distances Ezekiel gives are greater than the present land area, and if several additional miles are taken off of the present area by the Jordan becoming a lake, the discrepancy would become even greater. These considerations make the case against a literal and eschatological interpretation of these chapters conclusive. Therefore, we hold that these waters represent the ever widening movement of God's love and grace to all men, particularly from Calvary onward. It refers to the gospel age and the Church age—not to a future millennium.

The problems of these chapters discussed thus far pale in insignificance compared to the ones which are said to teach the restoration of Mosaic law, animal sacrifices, and the Old Testament priesthood. Had enemies of Christ concocted this absurd travesty, I could at least understand the motivation which prompted it. In accord with Agur's admission that some things were beyond this ken (Prov. 30:18-19), I must admit that the thinking of the men who teach this doctrine is utterly and completely incomprehensible to me.

Chapters 40-48 contain so many references to things of the law no effort shall be made to quote them. Only totals will be given. However, literalists who hold that these chapters refer to the millennium are forced to interpret them as a restoration of things Christ nullified through His atoning sacrifice. The priesthood of the Old Testament based on descent from Levi and Aaron is mentioned 21 times in these chapters. They offer the various Old Testament sacrifices of animals as burnt offerings and sin offerings. They are given laws to follow very much like the Old Testament requirements set forth by Moses.

But Christ abolished the Levitical priesthood. The Hebrew epistle clearly indicates that if the results God desired had been possible by the Levitical priesthood, then Christ who was not a descendant of Aaron would not have needed to come (Heb. 7:11). In the verses which follow the inspired writer declares that a change in the priesthood has been accomplished so that we now have an eternal being as our high priest. The Dispensationalists give us no answer regarding this eternal priesthood of Christ. The Aaronic priesthood could be set aside for it was not sealed with an oath, but God has sworn that Jesus' priesthood is eternal. This reestablishment of the Old Testament priesthood sacrifices Christ's priesthood in an effort to establish Him as an earthly sovereign. Praise God for His oath. No earthly priesthood will ever be substituted for His priesthood.

Sabbath keeping is mentioned six different times in these chapters. Of course, Jews have continued to honor the seventh day, but Christians accept the first day. That a Christ rejecting group (Jews) would worship on Saturday is recognized as part of their refusal to accept Jesus of Nazareth as the Messiah, but for Jews who do accept Him as the Messiah to worship on Saturday is without scriptural support. Will the distance one can travel on Saturday, and the restrictions on cooking be restored? No, for when Christ established a better covenant, He was not about to go back to the old one.

Worshipers must be circumcised in the flesh as well as the heart, according to Ezekiel 44:7, and 9. Now circumcision of the flesh was a type of circumcision of the heart. The gospel era made possible the true circumcision of the heart. Thus the antitype has replaced the Old Testament type. Shall the type be restored after its fulfillment has become a fact? Never, thank God. Paul plainly declares that one becomes a Jew through circumcision of the heart, and that of the flesh no longer has any significance. And it never will. In fact to go back to fleshly circumcision is to reject Christ. Paul indicated that to be circumcised would nullify their blessings in Christ (Gal. 5:2).

According to Judaistic-Premillennialism, not only will the Aaronic priesthood be restored along with the Levites who are mentioned eight times in these chapters; but the animal sacrifices of the Mosaic law will also again be offered. It is true that it is claimed these will be memorial sacrifices, rather than as a substitute for the blood of Jesus: but Ezekiel says nothing about them being memorial. This is an importation into the account by expositors. Ezekiel says they are for sin. Let us consider some of 14 different places where Ezekiel mentions these sacrifices. In several other texts he mentions burnt offerings. Most of the passages that speak of sin offerings also tell of trespass offerings.

Two passages of Ezekiel's prophecy indicate that these sacrifices had the same import as those of the Pentateuch. After listing the various kinds of offerings which included burnt offerings, peace offerings, and sin offerings, the promise is given, "and I will accept you, saith the Lord" (Ezek. 43:27). Now this word "accept" is a translation of the Hebrew *ratsah*. This Hebrew word includes in its meaning, to pay off or make compensation for and to conciliate as well as the meaning of acceptance or being satisfied. Thus these are not purely memorial sacrifices. They make the person acceptable to God.

The second passage is even more pointed. The "prince" is instructed to "prepare the sin offering, and the meat offering, and the burnt offering, and the peace offerings, to make reconciliation for the house of Israel" (Ezek. 45:17). A similar statement is made in verse 15 of this same chapter. Now the Hebrew word translated "reconciliation" in verses 15 and 17 is the word *kaphar*. The more common translation of this word is "atonement." In fact it is so translated no less than 70 times in the KJV. Atonement has an entirely different meaning than memorial. Dispensationalists contend that these sacrifices are to be memorial in nature, but Ezekiel says they are for purposes of atonement or reconciliation. This is but another instance where literalists are forced to abandon their literalism and impose a nonliteral interpretation upon their literalistic superstructure.

A review of the writings of the early Church fathers on Ezekiel indicates the following facts: 1. Not a single writer was found who used Ezekiel as a basis for teaching a future millennium. 2. The idea of a future restoration of Jews to Palestine was repeatedly and consistently opposed by the early writers. 3. The new covenant of Ezekiel was consistently applied to the Church. Not once was it applied to a millennial reign. 4. The teaching of a future physical battle of Armageddon is completely absent as far as their interpretation of Ezekiel is concerned. The only eschatological elements which the early writers found in Ezekiel were a resurrection of the dead (ch. 37) and a reference to heaven from the latter chapters. Thus all of them spiritualized the latter chapters as referring to either heaven or the Church. Not one was found who literalized these chapters.

Biederwolf, a millennialist, recognizes that not only the early Church fathers, but the prevailing view of the Church as a whole has been that Ezekiel's prophecy or visions should be interpreted symbolically and spiritually rather than literally.[135] He quotes Fausset whom he classifies as "a literalist of the pre-millennial school" as writing, "There are things in the vision so improbable physically as to preclude a *purely* literal interpretation."[136] Thus the present use of Ezekiel to support a Judaistic millennium is a Johnny-come-lately, theologically speaking.

---

135  Wm. E. Biederwolf, *The Second Coming Bible*, p. 199.
136  *Ibid.*

CHAPTER 11

# THE ESCHATOLOGY OF DANIEL

The book of Daniel contains the most fully developed apocalyptic material found in the Old Testament. Only the Revelation exceeds it in this respect even in the New Testament. And since apocalyptic literature is more subject to a variety of interpretations than is true of ordinary prophecy, Daniel inevitably became a controversial book prior to New Testament times, and even more so during the gospel era. No solution to the problems involved can hope to please every one, but it is hoped that what is said in this chapter will clarify some of the issues. Of Daniel's 12 chapters, only half of them will require consideration. These are 2, 7, 8, 9, 11, and 12. Although there is considerable overlapping, they shall be examined in the order given above.

## Daniel 2

In this chapter the vision comes to Nebuchadnezzar, and Daniel interprets it. In the other chapters Daniel receives the vision, and whatever interpretation is given is by an angelic being. Nebuchadnezzar dreamed of a great image composed of a head of gold, the breast and arms of silver, the belly and thighs of brass, and the legs were of iron, and his feet were part of iron and part of clay. It should be noted in passing that verses 32-35 say nothing of toes. It is the feet that are part of iron and part of clay, and the stone which was cut out without hands smote the image on the feet and not the toes.

The interpretation Daniel gave included the following points:

1. The vision included things which "shall be in the latter days" (v. 28).

2. The image represents four kingdoms of which Nebuchadnezzar or the Babylonian kingdom was first as symbolized by the head of gold (vv. 37-38).

3. The fourth kingdom, the Roman, was symbolized by the lower extremities of iron and clay. The iron indicates strength; the clay, weakness; the two together, a lack of cohesiveness.

4. Prior to the dissolution of the fourth kingdom ("in the days of these kings") the God of heaven was to establish an eternal kingdom which was to "break in pieces" the other kingdoms (v. 44).

5. The latter would be accomplished through a stone cut out without hands (v. 34) out of the mountain (v. 45) smiting the image on its feet—not its toes (v. 34). The stone was to become a mountain (v. 45).

First, what is meant by the "latter days" (v. 28)? The literal rendering of the Hebrew is "end of days." I know of no one who contends that this means the time when time (days) ceases to exist and eternity sets in. It is recognized that this refers to the time the kingdom will be established, and is interpreted accordingly. Those who hold that the kingdom was established at Christ's first coming interpret this as referring to the gospel age. Those who hold that the kingdom will be established at Christ's second coming interpret this as yet future. These give this chapter an eschatological interpretation making the latter days refer to the beginning of the millennium which they envision. Neither can be absolutely established by exegesis apart from interpretation, but the weight of evidence is against the eschatological interpretation.

The four kingdoms are generally recognized in conservative circles as the Babylonian, the Medo-Persian, the Grecian, and the Roman. Chapter 8 which has certain parallels with chapter 2 names the two middle kingdoms. In this chapter the Babylonian is placed first, and the description of the fourth is so plainly applicable to none other empire than the Roman that no refutation of the other position is considered necessary. History will testify to the fact that these four are the only empires extensive enough to meet the demands of the dream and its interpretation.

Our third item had to do with the iron and clay mixture of the image. Historians and churchmen alike recognized that this was applicable to the Roman empire during its two last centuries of existence. The Roman empire fell in A.D. 476, but its weaknesses were easily discernible many years prior to its demise. The description given in chapter 2 is fitting and appropriate.

The fourth statement listed above was to the effect that during the viable existence of these four kingdoms or empires, the everlasting kingdom would be established. If the four kingdoms mentioned in chapter 2 are accepted as the Babylonian, Medo-Persian, Grecian, and Roman, and most Premillennialists and Dispensationalists are in agreement with me at that point, then this prophecy must have its fulfillment prior to A.D. 476, at least as far as exegesis is concerned. The reason for this is that this prophecy mentions these four and these alone. It says nothing of the ten minor kingdoms, nor of a restoration of the Roman empire in any form. These cannot be established by exegesis of chapter 2. These teachings depend upon eisegesis and interpretation. The time limits of this chapter are from its utterance by Daniel (c. 603 B.C.), to the fall of Rome in A.D. 476.

The way Dispensationalists handle this passage is revealing of their disregard for hermeneutical principles. A. C. Gaebelein, one of the consulting editors of the *Scofield Reference Bible* actually inserts his interpretation in a quotation he gives of Daniel 2:44-45. The first lines of verse 44 read (KJV), "And in the days of these kings shall the God of heaven set up a kingdom, which shall never be destroyed." Now, the only kings or kingdoms which can serve as an antecedent to the expression "these kings" are the four kingdoms which we have mentioned. No other kings are mentioned in this prophecy. Dr. Gaebelein quotes the above with his parenthetical insertion making it read as follows: "In the days of these kings (the ten toes), shall the God of heaven set up a kingdom, which shall never be destroyed."[137]

Gaebelein has a right to interpret the word as he sees it, provided he refrains from making insertions such as the above into God's word. This shows a disrespect for God's word that is appalling. It is an effort to influence the reader that smacks of trickery and deceit. Daniel says nothing about the ten toes, if there were ten, for the number is not given by Daniel, except that the stone smote the image on the feet (v. 34) which would include the toes (vv. 41-42) and ground the whole image to powder. Not once does Daniel say the ten toes represent the ten minor kingdoms. Gaebelein is the one who says it.

Gaebelein makes other additions to Daniel's words. He contends that the two legs represent Rome east and Rome west. Daniel does not say this, and one has no right to add to what Daniel has given us. Had he said that he understood the two legs to have this significance, I would not object, but he says it as if it was a settled fact. In his effort to establish the futurity of the ten toes, he adds, "But when our Lord came the first time the Roman empire was a unit. The division into the East and the West Roman empire, seen in the two legs of the image, had not yet taken place."[138]

---

137  Arno C. Gaebelein, *The Prophet Daniel*, p. 32.
138  Ibid., p. 35.

This shows how improper it is to import ideas into one prophecy that are obtained from another prophecy or from one's imagination. According to Gaebelein's importations, this prophecy would have the Grecian kingdom divide into two divisions instead of the four which are clearly set forth in chapter 8. The Grecian kingdom was the portion of the image composed of brass. The brass portion included the belly and the thighs (v. 32). Now the thighs are defined as that part of the legs from the trunk or pelvis to the knees. Hence, if the two legs of the iron part mean division into east and west, Greece must have a similar division. But when Greece split up, she split into four divisions (Dan. 8:8 and 22). Does Daniel contradict himself? Not so. It is Gaebelein's importations that cause confusion.

It is admitted that ten minor kingdoms are part of the prophecy of chapter 7, but that should not be imported into the prophecy of chapter 2. As we have shown already, the latest possible date of fulfillment of the prophecy of chapter 2, at least insofar as the establishment of the kingdom is concerned, is A.D. 476. And there is no event other than the first advent of Christ which fits in with the time limits of this prophecy. Efforts to inject eschatological import into this chapter must be rejected. If this prophecy is read and understood as we would read and understand ordinary communications, no eschatological import would be found.

Another reason for rejecting the idea of the toes symbolizing the ten minor kingdoms is that it makes the image disproportionate in its dimensions or disconnected. If the toes are taken to mean the divisions that developed after Rome fell in A.D. 476, then the toes are longer than the entire image. From the prophecy to the fall of Rome we have roughly 1,075 years, whereas from the development of minor kingdoms until the latter part of the twentieth century, we have about 1,400 years. This makes the toes too long for the body to be one that is even reasonably well proportioned. It should also be remembered that the ten divisions which did grow out of the dissolved Roman empire are all from Rome west.

I have before me a drawing of this image that has been used by different authors. It depicts the legs as Rome east and Rome west. The ten toes are then designated by such names as Heruli, Lombards, Suevi, and two branches of Goths. All of this seems quite reasonable for such divisions did exist in Europe after A.D. 476. But the illogicalness of it all is evident when the designations of the five toes on Rome east are considered. Pray tell me how the Anglo-Saxons could by any stretch of the imagination be thought of as growing out of Rome east. Almost as impossible are the Burgundians, Franks, and Huns. It is impossible to connect these kingdoms with Rome east, historically, yet they are attached to the leg of the image entitled Rome east.

On the other hand if we consider the ten minor kingdoms as yet future, the problem is how they could have any connection with the image which has not existed since A.D. 476. When Rome fell, the image ceased to be. It vanished. The grinding to bits was completed. Should the common market or any other confederacy develop into a ten nation alliance, it would have no connection with the image which hasn't existed for about 1,500 years. Such a restoration would not be an image at all. It could not even be the toes, for the toes were also destroyed when the image was destroyed in A.D. 476. There is no logical or hermeneutical basis for a revived Roman empire composed of ten separate countries. First of all, it would not be an empire. Ten separate nations could form an *entente*, but not a true empire. Secondly, Daniel says nothing about a revival. The notion is foreign to the text.

We have yet to identify the stone, the mountain out of which it was cut, the demolishing of the image, and the mountain into which the stone grew. Many commentators refer the stone to Christ, and the cutting out without hands to the virgin birth. I do not reject this outright, but there are some illogical aspects to this explanation which militate against it. It is true that Christ is the one who establishes the kingdom, but the stone is identified with the kingdom rather than with its founder. For this reason I prefer to think of the stone and the mountain into which it grew as that kingdom which is so closely identified with the Church.

If this be accepted, then the cutting of the stone without hands refers to the divine creativity which produced the Church. The Church is not a human institution which was started and is perpetuated by mere human effort. It is a spiritual institution, and it is maintained by spiritual power and principles. It is entered into by the new birth. It is the body of Christ. Part of its constituency is in heaven or paradise, and part is living here upon earth. It is larger than any denomination, but only the saved of any denomination are in it.

In the earlier study of hermeneutics it was suggested that normally political events are symbolized by figures inferior to those that are used for religious events. The one exception noted was that any thing used in religious services or which had received religious labels of any kind always carried this religious meaning with it when used in apocalyptic writings. Thus an altar would refer to religious conditions or events even though made of stone. The stone and the mountain into which it grew appear to be an example of this principle.

The first mention of the stone (v. 34) does not say from whence it came. Then without previous mention it is said to have been cut out of the mountain. What mountain? To a Jew *the* mountain would almost have to mean Mount Zion. Keil understands it thus as he says it "can be only a reference to Mt. Zion."[139] There is reason, therefore, to take this unnamed mountain as Mt. Zion, and Mt. Zion is assuredly given religious significance both in the Old and New Testaments.

On this basis we hold that even though gold, silver, and brass, as well as the iron may be considered superior to a mere stone, this stone, because of its source, possesses qualities infinitely greater than do these metals. As the literal *qahal* (congregation of Israel) became the *ekklesia* (Church) of the New Testament; and as literal Jerusalem was a type of the New Jerusalem (the Church); so Mt. Zion of the New Testament is, we believe, connected with the Old Testament Mt. Zion through this prophecy as well as through various other passages.

Possibly the strongest argument against this being a prophecy of the growth and development of a spiritual kingdom, the Church, is the contention that this depicts "a great catastrophe" rather than the "peaceful extension of a spiritual kingdom."[140] Admittedly, such a conclusion is not contradictory to anything in the passage, but neither is it the only conclusion that can be reached. The Hebrew term *duq* used here is the same as that used in Exodus 32:20 where Moses ground "the golden calf to powder."[141] Thus the idea of repeated blows is not foreign to the passage.

And when the New Testament is considered, the idea of a catastrophic establishment of the kingdom must be rejected. Three parables of Jesus are cited to prove this. Mark tells us that the kingdom of God is like seed growing secretly (Mark 4:26-29). Matthew informs us that the kingdom of heaven is like leaven which spreads through a batch of dough (Matt. 13:33). Luke gives us the same information except he refers it to the kingdom of

---

139  C. F. Keil, *Biblical Commentary on the Book of Daniel*, p. 110.
140  Gaebelein, *op. cit.*, p. 35.
141  J. E. H. Thomson, *Pulpit Commentary on Daniel*, p. 73.

God. All three synoptic writers give the parable of the mustard seed which grew from a small seed into a tree (Matt. 13:31-32; Mark 4:30-32; Luke 13:18-19). Now Matthew refers this to the kingdom of heaven, but the other two say it refers to the kingdom of God.

The hermeneutical principle that requires that parallel passages be interpreted alike requires that all three of these refer to the same kingdom. And all three require that it be a process rather than a sudden catastrophe. Since Dispensationalists differentiate between the kingdom of God and the kingdom of heaven, it should be noted that this idea of a process is applicable to both the kingdom of God and to the kingdom of heaven. Hence, even though they violate hermeneutical principles in making such a distinction, they cannot avoid the fact that Mark and Luke make this process refer to the kingdom of God. Thus neither the kingdom of God nor the kingdom of heaven is to be begun by a catastrophic event.

It should be further noted that the kingdom which God was to establish at that time is one that "shall never be destroyed," and "it shall stand forever" (v. 44). It is impossible to construe these words as meaning for 1,000 years only. Does Daniel really mean it will last forever? One who believes the Old Testament was fully inspired must accept this statement at face value if he is at all consistent. Yet, Premillennialists constantly assert that the kingdom which they say is yet to be established is to last but one millennium.

Any effort to make the earthly millennium the initial phase of that heavenly kingdom which the faithful are to inherit after the final judgment is quite futile. The Amillennial position on this is legitimate for it states that a spiritual rule is now in progress, and that this spiritual rule will be perpetuated in heaven. But Premillennialism expects an entirely different kind of kingdom and rule during the millennium from that which will exist in heaven. It teaches that an earthly rule will be established and maintained by force, contrary to any heavenly rule existing now or in the future. Also, the priority of the Jews in the millennium is taught in violation of repeated statements that God is no respecter of persons; but for this partiality to be a part of our heavenly existence must be rejected as unthinkable.

Of the Ante-Nicene fathers, we found only four who left writings on this chapter. Of these, Hippolytus was the only one who interpreted it eschatologically. A casual reading of his comments might lead to the conclusion that he was a millennialist, but a careful study of his writings on Daniel 2 and elsewhere indicates otherwise. He did use the analogy of six days of creation representing six thousand years of earthly life, but the seventh day of rest was to be in heaven, rather than on this planet. Apparently he did not limit it to 1,000 years. He wrote in part, "... when the sixth day was completed [i.e., the 6,000 years represented by the six days] He might end the present life."[142] He also interpreted the toes (10?) as ten "democracies that were subsequently to arise."[143] His error of importing into chapter 2 from chapter 7 is still with us.

Irenaeus applied the stone cut out without hands to Christ and the virgin birth,[144] but he had little else to say about this chapter. Tertullian contended, as I do, that the Church Christ established was "that very stone in Daniel, cut out of the Mountain."[145] Elsewhere he linked Isaiah 2:2-4 and Daniel 2:34-35, 44-45 making both prophecies refer to the gospel age and the Church. He wrote, "Who else, therefore, are intended but *we* who, fully taught by the new law, observe these practices,—the old law being obliterated."[146] Cyprian explains Isaiah 2 and Daniel 2 in much the same fashion.[147]

Of the Nicene and post-Nicene fathers, not one was found who interpreted Daniel 2 as referring to a millennial reign, and only Jerome gave it any eschatological significance. Jerome believed "the stone" was Christ, the mountain out of which it was cut was deity, and that "without hands" referred to the virgin birth.[148] He considered the demolishing of the image to be the work of Christ over a long period of time. He wrote, "The inference is to be drawn, that the over-all interpretation of the dream applies to that final end when the image (D) and the statue beheld [in the dream] is ground to powder."[149] He does not posit a millennial reign at any point, and strongly opposed the teaching of the Jews whom he said taught that this chapter constituted a promise that the Jews would "be the strongest power at the end of the ages."[150]

---

142 Hippolytus, *Ante-Nicene Fathers,* vol. V, p. 179.
143 *Ibid.,* p. 179.
144 Irenaeus, *op. cit.,* vol. l, p. 453.
145 Tertullian, *op. cit.,* vol. III, p. 326.
146 *Ibid.,* p. 154.
147 Cyprian, *op. cit.,* pp. 523ff.
148 Jerome, *op. cit.,* vol. VI, pp. 29, 101. 133.
149 Jerome, *Commentary on Daniel,* p. 30.
150 *Ibid.,* p. 32.

Augustine held that the stone was Christ and that the development into a mountain was applicable to the kingdom and the Church. He even used the expression, "His kingdom which is the church."[151] He contended that verses 34 and 35 which involved the destruction of the image had already been fulfilled in his day.[152] Other early writers who wrote in a similar vein include Gregory of Nyssa, Cyril of Jerusalem, Aphrahat, and Gregory the Great. Thus the overwhelming opinion of the early Church writers is opposed to this chapter referring to a millennium, especially a Judaistic millennium, or to eschatological events of any kind.

## Daniel 7

This chapter has four wild beasts which the angelic messenger says symbolize four kings or kingdoms (v. 17). These four kingdoms were depicted in chapter 2, and the latter three are again seen in chapter 8. However, this chapter gives a great deal of information not contained in these other chapters. The additional information is not easily interpreted, and the different views which are advocated as the meaning of these portions conflict sharply with one another. This is especially true of verses 13 and 14 which are not explained by the heavenly visitor.

Three times in this chapter Daniel speaks of visions which he had seen in the night. This expression in verse 2 leads to his recounting of having seen three beasts which looked somewhat like three beasts which are known to men. The first was like a lion; the second was like a bear, and the third was like a leopard. It is generally recognized by conservative scholars that these are Babylon, the Medo-Persian, and the Grecian empires, comparable to the gold, silver, and brass of chapter 2.

The expression is found again in verse 7 which tells of an unusual beast with iron teeth. The iron teeth, as well as the order of appearance, identifies this fourth beast as the Roman empire. This verse further informs us that this fourth beast had "ten horns." Most will accept the interpretation of these ten horns as ten minor kingdoms which did grow out of Rome, or which shall in the future grow out of Rome. It can hardly be disputed that this chapter includes material beyond A.D. 476 and the dissolution of the Roman empire which occurred that year. Thus the extent of time covered by this chapter is greater than that of chapter 2 which placed the

---

151 Augustine, *op. cit.*, vol. VII, p. 26.
152 *Ibid.*, p. 467.

establishment of the kingdom which God was to establish prior to the dissolution of the Roman empire according to the interpretation previously given of that chapter.

Of particular interest is the little horn mentioned in verses 8 and 20-26. This little horn is different from the other ten in certain ways. First, it is not considered a basic outgrowth of the political kingdom out of which it in fact grew. The last three kingdoms of Medo-Persia, Greece, and Rome were yet future at the time Daniel saw these visions. The ten minor kingdoms were also future, but they are depicted by ten horns in the head of the fourth beast. Why, then, was not this little horn included, so as to make eleven horns? Why was it said to come up at a later time, when all of the horns were to come up at a later time than that of the writings down of the vision? Before considering these questions further, let us consider the description of this horn and activities which are not exactly political in nature.

From verse 8 we know that this horn has "eyes like the eyes of a man" and that it has "a mouth speaking great things." From verse 25 we know that it will "speak great words against the most High," and that it will "think to change times and laws." First, note that this horn has human characteristics. Its eyes are those of a man, and it speaks a communicable language such as humans use. No such activity or capability is attributed to any of the four beasts or the ten horns. This places the eleventh horn in a class by itself. This combination of beastly characteristics with human characteristics, as previously indicated, is considered the apocalyptic method of symbolizing an organization that combines political and religious power in a single body.

It cannot be denied that such an organization did develop during the middle ages. It eventually assumed the title of the Roman Catholic Church, although it was in existence many years before this became the official title of this body. It utilized an entirely different power structure than that used by the four empires of the ten minor kingdoms. Thus, in the second place, it is set apart from the ten horns as something that did not grow out of the four previous kingdoms. Had it not been for this difference in structure, it would have been a horn in the original vision rather than something which developed in an entirely different way than did the original ten horns.

Two other activities of the eleventh horn require consideration. It was prophesied that this horn would "think to change times and laws." Now one normal function of a legitimate government is to update its laws as conditions warrant. Then why should this be considered an improper activity of this horn? The first clause of verse 25 is taken as the answer to this query. This horn was to speak great "words against the most High." I hold that this was done through the usurpation of the authority of Christ and the Bible by the Pope and the Roman Catholic Church by holding that the Pope is the Vicar of Jesus Christ on earth and that the Roman Catholic Church has the authority to establish laws for the Church which are contrary to the teachings of the New Testament. Thus, this horn claims things which are blasphemous.

The other activity mentioned is that it would "wear out the saints of the most High" (v. 25). That the Roman Catholic Church did persecute many true Christians is common knowledge. Groups such as the Albigenses, the Waldenses, the Huguenots, and others were slain without mercy. The Inquisition was utilized to persecute dissenters, even those who by their own admission lived exemplary lives and possessed a strong faith in Christ. Men like Huss and Savonarola were killed. Had not Luther been protected by friends, he, too, would have been a victim of this persecuting power.

If it be accepted that the ten horns did develop after the dissolution of the Roman empire, then there is no great difficulty in locating the three horns which the eleventh horn uprooted. The temporal power of the Pope developed around the city of Rome. When the Roman Church actually assumed temporal and political power over a large land area and the people within that area through gifts by Pepin and Charlemagne, she ruled what had been occupied by the Heruli, the Ostrogoths, and the Lombards. Although political power had been exercised long before this, from this time onward she was definitely a politico-religious entity. Even today she rules over the Vatican and sends and receives ambassadors as nations do. Napoleon and Garibaldi took most of her political power from her, but it still exists to a limited extent.

The period of time the saints were to be "given into his hand" is stated in language that is subject to various interpretations, none of which can be advocated with great certitude. The two most accepted explanations are that it represents 1260 literal days or 1260 years with each day being a symbol of a year. Still others contend that it should not be interpreted as a specific period of time. According to this approach, whatever time works out in history is the time that is intended. I tend to lean towards the second and third explanations.

It can be shown that major persecution did cover approximately 1260 years. When Louis XIV revoked the Edict of Nantes in 1685, some 18,000 persons, mostly Huguenots, were slain. Although accomplished by the civil power, Pope Innocent XI recognized it as being done for the Roman Catholic Church. This can be considered as the period when persecutions of this sort generally came to an end. Counting back 1260 years, we come to that period when the primacy of the Popes was being firmly established. It was in A.D. 445 that Valentinian III made the rulings of the Pope to have the force of law. These dates are twenty years short of the 1260, hence are not used as doing more than indicating a possibility that the time element, generally speaking, can be applied to this period.

The judgment of verse 26 also fits into this picture. This judgment is not the final judgment for time is indicated as continuing. The taking away of his dominion was accomplished by degrees. The 16th century Reformation took much away. The Renaissance took some away. The refusal of Napoleon to recognize the Holy Roman empire took still more away. When Garibaldi freed Italy most of what was left was taken away. Vatican City is but a fragment of the dominion the Popes exercised at one time.

If it may seem that a disproportionate amount of attention has been given to certain details of this prophecy, justification for it is in the fact that Dispensationalists deny that the ten horns have yet appeared. From this position, they project a future fulfillment. Gaebelein states it in these words: "The Roman empire has never existed in this form...The Roman empire must therefore some day be revived politically."[153] I am prepared to grant that the "Roman empire" has not existed in this form, but that does not mean that this has eschatological significance. Daniel does not say the Roman empire will exist in this form. Rather he indicates that the Roman empire will break up into ten divisions, and a check of almost any history of the middle ages will indicate that it did break up into multiple divisions. There may be some slight difficulty in determining just which divisions are to be considered as the ten for the simple reason that the map of Europe is continually changing; but it can hardly be denied successfully that a group of ten branches of the Roman empire did spring into existence after the empire was dissolved in A.D. 476.

---

153 Gaebelein, *op. cit.*, p. 82.

I am prepared to agree with Gaebelein and others who hold that the judgment of verses 9-12 does not refer to the final judgment, but I am not prepared to concede that this judgment is yet future. As indicated in the preceding pages, I hold that the little horn of this chapter is the Roman Catholic Church which itself interprets the chapter to refer to the hierarchy. The taking away of her temporal power, especially that by Napoleon and Garibaldi, is considered the judgment set forth in verses 9-12. I can also agree with them that the little horn of this chapter and the first beast of Revelation 13 are the same; but instead of these being references to a supposed revival of the deceased Roman empire about which the Bible says not one word, I hold that these two prophecies can be shown to have been fulfilled in the past. There is no substantial basis for giving these prophecies an eschatological interpretation.

Verses 13-14 tell of one like the Son of man (Christ, we believe) receiving a kingdom from the Ancient of days (i.e., God, the Father). This kingdom is an "everlasting" kingdom, and it "shall not pass away." This kingdom cannot refer to a millennium here on earth, which is to last but 1,000 years according to most millennial advocates. Rather it refers to the kingdom Christ established at His first coming. Verse 18 indicates that the "saints of the most High" were to possess the kingdom "for ever, even for ever and ever." Gaebelein and others attempt to restrict this to certain Jews. The saints referred to here are said to be "the Godfearing Jews, who pass through the great tribulation and inherit the blessings and promises which God gave through their own prophets."[154] This restriction is not found in Daniel. It is imported into it by Dr. Gaebelein in an effort to make this passage conform to his plan of last things.

It should be apparent that these verses deal with the same everlasting kingdom—not a millennial reign of just 1,000 years—as that of chapter two. But it was shown that that kingdom was established at Christ's first coming (see also chapters 1-2 of this volume), hence it follows that the kingdom Christ was to receive became a reality during His first advent and is even now in existence. All of the essential aspects of a kingdom are evident in Christ's dominion over the Church. Christ is the ruling monarch; the Bible contains the law of the kingdom; the extent of the dominion includes both

---

154 *Ibid.*, p. 80.

heaven and earth; the subjects are those rightly related to God; sinners are like foreigners (tares in Matt. 13:24-30).

No millennial teaching based on this chapter was found among the writings of the early Church. In a section classified as containing dubious or spurious material, Hippolytus is said to have asserted that the Antichrist would "restore the kingdom of the Jews."[155] Inasmuch as Hippolytus left a strong polemic against Jewish aspirations, this statement certainly is not from his writings. Just who did write it will forever be a matter of conjecture.

In an authentic portion of the writings of Hippolytus, he said that at the second coming Christ will come as "God incarnate…coming from heaven as the world's Judge."[156] From this we know that he believed in a single judgment. A passage from those writings which were said to be dubious or spurious is quoted for what it is worth. It could be authentic for it is [in] line with the above.

And every kindred, and tongue, and nation, and tribe shall be raised in the twinkling of an eye; and they shall all stand upon the face of the earth, waiting for the coming of the righteous and terrible Judge…For both the righteous and the wicked shall be raised incorruptible: the righteous, to be honored eternally;…and the wicked to be punished in judgment eternally.[157]

Certain writers, of which Hippolytus was one, did hold portions of chapter 7 as eschatological. Cyril of Jerusalem agreed with Hippolytus regarding the reign of Antichrist.[158] Trypho interpreted the time element of this chapter in terms of centuries rather than days or years.[159] Although perfect harmony of interpretation of this chapter was lacking, no writer used it to support a millennial view.

## Daniel 8

It is not my belief that this chapter has any eschatological significance, but inasmuch as some inject such a significance into their interpretation, some consideration is necessary. It is generally conceded that the ram is a symbol of the Medo-Persian empire, and that the he-goat refers to Macedon or Greece. The notable horn is, of course, Alexander the Great, and the

---

155 Hippolytus, *op. cit.*, p. 246.
156 *Ibid.*, p. 189.
157 *Ibid.*, pp. 251-252.
158 Cyril of Jerusalem, *op. cit.*, pp. 107ff.
159 Trypho, quoted by Justin Martyr, p. 210.

four horns that arose when the notable horn was broken, refer to the four divisions of the Grecian empire following the death of Alexander the Great. There is also reasonable agreement that the little horn that arose (vv. 9-14) primarily refers to Antiochus Epiphanes who was the oppressor of the Jews during the Maccabean period. The problem is that Scofield and other Dispensational writers contend that Antiochus Epiphanes is a type of the Antichrist. On this basis certain aspects of this chapter are given eschatological import. This, however, is speculation—not exegesis.

Biederwolf cites numerous authorities which reject the day-year method of interpreting the 2,300 evenings and mornings of verse 14. I agree. This does refer to the period from 171 B.C. (some say 170) to the time when Judas Maccabeus restored the true worship after cleansing the altar and sanctuary. Nothing in this chapter indicates that it is a type of future events or persons. It is excessive typology to hold that it constitutes a type. The most that can be said is that some of the aspects of this chapter may be analogous to certain future circumstances. Personally, I see no sound basis for even going this far.

## Daniel 9:24-27

Seventy weeks are determined upon thy people and upon thy holy city, to finish the transgression, and to make an end of sins, and to make reconciliation for iniquity, and to bring in everlasting righteousness, and to seal up the vision and prophecy, and to anoint the most Holy. Know therefore and understand, that from the going forth of the commandment to restore and to build Jerusalem unto the Messiah the Prince shall be seven weeks, and threescore and two weeks: the street shall be built again, and the wall, even in troublous times. And after threescore and two weeks shall Messiah be cut off, but not for himself: and the people of the prince that shall come shall destroy the city and the sanctuary; and the end thereof shall be with a flood, and unto the end of the war desolations are determined. And he shall confirm the covenant with many for one week: and in the midst of the week he shall cause the sacrifice and oblation to cease, and for the overspreading of abominations he shall make it desolate, even until the consummation, and that determined shall be poured out upon the desolate (Dan. 9:24-27).

The verses quoted above constitute the most remarkable prophecy regarding the time of Christ's first advent. However, it has become one of the most controversial passages of the Old Testament. Such a variety of explanations of these verses has been given, and there are so many minor points of difference, that only the broad outlines can receive consideration. Some go so far as to reject this prophecy in its entirety. We have no sympathy for that position. Another group of commentators apply this to the time of Antiochus Epiphanes. This we must reject as untenable for both historical reasons and the content of the prophecy as well. The only acceptable view is that it is Messianic.

But even between two classes of interpreters who consider the prophecy to be Messianic, a great hiatus exists. The first disagreement is over the beginning point or *terminus a quo*. The edict which was generally accepted for many years was the one found in Ezra 7. It was made in the seventh year of Artaxerxes (Ezra 7:7-8), and was usually dated at 457 B.C. Another group of expositors believe the edict found in Nehemiah 2 is the starting point of the prophecy. This was given in the twentieth year of Artaxerxes and is usually dated at 445 B.C. Those who hold to the first date believe the seventy weeks or *heptads* are to be taken as 490 years, and that the first 483 years takes one to the beginning of Christ's ministry which is His baptism. By counting back, they come to the decree in Ezra.

Others contend that the only edict that meets the stipulations of the prophecy, especially in regard to the building the city of Jerusalem, is the one in Nehemiah 2. The twelve or thirteen years difference in the time of these two prophecies is explained in various ways. The possibilities are numerous. The uncertainties are many. It is our own opinion that it is impossible to prove with solid substantial evidence that any system of calculation is correct beyond a reasonable doubt. My reasons for saying this are these uncertainties mentioned above. To list them is to recognize the scope of variables that must be considered.

First, at least three different lengths may be assigned to the seventy sevens or seventy weeks of years. These are the regular Jewish year of 354 days (six 29 day months and six 30 day months), the so-called prophetic year of 360 days which had much support but which is not specifically established by Scripture, and the solar year of 365 1/4 days. Arguments may be advanced for one or the other of these years as the one intended in Daniel 9:24, but proving that these arguments are correct is quite another thing.

Chronology is a second area of uncertainty. It is known that the birth of Christ was some years prior to the date our calendar assigns for it, but authorities are not in agreement as to just how many. It is equally difficult to prove the year of Christ's crucifixion. Anyone who writes with absolute certainty on this point is probably fully convinced in his own mind, but that is not to be equated with absolute proof. Sir Robert Anderson has given a most detailed calculation of the time from the edict in Nehemiah 2 to Christ's triumphal entry into Jerusalem which he places in A.D. 32, but other authorities who have examined the same evidences Anderson has used place it as early as A.D. 29. And the 445 B.C. date for the edict is subject to some question. For these reasons Anderson's figures cannot be accepted as being proved.

It is not necessary to reject the importance of this passage simply because of the difficulties involved. There can be little question but that it is Messianic and that the first 69 weeks bring us to some point in the life of the Messiah. The greatest area of controversy is in regard to the seventieth week. Many hold that the 69 weeks end with the baptism of Christ, and that He was crucified in the midst of the 70th week, whereas other equally sincere persons hold that the 69 weeks of years takes us to Christ's triumphal entry into Jerusalem, and that the 70th week is yet future. Our approach is that this problem cannot be settled on the basis of historical evidence, hence must depend on exegesis and interpretation. It is my opinion that exegesis makes the futurity of the 70th week an utter impossibility.

Since this volume is concerned particularly with eschatological matters, our principal concern in this chapter of Daniel is the 70th week. If it was fulfilled in the week following Christ's baptism as most commentators claimed for many years, then it is improper to relate it to the time of the end. Only by playing fast and loose with hermeneutical principles and the grammatical significances of terms can the 70th week be projected into the future.

Possibly the most important determining aspect of this prophecy is the first clause of verse 24: "Seventy weeks are decreed upon thy people and upon thy holy city." The Hebrew term translated "decreed" means marked off or cut off as a block. It refers to a block of time. It is true that this block of time has three sections to it; seven weeks or 49 years, 62 weeks or 434 years, and one week or seven years. But there is nothing in this prophecy that justifies the separation of the last week from the other 69 weeks.

These 70 weeks constitute a block of time. No grammatical or hermeneutical principle exists which justifies throwing 1900 or more years into this prophecy between the 69th week and the 70th week.

A second very damaging fact to those who teach a deferred 70th week is their teaching that the death of Christ occurs during the period between the end of the 69th week and the beginning of the 70th week. Scofield makes the palm Sunday of Christ's triumphal entry into Jerusalem the end of the 69 weeks and the beginning of the great parenthesis. Sir Robert Anderson's figures which are generally accepted by Dispensationalists makes this date the *terminus ad quem* of the 69 weeks. Gaebelein quotes Anderson at some length on this point.[160] That he accepts Anderson's figures is shown by his later statement that Christ "appeared in Jerusalem on exactly the day on which the 69 prophetic weeks expired and a few days later He was put to death on the cross."[161] Now this fits in with the Dispensational theory of the stopping of the prophetical clock and the beginning of the parenthesis which they teach, but it does not agree with Daniel's prophecy.

The fact is that Daniel places the crucifixion within the 70 weeks. In verse 24 we find that one of the things to be accomplished during the 70 weeks—not during a so-called parenthesis—is "to make reconciliation for iniquity." Boutflower points out that the basic meaning of the Hebrew term used here is that of atonement.[162] The only work of atonement to which this could refer is Christ's sacrificial death on Calvary's cross. The cross of Christ seems to be the focal point of this entire prophecy. This distortion of prophecy to make it fit a particular eschatological scheme should be recognized as an instance where men's ideas are given precedence over the word of God.

Now that the atoning death of Christ is definitely placed within the 70 weeks by verse 24, let us consider verse 26. This verse says, "And after threescore and two weeks shall the anointed one be cut off." The traditional view as well as that of Dispensationalists recognizes that Christ's death did come after the end of the 69 weeks. But verse 24 places it within the 70 weeks, hence it *must be during the 70th week*. Thus exegesis establishes the beginning of the 70th week as the period immediately following the end of the 69th week. No hiatus of some 2,000 years is indicated. According to

---

160 Gaebelein, *op. cit.*, pp. 138ff.
161 *Ibid.*, p. 141.
162 Charles Boutflower, *In and Around the Book of Daniel*, p. 183.

the Dispensational scheme, it is only a week after the end of the 69th week that Christ was crucified, but even so it must be the 70th week despite their protestations to the contrary.

This proves that the 70th week began immediately following the end of the 69th week. It verifies the traditional interpretation of this prophecy. It strongly supports the view that the cessation of sacrifices (i.e., the need for further sacrifices of animals, v. 27) which occurred in the midst of the 70th week, has reference to Christ's atoning work, rather than an act of the Antichrist ostensibly after the Jews are supposed to restore animal sacrifices.

Before considering the time element held by the writers of the early Church, it is considered appropriate to give a brief digest of these verses. Most of this follows the traditional interpretations of the Church. Bare statements must suffice.

Verse 24: The 70 weeks or heptads of unstated length do refer to 70 weeks of years, although these years may be as short as 354 days or as long as 365 1/4 or in between at 360 days. These years were determined, decreed, or marked off in a single block. The prophecy was directed against Jerusalem. Transgressions are to be restrained (by Christ's sacrifice and the influence of the Church) rather than stopped completely. Sins which could not be removed by animal sacrifices were to be ended or removed by Christ's blood. Man was to become reconciled to God through the atoning work of Christ. A type of permanent righteousness (true holiness) was to be introduced. Old Testament prophecies, at least in the main, were to be fulfilled, and the new temple (the Church) or most holy place was to be dedicated.

Verse 25: The 70 weeks were to begin at the command found in Ezra 7 or Nehemiah 2. The first seven weeks (49 years) were to be years of trouble. After 62 additional weeks (434 years for a total of 483 years) the Messiah (Christ) was to appear. This has reference to the time He began His ministry following His baptism, rather than to His birth.

Verse 26: After the 62 weeks (plus the initial 7 weeks) the Messiah (Christ) was to be crucified not for Himself, but for us. At this point Daniel reaches beyond the 70 weeks to the destruction of Jerusalem in A.D. 70. The prince that would come was Titus and Jerusalem was destroyed following a long siege. The "sanctuary" or temple was also destroyed as Jesus said it would be in His Olivet discourse. Desolations did follow, especially toward the end of the war. Placing this in the future as something to be done by one who has been termed the Antichrist is completely rejected.

Verse 27: During this 70th week Christ would confirm the new covenant with many. In the midst of the week Christ would be crucified. This made animal sacrifices no longer essential, so they are said to end. Of course, Jews did continue their animal sacrifices until the destruction of Jerusalem in A. D. 70, but the need for them was removed at Christ's death. The desolation that followed the destruction of Jerusalem is the intent of the expression about abominations in this verse. The consummation of that determined is the capture and enslavement of the Jews following the destruction of Jerusalem. (See chapters 14-15 for additional material on this matter.)

How the early writers of the Christian era interpreted this passage is now considered—

Julius Africanus computed the time element from the regular lunar year which is only 354 days or 11 1/4 days short of the solar year. He used the prophetic *terminus a quo* as the edict from Nehemiah 2. This method indicated there were 487 years to the crucifixion which took place in the midst of the 70th week.[163] Augustine applied this passage to the gospel era and Christ's first advent.[164] Athanasius,[165] Cyril of Jerusalem,[166] and Eusebius did likewise. The latter specifically held that the abominations of desolation were fulfilled through the destruction of Jerusalem in A.D. 70.[167]

From the collection of writings which we have been using as our major source of information on the early Church, only two statements were found that could possibly be interpreted eschatologically. Athanasius who was not a millennialist did look for a future Antichrist, but when he expected him to appear is not clear.[168] The other reference is by John Cassian who held that the literal "abominations of desolations" were past (probably the destruction of Jerusalem in A.D. 70), but he did expect a future condition the Church would have to endure of which the destruction of Jerusalem was a symbol or type.[169] He did not say when he understood that this would be fulfilled.

However, another source of information gives the opinions of certain writers which are not incorporated in the three series of more than thirty

---

163 Julius Africanus, *Ante-Nicene Fathers*, vol. VI, pp. 134ff.
164 Augustine, *op. cit.*, vol. II, p. 380; vol. IV, pp. 37, 197.
165 Athanasius, *op. cit.*, p. 57.
166 Cyril of Jerusalem, *op. cit.*, p. 77.
167 Eusebius, *op. cit.*, pp. 90, 138.
168 Athanasius, *op. cit.*, p. 298.
169 John Cassian, *Post-Nicene Fathers*, second series, vol. X. p. 377.

large volumes which is our major source of material. I refer to *Jerome's Commentary on Daniel*. He quotes extensively from Africanus, but since that has already received consideration, nothing additional needs to be said. He gives two possible explanations from Eusebius, the first of which apparently is the one he accepted. This made Christ's crucifixion occur in the midst of the 70th week. The other ends with the destruction of Jerusalem in A.D. 70.[170] Apollinarius was one of the very early date setters. He began the 490 years with the birth of Christ and forecast the consummation 490 years later.[171] Since his prediction has long since been proved untrue, the fact that he interpreted this passage eschatologically is of little significance today. Nothing is said about a millennium.

Clement of Alexandria stretched the 490 years to cover the period from Cyrus to that of Vespasian and Titus.[172] Tertullian followed a similar pattern.[173] Origen would not venture an interpretation, but he did suggest that the period from the first year of Darius to the advent of Christ was the period which should be considered.[174]

Of the early writers considered thus far, not one has applied this passage to a millennium. The centrality of Christ's first advent and Christ's atoning work has been recognized by almost all of the early writers. One writer, however, is yet to be considered. This is Hippolytus who held to a deferred 70th week. He said that the first seven weeks were prior to the return of the Jews from Babylon. The 62 weeks, according to his interpretation, extended from the return to the birth of Christ. Jerome points out that these dates do not agree at all with the time limits of the prophecy. The important statement of this writer is in regard to the 70th week. Jerome says of him, "Moreover Hippolytus places the final week at the end of the world and divides it into the period of Elias and the period of the Antichrist." During the latter half of the week, "under the Antichrist the sacrifice and offering shall cease."[175]

Although present day Dispensationalists figure the first 69 weeks in a different manner than Hippolytus did, and although Hippolytus believed

---

170 Eusebius, quoted in *Jerome's Commentary on Daniel*, pp. 98ff.
171 Apollinarius, *op. cit.*, p. 104.
172 Clement, *op. cit.*, p. 105.
173 Tertullian, *op. cit.*, pp. 106ff.
174 Origen, *op. cit.*, pp. 105-106.
175 Jerome quotes Hippolytus, *op. cit.*, pp. 103-104.

the Church would endure the Tribulation[176] contrary to the view of Dispensationalists and the majority of Premillennialists, it appears that Hippolytus is the author of the theory that the 70th week is separated from the other 69 weeks. It should also be remembered that Hippolytus did not believe in a Jewish millennium. His *Dissertation Against the Jews* is one of the strongest polemics against the Jews on record. Thus only one of the writers of the early Church interprets Daniel 9 with any degree of conformity to that of Dispensationalism, and even so, there are more points of difference than there are similarities.

## Daniel 11

This chapter parallels chapter 8 in some respects, but the latter part of the chapter either goes into greater detail regarding the little horn of chapter 8, Antiochus Epiphanes, or some other explanation must be given. There is little or no controversy down to verse 24. From this verse onward, Jerome holds that in part the reference is to Antiochus Epiphanes as a type of the future Antichrist, and that some point directly to the Antichrist. Most commentators accept verses 24-30 as being applicable to Antiochus Epiphanes, but from that point onward there is little agreement.

The efforts to make this chapter refer to the years immediately preceding the second coming of Christ are rather weakly supported, although the verbal barrage is quite prolific. Verse 31 is the first important basis for an eschatological interpretation. This verse tells of "the abomination that maketh desolate." This is equated with the abomination Jesus mentioned in Matthew 24 which is in turn interpreted as yet future by many Premillennialists, rather than being fulfilled in the destruction of Jerusalem in A.D. 70. However, this is not crucial, for men like Tan and Gaebelein admit that Antiochus Epiphanes fulfilled this prophecy, and yet they hold that the latter portion of this chapter is to be interpreted eschatologically.

Considerable disagreement exists regarding verses 35-39, but the crucial verses are 40-45. If these latter verses are considered a continuation of the account in the sense of giving new and additional information, then it must refer to some person other than Antiochus Epiphanes, for certain statements in these verses cannot be applied to Antiochus except these verses be considered a summary of events already given. Biederwolf lists seven commentators who interpret these verses as a summary.[177] Several others

---

176  Hippolytus, *op. cit.*, p. 217.
177  Biederwolf, *op. cit.*, p. 231.

could be added to his list among whom are Barnes and Lange. Barnes' discussion is especially helpful on this chapter and these verses.

No ordinary book of literature would skip from describing one character and his activities to that of another without alerting the reader to the fact that the change was being made. However, this is what we are asked to believe is done in the book God has given us. It is difficult for me to understand how so many learned persons have perpetuated this error which goes back to the days of unrestrained typology. Note how careful Daniel is to inform the reader of changes in the person(s) being referred to in the earlier portions of this chapter: three kings and a fourth (v. 3), a mighty king (v. 3), not to his posterity (v. 4), one to stand in his estate (v. 7), and one to stand up in his estate (v. 20), and again one is to stand in his estate (v. 21).

This brings us down to Antiochus Epiphanes. Now if Daniel was careful to carry the reader along with these lesser changes, it is unreasonable to believe that he would skip over more than twenty centuries of time without at least indicating he was talking about a different person. It is far less difficult to show how verses 40-45 apply to Antiochus Epiphanes than it is to explain how verses 21 onward are about Antiochus Epiphanes but that verses 40-45 are about a yet future Antichrist.[178]

Only two early Church writers left discussions of Daniel 11. Hippolytus held that the abomination of 11:31 referred to Antiochus, but that the one in 12:11 referred to the Antichrist.[179] Jerome held that from verse 21 onward the primary reference was to Antichrist, although he recognized that certain portions did apply to Antiochus Epiphanes. He held, however, that whenever the reference was to Antiochus, he was but a type of the future Antichrist.[180] And since Jerome repeatedly referred to his views as the accepted view of his day, I accept them as such in spite of the dearth of evidence. However, it should be kept in mind that Jerome was not a millennialist. He was a contemporary of Augustine who pushed premillennialism into obscurity. Actually, belief in a future Antichrist is as compatible with amillennialism as it is with premillennialism. Belief in a future Antichrist tells us nothing of what one expects to follow his appearing.

---

178 Scofield makes verse 36 the point of transition.
179 Hippolytus, *op. cit.,* p. 184.
180 Jerome, *Jerome's Commentary on Daniel.* pp. 129ff.

## Daniel 12

Chapter 12 is a part of the same vision as chapter 11, hence this chapter is a continuation of the preceding chapter. The first words of chapter 12, "And at that time" evidently refer to the time of the closing verses of chapter 11. But since there is sharp disagreement as to whether the closing verses of chapter 11 refer to the time of Antiochus Epiphanes, or whether they refer to a future Antichrist, chapter 12 is interpreted along the same separate lines of interpretation begun in chapter 11. Dispensationalists refer verse 1 to what they call "the great tribulation" which they say the Jews must endure immediately preceding the visible appearance of Christ. But if the latter verses of chapter 11 refer to the time of Antiochus Epiphanes, as we have given reasonable arguments for, then the time of trouble was fulfilled in the time of Antiochus Epiphanes. That Antiochus was a baneful ruler who brought unprecedented tribulation to the Jewish nation cannot be gainsaid. The deliverance mentioned in this verse is applied to the deliverance wrought by Judas Maccabeus and his army.

Verses 2-3 have been generally interpreted as referring to the general resurrection. Certainly the language is appropriate to that event. However, the context indicates otherwise. The portion which precedes these verses has been discussed already. That which follows will be discussed shortly. With references to the time of Antiochus Epiphanes coming both before and after these verses, we can only interpret them as apocalyptic expressions in which language similar to that which would be used of the general resurrection is utilized.

As eminent a literalist as Gaebelein joins me in this assertion though for very different reasons. He writes, "Physical resurrection is not taught in the second verse of this chapter…We repeat the passage has nothing to do with physical resurrection. Physical resurrection is however used as a figure of the national revival of Israel in that day."[181] The essential difference in his interpretation and mine is that I place the fulfillment in the past, whereas he places it in the future. Such an interpretation from him is to deny the single hermeneutic of which Dispensationalists boast, whereas I have from the beginning stated that apocalyptic writings should be interpreted as symbols or figures of speech. Again, I recommend *Barnes Notes* as a balanced discussion of the way this should be understood.

---

181 Gaebelein, *op. cit.*, p. 200.

Verse 4 brings to an end the words which the heavenly visitor spoke directly to Daniel, but in verse 5 two other heavenly beings appeared. One of these asked the first angel, "How long shall it be to the end of these wonders?" (v. 6). The first angel answered, "It shall be for a time, times, and half a time" (v. 7). With "a time" considered one year of 360 days, and "times" the simple plural representing two years, and "half a time" equaling one-half a year, the total time involved is three and one-half years. But no starting point is given, which makes the interpretation depend on conjecture—not on exegesis.

Those who apply this period to the Antichrist point out that in the Revelation there is a similar statement, and they *assume* that the two periods are identical. But this does not necessarily follow. The time under discussion in Daniel chapter 12 is the time of Antiochus Epiphanes, I believe, whereas the same expression in the Revelation refers to a period beyond the first Christian century. I consider the similar reference in chapter 7 to be identical to the similar reference in the Revelation, for chapter 7 verse 26 is dealing with a time later than A.D. 476. The existence of the ten minor kingdoms proves this to be true. But we have no such clear indication of a later time in this verse, and when the time of this verse is considered in conjunction with the time of verses 11-12, objections to verse 6 referring to the time of Antiochus are answered.

If verse 11 is read carefully, it will be noted that two distinct events are mentioned. The first is the taking away of the daily sacrifice. The other is the setting up of the abomination that maketh desolate. From I Maccabees 1:59 and 4:52 we find that it was exactly three years from the time pagan sacrifices were made on the pagan altar until the altar was cleansed, but some six months earlier the daily sacrifice had been taken away. Josephus in his *Antiquities* (bk. XII, chap. VI, parag. 6) agrees with the three years mentioned above. But in his *Wars of the Jews* (bk. 1, chap. 1, parag. 1) he adds that Antiochus stopped the daily sacrifice for three years and six months. Thus the taking away of the daily sacrifice is the starting point of this prophecy rather than the setting up of the abomination that maketh desolate (I Macc. 1:54) and the actual sacrificing on it (I Macc. 1:59) which came roughly six months after the daily sacrifice was stopped. Thus the prophecy is shown to fit the time of Antiochus. This may not absolutely prove that it does refer to him, but the inference is very strong.

When verses 11 and 12 are considered, presumptive evidence is also available that these times refer to Antiochus and his activities. The three and one-half years, if each year is figured at 360 days, would be approximately 18 days short of three and one-half solar years. The exact date that the daily sacrifice was taken away cannot be ascertained, but it could easily have been 12 days earlier than the figures Josephus gives. His dates are only approximate at the best. By adding the 12 and the 18 a result is obtained that equals the 1290 days of verse 11 if the sum is added to the 1260 days already given. It is held that the 1260 days is an approximate figure from the taking away of the daily sacrifice to the cleansing of the altar, but that the 1290 figure gives the exact number of days.

The 1290 days ends with the cleansing of the altar in December of 165 B.C. It was in January or early February of 164 B.C. that Antiochus Epiphanes died. Although the exact date cannot be determined, the dates are sufficiently precise to remove any obstacle to the belief that his death is the terminus *ad quem* of the 1335 days. Thus no pressing need exists to interpret these verses eschatologically. Any who do so must draw on their imagination rather than any text of Scripture. Any effort to interpret these as years is equally futile.

Of the early Church writers, only two were found who discussed Daniel 12:1. These were Jerome and Hippolytus. Both interpreted this verse as referring to a future persecution under a future Antichrist. This sounds favorable to the Premillennial position, but when verses 2-3 are considered any advantage is eliminated and a strong minus is registered for that view. Every one of the several writers who discussed these two verses applied them to a *general resurrection*. Now bear in mind that at least two resurrections and a plurality of judgments are absolutely essential to the maintenance of the Premillennial position. And not a single one of the early writers support that view from this passage.

Verse 11-12 are discussed by Hippolytus and Jerome, only. Both held that the abomination of 11:31 refers to Antiochus, but that this one in chapter 12 refers to the Antichrist. Jerome bases his interpretation almost exclusively on the fact that the temple was polluted for only three years (I Macc. 4), whereas the prophecy speaks of three and one-half years.[182]

---

182 Jerome, *Jerome's Commentary on Daniel*, p. 151.

We have previously shown that the daily sacrifice was taken away six months before the pagan altar was erected, hence his objections have been answered already. Then for this prophecy to be applicable to future times, a restoration of the daily sacrifice is demanded. But any effort to prove that the Bible teaches a future restoration of Jewish sacrifices fails miserably. Yet much of the Premillennial teaching of today injects this restoration into their program of last things. These verses should be accepted as fulfilled by Antiochus Epiphanes.

CHAPTER 12

# THE ESCHATOLOGY OF THE MINOR PROPHETS

The Minor Prophets say little about things that can be related to the time of the consummation from a purely exegetical basis. The texts themselves say nothing about a millennium. But by devious reasoning they are given such meaning by millennialists, especially those who teach a revived Judaism. Therefore, this chapter, as most of those which precede it, will not be much more than a refutation of the claims others make about portions of these twelve books. A number of my former students hoped this volume would discuss all of the passages millennialists interpret eschatologically. As originally written it did this. However, space limitations necessitated a drastic reduction in this section. I regret this, but it was unavoidable.

In order to conserve space, listings of writers of the early Church will not include volume and page numbers unless a specific quotation is given. By consulting the scriptural index for any author, the reader will be able to find the page number for any particular reference he is interested in checking, provided he has access to such volumes.

### Hosea

Hosea 1:10-11 is applied by Scofield and many others to a future restoration of the Israelitish nation. Three possible explanations are evident. First, the return from the Babylonian captivity. This is hardly acceptable. It is too inadequate. A second view is the one that claims a future restoration of the Jewish hegemony. We reject this as contrary to New Testament passages which will be discussed later, and for other reasons which will be discussed next. The third possibility, and the one which this writer accepts, is that it has a spiritual fulfillment during the gospel age.

The reference to the children of Israel becoming "as the sand of the sea" has direct reference to the Abrahamic covenant, and we have shown that this was fulfilled through the gospel and the Church. The remainder of verse

10 is applicable to the conversion of Gentiles which has far exceeded the conversion of Jews. Those who were not "my people" are Gentiles. These are to become "sons of the living God." No one can deny that Gentiles have become sons of the living God.

This last view is the one generally held by the Church until recent times. The following early writers held this view: Tertullian, Cyprian, Irenaeus, Clement, Augustine, Chrysostom, Ambrose, and Ephraim Syrius. Not a single writer was found who opposed this view. Note that even Irenaeus refers this to the gospel age, even though he believed in a future millennium. Most of these writers held it had been fulfilled and/or was being fulfilled in this present Church age.

Between verses 13 and 14 of chapter 2, Scofield inserts the statement or caption "Israel, the adulterous wife, to be restored." This prophecy is couched in terms of literal Israel, but is fulfilled, as we have shown in relation to similar prophecies, by spiritual Israel. The betrothal (vv. 19-20) refers to Christ and the Church. It is done in "righteousness" which can never be said of literal Israel. And if it is applied to the remnant, that is nothing more than another term for the Church.

Verse 23 plainly shows that the reference includes the Gentiles. "Them which were not my people" (v. 23) must refer to Gentile Christians. Of the early Church writers, Tertullian, Clement, and Chrysostom make verse 23 apply to Gentile converts to Christianity. These join with Cyprian, Irenaeus, Ambrose, and Ephraim Syrius in assigning its fulfillment to the gospel age and the Church. Not a dissenting opinion was found.

## Joel

It has already been stated that Joel was probably the first of the apocalyptic writers. Among other things this infers that he uses literal or physical conditions or events to portray spiritual truths. Jesus told parables to convey spiritual truths. An apocalyptic prophecy is similar in that figures of speech are utilized in a way very similar to the way Christ used them in His parables. There is strong support for Joel 1 being an allegory in the writings of the early Church. Most of the older commentaries gave this interpretation. In recent years several commentators have revived this view. However, chapter 1 is not the focal chapter in Joel. It is in chapter 2 that the question of interpretation takes on great significance.

Regardless of whether chapter 1 is an allegory or whether it is factual, chapter 2 is built on it. Something analogous to the desolation of the palmerworms, the locusts, and the cankerworms is to occur at a time future to that of the writing by Joel. Scofield, Lindsey and others take such obscure passages as this one and link them together to establish an order of events just prior to the visible appearance of Christ to set up, as they say, His millennial kingdom. It appears far more reasonable to us to hold that Joel 2 is apocalyptic.

In support of this view we invite a comparison of Joel 2:10, and 30-31 with the apocalyptic passages from Isaiah 13:6-10; 34:3-6, 9-10; and Ezekiel 32:7-8. In all of these passages tremendous changes in the sun, moon and stars are depicted. The passages from Isaiah and Ezekiel are explained within those chapters as referring to temporal judgments against Babylon, Idumea, and Egypt (see chap. 4 of this volume). These have long since come to pass. Although Joel does not fully explain the meaning as these others did, Peter boldly proclaims that Joel 2:28-32 was being fulfilled at that very time. He even quoted the part about the sun and moon as included in what he meant (Acts 2:19-20).

And then he adds the first part of Joel 2:32, "And it shall come to pass, that whosoever shall call on the name of the Lord shall be saved." Paul applies these words to the gospel era (Rom. 10:13). Thus both Paul and Peter contend that Joel is referring to the Church age in this prophecy. Dispensationalists contend, however, that the Old Testament prophets knew nothing of the Church age. Therefore, it is necessary for them to posit a future fulfillment of which Pentecost was but a foreshadow. We hold, therefore, that Joel 2:10 and 30-31 were fulfilled in the impact Christianity had on Judaism, and that verses 28-29 referred to the outpouring of the Holy Spirit at Pentecost and since that time. Verse 32 refers to the general blessings that come to mankind through the gospel.

That Joel 3 continues in the apocalyptic style of chapter 2 is indicated by verse 15 which reads, "The sun and the moon shall be darkened, and the stars shall withdraw their shining." Any effort to literalize this passage and Joel 2:10 and 30-31 requires that a time of fulfillment be determined. But the time of fulfillment is not given. Hence, the interpreter must supply such a time without any real support from inspiration. If this passage were intended to be taken literally, additional guidelines regarding the time would have been given. Joel 3:10 is of special interest because it reverses the beating of swords into plowshares and spears into pruning hooks (Isa. 2:4; Micah 4:3).

Since swords and spears have long since been superseded by other weapons, it is illogical to apply either of them to literal conditions of the future. However, if both are recognized as figurative expressions, a beautiful harmony results. According to this interpretation, Isaiah and Micah refer to the peaceful, nonviolent aspects of the Church. The fight is not against flesh and blood with weapons of carnal warfare. Rather the warfare is spiritual in nature. But it is a warfare; hence Joel portrays this militant aspect of the activity of the Church in its opposition to the forces of evil. Jesus said that the gates of hell could not withstand this assault with spiritual power.

Little reference was found to Joel 3 in the writings of the early Church fathers. Tertullian applied 3:9-15 to the final judgment day. Irenaeus said verse 16 referred to Christ's first advent. Tertullian explained verse 18 as figurative. None of these writers mentioned a millennium in connection with his discussions of chapter 3.

### Amos

Amos 5:16-20 is given eschatological significance by some because of the appearance of the expression "day of the Lord," or "day of Jehovah" in verses 18 and 20. Scofield in his note on Revelation 19:19 makes the day of the Lord extend from Christ's appearance in glory at the close of the great tribulation to include the millennium and what is to follow according to the Dispensational claims. Now chapter 5 is directed to Israel. The inconsistency of the claims of Dispensationalism is that verses 18 and 20 pronounce woe and darkness to Israel for the duration of the day of the Lord, whereas the Dispensational claim is that the Jews will be exalted to a place of special prominence during the so-called millennial reign. Any tribulation the Jews endure is supposed to precede the day of the Lord, according to Dispensational theology.

Chapter 9, especially verses 11-15, are very important to the Premillennial teaching. (Sec chapter 3 for previous consideration of this passage.) It is our contention that "In that day" (v. 11) refers to the gospel age. James gives it that meaning in Acts 15. The efforts to force some other meaning on James' words are not built on sound exegesis of Acts 15. When read like any other book, Acts 15 can only be taken to mean that Amos 9:11-12 was then in the process of fulfillment. Instead of accepting the evident intent of James, as Dispensationalists often recommend that we do in reference to other passages, they go into an elaborate explanation that requires the injection of millennial ideas into Acts 15 which cannot be verified by sound exegesis.

Those who literalize verses 11-12 are embarrassed by the apparent figurative expressions which follow in verse 13. Very few are willing to take such expressions as "the plowman shall overtake the reaper, and the treader of grapes him that soweth seed; and the mountains shall drop sweet wine, and the hills shall melt" as anything but figurative. However, some still insist that verses 11-15, except for verse 13, must be taken literally. I prefer to believe that the extravagant language of verse 13 is designed to inform us that the entire passage is figurative. James indicated that the prophecy applied to the Church, rather than to literal Israel, but since Dispensationalists deny that the prophets foresaw the Church, they must explain this section in conformity with their established pattern of interpretation, even though it requires the use of unacceptable methods of interpretation.

## Obadiah

Verse 15 of this short prophecy mentions "the day of the Lord" (Jehovah). This is often taken to refer to the time of the end. The expression surely does mean that in certain instances, but it is denied that it always means this. Since this is closely connected with the doom of Edom (vv. 1-14) which occurred centuries ago, we take this passage to refer to the gospel age. Mount Zion (v. 17) is often used of the Church, and we hold that to be the intent of this passage.

Dispensationalists claim that Obadiah, as well as Ezekiel, tells of literal Israel during the so-called millennium. But a comparison of Obadiah 19-20 with Ezekiel 47:13-48:9 gives land occupancy details that cannot be reconciled. And neither of these gives land areas that extend to the Euphrates, the eastern border of the original promise to Abraham. Therefore efforts to make these refer to a future fulfillment of the Abrahamic covenant are fruitless regardless of the time element assigned to these passages from Obadiah and Ezekiel.

## Micah

In the discussion of Isaiah 2:2-4 (chap. 8) Micah 4:1-5 was also examined. A review of that portion will be helpful, for only the basic elements will be given here. The "mountain of the house of the Lord" (v. 1) is interpreted as referring to the Church. The ingathering of many peoples predicts the spread of the gospel (v. 2). The law going forth from Zion (v. 2) is the preaching of the gospel by churchmen. The changes made in certain weapons of warfare to implements of agriculture refer to the peace that Christ imparts to Christians (v. 3). Sitting under one's own vine and fig tree (v. 4) is a symbol of the Christian's security in Christ.

The early Church writers interpreted Micah 4 as well as Isaiah 2:2-4 as spiritual rather than literal. Not one was found who interpreted this passage in terms of a future millennium. Justin Martyr held that verse 3 was to be interpreted spiritually. He applied II Corinthians 5:17 to this verse. He did leave room for it to have a future application, but no mention was made of a millennium. Irenaeus applied verses 2-3 to the Church. Origen discussed the passage, but did not interpret it. Cyprian interpreted the law going forth (v. 2) as the preaching of the gospel. Lactantius did the same. Methodius interpreted the vine and fig-tree as I have done. Augustine and Chrysostom apply the passage to the gospel age. Millennialists can find no real support for their doctrine from the interpretations given by the early Church fathers of Micah 4. No support was found for the contention that verses 11-13 refer to a future battle called Armageddon.

Dispensationalists tend to interpret Micah 4:11-13 as yet future, and they also interpret 5:4-14 as referring to a millennial reign. This poses a problem for them regarding sequence. Just why would Micah write about a battle which is yet future to our time, then write about the birth of Jesus in Bethlehem, and follow this with a discussion of a millennial kingdom which is to follow the battle of Armageddon? The explanation is very simple. It is called a parenthesis. But can a legitimate reason be given for a parenthesis at this point? No. The explanation Scofield gives in his note on 5:1 is an illustration of how far some will go to defend an untenable position.

## Zephaniah

The book of Zephaniah is interesting for two reasons. First, it furnishes a strong argument against the claim that the day of the Lord always refers to a future judgment. In 1:14 the expression "The great day of the Lord" is found. Then in verse 15 the term "That day" appears. But instead of these referring to the future judgment, Scofield admits in his notations which introduce the book, that the major reference is to "The coming invasion of Nebuchadnezzar." He attempts to avoid an inconsistency by saying this constitutes "a figure of the future day of the Lord." But the damage is done. He admits that the expression is used other than of the final judgment.

# THE ESCHATOLOGY OF THE MINOR PROPHETS

The other interesting aspect of this prophecy is the section of chapter 3 that begins with verse 8. Scofield contends verses 8-13 refer to a judgment of nations based on his peculiar interpretation of Matthew 25 which will be discussed in the New Testament portion of this volume. He jumps from the time of Zephaniah which he admits is the intent of verses 1-7 to eschatological events. There is no transitional verse or sentence on which to base this tremendous leap in time. It is not likely that God would have Zephaniah make such a break without giving some indication of what he was doing.

Verse 9 is most interesting because of the unscholarly if not unethical way it is being used by Judaistic Premillennialists. This verse has certain people using a "pure language" (KJV). Hebrew scholars are unanimous in applying this to speech that is wholesome because it contains no evil aspects such as lying or cursing. It has no reference to "pure" in the sense of being grammatically correct, idiomatic, without slang expressions, or free from mixing with other languages. Wolfendale says it means "a pure life. The mouth speaks from the abundance of the heart. The lip was created by God, and should be used for his service and glory."[183] Keil translates the phrase, "Then I will turn to the nations a pure lip." His comments include, "God turns to the nations a pure lip, by purifying their sinful lips…Lip does not stand for language, but is mentioned as the organ of speech."[184] Many other authorities could be cited to prove this phrase has nothing to do with correcting accretions or mixed modes of expression.

In spite of the fact that the above interpretation cannot be denied, the paraphrased Living Bible gives the reading, "At that time I will change the speech of my returning people to pure Hebrew so that all can worship the Lord together." In note 3a in fine print the literal rendering is given as "… I will change the speech of the peoples to a pure speech.…" Four distinctions should be noted between the paraphrased reading and their literal rendition. "Peoples" (plural) is changed to "my people" (i.e., God's people—singular). The idea of this people "returning from some unnamed place to an unnamed place" is injected. Some of this may be justified by verse 10, but in that verse it is only to bring an offering—not to take up residence.

---

[183] James Wolfendale. *Preachers Complete Homiletic Commentary*, vol. II, Minor Prophets, p. 553.
[184] Keil, *op. cit.*, vol. II, Minor Prophets, p. 156.

The third change is the use of "pure" in a grammatical sense rather than an ethical sense. The fourth is the worst of all. It is the insertion of the word "Hebrew" which is without any justification whatsoever. It is assumed that the writers of this paraphrase have injected into this verse their own ideas of what Zephaniah intended to say. This kind of tampering with God's word is most reprehensible. We refrain from condemning this further, although stronger words would not be inappropriate. All persons involved in this would do well to make amends for this alteration of God's holy word.

The weakness of the Premillennial position, at least for those who insist on making a return of the Jews to Palestine an integral part of their eschatological program, is shown by the fact that they have taken this obscure verse and doctored it up as they have to bolster their claim that it is now being fulfilled. A real effort is being made to revive the ancient Hebrew language. Even if this is accomplished, it will not be a fulfillment of this prophecy. In addition to the reasons already given, the pure language was something from God. If the long-dead language of ancient Hebrew is restored by present methods, it will be an accomplishment of man—not something given of God.

Also, the question of the Jewish return to Palestine which has been blown up as a fulfillment of prophecy has taken a turn that these brethren did not anticipate. In 1974 more Jews left Israel than immigrated there. It is estimated that 22,000 fewer Jews returned to Palestine in 1974 than in 1973. Even more devastating is the fact that 15,000 more Jews emigrated from Israel than immigrated to Israel.[185] If this trend continues for many years, it will be fatal to the nation of Israel. It is interesting to note that many immigrants from Russia are so disillusioned that they are even attempting to go back to Russia.

The evil effects of this paraphrasing of Zephaniah 3:9 has been compounded by a film entitled *His Land* produced by the Billy Graham organization. This film received wide coverage through its appearance on T.V. This film evidently used the paraphrase of this verse from the *Living Bible*, for it used the word "Hebrew" in quoting this verse. It is the only translation (paraphrase or otherwise) that has added this word to this verse insofar as I know. In this film a strong emphasis on the resurrection of the formerly dead language of *pure* Hebrew came through loud and clear. It is regrettable

---

185 *Houston Chronicle*, issue of Jan. 10, 1975.

THE ESCHATOLOGY OF THE MINOR PROPHETS     205

that an organization which has been used of the Lord in a most remarkable manner would stoop to such means to promote a doctrine about which there is a considerable difference of opinion, especially a doctrine that is not essential to salvation. This author recommends that both the publishers of the *Living Bible* and the Billy Graham organization take steps to correct the erroneous impressions they have produced in the minds of many people. In doing so, they should admit the use of improper means in creating these erroneous impressions.

## Zechariah

It is generally agreed that Zechariah has more to say about the Messiah than any other of the Minor Prophets. But how much of this prophecy has eschatological content is a matter of considerable controversy. Premillennialists tend to interpret a large number of passages with this sense. Others interpret these same passages without such significance. Most of what is written depends on interpretation, for the time each prophecy is to be fulfilled is seldom clear within the prophecy itself. The fact that many passages are written in apocalyptic style is one of the reasons I tend to consider most of these prophecies as figurative or symbolic. Certainly some of them are quite literal, but others are patently not literal.

It is held that chapters 1-8 were written when Zechariah was a young man. Chapters 9-14 were written many years later, possibly as much as thirty years later. The most serious disagreements involve portions of these last six chapters, hence only these will be considered.

Zechariah 9:9-10 tells of Jesus entering Jerusalem in triumph on that first palm Sunday. As Jesus rode into the city on a lowly animal representative of peace, along with its foal just as Zechariah had prophesied, this text was fulfilled. Matthew specifically states that it was the fulfillment of verse 9 (Matt. 21:5). Now who was said to ride this animal? It was The King! However, Dispensationalists contend that He was not then king, and that He will not be king until He comes, as they teach, to establish a millennial kingdom. But Matthew and Zechariah say He came as King, then.

Scofield divides this chapter 9 as follows: Verses 1-8a tells of certain campaigns of Alexander the Great. Verse 8b is a promise yet to be fulfilled in the future millennium. Verse 9 constitutes an offer of the kingdom to the Jews, an offer which they rejected. From this he claims the kingdom was postponed. According to him, verses 10-17 refer to the future millennium. Now if 8b refers to the millennium, and verses 10-17 refer to the millennium, the insertion of Christ's triumphal entry into Jerusalem in between is unreasonable and illogical. Therefore, we must discard such far-fetched analysis as completely unacceptable. The main thrust of this chapter must he the first advent.

In accordance with the above reasoning we interpret verses 1-8a as referring to conquests of Alexander the Great. He could have conquered Jerusalem also, apart from divine intervention, but he did not molest Jerusalem. The prophet turns then from the fact that Alexander was to pass by Jerusalem (8a) to the safety and security we would enjoy in the kingdom of God (the Church) which Christ came to establish, and which He did establish. This is in line with the New Testament interpretation of the message of the prophets as found in Luke 1:67-79.

In these verses Zacharias, the father of John the Baptist, declared that the deliverance foretold by the prophets was salvation from sin and iniquity so that they were delivered from ethical and moral foes. The covenants made with Abraham and David were to find their fulfillment through people living holy and righteous lives. The salvation involved was from ethical foes that fight against the soul rather than physical foes using physical weapons. Thus the "that day" (9:16) is held to refer to the gospel day. It is now being fulfilled. It does not refer to a future battle fought with carnal weapons.

Since chapters 9-11 constitute a unit, the interpretation of chapter 9 is crucial to the interpretation of chapter 10. Taking 9:9 as the key text of that chapter, the remainder of the chapter was interpreted as referring to blessings of the gospel age. It should be kept in mind that verse 9 unquestionably refers to the first advent in general and to the triumphal entry into Jerusalem in particular. All are agreed on this. If this approach to chapter 9 is accepted, then it follows that chapter 10 also refers to spiritual blessings of the gospel age couched in terms of the physical.

On the other hand if chapter 9 is held to refer to the end of time with verse 9 a parenthetical expression with no vital connection with anything else that is said in this chapter, then it would follow that chapter 10 is also eschatological in significance. Scofield goes so far as to claim that the Church or present gospel age is not seen anywhere in Zechariah except in 9:9 (see note on 9:10 for confirmation). The reader must decide whether to follow this indefensible statement of Scofield, or the more reasonable interpretation given herein.

In chapter 11 the first advent is again the central theme. Verses 12-13 very definitely refer to the betrayal of Christ by Judas for thirty pieces of silver. Matthew quotes this in his account of the betrayal (Matt. 27:3-10). He also mentions the potter's field which is a portion of Zechariah's prophecy. Thus the New Testament affirms that this prophecy did have reference to the first advent. The fact that Matthew refers this to Jeremiah instead of Zechariah does not alter the fact that these words of Zechariah are said to have found their fulfillment in connection with Jesus' betrayal and death.

Another interesting and informative feature of chapter 11 is verses 10-11. They read in part, "And I took my staff, even Beauty, and cut it asunder, that I might break my covenant which I had made with all the people. And it was broken in that day." Those who teach a future union of Judah and Israel based on these chapters attempt to soften these expressions "break my covenant" and "And it was broken in that day." Scofield's note on verse 7 that it was "abandonment, for the time" has no exegetical basis in this chapter. It is an imported idea. Taken at face value, it means that God has no covenant with Israel or Judah. As Jeremiah told of God divorcing the Jews (Jer. 3:8), so Zechariah tells of God nullifying His covenant. Scofield's descriptive term "abandonment" is quite fitting except for his claim that it is only temporary.

In John 19:37 the inspired apostle informs us that Zechariah's statement, "and they shall look upon me whom they have pierced" had its fulfillment at Calvary. The force of the expression "that the scripture might be fulfilled" (John 19:36) carries over into verse 37 which refers back to Zechariah 12:10. This establishes the fact that at least one verse in Zechariah 12 refers to the first advent. If the remainder of chapter 12 is not interpreted in harmony with this verse, the result is a jumping from last things to Calvary and then back to last things again with no adequate basis for this jumping around.

Chapter 13 has two verses which inspiration applies to the first advent. These are verses 1 and 7. Verse 1 reads, "In that day there shall be a fountain opened to the house of David and to the inhabitants of Jerusalem for sin and uncleanness." That this refers to the shedding of the blood of Christ at Calvary needs no defense. However, some recognition must be given to the attempts to twist this text to give it an eschatological significance. Those who insist that "in that day" always refers to the time of the second coming must interpret this passage in the light of that claim even though it is done in violation of exegetical principles. The opening of the fountain cannot refer to the second coming. It was opened at Calvary.

It is confidently claimed by Premillennialists that 14:4 refers to the second coming of Christ. Among other things it states, "And his feet shall stand in that day upon the mount of Olives." Now, who will stand there? Is it Jesus, the Messiah? No! It is Jehovah who is to stand there. Both verses 1 and 3 indicate that Jehovah (Lord is Jehovah in the Hebrew in these two verses) is the person under consideration. Nothing is said of Christ, the Messiah. This verse says nothing about the second advent. Those who insist it must mean that, have to make Jehovah refer to Jesus. I recognize the deity of Christ, but the distinction between the Father and the Son is usually maintained in prophecy as well as in the rest of the Bible.

Verse 4 also contains the prophecy of the mount of Olives splitting and part going to the north and part to the south. This, along with the semidarkness of verse 6, is closely akin to the apocalyptic passages already studied from Isaiah and Ezekiel. Hence we take these physical disruptions to symbolize political and religious upheavals that accompanied Christ's first advent and the preaching of the gospel. This view is strongly supported by verse 8 which reads, "And it shall be in that day, that living waters shall go out from Jerusalem; half of them toward the former sea, and half of them toward the hinder sea: in the summer and in winter shall it be."

Those who insist that this is yet to be fulfilled, literally, have an insuperable problem. First, rivers do not flow in two directions. Yet, this river is said to flow into what is generally considered the Mediterranean and the Salt Seas. The second problem is that Ezekiel has the water flowing only into the Salt Sea. But if both Ezekiel and Zechariah are interpreted figuratively, then this water represents the outflowing of the grace and Spirit of God to a lost and dying world. The flowing in one direction, as in Ezekiel, or the flowing in two directions, as in Zechariah, in either case symbolizes the outflow of that living water which stemmed from Calvary—living water which Christ professed to be (John 4:10-11), and which the Holy Spirit brings (John 7:38).

Even some who teach a future millennium recognize the figurative nature of much of this chapter. Kenneth Grider is one of these. He denies that the gathering of all nations against Jerusalem (v. 2) is to be taken literally. Regarding verses 4 and 8 he says,

> Since the water is to flow in two directions from the same source, the water referred to is symbolical water. This is the water of redemption that Ezekiel saw (Ezek. 47), and that other Bible writers have seen (Joel 3:18; Rev.

22:1). These references, then, to a mountain splitting open, and to a river flowing in opposite directions from Jerusalem, are surely figurative; and they show that the prophet uses figurative language along with references to factual places and practices.[186]

It is unfortunate that Dr. Grider does not also see that the keeping of the feast of tabernacles (vv. 16-19) is also a figurative method of expressing the blessings of the gospel age. The problems of food, lodging, and transportation for all the people of the world to go to Jerusalem for this feast are far more illogical than for one stream to flow in opposite directions. The holiness of verses 20-21 is that of the gospel age—not of a future millennium.

## Malachi

How much of Malachi 3 and 4 is to be interpreted eschatologically has been a fruitful source of controversy from the first Christian century onward. Their significance regarding a millennial reign is minor, for persons of all millennial persuasions have interpreted them in an eschatological sense, while yet others of the same millennial persuasion have interpreted them as fulfilled in the first advent. Many combine the two. These say that some portions are fulfilled and others are yet future, or that the earlier fulfillment was but a type of the larger fulfillment which they anticipate in the future. The present writer considers all of Malachi to have been fulfilled in the first advent and the gospel age, hence it is without eschatological significance.

However, because various commentators claim that Malachi 4:5-6 has a fulfillment in Revelation 11 yet future, these verses are briefly considered. The Jews, being literalists, looked for a personal appearance of Elijah the Tishbite prior to the advent of the Messiah. Therefore, when they asked John the Baptist if he was Elijah, i.e., the Elijah that was taken to heaven in a fiery chariot, he correctly answered that he was not (John 1:21). Had they asked him if he was the fulfillment of Malachi 4:5-6, he no doubt would have said yes, for he did relate himself to a similar prophecy in Isaiah (Isa. 40:3-4; John 1:23). Jesus' statement is conclusive that John the Baptist was the Elijah (Elias) about which Malachi prophesied (Mal. 4:5-6; Matt. 17:10-13). There is no legitimate basis for expecting Elijah the Tishbite to return. Those who read such a return into Revelation 11 are mistaken.

---

186  J. Kenneth Grider, *The Wesleyan Bible Commentary*, vol. III, p. 786.

## A Summary of Old Testament Eschatology

The research for this book has included the reading of literally dozens of books in which the millennial concept is defended. Therefore, the following list of events which many millennia lists incorporate into their scheme of last things should not be taken lightly, even though I contend they have not proved their case. At this juncture no final judgment can be made for New Testament texts have not been fully explored; but it can be said that evidence from the Old Testament has not been sufficient to declare that any of the following statements has been proved true from the Old Testament. Of course, it is also believed that these statements cannot be proved from the New Testament, but no statement to that effect will be made until the teachings of the New Testament have been considered.

## Claims Held to be Unsubstantiated by the Old Testament

1. *That there will be a future millennium of earthly tranquility and universal peace, either before or after the second coming of Christ but prior to the end of time.* The Old Testament is completely void of any mention of a millennium. Of the dozens of millennial volumes read in my research, not a single writer quoted a text that within itself affirmed a millennial reign of any sort. All have depended on analogy which proves nothing according to the rules of logic, or on non-canonical statements, or on the single New Testament passage in Revelation 20. This lone passage from the New Testament which is from an apocalyptic book full of figurative expressions is the only passage inspiration furnishes on a millennial reign. And even it does not refer to an earthly reign as will be shown later.

2. *That there will be a return of the Jews to Palestine just prior to the second coming.* That a number of Jews have returned to Palestine is admitted, but it is denied that the Old Testament prophets mention this return. In 1974 15,000 more Jews emigrated from Palestine than immigrated into it. Thus the return that has been played up so much has gone into reverse. But none of this is a subject of prophecy insofar as I am able to discern. The special place Israel occupied in Old Testament times was temporary. With the coming of Christ and the gospel era, God obliterated the artificial distinctions between Jews and Gentiles. All men meet Christ on an equal level. No nation is preferred above any other nation. The returns that are the

subject of prophecy have been fulfilled already or else they are finding their fulfillment through the preaching of the gospel.

3. *That the Abrahamic covenant was unconditional regarding the physical posterity of Abraham, and that this covenant assures the Jews of one day reigning over the entire area from Egypt to the Euphrates.* It has been shown that the Abrahamic covenant did contain provisional aspects which involved the rejection of Ishmael, Esau, the sons of Abraham by Keturah, and their descendants. Likewise the nation of Israel was divorced which indicates the masses of the Jews of today have no promise of anything except through the acceptance of Christ. This means that no promises of geographical dimensions survive for the Jews. The immutable aspects of the Abrahamic covenant are fulfilled in Christ and the Church.

4. *That the Davidic covenant is yet future and will have its fulfillment in an earthly reign of Jesus on the throne of David.* Although some statements of this covenant seem unconditional, the Psalmist records that that covenant was broken. (Ps. 89:39). It also had aspects which were immutable as well as some which were provisional. Only the immutable aspects have any significance today. And this part of the Davidic covenant is now being fulfilled through Christ's reign over the Church. Christ now reigns from the throne of David. Peter's sermon on the day of Pentecost was shown to give this interpretation of the fulfillment of the Davidic covenant. Paul also interpreted the "sure mercies of David" as referring to the gospel age and the resurrection of Jesus (Acts 13:29-39). Thus the Old Testament does not prove a future reign of Christ on the throne of David, and the New Testament clearly places that reign as now in progress from Christ's mediatorial throne in heaven.

5. *That there will be a personal Antichrist.* Most of this doctrine is based on specific ways of interpreting New Testament passages. These will be considered in due course. Passages like Daniel 9 and 11 are interpreted in the light of these New Testament interpretations. The Old Testament simply fails to refer to an Antichrist as such. Exegesis alone cannot establish such a person from the Old Testament. Of course, it is also held that this cannot be done from New Testament texts, but it must be admitted that the evidence in favor of such a person is stronger in the New Testament than in the Old.

6. *That there will be a literally material battle with carnal weapons in Palestine involving armies of unparalleled size.* Texts most used for support of this doctrine are apocalyptic in nature whether in the Old or New Testament. For this reason they are subject to a variety of interpretations. Expressions in these passages are of such a nature as to indicate the battle is not fought with weapons of this world. Instead, the physical expressions are figurative expressions of the battle between good and evil and are spiritual in nature.

7. *That a group of Israelites will become exceedingly successful Christian evangelists in the years immediately preceeding the second-second coming of Christ.* The teaching is that the Church is to be raptured to heaven at a special second coming which is distinct from His real second coming to establish His kingdom. This first second coming is often said to be secret although the text most used to support it indicates it will be a noisy affair (I Thess. 4:13-18). It is also held that the Holy Spirit will be removed from His earthly activity at this time. And yet it is claimed that a group of Jews will evangelize more successfully during this period than the Church has been able to do with the Holy Spirit's empowerment. Certainly, nothing of this was found in the Old Testament, and it will be shown later that it is not a New Testament teaching either. The only coming of Christ mentioned in the Old Testament is the first coming.

No doubt this last statement will be challenged, but we have shown that the Old Testament passages which are said to refer to the second coming of Christ do not do so. The strongest text of this nature is Zechariah 14:3-5, and it has been shown that this is an apocalyptic expression regarding Jehovah. It says nothing of Christ, the Messiah. Other passages such as Isaiah 11 have been shown to refer to the first coming of Christ.

8. *That there will be several resurrections rather than a general resurrection.* The most important passage of the Old Testament regarding a resurrection of the body is Daniel 12:2. Premillennialists admit that this passage does not teach a multiplicity of resurrections. They either deny that it refers to the bodily resurrection, or else it is made to teach at least two resurrections by injecting at least one thousand years into the text about which the text says nothing.

9. *That the former enemies of Israel will be reestablished.* No Old Testament text can be presented that teaches this doctrine. It is a supposition built upon another supposition.

10. *That the Roman empire will be restored in the form of ten minor kingdoms.* Daniel 2 is the principal text used to support this doctrine, but that chapter has been shown to refer to a period that ended in A.D. 476. Daniel does not say that the toes represent minor kingdoms. The image was destroyed in A.D. 476, and the fulfillment of the establishment of the kingdom of God was already an accomplished fact.

11. *That there will be a judgment of nations as corporate entities.* No Old Testament text teaches anything of this nature. Many denunciations of specific nations are found in the Old Testament, but the idea of a general judgment of all nations, only some of which are said to be judged worthy of continuance into the so-called kingdom age, cannot be verified by Old Testament writings.

12. *That Israel is to undergo a future time of extreme tribulation just prior to the establishment of the kingdom.* This concept is mainly based on New Testament texts, but Jeremiah 30:7 and Daniel 12:1 are often interpreted as applicable to this expected event. However, Jeremiah speaks of either the destruction of Jerusalem by Nebuchadnezzar or Titus, and Daniel speaks of the persecution under Antiochus Epiphanes. Although this problem of a future time of great tribulation, like that of a personal Antichrist, is not vital to the millennial doctrine nor inimical to the opposing view, it has become so associated with Premillennialism that it has taken on the flavor of a basic element. For this reason it has been necessary to refute it.

## Writings of the Early Church on the Above Twelve Points

That a certain amount of millennial teaching existed in the early Church is admitted, but that this was the prevailing teaching in any previous period of Church history is denied. At this juncture the point in question is not how much millennialism there was in the early Church, but whether or not that which did exist was based on Old Testament teachings. This study has indicated that the Old Testament was not a major source of millennialism in the early Church.

Rather, the main sources of millennial teachings were from Jewish apocalyptical writings and analogical applications. These Jewish expectations were inevitably brought over into early Christianity just as circumcision, Sabbath keeping, and other Jewish teachings were. It required several centuries to throw off these accretions. Papias improperly attributed certain

Jewish fables to Christ. Irenaeus accepted what Papias wrote, thus perpetuating this concept through his extensive millennial writings. Thus the true source was not the Old Testament, but Jewish apocalypticism and other Jewish expectations which existed before the Christian era, some of which were carried over in the Church.

The accuracy of this observation is further supported by the fact that advocates of a millennium in the early Church seldom used Old Testament texts in support of their position. Only Tertullian made reference to the Abrahamic covenant in this connection, and he applied it to the Church as the true Israel, rather than to the genetic descendants of Abraham. Not one was found who based a millennium on the Davidic covenant. More millennial advocates interpreted Isaiah 2 as referring to the gospel age than to a millennium. More saw the animals of Isaiah 11 as symbols of changed personalities than of changes in lions and wolves. *Not one* advocated a Jewish millennium such as is being advocated in this the twentieth century.

The writers of the early Church who advocated a millennium did not teach a Jewish millennium such as is now being taught. Millennialists and Amillennialists alike were opposed to any Jewish expectations of a future Jewish return or the establishment of a kingdom in which the physical Jews would have the preeminence. Almost without exception, they interpreted the major passages of the Old Testament which are now being interpreted as referring to a future millennium as being fulfilled in the Church and the gospel dispensation.

The new covenant of Jeremiah 31 was uniformly applied to the Christian era. Likewise, Amos 9:11 was considered fulfilled through the gospel, even by writers claimed to be Premillennialists. Millennialists denied that Ezekiel prophesied of a return to animal sacrifices. A quotation from Justin Martyr, the one very early writer who was definitely a millennialist, is very pointed. It reads,

> And do not suppose that Isaiah or the other prophets speak of sacrifices of blood or libations being presented at the altar on his second advent, but of true and spiritual praises and giving of thanks.[187]

---

187 Justin Martyr, *op. cit.*, p. 258.

Thus, although the Church was not in full agreement as to whether or not there would be a future millennium, they were in full agreement that there would not be a Judaistic millennium such as is being advocated today. Had the millennialists of the first Christian centuries taught a revived Judaism such as leading Premillennialists are now teaching, they would have been classed with those Judaizers who insisted on circumcision and the keeping of the law of Moses. I can confidently affirm that if the millennialists of the first Christian centuries were now living, they would denounce the Judaistic millennialism of today as rank heresy. Various other emphases of the millennialists of today are unsupported by any of the early Church writers.

— PART THREE —

# THE ESCHATOLOGY OF THE NEW TESTAMENT

CHAPTER 13

# THE SECOND COMING OF JESUS CHRIST

In Part Two of this volume the key passages of the Old Testament were studied in the order in which they appeared in the Bible. In this, the New Testament section, the same plan will be followed except that this first chapter considers the second coming of Christ as a subject. Part Four, the last section of this volume, will deal with the several events which are often connected with the second coming. That section will consider each event as a special subject.

The resurrection of Jesus, which comes first chronologically, is considered in the chapter on the resurrection of the dead. It will not be practical to evaluate the teachings of the early Church on every text which is quoted, but the more important ones will be evaluated as they were in Part Two.

## The Promise of Christ's Return

The second coming of Christ is a prominent teaching of the New Testament. Jesus Himself promised to return both through His parables and through direct statements of positive intent to return. In the Acts the resurrection of Christ is affirmed, and our future resurrection is predicated on this fact. Paul's letters repeatedly refer to the return of Christ. I Corinthians 15 is the most extensive discussion of the resurrection of the dead, but I Thessalonians 4 has important material on the second coming. The Hebrew epistle mentions Christ coming a second time. Peter, James, and the Revelation all speak of His return through one means or another. In fact, most of the books of the New Testament include some material on the second coming or events connected with it.

A review of the early Church writers indicates that the second coming continued to be an important doctrine. It is true that considerable controversy developed over certain features of the second coming, but no writer contradicted the doctrine of a future return. It is doubtful if any other doctrine received as much consideration as that of the resurrection of the body, but since that was an event connected with Christ's return, any teaching on this subject was an affirmation of Christ's second coming.

The New Testament contains a variety of phrases which express the promise or hope of Christ's return. However, the expression *he deutera parousia* which came to he used of Christ's second coming during the second Christian century is not a biblical phrase. The nearest to it is found in the book of Hebrews to the effect that Christ would "appear the second time" (Heb. 9:28). But this promise has the word *ophthesetai* rather than *parousia*. Now *ophthesetai* implies visibility, and it can mean personal presence, but personal presence is not the essential meaning of the word. No doubt the writer of the Hebrew epistle intended to convey the idea of Christ's personal presence, but it could mean visibility at a distance as at the trial of Stephen (Acts 7:56).

The issue is further complicated by the fact that some of the expressions about Christ coming refer to events not involving His personal return. Seven of these possibilities and suggested meanings will be considered here—

1. Christ comes into one's heart and life in some manner when one repents and believes on Christ as his Saviour (Rev. 3:20).

2. In preparing the disciples for His death, Jesus informed His followers that He would not leave them comfortless or orphans, but that He would "come" to them (John 14:18). That this referred to His coming through the Holy Spirit on the day of Pentecost can hardly be denied.

3. There is a sense in which death involves a coming of Christ to the one dying (Acts 7:59). At least we enter His presence at that time (Phil. 1:23).

4. Although there is disagreement regarding which texts speak of Christ coming in judgment on the Jews in A.D. 70, there is general agreement that such a coming is implied in the Gospels, and that it was fulfilled in due time.

5. A secret second coming, or at least a coming that is not visible to all men. This teaching has three variations. Jehovah's Witnesses claim that Christ returned to this earth in 1914, and that He is now somewhere on the planet earth. The more common belief is that the Church will be raptured to meet Christ in the air. The contention is that only Christians will see Christ at this time. Two distinct teachings follow separate lines of thought from this point onward. Pretribulation rapturists hold that the Church will be

# THE SECOND COMING OF JESUS CHRIST

taken to heaven for a seven year marriage festival. At the end of this period the true second coming is said to occur. Posttribulationists hold that the rapture is simply to meet Christ on His way to establish His kingdom. Both hold that Christ then returns to the earth to establish a millennial kingdom. I reject as unbiblical any variation of this so-called secret coming of Christ.

6. Since pretribulation rapturists claim that there are two future comings of Christ, this item is inserted to list His second-second coming according to their scheme of eschatology. It is claimed that when He comes to rapture the Church to heaven, He only enters the atmosphere of the earth. The real second coming is seven years later at which time, they teach, He will return to establish the millennial kingdom. The two-phase second coming is rejected as is the millennial kingdom. Neither have adequate biblical support.

7. Amillennialists and Postmillennialists as well hold to one future second coming at which time all of the dead will be resurrected, all the living will be changed, a single judgment of all who have ever lived will occur, and appropriate rewards and penalties in heaven or hell will be meted out to all. Time, as we know it, will end, and eternity will begin.

Now this variety of views does not dim the promise of a personal return. Before considering the several words that are used of the second coming, the promise of a personal return must be established free of the technicalities of interpretation. Jesus said, "I will come again, and receive you unto myself; that where I am, there ye may be also" (John 14:3). Here Jesus promised to return in person for us. Implicit in this promise is a home with Him in heaven as the context definitely indicates. This is often applied to the so-called "rapture" by Premillennialists; but Jesus said nothing about a temporary occupancy of our mansion in glory followed by a 1,000 year absence from heaven during a kingdom age before our return to be with Him. Only by reading something into the text can this conclusion be reached.

The message of the two heavenly visitors following the ascension of Christ is even more forceful. They said that "this same Jesus, which is taken up from you into heaven, shall so come in like manner as ye have seen him go into heaven" (Acts 1:11). This passage indicates that Christ will return personally, bodily, and visibly. At least this much is included in the words "this same Jesus" would come "in like manner." Some of the other texts which refer to the second coming are Matthew 26:64; Mark 14:62; Luke 12:40; John 21:22; Philippians 3:20; I Thessalonians 1:10; 3:13; 5:23; II Thessalonians 1:7-8; I Peter 1:13; and II Peter 3:8-13. This is only a partial list of the texts on which Christians earnestly place their faith for a future return of Christ.

This is the "blessed hope" of the Christian faith. For those who accept the inspiration of the Bible, it is a certainty. It is admitted that there is disagreement over some of the events connected with His coming, but the promise of His coming is too strongly supported by the Scriptures for there to be any quibbling over the certainty of His return, at least among conservative scholars. Jesus *will return* some day. Our faith is not shaken by scoffers, existentialists, liberals, or men such as Albert Schweitzer who hold unacceptable views regarding Christ and the Bible.

## Could Christ Come at Any Moment?

It is certain that Christ could not have come at any moment during the very early days of Christianity, and this may be true of many later centuries, but it is my opinion that God has intended for each generation to anticipate His return during their lifetime. We know that Christ could not return prior to the destruction of Jerusalem for He foretold events connected with that destruction in A.D. 70. And Paul indicated a great apostasy would occur prior to the return, although he did not know just when it would come nor how long it would last. Many scholars believe that Paul anticipated the second coming during his lifetime when he wrote I Thessalonians (note the "we which are alive and remain" of I Thess. 4:17), but that he had ceased to expect it when he wrote the last letter to Timothy (II Tim. 4:6-8).

Also, if my interpretation of the Revelation is correct, then He could not return until the prophecies of that book were fulfilled, but since all prophecies are obscure to some degree, and especially those given in apocalyptic writings, these did not hinder persons living in the early centuries of Christianity from expecting the second coming during their lifetime. Repeated warnings to always be ready, and that He will come suddenly and unexpectedly, even as a thief in the night, have stimulated Christians down through the years to expect him to return while they were yet alive.

But the Bible also speaks of a delayed return. This is a paradox. There is a tension between the two ideas. In the parable of the talents (Matt. 25:14-30), the man who travelled into a far country and returned is a figure of

Christ's departure and return. He was to return "After a long time" (v. 19). However, in the Revelation it is said, "I come quickly" (Rev. 22:7, 12, 20). James brings out this tension in a single passage (James 5:7-9). In verse 7 we are encouraged to wait patiently for the "coming of the Lord," whereas in verse 9 he writes, "Behold, the Judge standeth before the door." In other words, we should be ready should He return today, but we should not become impatient if that coming is delayed.

To the question, could Christ come today? several answers are available. Dispensationalists contend that the "rapture" could come today but that the visible return of Christ could not. The reason they give is that there are seven years between these two events. Other Premillennialists say that the Antichrist must reign for seven years and the "great tribulation" occur before either the rapture or the visible return of Christ can occur. Postmillennialists say that Christ may come for us individually at death at any time, but that the visible return can come only after 1,000 years or a long period of peace and prosperity. Only Amillennialism says He can come soon or late and that His coming will be without any time warning, even as a "thief in the night."

## Greek Words Used of Christ's Second Coming

Before considering other aspects of the second coming, a study of the Greek words which are used of that coming is advisable. Some attention will be given to the texts where the several words appear.

### *Erchomai*

Of the Greek words used of the second coming, this verb is more nearly comparable to the English word "come" than any of the others. It usually signifies arrival or personal presence, but not in every instance. It is also applicable to comings which are spiritual, inward, invisible, and nonbodily insofar as the comings of Christ are concerned. It is so used of His coming through the Holy Spirit on the day of Pentecost (John 14:18). However, it is also used of that personal return of Christ which is yet future (see Matt. 24:42, 44, 46; 25:19, 31, and parallel passages in Mark and Luke; John 14:3, 28; Rev. 1:7).

### *Heko*

This verb includes the idea of arrival. It may be translated "has come" without doing violence to its meaning. Matthew and Luke both use this term in telling how Jesus stressed the necessity of obedience and watchfulness while we await His return (Matt. 24:50; Luke 12:46). Although this discourse is in the form of a parable, He unquestionably had His own return in mind. In both of these passages the unexpectedness of His return is emphasized. The servants represent the Church. Hence Christ's return will be unexpected even by the Church. This is in direct contrast to the present day emphasis that Christ *must* come during this generation. He *may* come during this generation, but to say He *must* come in this generation is to miss the mark.

Three Greek verbs are used incidentally of Christ's return. *Analuo* implies a return. As we wait for the Lord's return (*analuo*), we are to keep ready to open to Him when He cometh (*erchomai*) (Luke 12:36). *Hupostrepho* is used once of Christ's return. In the parable of the ten pieces of money, Christ depicts Himself as a nobleman who "went into a far country to receive for Himself a kingdom, and to return" (Luke 19:12). Note that the kingdom was to be received while He was away from His servants. Christ's return is to settle accounts with His servants—not to receive or establish His kingdom. *Ephistimi* means "to come." We are warned to take heed lest that day, the day of Christ's return, "come upon you unawares" (Luke 21:34).

### Epiphaneia

This noun is used of Christ's first advent (II Tim. 1:10), as well as His second. In the KJV it is consistently translated "appearing" (which is its basic meaning), except in II Thessalonians 2:8 where it is translated "brightness." This is an interesting verse which will be discussed under the next term which is defined.

### Parousia

This word and those which follow have assumed special significance since the two-phase second coming has been accepted by a significant number of expositors. As long as a single return was taught, little distinction was made between the several words that were used of Christ's return; but with the advent of a teaching that claimed there would be two future comings of Christ, an effort was made to apply certain words to the meeting in the air, and others to that coming which would be visible to all men.

The noun *parousia* is the word most frequently used of the second coming. It implies actual presence, arrival, or advent. It is clearly used in contrast to Christ's first advent in Matthew 24:3. The question of the disciples about His future *parousia* implies a departure and a return, for at that time Christ's bodily presence was with them. Matthew's use of *parousia* in this text, plus its frequent use by Paul and other New Testament writers, probably contributed to the coining of the phrase *he deutera parousia*. This phrase became the accepted form of referring to Christ's return during the second Christian century.

*Parousia* is used of Christ's second coming in Matthew 24:37, 39; I Corinthians 15:23; I Thessalonians 2:19; 3:13; 4:15; 5:23; II Thessalonians 2:1, 8; James 5:7-8; II Peter 3:4; I John 2:29. Matthew 24:27 includes an indirect reference by Christ to His return. The major emphasis of this portion of Matthew 24 is on the destruction of Jerusalem and events leading up to it. False Christs would appear and seek to draw disciples after themselves. Jesus instructed them to ignore all such claims for His *parousia* would be so luminous that all would see it, even as lightning is visible as it flashes across the sky (Matt. 24:27).

Dispensationalists and others who attempt to make *parousia* refer to the rapture, as well as the true second coming, should consider these words of Jesus more seriously than they have. It is also worthy of note that the plural form of *parousia* is never used when the return of our Lord is intended. The idea of two returns is foreign to the way this term is used in the New Testament. This is reinforced by the fact that the definite article is consistently used with *parousia*. It is not thought of as "a coming of the Lord," but rather *the* coming of our Lord.

Of special interest is II Thessalonians 2:8 where *epiphaneia* is used with *parousia*. *Epiphaneia* can have no other meaning than the actual presence of the person involved. Its use with *parousia* strengthens the idea that *parousia* must also involve the actual, visible presence of Christ whenever it is used of Him. Our conclusion is that whenever *parousia* is used of Christ's return, it signifies a personal, visible, bodily return and presence of Jesus who ascended that way. The early Church certainly used it this way when they coined the phrase, *he deutera parousia* which is translated, "The Second Coming" of Christ.

### *Apokalupto (verb) - apokalupsis (noun).*

These words refer to an unveiling or the revealing of something previously hidden. The last book of the Bible is sometimes called the *Apocalypse* from the Greek term meaning Revelation. The term is used of revelations by dreams or subjective insights from the Spirit (Gal. 2:2). It is used of Christ's second coming in the sense that He is now hidden from our view, but when He comes again, He will be revealed, i.e., He will become visible. These words are used nine times in relation to the second coming and to conditions or events connected with that second coming. The KJV utilizes five different English words in translating these Greek terms. But regardless of the English word used, the idea of revealing or unveiling is essential to a correct understanding of the author's meaning.

Four of the nine instances refer to the revealing of Christ's glory, or the glory that we will receive at the resurrection (Rom. 8:18-19; I Pet. 4:13; 5:1). Although these can hardly be dissociated from the second coming, especially the two from I Peter, they will not be considered further. The other five refer to the second coming in ways that make it fitting to consider them more carefully. The first of these is Luke 17:30.

In the verses immediately preceding Luke 17:30 Jesus pointed out that life had continued in its customary fashion or manner right up to the time the flood began which resulted in the destruction of all humanity except Noah and his family. A similar statement is made about Lot and the destruction of Sodom by fire. Then Jesus adds, "Even thus shall it be in the day when the Son of man is revealed." The two points Jesus emphasizes are:

1. Life will continue as usual right up to the time of His revelation. There will he no drastic changes or series of unusual events to warn of that revelation. If this clashes with your interpretation of Matthew 24, please reserve judgment until you have read the two chapters which follow.

2. Christ's revelation will include, among other things, His divine judgment on evil men.

Both of the above points are contradictory to the Premillennial scheme of eschatology, especially the two-phrase theory. According to that view, the righteous are to be raptured away to heaven seven years prior to the revelation, and the wicked will not see Christ at that time. Hence, the rapture and the revelation are separated by seven years, they say. But such an unusual event could not escape the close scrutiny of the unsaved who were left behind. Also, the next seven years are not to be normal or usual years, they say. The Antichrist is to appear, three and one-half years of severe persecutions of the Jews will follow, saved Jews will be effective evangelists (note how unusual that would be), then comes the battle of Armageddon with its unusual features just prior to the revelation. Also, Premillennialists place the judgment of the wicked after the millennial reign, whereas Jesus places it at the revelation.

It is true that most Premillennialists claim that Christ will destroy the armies of the Antichrist at the time of Christ's revelation, but it is not possible to make the destruction of the antedeluvians and the Sodomites as analogous to that event. The only thing Jesus could have had in mind in drawing this comparison is the final judgment of the wicked. It is also worth noting that the statement of "the one being taken, and the other left" (vv. 35-36) is usually applied to the rapture by Premillennialists, but Jesus applies it to the revelation which most Premillennialists say will come seven years later. No twisting of meanings can reconcile the intent of this passage with the Premillennial order of events, especially the two-phase second coming concept.

The second passage tells the Corinthians to wait "for the coming [revealing] of our Lord Jesus Christ" (I Cor. 1:7). If the two-phase second coming is indeed correct, this admonition is ridiculous. According to that teaching, the rapture of the Church is the all important event. It contends that the Church will be with Christ in heaven for seven years preceding the revelation, and that they will already be with Christ at the time of His revelation. This makes the revelation of minor significance to the Church. No doubt Paul would have urged them to wait for the rapture, if the rapture is to come seven years before the revelation.

The third passage tells of a time "when the Lord Jesus shall be revealed from heaven with his mighty angels, in flaming fire taking vengeance on them that know not God, and that obey not the gospel of our Lord Jesus Christ" (I Thess. 1:7-8). Again the revelation is an event which results in God's judgment being poured out on the wicked. This is a judgment on the wicked in general—not just the armies of the Antichrist. Thus the Scripture ties the revelation of Christ to the final judgment, rather than to the setting up of an earthly kingdom.

Two passages from I Peter chapter 1 remain to be studied. Peter wrote of "honour and glory at the appearing [revelation] of Jesus Christ" (I Pet. 1:7), and of "the grace that is to be brought unto you at the revelation of Jesus Christ" (I Pet. 1:13). Thus the Church is to be glorified at the revelation—not at the rapture. The first three passages studied linked the judgment of the wicked with the revelation. These two link the glorification of the Church with the revelation. Most Premillennialists contradict this teaching of the

Bible by placing the glorification of the Church seven years prior to the revelation, and the judgment of the wicked 1,000 years after the revelation.

According to the two-phase second coming doctrine, I Thessalonians 4:13-18 refers to the rapture of the Church to heaven for a seven year marriage festival. But Paul affirms that the coming of the Lord that he has in mind is His *parousia*, and this involves His visible presence. Similar conditions exist about I Corinthians 15:23. This passage indicates that Christ is the firstfruits of the resurrection, then "afterward they that are Christ's at his coming" (*parousia*). But the two-phase coming has the righteous resurrected at the rapture, rather than at the second coming. This text cannot be harmonized with a rapture of the Church prior to His visible appearance or *parousia*.

In considering the attempted distinction between Christ coming "for His saints" and "with His saints" it is important for it to be understood that in the Greek the term "saints" (*hagioi*) is a generic term. It is a descriptive adjective that is used of a variety of nouns. We read of the holy covenant, holy ground, holy Scriptures, holy hands, holy city, holy place, holy thing, holy One, holy mount, holy nation, and holy kiss. These are not especially important to this study except to show the variety of things described by this adjective. The fact that is important is that *hagioi* is applied to angelic beings as well as to human beings in at least half a dozen texts.

The term used to describe angelic beings in Matthew 25:31, Mark 8:38, Luke 9:26, Acts 10:22, and Revelation 14:10. It is also used of John the Baptist (Mark 6:20), of women (I Pet. 3:5), of the brethren (Heb. 3:1), of the prophets (Luke 1:70, etc.), and of the apostles (Eph. 3:5). But the term is also used many times without the being or object it is modifying being specifically stated in the text. The most common translation of these passages is to use the noun "saints" for the adjective *hagioi*. This is acceptable as long as only human beings are indicated by the context, but it is hardly acceptable for passages in which angelic beings may be intended or included. This problem is evident in the translations of Jude 14. The KJV has "saints"; the NEB has "angels"; but most translations simply read "holy ones." The reader thus is left free to decide on men or angels or both.

Although other passages are involved in the argument, I Thessalonians 3:13 is probably the key passage. The latter part reads, "at the coming of our Lord Jesus Christ with all his saints." *Parousia* is the Greek word translated "coming." The adjective *hagioi* (saints) is without a noun to modify.

Hence, the translation should be "holy ones" or "holy beings." It could refer to holy angels, holy persons, or both. Which is meant cannot be determined by exegesis. It is strictly a matter of interpretation. Actually, this leaves the two-phase second comers without any solid basis for insisting that this text demands that Christ come "for His saints" before He can come "with His saints." These He comes "with" may just as well be angels as people.

I Thessalonians 4:13-18 is even more devastating to their position. It should be remembered that those who teach the two-phase second coming uniformly interpret this passage as pertaining to the coming "for His saints" rather than "with His saints." This coming is the *parousia* (v. 15) which refers to the actual presence of Christ. The latter part of verse 14 reads, "even so them also which sleep in Jesus will God bring with him." The meaning is that Christ will empty paradise of all its disembodied spirits, holy persons or saints, and bring them with Him when He comes (*parousia*).

Therefore, it is quite acceptable to say that at this coming, He is coming "with His saints." But at the same time it is evident that He is coming "for His saints" in the sense of resurrecting their bodies. Thus, at a single coming He comes with His saints, and also for His saints. This nullifies completely the argument that He cannot come with His saints until He has first come for His saints. This entire passage will be exegeted more fully in a later chapter.

## The Purpose of Christ's Second Coming

When Christ comes again He will have more than one objective in mind. First, He will come to take us to be with Him. This is the essence of His promise, "I will come again, and receive you unto myself: that where I am, there ye may be also" (John 14:3). Our abode in the home He has prepared for us will be permanent—not just a seven year marriage festival as some contend. Paul makes this clear by saying that after we meet Christ in the air, "so [or after this manner] shall we ever be with the Lord" (I Thess. 4:17). Thank God for this blessed hope!

Christ will also come to judge all men. Paul tells us, "We must all appear before the judgment seat of Christ" (II Cor. 5:10). That this involves both good and bad is evident from the remaining portion of the verse which reads, "That every one [i.e., all men both good and bad] may receive the things done in the body, according to that he hath done, whether it be good or bad." Do not be fooled by the use of Romans 14:10 in the place of II Corinthians 5:10. The same word is used in both texts (*bema*), but the fact that all men appear there is more plain in the Corinthian passage. This could be the reason Tan uses Romans 14:10, but for some reason neglects to mention II Corinthians 5:10.[188] Other passages on the judgment will be discussed elsewhere.

The two purposes already given imply a resurrection of the dead. The judgment also implies that awards and penalties will be meted out to both good and evil. Just as the reward of the righteous is endless bliss, the punishment of the wicked is unending banishment from the presence of the Lord. And, of course, Christ's advent will be the consummation in a very real sense. It will bring to an end the world order under which we now exist. (See subsequent chapters for more detailed discussion.)

## The Manner of Christ's Coming

The two heavenly messengers indicated that Christ would return "in like manner as ye have seen him go into heaven" (Acts 1:11). The manner of His going included at least three features. His going was bodily, personally, and visibly. This third feature of visibility is a source of embarrassment to the two-phase advocates. The reason for this is their teaching that at the rapture, Christ will not be visible to the general populace. For this reason they must apply Acts 1:11 to the second phase of the second coming, and they are hard put to furnish an adequate explanation.

It is interesting to note that Luke uses the more common word for "coming" (*erchomai*). Had he used one of those more specialized words which denote actual presence as *heko* or *parousia* or words that imply visibility such as *apokalupsis* or *epiphaneia*, then their argument would be stronger; but Luke was led to use the term for "coming" that is most readily applied to an invisible type of coming. Surely, if two future comings are to occur, the Holy Spirit would have given us more specific data regarding it. But these messengers mentioned but one coming, and it is to be a visible coming.

Jesus indicated His visibility at His coming (*parousia*) by comparing it to lightning which flashes from the eastern sky to the western sky (Matt. 24:27). The Revelator indicates that "Every eye shall see him" (Rev. 1:7). The fact that He will function as a judge, and that He will divide people into two groups certainly implies visibility (Matt. 25).

---

188 Tan, *op. cit.*, p. 337.

And it will be "this same Jesus" who would return (Acts 1:11). It will not be a different Jesus. It will be the same one they saw go away. This must include His immortal body which had been resurrected from the tomb. In order to be the same Jesus, He must have the same body, and body tends to imply visibility. In turn visibility implies body. Paul also informs us that it will be "Jesus himself" who will come for us (I Thess. 4:16) to ever be with the Lord (v. 17).

In spite of the similarities of His going to His coming, there will be some differences. He left as our Saviour. He will return as our Judge. He left alone. He will return with the disembodied souls of the righteous dead to be reunited with their resurrected bodies (I Thess. 4:14). He left with death only partially conquered through His own resurrection. At His return death will be annihilated. He left only partially triumphant. He will be fully and completely triumphant at His return. At His ascension His humanity still veiled His deity to some extent. On His return His deity will be evident to all. At His departure only a small group accepted His lordship. On His return He will be acclaimed by millions. His leaving was an historical event. His return will bring an end to the history, and time, as we know it, will be replaced by eternity.[189]

## The Time of Christ's Coming

The aspect of Christ's coming mentioned most frequently in the New Testament is that He will come quickly, suddenly, unexpectedly, and without any additional warning beyond the command to watch. This statement is sure to be challenged by those who claim that Jesus gave very definite signs by which we could know that His coming was soon to become a reality. The so-called signs of His coming will be considered in the chapters on the Olivet discourse. A this juncture we simply point out that if definite signs were given, then the several texts in that discourse which indicate that He will come unexpectedly become meaningless if not an outright contradiction of the signs.

Consider the emphasis on the unexpectedness of Christ's return within the Olivet discourse itself. After answering the disciples' question about the destruction of the temple (Mark 13:1-30), Mark quotes Jesus in regard to His second coming—

---

[189] The unexpectedness of Christ's coming would be appropriate under either The Manner or The Time Of His Coming. I chose the latter.

> But of that day and that hour knoweth no man, no, not the angels which are in heaven, neither the Son, but the Father. Take heed, watch and pray: for ye know not when the time is...Watch ye therefore: for ye know not when the Master of the house cometh, at even, or at midnight, or at the cockcrowing, or in the morning: Lest coming suddenly he find you sleeping. And what I say unto you I say unto all, Watch (Mark 13:32-33, 35-37).

The time of Christ's coming is the most carefully kept secret of the ages. The Father reserved this knowledge unto Himself alone. Men, angels, and even the Son during His incarnation were not permitted to have information on this event. The word "time" of verse 33 of the above quotation is from the Greek *kairos*. It can refer to any marked off period of time, regardless of its length. Note how Mark uses it in the following: "But he shall receive an hundredfold now in this time [i.e., in this age or this life]...and in the world to come eternal life" (Mark 10:30). Therefore, it is not improper to say that we cannot know what age or what generation Christ will come.

It is true that exegesis does not demand that verse 33 refer to this age or a generation, but since it could have this meaning, one should be cautious about setting even a century in which Christ will come. So many have been proved wrong in the past that only a rash person would do it. But Lindsey deduces that "within forty years or so of 1948, all these things could take place."[190] Elsewhere he says they must take place while there are persons living who were born prior to the creation of modern Israel in 1948. Mark 13 and other passages like it prove Lindsey and those who follow him to be false prophets.

The "these things" of the above quotation from Hal Lindsey includes the rapture, the reign of the Antichrist, the great tribulation, and the battle of Armageddon. These events cover a seven year period, according to Lindsey, and many others. Only after "these things" have come to pass can the second coming occur, so they say, and seven years from the rapture the second coming must occur. But if this be true, it is not the second coming that will come suddenly or unexpectedly; it is the rapture. If all one has to do is count seven years from the rapture to pinpoint the second coming, the time of the second coming would become common knowledge to saint and sinner alike. This is not the picture painted by the Bible. The Bible says the second coming, not the rapture, will come unexpectedly. Of course, if the

---

190 Lindsey, *op. cit.*, p. 54.

rapture and the second coming are but aspects of a single return, as Amillennialists generally accept, the problems created by the two-phase second coming concept simply cease to exist.

The suddenness or unexpectedness of Christ's second coming is stressed in Mark 13:36. The Greek term used means suddenly, unexpectedly or without warning. Luke is the only other New Testament writer to use it. He uses it of the angels appearing to the shepherds to announce the birth of Christ. Certainly, this was an unexpected event—one that came without any warning signs (Luke 2:13). Twice Luke uses it of the light which appeared unto Saul (Paul) on the Damascus road (Acts 9:3; 22:6). This event surely caught Paul and every one else by surprise. No warning signs of any kind were given.

Even in the same chapter in which it is claimed that Matthew lists a number of signs (Matt. 24), strong indications are given to the contrary. Only the Father knows when the return will occur (Matt. 24:36). We have no knowledge of the hour "our Lord doth come" (Matt. 24:42). Christ affirmed that His coming would be "in such an hour as ye think not" (Matt. 24:44). Does this not also mean in such an hour as Mr. Lindsey thinks not? Jesus adds, "The Lord of that servant shall come in a day when he looketh not for him, and in an hour that he is not aware of" (Matt. 24:50). The sudden, unexpected, and without warning aspect of Christ's coming is inherent in the seven passages in which His coming is compared to that of a thief. Thieves give no warning of their coming.

## The Certainty of Christ's Coming

The fact that Christ is depicted as coming in more ways than in *he deutera parousia* (the second coming) should not lead one to question the certainty of His coming again. The many clear references to a personal, visible, bodily coming or presence make it an important aspect of divine revelation. The fact that these references are scattered throughout the New Testament adds strength to the certitude of Christ coming again.

That at least eight different Greek words are used in relation to the second coming also strengthens the case for a return. Six of the eight words used can hardly mean anything else than a real return, at least in the contexts where they are found. The many casual or indirect references to the second coming contribute much to the certainty of His coming. Even though the time of His coming is uncertain, the fact of His coming is free of any doubt.

## Living in Expectation of That Coming

Christ's repeated command that we watch implies a period of waiting. While we wait, we are enjoined to watch. Waiting is frustrating unless one is busy. Therefore, it is imperative that we keep busy about the Lord's work. To watch does not mean to peer with the eyes or with binoculars. Nor should we go out on a mountain side the better to see Him when He does appear. He calls that servant "faithful and wise" as well as blessed who would be found performing those tasks assigned to him (Matt. 24:45-46). Has God called you to preach, visit the sick, teach, or do personal work, then see that you zealously work at that calling year in and year out. Sporadic effort is not adequate. Our major concern should be with faithful performance, rather than worrying about just when He will come.

In the great commission (Matt. 28:19-20), evangelism is Christ's imperative to the Church. In the KJV the emphasis appears to be on the going, but in the Greek text the going, the baptizing, and the teaching are all participles. The important finite verb is *matheteusate* which means to make disciples or simply to disciple all nations. This verb is in the imperative mood. It is a command. Christians who maintain the correct attitude towards the second coming will by one means or another be busy winning souls for Christ.

Dr. Ray Summers, in emphasizing this point, wrote—

"One of the greatest needs of our day is that of genuine piety. Not an assumed, artificial, or superficial piety, but genuine goodness which the living Christ would produce in men."[191] Men who profess the name of Christ, but who "in works deny him" (Titus 1:16) are unworthy of the name they profess. This type of Christian (?) cannot do effective work in the field of evangelism. Actually, they are a hindrance.

John in writing of that blessed hope of Christ's second coming and what a realization of that hope would mean to the Christian declared, "And every man that hath this hope in him purifieth himself, even as he is pure" (I John 3:3). Persons living impure lives may claim to have that hope, but John plainly states that they do not in fact possess that hope.

Peter, writing of the dissolution of all things at the consummation, warned that these truths proved the need for "holy conversation and godliness" (II Pet. 3:11). Now, various texts of the Bible demand uncorruptness of speech,

---

191 Ray Summers, *The Life Beyond*, p. 139.

and this text is one of them; but Peter did not stop at pure speech. The Greek word translated "conversation" refers to one's manner or pattern of life. Our conduct in its totality is meant. We must be holy in all of our relationships and activities of life. Only by diligent and earnest effort on our part "may we be found of him in peace, without spot, and blameless" at His coming (II Pet. 3:14). The Greek term implies energetic effort, but it must be more than human energy. Spiritual forces of faith, commitment, adherence to the Bible's standard of conduct, and reliance on God and His power will enable one to measure to this standard.

This watchful waiting demands patience. The sentry or guard may be less alert in the wee hours of the morning than he was at the beginning of his watch. Jesus warned against lassitude in our watch for His return. In the New Testament patience usually refers to the need to stand firm against such pressures as doubt, temptation, sorrow and opposition. Paul informs us that these pressures, if resisted, "worketh patience; And patience, experience: and experience, hope" (Rom. 5:3-4). He who is deficient in patience (endurance) is also deficient in hope.

## The Early Church on the Second Coming

The early Church writers are agreed that there will be a second coming of Christ. Not one questions the certainty of that event. No witnesses were found who doubted the validity of the Christian hope. Some disagreement existed regarding certain details of His coming and of events connected with that coming, but none questioned that Christ would come again some day. It is worthy to note that the two-phase second coming (the rapture of the Church, then seven years later the revelation or unveiling of Christ) has absolutely no support from any of the Church fathers. If that doctrine has any validity, it is very strange that the Church knew nothing about it for eighteen centuries. Darby and his associates were first to propagate it in the nineteenth century.

## Concluding Remarks

Christ will return. The New Testament is replete with emphatic statements which cannot be questioned. The time of His coming is uncertain in spite of voices to the contrary. The fact of His coming is as certain as though it had already occurred.

CHAPTER 14

# THE OLIVET DISCOURSE

Few portions of Scripture have been divided and subdivided into mere fragments, then reconstructed to suit the views of the various persons doing the segmenting, as is true of this passage. The hodge-podge which often results makes it appear that Jesus spoke in a wandering, erratic manner such as a confused person might use. But Jesus was not confused, and if we will but utilize the keys inspiration has made available to us, it is not necessary for us to be confused. These keys make the discourse orderly and logical in its development, and they dispel the smog that has hindered our vision for many years.

These keys are five in number. The first of these is what Kik has designated the "time-text" of this discourse.[192] It is his contention that the expression of Jesus to the effect that "This generation shall not pass away, till all these things be accomplished" (Matt. 24:34; Mark 13:30; Luke 21:32) should be taken in its obvious sense. Its obvious sense is twofold. First, it means that some people then living would still be living when the things he had talked about thus far were fully accomplished. This points to A.D. 70 as the time of fulfillment. Secondly, it divides the discourse into two divisions. Up to that point He had discussed the destruction of the temple. From that point onward He discussed matters of a different nature.

The second key supports the above conclusions. In listing the questions asked by the disciples (Matt. 24:3; Mark 13:4; Luke 21:7) only Matthew mentions the second coming and the end of the world. The obvious significance of Mark and Luke failing to mention these questions which involve the consummation is that the main thrust of what they wrote had to do with the destruction of Jerusalem, and very little they wrote should be taken as

---

192 Marcellus Kik, *Matthew Twenty-Four*, p. 9.

referring to eschatological events. But when Mark and Luke are compared with Matthew, most of what commentators often apply to future events in Matthew 24:4-33 is also found in Mark or Luke or both. In this way, Mark and Luke support the thesis that the so-called signs (?) of the end of the age are to appear before the destruction of Jerusalem, and have no connection with the consummation.

The third key is the nature of apocalyptic language. In the chapters on hermeneutics it was shown that the Old Testament prophets used expressions regarding the stars falling or being darkened, and the sun and moon failing to give their light (Isa. 13; Ezek. 32:7-8) as terms referring to the destruction of such nations as Babylon and Egypt. Similarly, these terms in Matthew 24 should not be taken literally. Just as Isaiah and Ezekiel used such expressions to refer to destructions of heathen nations, Christ uses them here to refer to the destruction of the Jewish nation in A.D. 70.

The fourth key is the fact that all three Synopticists follow the "time-text" with an affirmation of the certainty of the prophecies Jesus had just made being fulfilled in due time. The statement, "Heaven and earth shall pass away: but my words shall not pass away" (Matt. 24:35; Mark 13:31; Luke 21:33) serves as a connecting sentence between the first portion of the discourse which spoke of the destruction of Jerusalem, and the second part which deals with the consummation.

The fifth key is the fact that all three accounts move from that which pertains to the destruction of Jerusalem to that which involves the second coming. Matthew and Mark make the contrast very emphatic. Both show a definite change of content by the use of the adversative *de* which is translated "But." "But of that day," i.e., the day of the return of Christ and the end of the world, He said was known only to the Father (Matt. 24:36; Mark 13:32). Luke is not so clear, but he, too, wrote of the need to watch, lest "that day" come on them unawares.

It should be further noted that Mark and Luke have very little to say about this new subject. This fits in with the fact that they did not list any questions about last things as matters being discussed. It was Matthew only who listed eschatological questions, and he is the only one of the three who deals with such matters in detail. Matthew discusses these questions at some length in the remainder of chapter 24 and on through chapter 25.

## Matthew 24:3-14; Mark 13:3-13; Luke 21:7-19

Most commentators have tended to take Matthew as the basic account, then, on the basis of interpretations made of Matthew, they have tended to force Mark and Luke to fit into their interpretations. The fact that Mark and Luke are in agreement on the major questions the disciples asked Jesus demands that their accounts take precedence over Matthew's. This is not to say that Matthew recorded questions which were not asked. A proper view of inspiration makes such an explanation absolutely unacceptable. But the fact that Mark and Luke fail to record some of the questions given by Matthew should show their emphasis or point of importance was the destruction of Jerusalem, instead of matters pertaining to the consummation. A comparison of the questions asked is very revealing.

> And as he sat upon the mount of Olives over against the temple, Peter and James and John and Andrew asked him privately, Tell us, when shall these things be? and what shall be the sign when all these things shall be fulfilled? (Mark 13:3-4)

> And they asked him, saying, Master, but when shall these things be? and what sign will there be when these things shall come to pass? (Luke 21:7)

> And as he sat upon the mount of Olives, the disciples came unto him privately, saying, Tell us, when shall these things be? and what shall be the sign of thy coming, and of the end of the world? (Matt. 24:3)

A review of the verses immediately preceding the above material indicates that the disciples had with a sense of pride asked Jesus to observe carefully the large and ornate buildings generally known as Herod's temple. Jesus had responded to this by informing them that at some future date these buildings would be completely destroyed. Jesus used the Greek term *tauta* in all three accounts. This expression is translated "these things" in Matthew and Luke. Mark supplies the objects to which the demonstrative pronoun refers, "great buildings," hence his account reads "these great buildings" instead of "these things." There is no room for argument about the subject matter thus far. It had to do with Herod's temple, and its future destruction.

An analysis of the verses quoted above shows that the disciples, according to all three accounts, utilized the same expression "these things" in their questioning of Jesus. The first question, according to all three accounts, is "when shall these things be?" The thing uppermost in their minds was the question of when would Herod's temple be destroyed. The second question asked for a sign, according to all three accounts. Mark and Luke agree that the disciples asked for a sign when "these things" would come to pass or be fulfilled. Both of these writers still place the main question on the destruction of Herod's temple. We are on solid ground, then, when we say that the signs found in Mark and Luke are signs of the destruction of Jerusalem and the temple, rather than signs of the second coming of Christ. Sound exegesis demands that we accept the import of each author's own statements.

Matthew adds the questions regarding signs of Christ's *parousia* or second coming, and of the end of the world. And Matthew discusses those matters in Matthew 24:36 and onward. It does violence to the total picture to insist that Matthew deals with last things in the first 35 verses of Matthew 24. If the five keys already given are properly used, it will eliminate the mutilation and patchwork reconstruction frequently performed on Matthew 24.

The conclusions an author reaches are important keys to understanding what he is trying to say. We have already shown how the "time-text" (Matt. 24:34: Mark 13:30; Luke 21:32) is a concluding statement that places all which had been said up to that point as referring to the destruction of Herod's temple. But it is not the only statement that is helpful in this way. Matthew 24:13-14, Mark 13:13, Luke 21:18 constitute a halfway or intermediate conclusion which strongly supports the division we are making of this account. I have particular reference to the identical statement by Matthew and Mark: "But he that shall endure unto the end, the same shall be saved."

The force of this statement can only be recognized by comparing all three accounts. Since Matthew listed questions regarding last things, it would not be wild speculation to consider this a reference to the end of the world. But Mark did not insert these questions found in Matthew. We conclude that Mark refers this to the destruction of the temple and the whole Jewish commonwealth as "the end" under consideration. And if that is what Mark meant, it is also what Matthew meant, for the two accounts are parallel. This interpretation is further strengthened by Luke's account. Like Mark, he did not say he was discussing questions related to the second coming. His questions and answers referred to the destruction of the temple and signs of when that event would occur.

At the point in the discourse where Matthew and Mark write about enduring to the end, Luke says, "But there shall not an hair of your head perish" (Luke 21:18). It should not even be necessary to point out that this refers to physical deliverance. And if Luke refers to deliverance from the sufferings others endured during and after the siege of Jerusalem, then so does Matthew and Mark. Thus the "end" in those statements regarding the end in Matthew 24 and Mark 13 refers to the end of the Jewish commonwealth and the destruction of Jerusalem. The time of the deliverance was, of course, prior to the destruction of Jerusalem in A.D. 70. Christians did flee to Pella and freedom in accordance with Jesus' instructions to them in the Olivet discourse.

Having shown that Matthew 24:14, Luke 21:18 and Mark 13:13 refer to the end of the Jewish nation, and not to the end of the world, it is logical to assume that what Jesus had said in the verses immediately preceding those listed above are related to the destruction of Jerusalem and the Jewish state. We conclude, therefore, that the signs, if indeed they are signs, are signs of the desolation of Jerusalem, rather than of the second coming of Christ.

In the verses presently being considered, all three accounts tell of false Christs, wars, earthquakes, pestilences, and persecutions. But since Mark and Luke address their remarks to questions relating to the destruction of Jerusalem and the signs which would precede it, an interpretation that started with Mark and Luke instead of Matthew would naturally conclude that these things were of events related to the destruction of Jerusalem, rather than the second coming. And although Matthew's perspective is broader than that of Mark and Luke, these events are parallel to those of Mark and Luke, hence must be interpreted as parallel. To do otherwise violates rules of biblical interpretation.

There is general agreement that most of the events listed in the three accounts did occur prior to A.D. 70, but questions are raised regarding two statements of Jesus. The first of these reads, "For many shall come in my name, saying, I am Christ; and shall deceive many" (Matt. 24:5). It is claimed that no one actually claimed to be the returned Jesus of Nazareth who was called Christ until after A.D. 70. But it is questionable whether Jesus meant that. For one to come in His name implies a separate personality. Jesus spoke of His disciples meeting "in my name," doing miracles "in my name," and giving a cup of water "in my name" (Matt. 18:20; Mark 16:17; 9:41). When we preach the gospel, we do so "in his name" (Luke 24:47), according to the words of Jesus.

We conclude that when Jesus said, "For many shall come in my name," He meant that they claimed to be ambassadors sent by Him, rather than that they claimed to be Jesus in person. To harmonize this conclusion with the statement that these would say, "I am Christ," requires that we consider the meaning of Christ (*Christos* in the Greek). It simply means "anointed." Jesus' words mean no more than that they claimed to be anointed of God. This claim was necessarily false, as was their claim of truly coming in the name of Christ, i.e., as His representatives. The expression "false Christs, and false prophets" (Matt. 24:24) incorporates these two ideas. Their claim of being anointed of God was false, and their claim of being spokesmen (prophets) of God was also false.

The other point of contention is, "And this gospel of the kingdom shall be preached in all the world for a witness unto all nations; and then shall the end come" (Matt. 24:14). What is the end Jesus had in mind when He said this? It has already been shown that "the end" in the preceding verse referred to the end of the Jewish state. There is no reason to hold that this verse has any other meaning. And when Mark is considered this becomes a certainty. Mark quotes Jesus as saying, "And the gospel must first be published among all nations" (Mark 13:10). Since Mark addressed his remarks to questions about the destruction of Jerusalem, it is evident that this was to precede that end. The end Mark had in mind was *not* the end of the world. The statement in Matthew is, of course, parallel to that of Mark.

But was the gospel preached to the extent indicated before A.D. 70? First, it should he noted that it does not say that every nation shall be fully evangelized before the end comes. Only a limited hearing is indicated. Only a few in each nation had to hear it as a "witness" to each nation. This did occur without question prior to A.D. 70. Luke tells us that "devout men, out of every nation under heaven" (Acts 2:5) dwelt in Jerusalem at the time of the first Christian Pentecost. These evidently heard the gospel on that day. This alone is a fulfillment of Jesus' words. But much more can be said.

That the gospel spread over much of the known world of that day is told in the Acts of the Apostles. Samaria, Syria, Asia Minor, Macedonia, Italy, and portions of Africa are clearly shown to have received the gospel before

A.D. 70. Other sources indicate that Thomas carried the gospel as far east as India, and that Paul may have preached as far west as Spain and the British Isles. This is not absolute proof that the preaching mentioned in Matthew 24:14 was fulfilled before A.D. 70, but it definitely supports that view. And with the further biblical evidence that can be introduced, it does reach a point which, at least to this writer, is conclusive.

Our first task is to determine the meaning of the expression "to all the world." This author agrees with Murray that it refers to the Roman empire of the first Christian century. He writes,

> Many people have the impression that this applies to the modern world, and that Christ cannot come again until the gospel has been preached to the (modern) world. Let us inquire as to what He meant and what His disciples understood by these words of His. It can be proved beyond contradiction that to the disciples of Jesus Christ the world was simply the Roman Empire.[193]

Murray uses the following texts in support of his position. In Luke 2:1-3 Caesar Augustus issued a decree that "all the world should be taxed." "All the world" in this passage can have but one meaning—the Roman empire. The same writer in Acts 2:5 states that "devout men, out of every nation under heaven" were in Jerusalem on the day of Pentecost. There are nations now existing who did not hear the gospel on that day, but all the nations of that generation did hear it. Then in Romans 1:8, Paul affirms that the faith of the Roman congregation was "spoken of throughout the whole world." Is not this "the whole world" the same "whole world" that Jesus mentioned in Matthew 24:14?

Other passages of Scripture which teach that the gospel did go to "all the world" of the first Christian century are found in Paul's letter to the Colossians. Paul indicated that the same "word of truth" which they had heard, had come into "all the world" as it had unto them (Col. 1:6). Further down in this same chapter Paul affirms in no uncertain terms that the "gospel which ye have heard" was also "preached to every creature which is under heaven" (v. 23). These texts are so plain and comprehensive that it is possible to claim with every assurance of accuracy that Matthew 24:14 has already been fulfilled. The burden of proof that it has any reference to the second coming rests upon those who propagate that teaching.

---

193 Geo. L. Murray, *Millennial Studies*, pp. 113-114.

Of course, some hold to a dual fulfillment. These accept the fact that Matthew 24:14 was fulfilled prior to A.D. 70, but they attach a future fulfillment to it. But if this is done, it changes the meaning of "the end" that was to come. Jesus meant the end of the Jewish nation, as has been shown, not the end of the world.

The question of whether the events to come which are given in these verses are to be taken as signs has been raised already, but a closer look is needed. If the events mentioned in the verses being considered are signs of anything, they are signs of the destruction of Jerusalem. But most of these are natural phenomena or recurring types of events, such as wars, which by their very nature are not signs. Wars, famines, and earthquakes can no more be signs of something, than the setting of the sun or the change of seasons could constitute a sign. Kik takes issue with those who teach that national and international calamities are decisive proof that the world is near its end. The Lord teaches that these signs did not even indicate the near end of Jerusalem. As He states: "But the end is not yet." Hence the disciples were not to be troubled by these things.[194]

Meserve points out that Jesus did not give a single sign of the second coming, and that those who claim such things as wars and rumors of wars are signs of the coming of Christ are using these terms "in exactly the opposite meaning than that which the Lord intended."[195] For an event to be a sign, it must be distinctive. Events such as wars, famines. pestilences, and earthquakes have been common occurrences throughout human history. By their frequency, they lack the essential nature of a sign. And, as Kik points out, after listing these events Jesus told them these things were not signs, for "the end is not yet." Jesus is saying in effect that these are not signs of the end of Jerusalem, or of any other end.

We conclude that the only event in the verses now being considered that can be called a sign is that found in Matthew 24:14. This verse indicates that something would come to an end after the gospel had been proclaimed to all nations. It has been shown already that this "end" is the end of the Jewish state and the Jewish sacrificial system. Kik calls this "the approximate sign of the end of Jerusalem."[196] This statement by Jesus is too indefinite for it to

---

194 Kik, *op. cit.*, p. 36.
195 Albert Dallas Meserve, *The Olivet Discourse*, p. 21.
196 Kik, *op. cit.*, p. 41.

constitute an unequivocal time signal. Nor does it have any relation to the second coming of Christ. It certainly is not a sign of that event.

## Matthew 24:15-22; Mark 13:14-20; Luke 21:20-24

That some of the above refers to the destruction of Jerusalem is recognized by all commentators, but from that point onward confusion prevails. One says these passages refer to the destruction of Jerusalem as the immediate fulfillment, but that a future fulfillment is also indicated. Another contends that Matthew and Mark write of the second coming, and that only Luke writes of the destruction of Jerusalem. Biederwolf lists 28 commentators who refer these verses to the destruction of Jerusalem in A.D. 70. He considers this as "perhaps the great majority of commentators." He includes most of the fathers of the early Church in this category.[197] But if the mass of recent Premillennial writers is included, that majority may have diminished into a minority.

In the portions now being considered, we move from the sign which was an approximate sign of the destruction of Jerusalem to the real sign—the sign that was to serve as a warning to the Church that they should hasten to get outside the city while opportunity to do so was unrestricted. Thus we move from that which gave a hazy sense of the time element to a very definite statement of the time. But the time of what? The answer to that question has traditionally been that of the destruction of Jerusalem by Titus in A.D. 70; but in recent years an explanation has become widely accepted that contradicts the older interpretation.

Many Premillennialists now claim that only Luke refers to the destruction of Jerusalem.[198] This violates the rule of how parallel passages should be interpreted. When similar statements are made in passages that are parallel, the rules of hermeneutics demand that these passages be interpreted as having the same meaning. The claim that Luke refers to A.D. 70, and that Matthew and Mark refer to what they term "the great tribulation" of the future is unacceptable. Tan avoids the basic issue by failing to quote Mark. By ignoring Mark's account, he proposes an explanation that would have some merit were these two the only accounts of the Olivet discourse, but when Mark is considered, his seeming harmony strikes a very discordant note. This will be explained as our study progresses.

---

197 Biederwolf, *op. cit.*, p. 332.
198 Tan, *op. cit.*, p. 348.

Luke furnishes us with a plain statement regarding the time element. He says, "And when ye shall see Jerusalem compassed with armies, then know that the desolation thereof is nigh. Then let them which are in Judaea flee to the mountains" (Luke 21:20-21). He follows with instructions and comments which are almost identical to those found in Matthew and Mark. Now, it is a rule of hermeneutics that plain passages take precedence over passages that may be subject to more than one explanation or which lack clarity for any reason. For this reason, we take Luke's account as the basic text regarding the time of which Jesus spoke.

In the following quotations the reader should note the relation of the command to flee to the mountains to that which precedes it, and compare this with Luke's statement given above.

When ye therefore shall see the abomination of desolation, spoken of by Daniel the prophet, stand in the holy place. (whoso readeth, let him understand:) Then let them which be in Judaea flee into the mountains. (Matt. 24:15-16).

But when ye shall see the abomination of desolation, spoken of by Daniel the prophet, standing where it ought not, (let him that readeth understand,) then let them that be in Judaea flee to the mountains (Mark 13:14).

The command to flee to the mountains is certainly parallel in all three accounts. The statements which follow are so similar that no question of them being parallel should be raised. It follows, then, that the "abomination of desolation, spoken of by Daniel the prophet" as given in Matthew and Mark is parallel to, or has the same meaning as, Jerusalem being surrounded by armies according to Luke. Thus, if we permit the Bible to interpret itself, then the Roman legions which did surround Jerusalem do in fact constitute the abomination of desolation Jesus had in mind. Those who wish to have this confirmed are invited to study those commentaries which discuss how the Roman eagle as an ensign, and other arguments, make the Roman army a fit object of the appellation of the "abomination of desolation." It did make desolate the city of Jerusalem. But for myself, I simply accept Luke's statement as an explanation of what the abomination really was.

Apart from Luke's explanation, the question of the "the abomination of desolation, spoken of by Daniel the prophet" is a very debatable matter. The problem is twofold. First, Daniel mentions an abomination of desolation in three different places, and the interpretations given these three vary from commentator to commentator. If interpretation of Daniel is the basis for interpreting Matthew 24:15 and Mark 13:14, then a consensus of opinion is impossible; for the opinions regarding Daniel are such that any substantial change is not likely to occur apart from a complete revolution in one's concept of last things.

Of the three statements in Daniel, there is a reasonable amount of agreement that the reference in Daniel 11:31 is to Antiochus Epiphanes. But the gap is great on the other two. The abomination of desolation in Daniel 9:27 is referred to the future Antichrist by most Premillennialists. Most other commentators take it to refer to the destruction of Jerusalem in A.D. 70. The major point of conflict is over whether the 70 weeks of Daniel 9:24 run consecutively, or whether the seventieth week is yet future. In spite of the illogicality of the claim that the seventieth week is yet to come, many able expositors hold to this interpretation. The third reference is in Daniel 12:11. This is said to refer to Antiochus Epiphanes directly, or to him directly but to the future Antichrist indirectly, or to the future Antichrist as the primary object of the prophecy.

Those who understand Daniel 9:27 and 12:11 to refer to a future Antichrist generally interpret Matthew 24:15 as referring to this expected personage also. But how they harmonize this with what Mark and Luke have to say varies form person to person. The more common method is to accept Matthew and Mark as parallels at this point. Both are said to refer to the expected "great tribulation" during the expected reign of him who is called Antichrist. Of course, when this is done, they have to force Mark to be commenting on things he did not say he was mentioning. Mark and Luke preface their remarks with questions relating to the destruction of the temple then standing. Unless it can be proved that they discussed other areas, it should be assumed that they confined themselves to these questions. And Luke who is parallel with Mark regarding the questions being considered, explains this point by mentioning the Roman armies, rather than the abomination of desolation. But this means that the Roman armies and the abomination of desolation are one and the same thing. For this reason, Matthew's use of the abomination of desolation must also refer to the Roman army of A.D. 70.

Tan evades this problem by failing to discuss Mark. He writes, "The answer to the disciples' first question [regarding the destruction of the temple] is given in Luke 21:20-24. The disciples' second question [regarding last things] is covered by Matthew 24."[199] Again we take issue with this arbitrary switching of the meanings in parallel accounts, but especially for his failure to consider Mark's account. Mark phrases his questions just like Luke, but his discussion utilizes the expression "abomination of desolation" just as Matthew does. When Mark is considered, there is no way of avoiding the conclusion that the verses under consideration in all three accounts refer to the destruction of Jerusalem in A. D. 70 and to that alone.

This switching of parallel passages is very tricky. Unless you see the total picture, the piecemeal tactics used may fool you, just as sleight of hand artists fool us. Tan, for example, admits that Luke 21:20-24 refers to A.D. 70, then he makes the assertion that Matthew 24:20 refers to a future time in which the old Sabbath day laws would be revived and enforced. A comparison of Matthews account and that of Luke at this point is quite interesting.

Then let them which be in Judaea flee into the mountains; Let him which is on the housetop not come down to take any thing out of his house: Neither let him which is in the field return to take his clothes. And woe unto them that are with child, and to them that give suck in those days (Matt. 24:16-19).

Then let them which are in Judaea flee to the mountains; and let them which are in the midst of it depart out; and let not them that are in the countries enter thereinto. For these be the days of vengeance, that all things which are written may be fulfilled. But woe unto them that are with child, and to them that give suck in those days! for there shall he great distress in the land, and wrath upon this people (Luke 21:21-23).

It is doubtful if any fair minded person reading the above accounts for the first time would conclude that they were about two separate and distinct events. There are too many points of agreement for this. Both tell of the need for haste in fleeing to the mountains, and both point out the distress which mothers of young children and expectant mothers would endure. And when it is remembered that both are recounting the same conversation between Christ and some of His disciples, it seems sheer folly to claim that these two accounts refer to two different times and occasions. But various writers present this view in all sincerity (see Scofield's notes on Matt. 24:3, 16).

Following the verses quoted above, Matthew includes a statement not found in Luke. It reads, "But pray ye that your flight be not in the winter,

---

199 *Ibid.*, p. 348.

# The Olivet Discourse 249

neither on the sabbath day" (Matt. 24:20). Such differences are common and should not be taken to indicate any real distinctions in the accounts. Mark has the remark about the winter, but does not mention the Sabbath day. The similarities show all three evangelists are talking about the same event or events in the verses being considered.

But Tan makes a great deal out of Matthew 24:20. He states,—

> In the New Testament, Christ Himself certainly foresees the reinstitution of Jewish ritualism when He urges tribulation saints to "pray that your flight be not in the winter, neither on the sabbath day" (Matt. 24:20), for Jewish ritualistic travel regulations would hinder escape on the Sabbath.[200]

Has Tan or anyone else proved that Matthew 24:20 refers to tribulation saints, rather than to the flight to Pella following its encirclement by the Roman legions under Titus? The answer is a positive no. Such cannot be done, for these verses have been shown to be parallel. Not only were the verses immediately preceding Matthew 24:20 parallel in all three accounts, but all three indicate great distress will occur at that time. The wording differs, but the meaning is the same. The three accounts read as follows:

> For then shall be great tribulation, such as was not since the beginning of the world to this time, no, nor ever shall be (Matt. 24:21).

> For in those days shall be affliction, such as was not from the beginning of the creation, which God created unto this time, neither shall be (Mark 13:19).

> For there shall be great distress in the land, and upon this people. And they shall fall by the edge of the sword, and shall be led away captive into all nations: and Jerusalem shall be trodden down of the Gentiles, until the times of the Gentiles be fulfilled (Luke 21:23-24).

It should be evident that these passages are parallels in spite of certain differences that can be noted. Matthew and Mark are more closely parallel than these are with Luke, but Mark and Luke are more closely parallel regarding the questions under consideration. All three mention the tribulation, affliction, or great distress that was to come upon these people. Mark and Matthew use the same Greek word (*thlipsis*) for this distress. Mark uses *anagke*, but the meaning is the same. All the imported arguments cannot

---

200 *Ibid.*, p. 294.

shake the evidence that these three accounts are parallels. All three refer to the destruction of Jerusalem in A.D. 70.

The one portion of the above quotations that does require special consideration is, "and Jerusalem shall be trodden down of the Gentiles, until the times of the Gentiles be fulfilled" (Luke 21:24). Various preachers and commentators of the present make much of the recent reoccupation of Jerusalem by the Jews as marking the time or event Jesus had in mind when He uttered these words. It is not uncommon for the times of the Gentiles to be set as from the destruction of Jerusalem by Nebuchadnezzar to its recent occupation by Israel. But a number of reasons makes these claims unacceptable.

The first of these reasons is the language Luke uses. The words "trodden down" is a translation of the Greek *patoumene* from *pateo*. This word means to trample upon with the feet or to crush by trampling upon with the feet. Taken very literally, this would mean that the Gentiles would actually trample on the Jews for whatever period is involved. Of course, Premillenialists plead a symbolic meaning of oppression, which is all right with me; I ask only that they accord me the same privilege when I insist that some of their so-called literalisms be interpreted as symbolic.

*Pateo* implies more than mere occupation. It implies severe oppression. Such cannot be substantiated by history. At various times between A.D. 70 and 1967 the Jews enjoyed peace and security. Under the British mandate from 1923 to 1948, Jerusalem and the Jews had relative freedom; and under the Saracens and Turks, the Jews probably received better treatment than Gentile Christians. Therefore 1967 and the reoccupation of Jerusalem by the Jews is not foretold in this prophetic utterance of Jesus.

This is substantiated by the use of the plural "times," instead of the singular "time." Although some contend the plural has no significance, it is not logical that the plural would be used if the reference was to a single event such as the reoccupation of Jerusalem by the Jews. This is reinforced by the word used for "times." One would normally expect *chronos* if a space of time is all that is intended, but instead we find *kairos* which includes the idea of opportunity, advantage, and suitability, as well as seasons of various kinds. Biederwolf lists six who take it to mean the time when Gentile domination of Jerusalem would end, and six who hold that it refers to "the period of grace during which the Gospel is offered to the Gentiles."[201]

---

201 Biederwolf, *op. cit.*, p. 384.

But neither of these answers is acceptable. The first would require the singular, time instead of times, and the idea that the gospel will one day be withdrawn from the Gentiles conflicts with the fact that the gospel is universal in its call and without partiality in its benefits. It recognizes no distinctions in men based on race, nationality, or position in life. The distinction between the Jew and the Gentile is obliterated in Christ. Outside of Christ, the distinction will, of course, continue to exist. Hence, it was in this latter sense that Jesus spoke of the "times of the Gentiles" ending.

It is assumed by many that when the "times of the Gentiles" comes to an end that a special time for the Jews will commence. But this is only an assumption. The text says nothing of the relation of the Jews to the Gentiles after the "times of the Gentiles" is ended. Scofield places the beginning of the "times of the Gentiles" with the fall of Jerusalem to Nebuchadnezzar (see note on Luke 21:24). Lindsey accepts a similar date for he writes of 2600 years of dispersion being ended by the establishment of a Jewish state in 1948.[202] But this ignores the periods when the Jews had relative freedom as they did during and following the reign of Cyrus, and during the Maccabean period, by lumping the total period into a single period of "time of the Gentiles."

This effort to establish a period of time prior to A.D. 70 as the "times of the Gentiles" is futile. Jesus did not say that Jerusalem had been "trodden down of the Gentiles" for several centuries, and that it was then being "trodden down," and that it would continue to be "trodden down" until the "time of the Gentiles" was fulfilled. He spoke (future tense) only of conditions after A.D. 70. At the time Jesus spoke these words, Jerusalem was subject to Rome, but the kind of oppression indicated by the term "trodden down" did not exist. Yet in the war that eventuated in the fall of Jerusalem and in the oppression that was an aftermath of that war, the people of Jerusalem could be appropriately termed "trodden down." But as Rome disintegrated into smaller nations, this oppression became less severe, and eventually ceased altogether.

Jerusalem was then conquered by the Saracens. They were quite ruthless in their conquests, and as long as Jerusalem refused to pay tribute, the oppression was severe; but Mohammed had commanded his followers to be tolerant of the "people of the Book" provided they paid tribute. This edict

---

202 Lindsey, *op. cit.*, pp. 43ff.

applied to both Jews and Christians, hence the Saracen oppression was mild during much of the time they ruled Jerusalem. During the Crusades, Saracen rule was broken for a time. It can hardly be claimed that Jerusalem was trodden down during this period of time.

In the course of time Saladin restored Saracen control. As the unity of the Saracens was replaced by division, any oppression they had exercised became less severe, but then the Ottoman Turks took up where the Saracens had left off. The Turks ruled oppressively whether it was in Palestine or Europe. They, too, weakened, however, and Turkey became known as "the sick man of Europe." Russia would have taken over all of Turkey during the 19th century, except for the interference of France and England. Turkish oppression became less brutal as her power diminished.

Following the defeat of Germany in World War I, Turkey, which was an ally of Germany, had Palestine taken from her. From 1923 to 1948, Jerusalem functioned politically under a British protectorate or mandate. If the British are descendants of the ten lost tribes of Israel, as Armstrong claims,[203] Jewish rule was restored in 1923, and even if the British are Gentiles, they were favorable to the Jews, rather than oppressive. Thus the oppression of Israel cannot be established for several periods of her history since the time of Nebuchadnezzar, and most certainly not since 1923. As for Jerusalem being "trodden down of the Gentiles until the times of the Gentiles be fulfilled," 1923 seems to be a more significant date than either 1948 or 1967.

What, then, is the true significance of Jerusalem being "trodden down" and of the "times of the Gentiles"? The "times of the Gentiles" has no reference to the totality of the Gentile nations. It does not pit Jew against Gentile, as many contend. Rather it refers to the three nations which have actually, although not literally, "trodden down" Jerusalem for a period of time. The time of the Roman Gentiles began about A.D. 70 and ended prior to the dissolution of the Roman empire in A.D. 476. The time of the Saracen Gentiles was from A.D. 640 to whatever time they ceased their severe measures. Their control was lost for portions of the 12th and 13th centuries, hence was not continuous. The time of the Turkish Gentiles was from A.D.

---

203 Herbert W. Armstrong. *The United States and British Commonwealth in Prophecy*, p. 161.

1517 until it was occupied by the British in World War I.[204]

Some may contend that the present, passive, participle *patoumene* which is translated "trodden down" implies continuous action. But it must be remembered that the linear action of the present tense may also indicate repeated action. The context in this instance favors repeated action through the use of the plural "times of the Gentiles," rather than the "time of the Gentiles." The latter could be construed as a single block of time had Jesus used it, but He saw fit to use the plural. At least three nations have oppressed Jerusalem since these words were uttered. Has the end come? The Bible doesn't say. Many commentators insist the end has come, but not one prophecy of the Bible would be broken if Russia, China, Egypt, or some other nation again oppressed the Jews. It would simply extend the "times of the Gentiles" to a future era.

Some hold that there have been times of greater tribulation since A.D. 70 than occurred at that time. This is used as grounds for holding a future fulfillment of Matthew 24:21-22 and Mark 13:19-20. That great tribulation did occur in A.D. 70 is admitted by all. But was it the most severe affliction of all time? Josephus is our principal source of information regarding the afflictions of A.D. 70. In books previously mentioned by Kik and Meserve, copious quotations from Josephus are given in support of that being the greatest of all tribulations. For those who are interested, you are referred to these books. In Josephus, the beginning of the war is found in book II, chapter XVII, and the account continues through book VII, chapter II. Space limitations prohibit the inclusion of the gruesome details in this hook. Only the basis for considering it the greatest will be considered.

It was not the greatest in numbers killed. World War II resulted in more deaths than occurred in A.D. 70. Whether Hitler's efforts to annihilate the Jews be considered separate to that war, or a part of it, is immaterial. The Jews suffered greatly during those years. But a combination of factors made A.D. 70 worse than what Hitler did. Regardless of how many went to the gas chamber, what occurred in Jerusalem was worse, for some things are worse than death.

---

204 Egypt controlled Jerusalem for a period prior to 1517, but no indication of severe oppression is found.

Some of the conditions that justify the superlative Jesus used of the destruction of Jerusalem in A.D. 70 include the following:

1. Fear was unusual. The mass of people in Jerusalem was split into several factions. The Idumeans and Zealots were especially brutal. It was impossible to know friend from foe in many instances. The populace lived in constant fear of those within the city more than of those besieging the city from the outside.

2. The famine reduced many to the level of beasts. Josephus records where one woman slew her child and ate part of it after cooking it. This was done without shame or remorse. Parents slew their families to avoid living under such horrible conditions. Children took food from parents and parents from children without compunction. In this way, this was a most unusual condition.

3. The brutal, bloodthirsty, senseless killings made it unusual. Had these killings come from the Romans, it could have been comparable to many other wars and the brutality that barbarians sometimes manifested. But this wantonness was wrought by persons who should have been defending the city.

4. The dishonor shown the dead made it unusual. The Jews paid every respect to their dead, ordinarily, but during this time, hundreds of dead bodies were piled together without any attempt at burial. These were allowed to putrefy with a callous disregard for what was appropriate.

5. The expectation of a miraculous deliverance by divine power made this a time of blasted hopes. A false prophet encouraged a large number of people in this expectation, but it resulted in their death. Many were burned to death, and others were killed by jumping from burning buildings, as well as by weapons of warfare.

There remains the question of Old Testament prophets. Daniel tells of a time "of trouble such as never was since there was a nation" (Dan. 12:1). Premillennialists generally hold that this refers to a future tribulation under Antichrist. Our interpretation of this was in reference to Antiochus Epiphanes, but it could refer to the destruction of Jerusalem. If that be the case, then it would parallel the verses of the Olivet discourse being considered. Whatever is involved in the 12th chapter of Daniel, it ends in the scattering or shattering of "the power of the holy people" (Dan. 12:7). The Premillennial scheme contradicts Daniel. At the point where Daniel says "the power of the holy people" would be scattered, a restoration of power to the Jews is proclaimed by them. On the other hand, what Titus did in A.D. 70 harmonizes perfectly with the scattering Daniel foretold.

Jeremiah 30:7 speaks of Jacob's trouble as an unusual time of difficulty for the Jews. He says "that none is like it." This indicates the problem has to do with the "kind of trouble" just as we have explained in the preceding paragraphs. But Premillennialists ascribe this to a future time of tribulation during the expected reign of Antichrist. It is argued that Jeremiah said that Jacob "shall be saved out of it" i.e., out of the trouble just mentioned. It is further argued that Jacob was not saved out of the destruction of Jerusalem. Instead, they say, he was either killed or taken captive.

But this is not necessarily the correct interpretation. Many Premillennialists believe in the idea of a remnant. Even Scofield admits a remnant as distinct from the total Jewish population. He goes so far as to say, "During the church-age the remnant is composed of believing Jews (Rom. 11:4-5)" (see note on Rom. 11:5). And this remnant, the Church, was saved from the tribulations which came upon those in Jerusalem. Eusebius, the Church historian, describes it in the following words:

The whole body, however, of the church in Jerusalem, having been commanded by a divine revelation, given to men of approved piety there before the war, removed from the city, and dwelt at a certain town beyond the Jordan, called Pella.[205]

Thus, even according to Scofield's own admittance, the godly remnant, the believing Jews were saved. Did Daniel 12:1 refer to all Israel being saved? No. Only those "that shall be found written in the book" (Dan. 12:1). What book? Our answer is the book of life. Similarly, we hold that only believing Jews, the Church if you please, were to be saved in the time of Jacob's trouble. That these were saved, we have just proved. There is, therefore, no logical reason to place the fulfillment of Jeremiah 30:7 at some future date. It was fulfilled during the first Christian century.

It is believed that the shortening of the days "for the elect's sake" (Matt. 24:22) refers to those at Pella, rather than those in Jerusalem. Unbelieving Jews who merited the wrath of God and who crucified their Messiah

---

[205] Eusebius, *op. cit.*, p. 86.

and King were rejected by Christ and God. The afflictions they suffered in A.D. 70 was the fulfillment of the prediction of Jesus,—

> That upon you may come all the righteous blood shed upon the earth from the blood of righteous Abel unto the blood of Zacharias son of Barachias, whom ye slew between the temple and the altar (Matt. 23:35).

Logic and sound exegesis make it impossible to conceive of Christ speaking of these people in this fashion, then, a short time later, referring to them as "the elect." But had the siege continued for as long as the Jewish capability would have indicated it might, the Romans would have ravished the surrounding country, even unto Pella, the refuge of the remnant, the believers, the Church, the elect.

CHAPTER 15

# THE OLIVET DISCOURSE (CONTINUED)

## Matthew 24:23-31; Mark 13:21-27; Luke 21:25-28

Probably no other portion of this discourse which precedes the "time-text" (Matt. 24:34) is as frequently connected with the second coming of Christ as are the apocalyptic expressions found in verses 27-31. According to this "time-text," it has been set forth in this volume that everything Jesus said down to verse 34 refers to events of the first Christian century, A.D. 70 in particular. And since Mark and Luke mentioned questions relating only to the destruction of Jerusalem their inclusion of most of what Matthew had in these verses, Mark especially, strongly supports the thesis that these verses were fulfilled during the first Christian century.

Jesus again warns against false Christs and false prophets. Basically these are the same. Anyone who claimed to be anointed of God with a message for the people would be a false christ (anointed person) or false prophet (spokesman for God) if his claims were not valid. However, Christ's first warning (Matt. 24:4-5) appears to be of such false persons prior to the siege of Jerusalem, whereas the warning given at this point is against false persons after the siege. Meserve and Kik both hold that this pertained to the time the siege was in progress; but I must disagree, even though Josephus tells of a false prophet who claimed God would miraculously deliver Jerusalem, and of "a great number of false prophets" who prophesied during the siege.[206] The words of Jesus, "Wherefore if they shall say unto you, Behold, he is in the desert; go not forth" (Matt. 24:26), are remarks totally unsuited to the conditions inside Jerusalem during the siege. It was impossible to go out to the desert, for those inside the city were effectually sealed up or imprisoned within its walls.

Following these words of warning about false christs and false prophets,

---

206 Josephus, *Wars of the Jews,* bk. VI, chap. v.

Matthew adds a verse not found in either Mark or Luke. It reads, "For as the lightning cometh out of the east, and shineth even unto the west; so shall also the coming of the Son of Man be" (Matt. 24:27). Does this refer to Christ coming in judgment against Jerusalem in A.D. 70, or does it refer to His second coming at the end of the age? Kik and Clarke say this refers to Christ coming in judgment of Jerusalem. This is suited to the "time-text" idea previously given. Most commentators apply it to the second coming.

But Meserve approaches it somewhat differently. He accepts the "time-text" division made by Kik. He believes that all Jesus said in the verses down to Matthew 24:34 that is primary was fulfilled in connection with the destruction of Jerusalem in A.D. 70. He denies that this verse is of primary significance. It is somewhat like an aside remark or a parenthetical expression. He contends, "It is brought in here only as a contrast to His coming in judgment on Israel and Jerusalem in the preceding verses."[207] Meserve's position is well taken. Christ, according to this view, refers to His second coming incidentally. It is as though Christ said, "If you are told Christ has come, you can know it is false. No one will have to be told about my coming, for all will see me at that time." This preserves the "time-text" division of the discourse without making a forced explanation of the verse.

This view is further strengthened by the fact that Matthew uses the Greek term *parousia* of Christ's coming in verse 27. It has already been pointed out that *parousia* involves the real presence of the person involved. It was used of Christ's first advent which involved His presence in a bodily, visible form. When used of His future coming, it must also involve His personal, bodily, visible return. It is contended that those who apply this term in I Corinthians 15:23 and I Thessalonians 4:15 to an invisible, secret coming which they call the "rapture" are using forced exegesis. I am not about to follow their example in this respect. It is my opinion that *parousia*, when used of a future coming of Christ, can apply only to that final coming at the end of the age.

Matthew is the only one of the three evangelists who records as part of the Olivet discourse the statement by Jesus, "For wheresoever the carcass is, there will the eagles be gathered" (Matt. 24:28). In this context the only legitimate interpretation is that the reference is to the destruction of Jerusalem in A.D. 70. Robbers, Zealots, Idumeans, and the Romans all attack the decayed

---

207 Meserve, *op. cit.*, p. 52.

Jewish nation in fulfillment of this verse. The thought picks up from verse 22 with the intervening verses either explanatory or parenthetical.

Biederwolf lists eight different explanations of Matthew 24:29-31.[208] This shows how confused expositors are over this portion of prophecy. But if the keys that are presented in this volume are utilized, all of this confusion is dissipated. One of the keys for this passage is the "time-text" key of verse 34 that "this generation shall not pass, till all these things be fulfilled." So we can know that what Jesus said here was fulfilled during the first Christian century, even if the words are difficult to assign to that period. The second key involves the nature of apocalyptic language which was discussed in an earlier chapter. Some repetition is unavoidable at this point. Let us compare the words of Jesus with the words of the prophets.

In a prophecy of the destruction of Babylon (Isa. 13:1), he said, Behold the day of the Lord cometh ..., and he shall destroy the sinners thereof out of it. For the stars of heaven and the constellations thereof shall not give their light: the sun shall be darkened in his going forth, and the moon shall not cause her light to shine (Isa. 13:9-10).

Taken out of context, this might well be taken for the end of time, but Isaiah, the prophet who uttered these words, says it refers to the destruction of Babylon. To literalize this or to make it refer to some future occurrence is to reject part of what the author says, while claiming to accept the rest. This was not literally fulfilled, but Babylon was destroyed, just as Isaiah said it would be through these apocalyptic expressions.

Again Isaiah prophesies of the destruction of Edom (Idumea and Bozrah, Isa. 34:5-6) in similar terms. It reads in part,

The mountains shall be melted with their blood. And all the host of heaven shall be dissolved, and the heavens shall be rolled together as a scroll: and all their host shall fall down, as the leaf falleth off from the vine, and as a falling fig from the fig tree (Isa. 34:3-4).

Once again this sounds like the end of the age, but Isaiah contends that it refers to the fall of Idumea and its principal city of Bozrah. This has never taken place literally, and it never will. There is no more reason to expect literal mountains to be melted by human blood than for literal rivers of milk and honey to spring up in Palestine.

Ezekiel speaks in similar terms of God's judgment on Egypt. He expresses

---

208 Biederwolf, *op. cit.*, pp. 340-342.

it in these words:

> Son of man, take up a lamentation for Pharaoh king of Egypt, and say unto him...I will lay thy flesh upon the mountains, and I will fill the valleys with thy height [heap of corpses]. I will also water with thy blood the land wherein thou swimmest, even to the mountains; and the rivers shall be full of thee. And when I shall put thee out, I will cover the heaven, and make the stars thereof dark: I will cover the sun with a cloud, and the moon shall not give her light. All the bright lights of heaven will I make dark over thee, and set darkness upon thy land, saith the Lord God (Ezek. 32:2, 5-8).

Various other passages from Isaiah, Daniel, Joel and the Revelation could be cited in support of apocalyptic expressions such as Jesus used on this occasion. Uniformly, they referred to the destruction of nations in figurative terms which were not intended to be taken literally. The Revelation is especially replete with apocalyptic expressions which allude to the heavenly bodies to express political and religious events. Anyone who literalizes expressions like a dragon whose tail "drew the third part of the stars of heaven, and did cast them to the earth" (Rev. 12:3-4) is in a class of those who contend that the earth is flat.

The question that faces us at this point is whether or not Jesus spoke in apocalyptic terms or factual terms in verses 29-31 of Matthew 24 and the parallel passages in Mark and Luke. I may not be able to prove this to the satisfaction of everyone, but there are strong indications that He did speak apocalyptically. In the verses preceding those under consideration, He did speak of the destruction of Jerusalem in A.D. 70. Also, the time-text (Matt. 24:34) indicates that all Jesus said prior to verse 34 did pertain to events of the first Christian century. And being a prophet, it would be expected that He would prophecy of the destruction of the Jewish nation in terms similar to those utilized by those earlier prophets who had foretold of similar disasters in apocalyptic terminology. Thus we have three good reasons for considering these verses as apocalyptic expressions which should not be interpreted literally. When interpreted literally, the whole point of the prophecy is missed, and confusion follows.

Matthew states that "immediately after the tribulation of those days" (Matt. 24:29) certain things would occur. The word "immediately" is a problem for those who claim the tribulation involved was that of A.D. 70, but that the remainder of verse 29 and the next two verses refer to the second coming of Christ. Possibly the majority of commentators fit into this category. For those who contend Matthew and Mark tell of the future tribulation, and that only Luke refers to the events in A.D. 70. no serious problem is encountered regarding this word. Their problem is that they are unable to disprove the fact that all three accounts are parallels.

Also, for those who interpret Matthew 24:29-31 as apocalyptic, no real problem exists. The reason for this is that the further words of Jesus are taken to refer to the destruction of the Jewish nation, rather than to the consummation. The fact that the Jewish nation was destroyed along with the city makes the expression "immediately," or at the conclusion of the tribulation, in full accord with the facts, if the tribulation meant was indeed that of A.D. 70.

If the remaining portion of Matthew 24:29 is compared with the apocalyptic expressions from Isaiah and Ezekiel quoted above, their similarity will be evident. All three speak of the darkening of the luminous bodies of the astral heavens including the sun, moon, and stars. It is not accidental or coincidental that the language of the prophets and that which Christ uses are almost identical. This form of expression was well known to the Jews. They understood what Jesus meant. Until expositors of our day are able to interpret these verses in the light of the thought patterns of that day, the present confusion will continue to exist.

Many expositors are prepared to accept the fact that verse 29 applies to A.D. 70, but very few can accept the same for verses 30 and 31. But if Jesus switches from one subject to another without giving adequate indication of the change, He is guilty of creating confusion. It leaves one with the impression that Jesus' own thinking was disorganized, an impression which must be rejected. The divisions we have given structure this discourse in an orderly manner. Any other division makes for confusion and misunderstanding.

"And then shall appear the sign of the Son of Man in heaven" (Matt. 24:30). This is usually read, and in several instances even translated as though it is read, "And then the sign of the Son of man shall appear in the heavens or sky." But that is a faulty reading. If that were what Jesus really said and meant, He phrased it in a most awkward manner, whether one reads from the Greek or the English. The expression "in heaven" is in the locative case. It locates whatever it modifies as being in heaven, but it cannot be determined with absolute certainty whether it modifies "sign" or "Son of man." However, the fact that it follows "Son of man" favors the view that it locates the Son of man as being in heaven.

Thus we conclude that the "sign" is something that occurs on earth which is proof of Jesus being in heaven. The sign could not appear in the heaven of heavens, for Christ is there. The words which are often taken to mean the sign will be in the aerial heavens do not place it there at all. Rather, it locates the Son of man in the heaven of heavens. Two conclusions stem from these facts. First, the sign is not a sign of Christ's second coming. Instead, it is a sign of His being in heaven. Secondly, the sign appears on earth as evidence that Christ was transported into glory at the time of His ascension.

Several occurrences of the first Christian century point to the fact that Christ was then in heaven. He promised to send the Holy Spirit upon His followers after His arrival in heaven. This promise was first fulfilled on the day of Pentecost. Each person who has received that infilling of the Holy Spirit since that day is further evidence of Jesus being in heaven. Another statement made by Jesus was to the effect that they would do greater works than He had done, "because I go unto the Father" (John 14:12). More people accepted Christ on the day of Pentecost than had believed on Him during His entire ministry. The rapid spread of the gospel during the first century and following was evidence of Christ being with His Father.

But the sign Jesus probably had in mind was the fulfillment of His curse upon Jerusalem and the Jewish nation. As Jesus wept over Jerusalem, He lamented because they refused to permit Him to bless them as He desired to do. Then He said, "Behold, your house is left unto you desolate" (Matt. 23:38). This was the sign, visible to all men, that "the Son of man in heaven" did rule in the affairs of men.

But it will be claimed that the rest of verse 30 does speak of Christ's second coming. It is admitted that a coming of Christ is mentioned in verse 30, but it is denied that it refers to Christ's second coming. The second clause of this verse reads, "and then shall all the tribes of the earth mourn." Two Greek words require consideration in this clause. Tribes is a translation of the Greek *phulai*. Although its definition includes the idea of a nation or a people, its frequent use in relation to the twelve tribes of Israel requires that this idea be eliminated before any text is interpreted as having a broader significance. Nineteen times the singular form is used of a single tribe of Israel. Not once is the singular used of another nation or country.

In the KJV the plural form is translated "tribes" in five instances, and in four of these the twelve tribes of Israel are the tribes referred to without question. Of these instances, only Matthew 24:30 can be questioned as having this significance. Our contention is that it is not an exception after all. It does refer to the twelve tribes, rather than the world population.

In six cases the plural form is translated "kindreds." In all of these save one, two or more additional terms are added to indicate the total population of the earth is intended. These additional words are tongues (or languages), nations, and people. Thus it is conceivable that the term *phulai* was so closely connected with the tribes of Israel that additional words were required when the scope of the utterance reached beyond the twelve tribes of Israel.

It may be contended, of course, that the expression "all the tribes of the earth" constitutes such an extension. But this need not be so. The Greek *ge* is often translated by our word "land." Thus we have the land of Egypt or the land of Judah. And since *phulai* is most often applied to the tribes of Israel, rather than to people in general, "all the tribes" refers to the twelve tribes; and the earth or land indicates Palestine or that land distributed to the twelve tribes by Joshua and Moses.

The foregoing is designed to help in determining the time the tribes would "mourn." There is no adequate reason for considering the time to be any time other than the time the temple was destroyed in A.D. 70. This mourning was over the destruction of Jerusalem and the temple, the privation so many had suffered, the deaths of friends and relatives, and the enslavement of themselves and others who survived the ordeal of the siege. Thus all Jews had ample reason to mourn, even if they had been spared the tribulations so many had to endure.

The remainder of verse 30 which reads, "and they shall see the Son of man coming in the clouds of heaven with power and great glory" is generally ascribed to the second coming of Christ. In a different setting this might be acceptable, but since verse 34 indicates that what is said prior to that verse refers to the destruction of Jerusalem, we must explain this statement in the light of that declaration.

Our first observation is that the coming mentioned here uses the Greek term *erchomai*. It will be recalled that this is the word for coming that can most easily have reference to an invisible coming as in judgment. However, this verse states that "they shall see the Son of man coming." But even this is not conclusive. The reason for this is that the term translated "shall see" is equally capable of referring to mental perception as it is to visual perception. It is perfectly legitimate for a totally blind person to say, I see, in the sense of perceiving mentally that which he had not understood before.

Two other statements by Matthew should assist in enabling you to see what I mean. Jesus said, "Verily I say unto you, There be some standing here, which shall not taste of death, till they see the Son of man coming in his kingdom." The "seeing" in this verse can hardly be considered other than seeing with the mind—not with the eyes.

Jesus also told Caiaphas during His trial, "Hereafter shall ye see the Son of man sitting on the right hand of power, and coming in the clouds of heaven." Seeing Christ "sitting on the right hand of power" is not applicable to the second coming. And considering how antagonistic Caiaphas was to Christ, it can hardly refer to a heavenly vision. Hence, it must refer to a mental concept that eventually came to Caiaphas. And keep in mind that Caiaphas was to see Christ coming "in the clouds of heaven." The expression "coming in the clouds of heaven" is expressed in identical terms in Matthew 24:30 and in 26:64.

Now if Caiaphas saw Christ coming in the clouds of heaven, and Jesus' words were fulfilled, then the coming in the clouds of heaven in Matthew 24:30 is of the same nature. No doubt Jesus was here using apocalyptic language to express the judgment that would be heaped upon the Jews. He certainly came in power and great glory on that occasion. Josephus believed that in the case of the impregnable towers of Jerusalem, the Jews were "ejected out of them by God himself."[209] Even the pagan Titus admitted as much. Josephus quotes him as follows:

> We have certainly had God for our assistant in this war, and it was no other than God who ejected the Jews out of these fortifications; for what could the hands of men or machines do towards overthrowing these towers?[210]

No doubt some will say that Jesus meant that at the second coming Caiaphas would see Him come in the clouds of heaven. But if this approach is accepted, it conflicts with the Premillennial teaching that the wicked will not be resurrected until after the so-called millennial reign. Thus Caiaphas who was not a Christian will be in his grave at the time of the second coming, according to this teaching. If those who teach the two-phase second coming concept deny that Caiaphas saw Christ coming in the clouds of heaven

---

[209] Josephus, *op. cit.*, bk. VI, chap. VIII.
[210] *Ibid.*, bk. VI, chap. IX.

during his lifetime, then they must admit that he will be resurrected at Christ's second coming. And if Caiaphas saw Christ coming in the clouds of heaven during his lifetime, there is no reason for rejecting the idea that Matthew 24:30 also refers to events of the first Christian century.

Admittedly, the gathering described in Matthew 24:31 sounds very much like the gathering at the end of time, but it cannot have this meaning. The word "immediately" in verse 29 does not allow for such an extended period of time between the destruction of Jerusalem and the gathering of verse 30. Also, verse 34 states that "this generation shall not pass, till all these things be fulfilled." The things to be fulfilled before the generation then living should all die include the gathering of verse 30. Therefore we are on solid ground in interpreting verse 30 as an apocalyptic expression.

The angels who do the gathering need not be bodiless, spirit beings. The Greek term translated angels is from *aggelos* or *anggelos*. In a number of places it definitely refers to human beings. In most of these instances the translation is "messengers" rather than "angels." John the Baptist was an *anggelos* (Matt. 11:10; Mark 1:2; Luke 7:27), as were the men he sent to question Jesus (Luke 7:24). Some of Jesus' disciples would have been called "angels" except for the fact that the translators used the word "messengers" instead. According to the Greek, the two spies Rahab protected were angels. It is commonly recognized that the angels of the churches in Revelation 2 and 3 are not spirit beings. Rather they are the pastors or some other representatives of the seven churches mentioned in these two chapters.

Consequently it should not be assumed that the angels of verse 31 are other than physical messengers. Only after careful examination of the text and context should the idea of physical messengers be ruled out. And since verse 29 indicates a very short period of time was to elapse before this gathering was to occur, and since verse 34 indicates that it was to happen while some then living were still living, we are not being illogical in applying the angels of this verse to the ministers of the first Christian century who proclaimed the gospel to their generation.

But what about the trumpet? Doesn't that indicate the second coming? It does in some places, but it need not do so. It is also used of the year of jubilee (Lev. 25:8-10), and the year of jubilee is a type or symbol of, the gospel age. At the beginning of the year of jubilee, in the institution of the year of jubilee, Moses instructed, "Then shalt thou cause the trumpet of the jubilee to sound on the tenth day of the seventh month, in the day of atonement shall ye make the trumpet sound throughout all your land" (Lev. 25:9). That the day of atonement was a type of Christ's atoning sacrifice is generally recognized, and it is closely associated with the year of jubilee.

Isaiah brought out the significance of the year of jubilee in his prophecy of Jesus (Isa. 61:1-2). Jesus declared that this prophecy which speaks of liberty, deliverance, healing, and restoration was a prophecy regarding Himself and the launching of the gospel era. The expression "acceptable year of the Lord" ties this in with the year of jubilee (Luke 4:17-21). What Moses commanded regarding the year of jubilee was for the Jews to observe, but in its antitypical fulfillment it was for all people. This is indicated by the extent of the gathering Jesus indicated. The four winds means universal activity. The gospel was designed to touch the lives of men in all parts of the world.

But Jerusalem was a hindrance to the spread of the gospel. As long as the animal sacrifices and the temple worship continued, there would be those who would continue to look to those things as the basis for their faith. Therefore, Jerusalem had to go, and its going marked a milestone in the advance of the gospel. It is probably what is intended by the "great sound of a trumpet." Since Jesus is speaking apocalyptically, we must recognize that much of what He says is expressed in figurative rather than literal terms. It is the same trumpet Isaiah had prophesied in an earlier prophecy which reads:

And it shall come to pass in that day, that the great trumpet shall be blown, and they shall come which were ready to perish in the land of Assyria, and the outcasts in the land of Egypt, and shall worship the Lord in the holy mount at Jerusalem (Isa. 27:13).

Now, no single trumpet was blown which was heard in both Assyria and Egypt, but the gospel message has been carried to both, as was the news of the destruction of Jerusalem. From Hebrews 12:18-22 we learn that both Zion and Jerusalem are types of the Church and the gospel, and in a somewhat similar way the trumpet is a symbol of the preaching of the gospel. Thus the gathering of verse 31 is not at the end of the age. Rather it is that gathering which took place during the first Christian centuries. The angels are the preachers of the gospel who turned the world upside down during those early years. If this seems unacceptable, just remember that Jesus indicated in verse 34 that these things would occur during the lifetime of some then living.

## Matthew 24:32-34; Mark 13:28-30; Luke 21:29-32

This passage contains the parable of the fig tree. Lindsey describes this as the *"Perfect Parable."*[211] He and others apply it to the restoration of the nation of Israel. I have no objection to this parable being termed perfect, for all of Jesus' parables could bear that descriptive term without misrepresentation, but the interpretation given by Lindsey is decidedly imperfect. In plain language it is incorrect, erroneous, false, illogical, and exegetically indefensible.

Only by interpretation can Christ's meaning of the "fig tree" be determined. Lindsey and others say it represents the nation of Israel which was established in 1948. Others say it has reference to the kingdom of God and the gospel era. Starting with the assumption that Christ is orderly and logical in His presentation, it is evident that the interpretation Lindsey gives places this parable in the wrong place. It does not fit in with the progress of the discourse. Let us for the moment consider the sequence of events in the discourse as related to the sequence of events espoused by Scofield, Lindsey, Tan, and many other Premillennialists.

According to the above mentioned teaching, the establishment of the nation of Israel in 1948 is the first link in a chain of major events. Lindsey and many others not only interpret this parable as foretelling the establishment of the country of Israel, but they also interpret the generation of Matthew 24:34 as the generation living in 1948 at the time the new nation was formed.[212] From this sandy foundation, they contend that the Roman empire will be restored with ten nations composing it, that the rapture will occur, that the Antichrist and the great tribulation he will bring will take place, that the temple will be rebuilt, that the Jewish law will be practiced once more, and that the battle of Armageddon will be fought.

The contention is that all of these events will be literally fulfilled during the life span of the generation living in 1948. But if this is the order of future events, and if the parable does refer to the state of Israel, then the parable is not in the proper order. If it is the first link in a chain of events, then it should come at the beginning of the chain, rather than at the opposite end of the chain. The proper place for the parable, according to Lindsey's interpretation, would be prior to verse 15 where the abomination of desolation is

---

211 Lindsey, *op. cit.*, p. 53.
212 *Ibid.*, p. 54.

mentioned. According to this interpretation, verse 15 is future, but verse 32 is already fulfilled. This is not an orderly arrangement.

But to what does the fig tree refer? It refers to the kingdom of God or the Church. Some have pointed out that the fig tree is sometimes used as a symbol of the Jews, but it is also true that literal Israel is used as a type of the Church; hence the fig tree is as suitable a symbol of the Church as it is of literal Israel. And there can be no question but that the productive season for the Church or the kingdom, as symbolized in the parable by the summer season, did come in the years following the destruction of Jerusalem in A.D. 70. But if the preceding verses are interpreted as referring to the personal appearance of Christ at the *parousia* (second coming), then verse 33 is as much out of place as a dislocated joint.

Verse 33 reads, "So likewise ye, when ye shall see these things [the things mentioned in the preceding verses] know that it is near, even at the doors." The "it" that is near is interpreted, on the one hand, as the destruction of Jerusalem. It is interpreted by others as referring to the second coming. The following events are depicted in the three verses immediately preceding the parable of the fig tree:

1. The sun and moon will be darkened.

2. The stars shall fall from heaven.

3. Certain powers shall be shaken.

4. The sign of the Son of man appears.

5. Tribes shall mourn.

6. People will see the Son of man coming in the clouds of heaven with power and great glory.

7. A trumpet shall sound.

8. The angels will gather the elect together.

If items 6, 7, and 8 are interpreted as most commentators interpret them, Jesus will have already arrived. The second coming will have become a reality. It will not just be "near, even at the doors." It will have burst upon the human scene in all its fullness and splendor. Hope will have been lost in sight. Expectation will have been replaced by the actual presence of our Lord and Saviour, Jesus Christ. This makes the literal explanation untenable. These verses must be interpreted as apocalyptic expressions of the judgments of God on rebellious Jerusalem.

But if the abomination of desolation (Matt. 24:15) is interpreted according to Luke 21:20 as the armies of Rome, and if the tribulation of Matthew 24:29 is made to refer to the siege of Jerusalem and the sufferings which occurred in that connection, and if the rest of verse 29 and verses 30-31 are considered apocalyptic expressions of God's judgments on the Jewish nation, then everything fits perfectly into place. The parable of the fig tree makes sense according to this interpretation. It is a message to the Church not to despair at the destruction of Jerusalem. Instead of it being a calamity to the Church, it was a necessary amputation to enable the Church to grow and develop relatively free of the detrimental effects which Judaizers produced prior to the destruction of Jerusalem.

These verses are almost identical in Matthew and Mark, but Luke has two verses that require consideration. Instead of the angels gathering the elect, Luke states, "And when these things begin to come to pass, then look up, and lift up your heads; for your redemption draweth nigh" (Luke 21:28). If the "Son of man coming in a cloud" (Luke 21:27) refers to the second coming, then their redemption would not be "nigh." It would be a reality. And for this reason it must have a different significance. But if the expression that "then shall they see the Son of man coming in a cloud" is taken as an apocalyptic expression, it agrees nicely with the idea of a release from Judaistic influences.

Then in Luke 21:31 a significant statement is added to the closing thought of the parable of the fig tree. Matthew and Mark do not define what is nigh as clearly as Luke does. Luke 21:31 reads, "So likewise ye, when ye see these things come to pass, know ye that the kingdom of God is nigh at hand." In connection with the preceding verse, I take this to mean that the summer time or growing season of the kingdom of God is at hand. That the kingdom of God was established at Christ's first coming has already been proved.

## Matthew 24:34-35; Mark 13:30-31; Luke 21:32-33

The generation which was not to pass away until certain things were accomplished is classified in as many as eight different ways.[213] Only four will be considered here, one of which is not included in the listing just mentioned.

1. The total group of Jews then living. This is the obvious meaning, as has been stated already.

---

213 Biederwolf, *op. cit.*, p. 347.

2. The Jewish race. These translate the Greek *genea* as race instead of generation.

3. A body of believers or the Church.

4. The population (generation) living in 1948 at the time the nation of Israel was formed.[214] The meaning of *genea* (generation) is very important in determining the meaning of the Olivet discourse.

Scofield applies it to the family of Israel. He contends that the verse means the Jewish race will not cease to exist until the second coming. In his note on Matthew 24:34 he says, "Gr. *genea*, the primary definition of which is, 'race, kind, family, stock, breed.' (So all lexicons.)" This is deceptive. The primary meaning of the term is to beget. It also refers to that which is begotten. A check of the lexicons reveals that "race" is one of the definitions, but hardly the primary one. Regardless of the basic meaning, our task is to determine how it is used in the New Testament, especially in the verses now being considered.

*The Theological Dictionary of the New Testament* is a voluminous and scholarly study of the Greek New Testament. It records that *genea* in the New Testament "mostly denotes 'generation' in the sense of contemporaries." This is, of course, the sense in which we use the word "generation." It refers to those who live at the same time or age. The term is used some 40 times in the New Testament. Although some instances may have a broader meaning than the above, there is not one case where such is demanded. In every instance it could refer to the people of a single life span.

Consider some of the ways Jesus used this word. Jesus declared that the men of Nineveh would rise up against "this generation" (Matt. 12:41; Luke 11:32). He could not have meant the Jewish race in this instance for He adds, "because they repented at the preaching of Jonas; and, behold, a greater than Jonas is here." Now, only Christ's contemporaries heard Jesus, hence only His contemporaries could be intended by this denunciation. The Jews then living are intended. A very similar statement is made in regard to the queen of the South condemning that generation (Matt. 12:42; Luke 11:31), and again He points out that one greater than Solomon was then present. Jews then living is the only meaning possible for these verses.

Jesus' denunciation of the scribes and Pharisees followed by His lament over Jerusalem is even more pointed. Jesus concludes His denunciation by

---

214 Lindsey, *loc. cit.*, p. 54.

placing all of the blood of righteous people, which previous generations had shed, upon the generation then living. This was no doubt based on the fact that He, Christ, was greater than all others who had been slain; hence the generation which crucified the Son of man was guilty of all others who had been slain before Him. His words are, "All these things shall come upon this generation" (Matt. 23:36; Luke 11:50-51). That Jesus was denouncing the Jews living at that time is not subject to debate. Unquestionably He meant His contemporaries—those who were plotting His death.

Just as "this generation" in the foregoing texts had reference to Christ's contemporaries, so is the meaning in that verse which has been designated the "time-text" of the Olivet discourse. When Jesus said, "This generation shall not pass, till all these things be fulfilled," He meant that all He had said down to that point would be fulfilled during the life span of some then living. The idea that it refers to the Jewish race, or to the body of believers is untenable in the face of the above.

Lindsey and certain others have departed from the original Dispensational teaching that generation means the Jewish race in Matthew 24:34. As has already been noted, he claims that it refers to the generation living in 1948. His words are, "What generation? Obviously, in context, the generation that would see the signs—chief among them the rebirth of Israel."[215] He adds that a generation in the Bible covers about 40 years. From this he deduces that the rapture, the tribulation, and the second coming will be by 1988 or shortly thereafter. This kind of date setting is rash or worse.

Lindsey's claim for contextual support for his position is void of any validity. The only acceptable meaning is this *present* generation. Had Jesus meant a future generation He would have had to use a different demonstrative pronoun. Just as we have the term "this" for something close at hand, and "that" for something at a distance, so did the Greeks. Jesus said, "This [Greek *haute*] generation shall not pass, till all these things be fulfilled." For Him to have meant a future generation, He would have had to have used *ekeine* which has the significance of "that." Thus the "time-text" stands. The things mentioned prior to our "time-text" had to be fulfilled while the generation living at the time Jesus spoke these words still possessed physical life here on this earth.

---

215 *Ibid.*

Following the "time-text," all three Synoptic writers have the verse, "Heaven and earth shall pass away: but my words shall not pass away." This verse connects the two main divisions of this discourse. That which preceded the "time-text" was concerned about events connected with the destruction of Jerusalem. That which follows has reference to last things. However, in accord with the fact that only Matthew mentions the second coming, Mark and Luke have very little to say on that subject. Matthew, on the other hand, discusses the second coming rather extensively.

### Matthew 24:34-51; Mark 13:32-37; Luke 21:34-36

The transition from things pertaining to the destruction of Jerusalem to the second coming is marked quite definitely in Matthew and Mark. Both have the words, "But of that day and [that] hour knoweth no man" (Matt. 24:36; Mark 13:32). Mark indicates that even Jesus in His incarnate state did not know the day. That was reserved for the Father's knowledge. Angels are as uninformed as we are.

In Matthew's account the second coming of Christ is compared to the coming of the flood. Conditions were as they had been right up to the day the waters came and took them away. No spectacular signs in the heavens came to warn them of what was about to happen. Those who teach that the signs in the early part of this discourse are signs of the second coming have an impossible task in harmonizing that teaching with these words of Jesus. No cross will appear in the sky to warn people of the second corning. It is believe the gospel now being preached or be damned, just as it was believe the preaching of Noah or be drowned.

Matthew then speaks of the selectivity that will be involved in the end. Some will be taken and others left. It is commonly held that these verses refer to the rapture; but that would put the rapture at the end of the age, not at the beginning of the reign of Antichrist or the tribulation period, nor of a thousand year reign. If the parable of the trees is designed to teach anything at all, it is designed to teach that there will be no separation of the good and the bad until the end of the age (Matt. 13:24-43).

It should also be noted that the two parables which deal with the separation of the wicked and the righteous picture the wicked as being taken out from among the righteous, rather than the reverse. In the parable of the tares, the angels gather the tares—not the righteous—and the tares are cast into the fire. Verse 30 pointedly states that He will instruct the reapers,

"Gather ye together first the tares." Thus those taken will be the tares and not the righteous. Also, in the parable of the net (Matt. 13:47-52), it is the bad who are gathered out from among the good. Rapturists, on the other hand, predict that the good will be removed from among the evil.

Some have tried to evade this problem by saying that the separation involved in Matthew 24:40-41 is at the end of the millennium, but this works no better than the other explanation. In the comparison to the days of Noah (Matt. 24:37), and in verse 39 just before the verses about one being taken and the other left, Jesus classifies these events as being connected with His *parousia* or second coming. It has already been shown that the term *parousia* does refer to the second coming. Neither of the Premillennial explanations fits the Bible demands. The separation comes at the *parousia*. It does not come at a so-called secret coming to rapture His saints away. Nor is it after an anticipated millennial reign. Rather, it will be at Christ's *parousia*. This is unquestionably what Jesus said.

The admonition, "Watch therefore: for ye know not what hour your Lord doth come" (Matt. 24:42) is hardly in keeping with time schedule to which most Premillennialists subscribe. Remember that the watching Jesus had in mind was not looking for signs such as the Antichrist, and the great tribulation. He meant for us to be faithful in preaching the gospel and living holy lives. The admonition to watch is repeated in Matthew 24:43-44 for emphasis. Let us not forget it. Those who claim to know when the second coming will occur are false prophets.

All three evangelists record the need for us as servants to perform faithfully the duties which have been assigned to us (Matt. 24:45-51; Mark 13:34-37; Luke 21:34-36). Also, all three warn us to be watchful for that coming will be sudden and unexpected. Matthew and Mark both use the illustration of a landlord leaving for an extended trip. His servants were assigned certain tasks to perform while he was away. At the return, there was to be an accounting. The return (from *heko* in Matt. 24:50) involves punishment of the unfaithful servant (v. 51). This disagrees with those Premillennialists who place the resurrection and punishment of the wicked dead after the millennium.

## Matthew 25

Approximately two-thirds of Matthew 25 is taken up with two parables which add little to the eschatological picture. The first is that of the ten virgins or maidens. It does indicate Christ will return, and it involves a marriage.

No doubt the five wise virgins constitute a figure of the true believers, the Church. The foolish virgins probably represent professed Christians who are not truly regenerate persons. In Revelation 19:7-10 the Church is represented as marrying Christ. In this parable the Church attends the marriage feast as in Matthew 22:1-14, rather than being figured as the bride. Both symbols have their application. Premillennialists usually interpret this parable as referring to the time Christ is supposed to come and set up His millennial kingdom. Amillennialists and Postmillennialists refer it to the final judgment. It closes with an admonition to "watch."

The parable of the talents again emphasizes the need for diligently applying ourselves to the tasks assigned us. The servants received differing amounts according to their capabilities. They were to use them for the benefit of their master. Two were rewarded for doubling their capital, whereas one was punished for burying his one talent. Since the servant that was punished was cast into "outer darkness," he can only represent an outright sinner or a hypocrite. It should be noted that both the good and the bad, the obedient and the disobedient were rewarded and punished at the same time. He did not take an account of the obedient at one time, then years later take an account with the disobedient servant. The reason for this last statement will appear in the discussion which follows.

Matthew 25:31-46 gives a word picture of the second coming. Before discussing these verses it is necessary to explain that Dispensationalists and other Premillennialists deny a general judgment. Scofield's note on Revelation 20:12 lists seven important judgments. Four of these are judgments of God, and people are the beings which are judged. These are a judgment of believers, another of Israel, a third of the Gentile nations, and a fourth of deceased sinners. Tan adds a judgment of the living wicked at the time of the second coming.[216] The important question to be answered is, who is judged in these verses? Scofield says it is the Gentile nations. I am among the many others who say it is the general judgment which takes place when Christ comes again.

A somewhat abbreviated version of Matthew 25:31-46 is given below to serve as a guide in the study which follows.

When the Son of man shall come in his glory, and all the holy angels with him, then shall he sit upon the throne of his glory: And before him shall

---

216 Tan, *op. cit.*, p. 339.

be gathered all nations: and he shall separate them one from another, as a shepherd divideth his sheep from the goats: And he shall set the sheep on his right hand, but the goats on the left.

Those on the right hand were to "inherit the kingdom prepared for them from the foundation of the world." In answer to their questions regarding the basis of this judgment, they were told, "Inasmuch as ye have done it unto one of the least of these my brethren, ye have done it unto me." Those on his left hand were told to, "Depart from me, ye cursed, into everlasting fire, prepared for the devil and his angels." The basis of judgment was their failure to have ministered unto him through "the least of these" with "my brethren" understood. The passage ends with, "And these shall go away into everlasting punishment, but the righteous into life eternal."

The solution to the controversy hinges, in the main, on the meaning of *ethne*, a plural form of *ethnos* which is translated nations. It is true that this term is sometimes used in contrast to the Jewish nation, but it is also used as including them. The contention that *ethne* must refer to the Gentile nations only, cannot be sustained. Thayer indicates the term may mean a multitude of individuals, a swarm, a race, a nation, as well as Gentiles or pagans. He points out further that the term is used of the Jewish nation in Luke 7:5; 23:2; John 11:48, 50, 51, and 52; 18:35; Acts 10:22; 24:2, 10; 26:4; 28:19. With these numerous passages where the term is applied specifically to the Jewish nation, it is folly to say the Jews cannot be included in the meaning of the term. Thus the expression "all nations" means just that. It refers to the Jewish people just as well as the Gentiles.

Scofield contends that three groups were represented at this judgment: the goats, the sheep, and Jesus' brethren. He interprets "brethren" as meaning the Jews. This is untenable for two reasons. First, the term all nations included the Jews as shown above. They were being judged just as much as the other nations. In the second place, Jesus refused to recognize blood relatives as His brethren. Rather, He contended that His disciples, those who obeyed God, were His brethren (Matt. 12:46-50). Now if any nation is to be classified as one that has rejected Christ, the Jewish nation is the one. Scofield's position is not defensible, yet men like Tan are still advocating it.[217]

---

217 *Ibid.*, p. 350.

The fact that these nations are judged as individuals is evident from the fact that the awards and penalties are eternal in nature. God has, on occasion, punished a nation that was wicked; and the good may have suffered along with the evil: but God will never send the righteous to "everlasting fire" (v. 41), and to "everlasting punishment" (v. 46). Nor will God allow wicked people to live within a nation which is largely righteous to inherit the kingdom of God (v. 34) or "life eternal" (v. 46).

Premillennialists are forced to leave their avowed literal interpretation in making this an earthly judgment of nations, instead of a heavenly judgment, the last judgment if you please, of all men who have ever lived. If these verses are read and interpreted the way one would read and interpret ordinary literature, one must conclude that this is the judgment that determines the eternal destiny of all men. This is a picture of where time as we know it ends and eternity begins. It is true that nothing is said of a resurrection in chapter 25, but neither is anything said of the rapture, the Antichrist, or the great tribulation. The fact that Christ did not mention a resurrection does not prove such a resurrection was not involved. Omissions like that are often made.

## Views of the Early Church on the Olivet Discourse

Certain things being taught today were conspicuous by their absence. The idea that Matthew and Mark tell of a future siege of Jerusalem and that Luke tells of the A.D. 70 siege was not even hinted in the 38 volumes used for checking. Augustine, in his *Harmony of the Gospels,* defended the thesis that all three accounts are parallel. A similar condition exists regarding the claim that Matthew 25:31-46 is a judgment of nations, rather than of individuals of all nations. Every reference to this part of the discourse placed it at the end of the age so that it involved a general judgment at which the righteous were separated from the unrighteous, just as the account indicates when read like any other literature. And the idea that the "brethren" of this portion was a reference to the Jews was not mentioned even once.

However, some of the interpretations I have given were not well supported either. Matthew 24:13, "But he that shall endure unto the end, the same shall be saved" was consistently referred to as Christian perseverance during any age. Often it was impossible to determine if the writer was saying this is what Jesus meant, or if he was only making an application of this statement to other conditions of life. Also, the preaching of the gospel to the whole world after which the end would come was sometimes applied to the end of the world. Chrysostom placed it in the past; Victorinus seemed to place it in the future; and Clement considered it past but also having reference to the end of the age.

Mixed reactions were found regarding the "abomination of desolation" and the "great tribulation" which was to accompany it. Irenaeus applied them to the time of the Antichrist. Eusebius applied them to A.D. 70. Tertullian applied them to both A.D. 70 and to a future time. Thus the lack of agreement which exists today on these matters is not a new thing at all. It has been with the Church for most of its existence.

Matthew 24:29-31, which I considered apocalyptic, was usually interpreted otherwise. But Premillennialists have little cause for jubilation in this fact, for invariably those who interpreted these verses as related to the second coming went on to include a general resurrection, a general judgment, and/or the end of the age. For this reason these interpretations are more favorable to Amillennialism than they are to Premillennialism.

I was surprised that so little attention was given to the problem of the meaning of the term "generation" (Matt. 24:34). Kik and others have designated this as the "time-text." The only reference I found to this was Clementina, and he interpreted it as I have. The events set forth in the verses prior to verse 34 were thus applied to the destruction of Jerusalem in A.D. 70.

Most of the comments on Matthew 25:31-46 were admonitions for all professed Christians to be charitable and hospitable towards others. However, when the authors did refer to the time element in the passage, they uniformly placed it at the end of the age which involved a general judgment. It was *people* who were the sheep and goats or kids, as it was often written, rather than nations.

CHAPTER 16

# THE ESCHATOLOGY OF CHAPTERS 9-11 OF ROMANS

Romans 9-11 constitute a unit. The trend of thought carries through. The arguments are linked together. Although chapter 11 is the major area of controversy, it is built on the foundation laid in the two previous chapters. The basic thrust of this passage is contemporary, rather than eschatological. Paul wrote this book to a church composed of both Jews and Gentiles. He was attempting to get across the idea that neither Jew nor Gentile had any significance. An interpretation of Romans that ignores this fact misses a very important aspect of the book.

## Romans 9

The designation "Israel" appears repeatedly in these chapters, but it does not always have the same significance. Therefore, in order for one to interpret Paul correctly, he must first ascertain just what people are involved in the term in each particular context. He also uses the term "Jews" with different meanings. In chapter 2 Paul moves from the use of the term "Jew" as referring to the descendants of Jacob to that of the Church or believers in Christ. These were regenerate persons whose lives had been changed by repentance and faith in Christ. Romans 2:28-29 reads:

For he is not a Jew, which is one outwardly; neither is that circumcision, which is outward in the flesh: But he is a Jew, which is one inwardly; and circumcision is that of the heart, in the spirit, and not in the letter; whose praise is not of men, but of God.

In a similar vein Paul writes, "For they are not all Israel, which are of Israel" (Rom. 9:6). The meaning here is that not all physical descendants of Jacob or Israel, are a part of the true Israel, the Church. This is sure to be contested, but the line of argument is quite plain. Isaac was the only son of Abraham who was accounted worthy (v. 7). Ishmael, and the several sons of

Keturah were rejected, even though they were begotten by Abraham. In the verses which follow Paul contends that not all of Isaac's posterity received the promises. Israel, or Jacob, was the only one to receive the favor of God. Esau was rejected. Those who were rejected were called children of the flesh (Rom. 9:8), rather than children of God.

What Paul's argument is designed to prove is that just as Abraham and Isaac had children of the flesh who failed to participate in the promises, so did Israel. Romans 9:7-24 constitutes a commentary on Romans 9:6 which is quoted a second time with explanatory notes added: "For they are not all Israel [children of God, partakers of the promise, believers, the Church, children of the spirit rather than the flesh], which are of Israel" (or who are lineal descendants of Jacob or Israel). In other words, that which held true regarding Abraham and Isaac having two kinds of descendants is likewise true of Israel.

Both John the Baptist (Matt. 3:9) and Jesus (John 8:33-44) made it clear to the Jews of their generation that lineal descent from Abraham was meaningless if they were not rightly related to God. The point Paul is making is similar. Only some Jews will be saved. Only the "children of the promise are counted for the seed" (Rom. 9:8). These "children of the promise" were "vessels of mercy, which he had afore prepared unto glory, even us, whom he hath called, not of the Jews only, but also of the Gentiles" (Rom. 9:23-24). Thus, this blessed group, the true Israel, the Church, is composed of both Jews and Gentiles.

Many passages could be presented which support this conclusion. Only two will be given at this point. Paul elsewhere indicated, "And if ye be Christ's, then are ye Abraham's seed, and heirs according to the promise" (Gal. 3:29). In the preceding verse Paul contended that Jew and Gentile shared equally in this promise for the distinction between them had been broken down. Again Paul says, "Now we, brethren, as Isaac was, are the children of promise" (Gal. 4:28). Paul is making the same argument in the Galatian epistle that he makes in Romans 9. Those who accept Christ and faithfully serve Him are the true children of promise, whether we be Jew by birth or Gentile. Thus, we see, that the Church is the true Israel. It is true that sometimes Paul uses the terms Jew and Israel in the sense of race, but it is also true that he uses them of the true believers, the Church.

# The Eschatology of Romans Chapters 9 - 11

Paul further emphasizes the oneness of Jews and Gentiles in Christ by quoting from Hosea 2:23 (Rom. 9:25-26). Paul interprets Hosea as meaning that the Gentiles who formerly were not considered the children of God would, through Christ, "be called the children of the living God." The emphasis is on the fact that Gentiles would be converted and become children of God. But what about the Jews? Paul discusses this in the next verse which reads, "Esaias also crieth concerning Israel, Though the number of the children of Israel be as the sand of the sea, a remnant shall be saved" (Rom. 9:27). The meaning comes through loud and clear that *not all of the Jews will be saved.* Only a portion, a remnant, a few of the physical descendants of Jacob will ever be saved.

This appears to be in direct contradiction to Romans 11:26 which states in part, "And so all Israel shall be saved." But this conflict is more apparent than real. It is a paradox. When properly interpreted, these are shown to be harmonious statements rather than being incompatible. How this seeming inconsistency is resolved will be considered in our study of chapter 11. Until then, the reader is urged to keep in mind that Romans 11:26 should not be interpreted as meaning that all persons of Jewish descent will be saved until a satisfactory explanation is found for Paul's statement in Romans 9:27 to the effect that only "a remnant shall be saved."

## Romans 10

This chapter begins with an expression of strong desire for the salvation of the Jewish race, but it closes with an admission that, in the main, the Jews were a "disobedient and gainsaying people." In between these two observations, Paul explains how people, both Jews and Gentiles, get saved. One becomes righteous or saved by submitting to God (v. 3). Christ is the end of the law to all believers whether Jew or Gentile (v. 4). Then in verses 9 and 10, Paul tells one and all, Jew and Gentile, how to get saved. The simple formula given in these verses is that one must believe on Christ from the heart, and that he must confess this belief with his mouth. Believing from the heart is more intense and profound than mere intellectual assent. It means to repent of one's sins and live in obedience to God's demands.

Paul makes it quite clear that this is the plan for both Jews and Gentiles to get saved in verses 12-13. These read:

For there is no difference between the Jew and the Greek: for the same Lord over all is rich unto all that call upon him. For whosoever shall call on the name of the Lord shall be saved.

How is it that so many continue to say there is a difference between Jew and Gentile, when Paul affirms that there is no difference? Does Paul indicate that the old difference will be restored? Not at all. Such a restoration would be a repudiation of the work of Christ who broke down the middle wall of partition (Eph. 2:14). The claim that that old wall will be erected in later years is totally unacceptable, because it cuts across biblical truths, and reverses the progression in God's plan of redemption.

Verses 14-15 tell of the importance of preaching in producing belief that is seated in the heart. Paul asserts the close relationship of preaching to believing in writing to the Corinthian church. He wrote, "it pleased God by the foolishness of preaching to save them that believe" (I Cor. 1:21). But if the Church is raptured to heaven just prior to the expected great tribulation, the group of believing Jews who are envisioned as exceptionally good evangelists is an impossibility. If they are believing Jews, they will be raptured to heaven as part of the Church, according to premillenarian theology. Therefore, this teaching must be recognized as a product of an over active imagination, rather than biblical exegesis.

In summing up chapter 10, it can be properly said to contain the basic elements of the plan of salvation. Whoever gets saved, both now and later, whether he be Jew or Gentile, will get saved because he has heard the gospel and as a result of this hearing, he has believed on Christ from his heart. If all Jews are to be saved, as it is contended by some, it will be because they respond from the heart to the preaching of the gospel—not because the glorified Christ appears to them at the end of the great tribulation.

## Romans 11

Paul begins this chapter by asking the rhetorical question, "Hath God cast away his people?" (Rom. 11:1). Paul argues that the fact that he has been accepted of the Lord proves the totality of the Jewish race had not been cast aside. Had all Jews been rejected, then he could not have been saved. That many Jews had been cast off, he readily admitted; but according to verse 5, there was a remnant accepted by the Lord. Paul considers himself and other Jewish believers in Christ as that remnant. This remnant was not cast aside; they heard the gospel and believed from the heart, according to chapter 10.

The rest of the Jews were cut off because they did not believe what they heard in the gospel of Christ.

In verses 6 and 7 Paul explains why most of the Jews were cut off, even though they sought the favor of the Lord. They sought by works rather than by grace. Because of this, the main body of Jews failed to obtain salvation. Paul says, "Israel hath not obtained." Israel cannot refer to all Jews, for Paul had argued in verse 1 that he was saved, and he was an Israelite after the flesh. Therefore, it appears evident that in verse 7 Israel refers to the unbelieving Jews. The reason for this is that "the election" (*ekloge* in the Greek) is used in contrast to Israel. This proves that Paul does not always refer to the great body of Jews when he uses the term translated by the English "elect" or "election." It may even exclude the main body of Jews as is true in this particular verse.

Whether the "election" refers only to the believing Jews, or whether it includes the believing Gentiles is immaterial at this point. It does refer to the "remnant," and that remnant does include the believing Jews to the exclusion of the great body of Jews. Although Paul does not mention the two olive trees until verse 17, he begins to build his argument based on this analogy as far back as verse 8. In verse 11 the stumbling of the Jews is pictured as the means by which the Gentiles could be converted. It should not be assumed that Paul is saying the atoning work of Christ would not have been available to the Gentiles apart from the Jews rejecting Christ. Such a view would depreciate the efficacy of Christ's death on Calvary. But according to the analogy he anticipates using, the only way a wild olive branch could be grafted into the tame olive was for a tame olive branch to be cut off. It is in this sense that Paul uses the stumbling of the Jews as necessary to the conversion of Gentiles.

In verse 11 Paul indicates the purpose God had in mind in the stumbling (disbelief and disobedience) of the Jews was not the casting away of the Jews, but rather as a means of reaching the Gentile people. Then in verse 12 he contrasts the falling and diminishing, in number, of the Jews to their fullness. Just what this fullness is can only be conjectured. Paul does not explain what he means. It is evidently the opposite of the diminishing, but absolutely nothing is said of when this fullness would occur, nor is anything said about how many would be involved. This text certainly does not say that it refers to a time when the total Jewish population will be saved. One who holds this view must transplant ideas from other sources into this text to get this answer.

The best explanation is that this fullness was realized during Paul's lifetime. In Acts 21:20 Luke informs us that there were myriads of Jews who believed. This is usually translated "thousands," but a literal translation would be "tens of thousands," for the word myriad means ten thousand. Many sources could be presented to prove that a sizable segment of the Jews did accept the Christian faith during the first Christian century. There is no adequate basis for contending that this refers to some future change in the Jewish attitude.

That he is not referring to an acceptance by the total Jewish population is indicated in verse 14 which reads, "If by any means I may provoke to emulation them which are my flesh, and might save some of them." Paul only anticipated a few Israelites after the flesh to get saved. Had he expected the total population of Jews to ever believe on the Lord, no doubt he would have expressed something of that belief at this point. It is generally recognized that Paul anticipated the second coming during his lifetime, and if all Jews were to be saved at that second coming, the saving of just a few requires considerable explanation to make it accord with that teaching.

The "receiving of them" (v. 15) cannot be made to apply to some future general acceptance by the Jews without doing violence to this passage. Paul refers to those who believed through his preaching (v. 14) as the "receiving of them" in verse 15. It is as though he said, "I hope to be instrumental in saving a few of the Jewish race," (v. 14), "and since these were cut off because of unbelief, receiving them into the Christian community would be 'life from the dead!' " (v. 15). The context does not support the idea of some future general acceptance of Christ by the Jewish population of that time. Rather it supports the idea that these Jews being influenced by Paul were a part of the fullness he mentioned in verse 14, and these were a part of those being received as from the dead (v. 15).

Verse 16 is a commentary on the unity that exists throughout the organism or substance. Two analogies are given. The first indicates that if the first grain that is gathered be holy, the dough made from those grains is also holy. And if the root of a tree be holy, then the branches will also be holy. The meaning is that the Church Jesus established here on earth is composed of holy persons only. Since Christ is the head, and without question He is holy, then the members of His body must also be holy. In the parable of the vine and the branches (John 15:1-8), branches that did not produce (holy) fruit were excised (John 15:2).

In the several verses following verse 16, Paul gives his analogy of the two olive trees. The wild olive tree is analogous to the Gentiles. The (good) olive tree is analogous to the Jews. The branches are analogous to people. As Paul develops this topic, he moves from the position of the good olive being Jews to it representing the Church. The part about branches being cut off makes this clear. Unbelief did not cut one off from national Israel. An unbeliever was just as much a physical Jew in unbelief as he would be were he a believer. But the unbelieving Jew was cut off from the election and the Church.

The unity of the entire organism was stated back in verse 16. In the verses that follow, unity is also stressed. Verse 17 indicates that the branches from the wild olive tree were partakers of "the root and fatness of the olive tree." Since the root was holy, so were these new branches which were analogous to the Gentile converts. This unity is further stressed in verse 24 where it is stated that the wild olive branches (Gentiles) were "grafted contrary to nature into a good olive tree." It is a well known fact that ordinary grafting does not change the nature of the fruit a branch bears. According to nature, a wild olive branch grafted into a tame olive would continue to bear wild olives, even though the rest of the tree bore tame olives. For this reason, Paul had to insert the phrase "contrary to nature" to show that the very nature of the wild olive branch was changed so that it coincided with the nature of the other branches.

There is an essential unity between what Paul says here and what is found in Ephesians 2. In that chapter Paul wrote of Jews and Gentiles being one in Christ. Gentiles who were "Miens from the commonwealth of Israel, and strangers from the covenants of promise" (Eph. 2:12) ceased to be "strangers and foreigners, but fellow citizens with the saints, and of the household of God" (Eph. 2:19). Words could hardly express the unification of Jews and Gentiles any stronger, yet certain writers in an effort to refute the plain intent of Paul's statements insist that this oneness is temporary during what they call "the church age." The basis for this is that Paul speaks of this union as constituting a "new man" (Eph. 2:15).

But in Romans 11 nothing is said of a "new man" or a different man. Therefore, the tactic used to explain away a truth found in Ephesians 2 is discredited by Romans 11. In Romans 11, the good olive represents nothing that is not Jewish. The root, the fatness, the branches, the fruit are all essentially Jewish, for these are in contrast to the wild olive which figure represents the Gentiles. When a wild olive branch is grafted into the tame olive tree, it partakes "of the root and fatness of the olive tree" (Rom. 11:17). And since it becomes like the original branches (Rom. 11:24), any distinction that had existed in the past is lost. Thus Jew and Gentile become one in fact; not just in theory or for a period of time. The difference between Jew and Gentile is completely and forever obliterated. They are one.

The regrafting of the Jews (Rom. 11:24) is not an eschatological event. Every Jew that became saved during the first Christian century was such a regraft. Each of the tens of thousands of Jews who had believed on Jesus (Acts 21:20) were regrafts into the tame olive tree. These had been cut off because of unbelief and disobedience. As they accepted Christ, they were regrafted into the tame olive. They had been rejected because, even though they were Jews, they did not possess the essential nature of a true branch. The root that bore them was holy, but they were unholy. For them to have remained a part of the tree would have destroyed the essential oneness of the root, fatness, and branches of the tree.

On the other hand, when a Gentile believed on Christ, his nature was changed so that he could be grafted into the tame olive without destroying the unity of the tree. Likewise, when a Jew rejected his former unbelief which made it necessary to excise him, he could be restored as a branch, for now his nature was changed so that he was like the other branches. Thus, the basis for being grafted into the tame olive was the same for a Jew as it was for a Gentile. When either believed in Christ, he was grafted into the tame olive where only those who partook of the nature of the root (holy from Rom. 11:16) were eligible.

The meaning of verse 25 is debatable. It reads in part, "that blindness [hardness or callousness is better] in part is happened to Israel, until the fulness of the Gentiles be come in" (Rom. 11:25). Israel, in this verse, undoubtedly refers to the Jews in general. A consensus of opinion exists at this point. This blindness or hardness was not complete for it existed only in part. Although other meanings are advanced, the apparent meaning is that not all Jews were blinded, hardened, or calloused. The large number of Jewish Christians attested to the fact that only a part of the Jewish people were hardened. Paul was one of these Jews who were not hardened at the time of this writing, although at one time he had been hardened.

Before considering the duration of this hardness and what is to follow, let us examine the phrase "fulness of the Gentiles." Apparently it refers to something distinct from the "times of the Gentiles." The term Paul uses is *pleroma*. It has a variety of meanings such as fullness, completeness, fulfillment, abundance, that which makes up a deficiency as of a number. Thayer informs us that etymologically it is passive. What he means is that originally it referred to that which filled something else, as a ship is filled with its cargo. *Pleroma* is so used several times in the New Testament.

A striking example is, "For the earth is the Lord's and the fullness thereof" (I Cor. 10:26). If *pleroma* is used in the same way in Romans 11:25, then it refers to filling or satiation of the Gentiles, rather than to a quota or specific number of Gentiles. But Paul uses *pleroma* of the number of Jews who accepted Christ in this same chapter (Rom. 11:12), and we take it that he is using the same word here in verse 25 of the Gentiles in the same way he had used it of the Jews. In verse 12 we understand that Paul means the total number of Jews who could be considered believers of all ages past, present, and future, and the "fulness of the Gentiles" in verse 25 has the same meaning for the Gentiles. This interpretation is founded on the idea of completeness being the meaning of *pleroma* in both verses.

If this view is accepted, the duration of the hardness or blindness of the Jews naturally follows as continuing right up to the end of the age; for the number of converted Gentiles will not be complete or full (*pleroma*) until the consummation. Thus, instead of pointing to a point in history, it actually refers to the end of history. Scofield agrees that the "fulness of the Gentiles" refers to "the completion of the purpose of God in this age" (see note on Rom. 11:25), but his meaning and mine are by no means identical.

Scofield's note on Revelation 7:14 claims that during what he terms the "great tribulation" "an innumerable multitude of Gentiles" will be saved through the activity of a select group of Israelites. His claim will be refuted later. At this juncture all we wish to say is that if an "innumerable multitude of Gentiles" are to be converted during the interim he posits between the so-called rapture and the second coming of Christ, then he should move his *pleroma* ("fulness of the Gentiles") forward enough to at least include this period of salvation work. It is quite illogical to assume that the fulness of the Gentiles has been reached when within the short span of seven years a group too numerous to count is to be saved.

Of course, some will contend that this verse teaches a softening of the Jews after the "fulness of the Gentiles" has been reached, but this is an invalid conclusion or interpretation. Our attention is focused on *achris*, or *achri*, as it is more frequently spelled. It is translated "until" in reference to Israel's hardness or blindness, which was to continue "until the fulness of the Gentiles be come in" (Rom. 11:25). This word is translated by such words as till, until, to, unto, and while. The word itself says nothing about future conditions. Any deductions about the future must be determined from the context not the word itself. If a change does occur or is indicated, it can be in either direction. Note the following instance where the condition was more severe after the "until" than it was before.

"For until [*achri*] the law sin was in the world" (Rom. 5:13). No one would contend that sin ceased to exist after the law was given, for Paul argues that "the law entered, that the offence might abound" (Rom. 5:20), and "that by the commandment sin might become exceeding sinful" (Rom. 7:13). Taking this example as our pattern would mean that the blindness or hardness that had come upon Israel would become more severe after the fullness of the Gentiles became a reality than it had been previous to that. But since we believe that the fullness of the Gentiles takes us to the utmost limits of time as we know it, we conclude that Paul is saying the blindness or hardness of Israel would continue to be "in part" right up to the end of the age and the beginning of eternity without reference to what it would be afterwards. After an excellent discussion of some length, Lenski concludes, "The idea that 'until' means that the petrification will be converted into softness is untenable."[218]

Romans 11:26 may well be considered the crucial verse of these three chapters. The first clause, "And so all Israel shall be saved," is the basis for Scofield and other Dispensationalists, as well as Premillennialists in general, to hold that at the second coming of Christ the total Jewish world population will be converted. The Dispensational view is that the Jews will be regathered into Palestine before the second coming and in a state of unbelief. Then, at the revelation of Christ, the entire nation will repent and believe on Him. Much of this view is very far-fetched, and the biblical basis on which it is constructed is very tenuous. This position cannot be maintained when this verse, its context, and the full scope of the Bible are considered.

---

218   R. C. H. Lenski, *The Interpretation of St. Paul's Epistle to the Romans*, p. 721.

First of all, elsewhere in this section Paul indicates that he anticipated no more than "some of them" becoming saved (Rom. 11:14). Even more forceful is his statement that "the wrath is come upon them [the Jews] to the uttermost" (I Thess. 2:16). Moffatt renders it, "But the Wrath is on them to the bitter end!" The Amplified Bible reads, "But God's wrath has come upon them at last—completely and forever!" The NASB renders it much like the KJV, but in the margin the meaning is given as "forever; or altogether." This indicates that most of the Jews will experience the "wrath to come" (1 Thess. 1:10), as well as temporal wrath which has been poured out on them from time to time.

The plain intent of these passages is that there will be no mass conversion of the Jews such as Dispensationalists and many other Premillennialists envision. They will, as a nation, be among those upon whom Christ will descend, "In flaming fire taking vengeance on them that know not God" (II Thess. 1:8). When Christ comes the second time, He will not come as a Saviour of the Jews or any other people. He will come as Judge. This being true, we must look for some other meaning for Romans 11:26 than a mass conversion of the Jews; otherwise we have truth contradicting truth, and this is completely unacceptable.

At least three considerations engage our attention in exegeting Romans 11:26.

1. What is the meaning of *houtos* which is translated by "so" or "thus" in the clause, "And so all Israel shall be saved"?
2. What is the meaning of Israel in this same verse?
3. What is the connection between this clause and its context?

These will be considered in the above order.

Thayer states that *houtos* "refers to what precedes; in the manner spoken of; in the way described"; as well as "thus, so." Now just how was Israel being saved at the time Paul wrote this letter to the Romans? They were being saved in small numbers (Rom. 11:14), and these were being saved through the preaching of the gospel (Rom. 10:12-16). Therefore, we conclude that Paul is saying that all of Israel that become saved will become saved after this fashion, or according to this pattern, or in the manner just described.

This being the case, Paul is not saying that at some future time the total Jewish population will accept Christ; nor is he saying that the present hardness or blindness will be changed to softness and proper vision. Instead he is saying that the present hardness, except for a few, will continue to be the case until the consummation. Further, he is not saying that when Christ comes again that Jews will be saved by this revelation of Christ. Rather he is saying that all Jews who do become saved will be saved through the preaching of the gospel. Paul contends that there is no distinction between Jews and Greeks (Rom. 10:12) All salvation comes through the preaching of the gospel. No other means is offered then, now, or in the future.

Those who teach a future conversion of the total Jewish population at the second coming, translate *houtos* as though it were an adverb of time. These render it as though Paul were saying, "And at that time," or "Then all Israel will be saved." But this interpretation is not justified. Had that been Paul's meaning, surely he would have used *tote* which is an adverb of time. Had he done so, he would have meant that at some future time all Israel would be saved. But *houtos* does not say that, and it is improper and misleading to attempt to force such an interpretation of what Paul did write.

And now we consider the meaning of "Israel" in this verse. It has been shown that Paul uses Israel in different ways. It may mean the Jewish people as a whole; it may mean the remnant; and it may refer to the Church. In verse 26 it cannot refer to national Israel, the Jewish nation, or the total Jewish population for several reasons. First, if it means the totality of the descendants of Jacob, men like Saul who were utterly rejected by God will somehow be saved. Few will go so far. But once it is admitted that "all Israel" does not mean every descendant of Jacob, the literal interpretation has been abandoned. Those unwilling to include evil Jews who are already dead as being included in the expression, usually narrow it down to that generation of Jews which is living at the time of the second coming.

But this interpretation is untenable. Paul says nothing about a generation of Jews being saved. He says, "all Israel." His statement is to the effect that after the manner then existing of most of Israel being blinded or hardened with relatively few being saved, "all Israel" would be saved. The meaning is that all descendants of Jacob that are worthy of the name will be saved. Those who are blinded or hardened are not worthy of the name Israelite. Part of this unworthy group is a segment of Jews of whom Jesus said, "Ye are of your father, the devil, and the lusts of your father ye will do" (John 8:44). Although these were descendants of Abraham, and Israelites in the fleshly sense, they were not of spiritual Israel, the true Israel, or "the Israel of God" (Gal. 6:16).

Now that it has been determined that *houtos* points to the manner or way by which Jews will be saved, rather than to a time when all Jews will be saved; and since all Israel has been shown to refer to the believers within national Israel, rather than to the totality of the Jewish population; it is now appropriate to look into the relationship which the statement, "And so all Israel shall be saved," bears to its context.

Romans 9-11 deals with the Church and the way that Jews and Gentiles become a part of it. Not all Jews are believers or persons worthy of the name of Israel. Paul declares, "For they are not all Israel, which are of Israel" (Rom. 9:6). The Church is composed of believers from among the Gentiles as well as the Jews. Paul states it includes, "Even us, whom he hath called, not of the Jews only, but also of the Gentiles" (Rom. 9:24). Chapter 10 sets forth the manner by which both Jews and Gentiles are converted and brought into the Church. It is through belief in the preaching of the gospel of Jesus Christ. This is the manner by which "all Israel" mentioned in Romans 11:26 is to be saved. It will not be by the appearance of Jesus Christ at His second coming. The manner of their salvation is clearly set forth in chapter 10. This must not be omitted in interpreting Romans 11:26.

In the early verses of chapter 11, Paul contends that Israel has not been cast away for he and other Jewish Christians constitute the remnant. But note that he never holds out the idea of national Israel accepting Christ. In verse 14 he recognizes that only "some of them" will be saved. The regrafting of the Jews (vv. 22-24) refers to the regrafting then going on—not a regrafting of the entire nation of Israel. Paul was such a regraft. James, the brother of Christ, was an unbeliever until after the resurrection of Christ. He, and all other subsequent believers in Christ from the Jewish population were regrafts. Nothing in these verses implies a mass regrafting.

The "mystery" of verse 25 is often said to refer to a future mass conversion of the Jewish nation, but this is not the intent. The idea of the Jews being God's preferred people was so deeply imbedded in the thinking of the Jewish nation that the ascendancy of the Jews in this respect would not have constituted a mystery. They interpreted Old Testament prophecies in a way favorable to the Jews, even when the intent was very plainly that the Gentiles would also be blessed by the atoning work of Jesus Christ. Therefore, the mystery was that only a few Jews would accept Christ, although they had the first opportunity to receive Him. The hardness or blindness was to remain on the mass of Jews, even until the last Gentile convert came to Christ. And this, of course, brings us to the time of the consummation. In other words, there would be no softening of the attitude of the Jews as a whole as long as this age lasts.

Lenski states this truth as follows:

> What the future will show to the very end of time is the mystery regarding which Paul offers the revelation he has received. They [the Jews] will endure until the last Gentile is brought into the kingdom and the Lord returns for the great judgment. Yea, they will endure—strange to say! to the very end just as Paul and the Romans saw them at their time, petrified in unbelief, but ever only in part and never as a whole, and so, with this situation prevailing, with a part ever being reached by God's grace despite the petrification of the rest, all God's true Israel, all of it that really deserves the name will be saved.[219]

In this way Lenski interprets "all Israel" as referring to the total number of Jews who accept Christ or who are rightly related to God. Israel, in this sense, refers to the true Israel, rather than to national Israel which remains hardened to this day.

We now turn to that part of the context that follows the statement, "And so all Israel shall be saved." The latter portion of verse 26 points to the first coming of Christ. Scofield, in his center column references, places this at the second coming. But the second coming will not be to deliver from sin. The second coming will be to receive those who have been freed from the bondage of sin through the gospel, and to take vengeance on those who rejected that gospel. The teaching that Christ will come a second time to save the Jews is a misconception of biblical truth.

This perversion of the truth by Dispensationalists and other Premillennialists who foresee a future time when national Israel shall become followers of Christ is accomplished by claiming that the gospel is not the fulfillment of the new covenant. Walvoord points out that Premillennialists who anticipate a future time of universal Jewish acceptance of Christ do so on the basis of the new covenant having a special significance to the Jews at a later time as well as to the Church in this present age, or as of two new covenants, one for the Church and another later one for Israel. He adds,—

---

219 *Ibid.,* pp. 718-719

"Romans 11:27 refers the detailed fulfillment of the covenant of Jeremiah to the second coming of Christ and the deliverance of Israel, a passage which amillenarians characteristically avoid as the plague."[220]

If Amillennialists have avoided verse 27, it is because they feel they have made their point by proving that "all Israel" of verse 26 does not refer to national Israel and a specific generation of national Israel. And if "all Israel" simply refers to those who accept Christ through the gospel, the true Israel if you please, then the idea of verse 27 referring to a future salvation of the Jews has no foundation. But since Walvoord, Tan, and others accuse us of avoiding that verse, it will be considered in detail.

That the new covenant is for both Jew and Gentile is evident from Romans 3:9 and 11:32. Paul insists that both Jews and Gentiles are in bondage to sin until released through faith in Christ. That he comes back to this statement first made in Romans 3:9 after mentioning the covenant in Romans 11:27 proves that the covenant he has in mind includes both Jews and Gentiles. Any effort to make it refer to the Jews in a special way is excluded by the context. There is no solid basis for anticipating another covenant, nor is there any reason to expect a different kind of application of the present covenant to the Jews. Our investigation is to determine whether the gospel is the fulfillment of the Old Testament prophecies of a new covenant or is there something yet to be fulfilled regarding the Jews.

It has already been shown that the hardness, in part, of the Jews would continue to the very end. It has also been shown that "all Israel" of Romans 11:26 refers not to national Israel but to the true Israel of believers. The covenant Paul mentions in verse 27 is nothing other than that which is based on Christ's atoning work on Calvary. The words that Paul quotes are from Isaiah 59:20-21 and 27:9. He does not refer directly to Jeremiah 31:31-37 in which this covenant is called a "new covenant," but since Isaiah and Jeremiah both refer to the same covenant, there can be no objection to thinking of Paul's words as including the passage from Jeremiah.

Paul's words are: "There shall come out of Sion the Deliverer, and shall turn away ungodliness from Jacob: For this is my covenant unto them, when I shall take away their sins" (Rom. 11:26-27). Were the conditions set forth

---

220 Walvoord, *Israel in Prophecy*, p. 55.

in these quotations fulfilled at the first advent? If they were, then there is no basis for contending for a future fulfillment. An examination of the specific prophecies will show that each has already had its fulfillment.

Did the Deliverer come? Who can deny that Jesus Christ is the Deliverer prophesied by Isaiah and referred to by Paul? Even those who look for a future fulfillment recognize that it is Christ who is the Deliverer, and they cannot deny that He did come as a Deliverer. Jesus proclaimed the fact that He was commissioned "to preach deliverance to the captives" (Luke 4:18 and Isa. 61:1). Did He come out of Zion? He did. Whether Zion is taken to mean Mt. Moriah and the temple area or Jerusalem is immaterial. He came out of both. Simeon found Him in the temple (Luke 2:25-35). Anna met Him there in the temple (Luke 2:36-39). He met the doctors of the law there (Luke 2:46).

That He spent many hours in the temple is indicated by His words, "I sat daily with you teaching in the temple" (Matt. 26:55). That He cleansed the temple is admitted by all. The picture painted by those who look for a future advent to bring deliverance to the Jews has Christ coming out of heaven to deliver—not out of Zion. Now this writer recognizes that Christ will return from heaven at His second coming, but he denies that Christ will bring physical deliverance to the Jews or any other people at that coming. The coming Paul wrote about has the Deliverer coming out of Zion—not out of heaven. By this means we can know that Paul and Isaiah were writing of the first advent, not the second one.

Did Christ turn away ungodliness from Jacob? He certainly did for those Israelites who would accept Him and His message. His followers were taught to "hunger and thirst after righteousness" (Matt. 5:6), and that their righteousness must "exceed the righteousness of the scribes and Pharisees" (Matt. 5:20). He taught that the Holy Spirit whom He would send would "reprove the world of sin and of righteousness" (John 16:8). His disciple, John, tells us that the blood of Christ cleanses from all sin, if we walk in the light (I John 1:7), and that he will even cleanse us from "all unrighteousness" (I John 1:9).

Did Christ establish a new covenant at His first advent? He did. It should be borne in mind that God's covenants are unilateral offers. Man cannot bargain for better conditions. He can only accept or reject. The Bible terms for God's covenants are *berith* (Heb.) and *diatheke* (Greek). In the New Testament *diatheke* is often translated by testament rather than covenant.

Except in the Hebrew epistle, covenant is a better translation. Actually the two divisions of our Bible should be thought of as the Old Covenant and the New Covenant, rather than the Old and New Testaments. Strangely, Dispensationalists make Christ's sacrifice the foundation for the new covenant, but they insist that the Church of today does not operate under it. According to their teaching, the new covenant does not become effective until the second coming of Christ.

The New Testament has four places where it is recorded that Jesus referred to the fruit of the vine which they drank at the institution of the Lord's supper as His blood and the "new testament" (Matt. 26:28; Mark 14:24; Luke 22:20; I Cor. 11:25). Thus every time we take communion we testify to the fact that Christ did establish a new covenant, and that the Church does operate under that covenant. In each instance testament is a translation of *diatheke*.

Paul recognized two covenants in the letter to the Galatians. It cannot be denied that these two covenants refer to the Mosaic covenant and the covenant under which the Church functions, the new covenant (Gal. 4:24). The covenants mentioned in Ephesians 2:12 are these same two covenants. Paul was an able minister of "the new testament" (*diatheke*, I Cor. 3:6). The Hebrew epistle has so much about the new covenant Jesus gave us that only portions will be noted. Chapter 8 has already been discussed elsewhere showing that the new covenant of Jeremiah 31:31-34 was the same as the new covenant discussed in that chapter, and that it was in effect at that time.

Chapter 9 of Hebrews continues the comparison of the old covenant with the new. In verse 12 it is stated that Christ "obtained eternal redemption for us" through the shedding of "his own blood." Christ is now "the mediator of the new testament" (*diatheke* Heb. 9:15). The inspired writer again quotes Jeremiah 31:33 to show that the covenant he has in mind is the one Jeremiah wrote about (Heb. 10:16). It reads, "This is the covenant that I will make with them after those days, saith the Lord, I will put my laws into their hearts, and in their minds will I write them." Verses 19-20 indicate that a "new and living way" has been the result of the shedding of "the blood of Jesus." Then in verse 29 "the blood of the covenant" indubitably refers to the shed blood of Jesus. The context proves beyond a shadow of a doubt that that covenant is now in effect, and that it is possible to violate the provisions of that covenant.

Then in Hebrews 12:22-24 this new covenant is connected with the Church in such a way as to make it evident that the Church does now function under that new covenant. These verses read:

But ye are come [perfect tense being accomplished in the past but presently effective] unto Mount Sion, and unto the city of the living God, the heavenly Jerusalem, and to an innumerable company of angels, To the general assembly and church of the firstborn, which are written in heaven, and to God the Judge of all, and to the spirits of just men made perfect, And to Jesus the mediator of the new covenant, and to the blood of sprinkling, that speaketh better things than that of Abel.

In the above, persons have come into the Church through the mediatorial work and the shed blood of Christ. The only conclusion that can be reached from these verses is that the Church is the outgrowth of the new covenant which is presently in effect.

Not only did Christ establish a new covenant at His first advent, but He established it with the Jews (Israel). Paul informs us that Jesus was "made under the law" (Gal. 4:4) in order that he might "redeem them that are under the law" (Gal. 4:5). He declared, "I am not sent but unto the lost sheep of the house of Israel" (Matt. 15:24). His command to the twelve prior to the establishment of the new covenant at Calvary was, "Go not into the way of the Gentiles, and into any city of the Samaritans enter ye not: But go rather to the lost sheep of the house of Israel" (Matt. 10:6). Only after the covenant was confirmed by His death (Heb. 9:16-17) did He commission them to go to all nations (Matt. 28:19-20).

The institution of the Lord's supper is quite pointed in this respect. That this meal pointed to the confirmation of the "new testament" (*diatheke*-covenant) is witnessed to by all three synoptists and Paul. And what nationality were the men who partook of this meal with Christ? All were Jews or Israelites. And what right did they have to accept this covenant (*diatheke*) which Christ offered? They had been hand-picked by Christ to be the representatives of the new Israel, the Church, which He was forming out of old national Israel.

The last provision of Paul's quotation (Rom. 11:26-27) was that he would "take away their sins" (Rom. 11:27). The reason that the name given to Christ was Jesus was because "he shall save his people from their sins" (Matt. 1:21). That Christ did forgive sins is amply verified by the Scripture. That He continues to remove the sins of penitent men is true beyond question.

# The Eschatology of Romans Chapters 9 - 11

Thus we see that every portion of the prophecy found in Romans 11:26-27 has been fulfilled already. No sound basis exists for holding that a future fulfillment is intended.

The basis upon which it is insisted that a future fulfillment is involved is a mental concept that demands that national Israel must respond to Christ in a favorable manner. But this is a concept that is not supported by the Bible. Adequate reasons for rejecting this concept have been given repeatedly in this volume. It cannot be established exegetically from Romans 11:26-27 or any other portion of the Bible.

## Concluding Remarks

Not a single instance was found among the early writers where chapter 9 of the Roman epistle was interpreted other than as it is interpreted in this volume. All agreed that Paul was distinguishing between national Israel and spiritual Israel in chapter 9. Verse 6 was consistently interpreted as meaning, "They are not all of the true or spiritual Israel who are a part of national Israel or Israel after the flesh." In most instances the Gentile converts were considered a part of the remnant or spiritual Israel. No significant passages were found from their writings on chapter 10.

Origen was the only writer found who interpreted the "fulness" of the Jews as meaning that all Jews would be saved at some future time, and he phrased it in the subjunctive "may" as if he had reservations at this point.[221] References were meager on Romans 11:15-24. Irenaeus says that the "lump meant us," but he does not elaborate on just who is meant by "us."[222] Tertullian does write of the "remaining expectation of Israel," but just what that expectation was, and whether it would be fulfilled is not stated.[223] The only reference on these verses that was found which pointed to a day when Israel would believe was in the *Testaments of the Twelve Patriarchs*. It did include the words, "a day on which Israel shall believe."[224] Just when this was to be is not stated.

Apparently none of the very early writers discussed Romans 11:26. Origen was the first writer to make a significant statement on the "all Israel" of this verse, at least so far as was found. He did write: "If fulness of the

---

221 Origen, *op. cit.*, vol. IV, p. 610.
222 Irenaeus, *op. cit.*, vol. I, p. 327.
223 Tertullian, *op. cit.*, vol. IV, p. 82.
224 *Ibid.*, vol. VIII, p. 26.

Gentiles be come in, all Israel shall be saved."[225] I take this to mean national Israel, for he implies that although God had divorced national Israel, He could take her back in spite of His prohibition that men not do this. It has been shown before that this position is untenable. Chrysostom makes one's ancestry of no significance.[226]

No intimation was found that a future covenant with Israel was taught in Romans 11:27. This tenet of Dispensationalism dates from the time that Dispensationalism itself originated during the first half of the nineteenth century. This teaching should be relegated to the theological scrap heap.

Nothing was found in the writings of the early Church fathers that linked Romans 9-11 with a millennium. Apparently the millennialists of the early centuries based their teachings on other texts, rather than on these three chapters. Thus the writings of the early Church fathers do not mention two of the three major issues based on Romans 9-11. They say nothing of a millennium, and they say nothing of a new covenant with Israel. Some evidence for a belief that national Israel would be saved was found, but this was counteracted by other writings against such a view. The total impact is to discredit the Dispensational view, rather than to support it.

---

225 Origen, *op. cit.*, vol. X, p. 508.
226 Chrysostom, *op. cit.*, vol. XI, pp. 493-494.

CHAPTER 17

# THE ESCHATOLOGY OF THE CORINTHIAN LETTERS

Only two passages from Paul's letters to the church at Corinth are of sufficient length and importance to receive consideration in this chapter. These are I Corinthians 15, especially from verse 20 onward, and II Corinthians 5:1-10. The first of these is the longest and most complete passage in the Bible on the resurrection. Some interesting side lights are also found therein. The second passage deals with the intermediate state which I prefer to call the disembodied state.

## I Corinthians 15

Two words used in this chapter require our consideration at the very beginning of this study. These are *anastasis* and forms of *egeiro*. Paul uses *anastasis* four times in this chapter, and each time it refers to the future resurrection at the end of the age. Forms of *egeiro* are used 19 times, and it is used of Christ's resurrection as well as the future general resurrection. This can be seen by reading verse 16. "For if the dead rise not, [at the end of the age—*egeiro*] then is not Christ raised" (or resurrected from the dead—*egeiro*). It is impossible to inquire into the reasons Paul may have had for using *egeiro* more often than *anastasis*. Elsewhere Paul does use *anastasis* of Christ's resurrection (Rom. 1:4), but in this passage he uses it only of the general resurrection.

In verses 1-19 Paul lays the foundation for his discussion of a future resurrection of the dead. His thesis is that our hope of a bodily resurrection is based on the bodily resurrection of Jesus. He testifies to the bodily resurrection of Christ, then contends that if this be not true, he and others are false witnesses; we are still in our sins, and there will be no future resurrection. Throughout the chapter, Paul's main consideration is of the "saints." He does not consider the wicked except incidentally.

Christ is classified as "the firstfruits of them that slept" (v. 20). Resuscitations to physical life had occurred in the past, but Christ was the first to be raised with an immortal body. Those who arose (*egeiro*) after Christ's resurrection could have been given immortal bodies at that time (Matt. 27:52-53) as far as this verse is concerned, but the order given "afterward they that are Christ's at his coming" (*parousia*) (v. 23) militates against this view. If they did receive immortal bodies, they constitute a unique group.

We take verses 21-22 to mean that as physical death comes to all through Adam, the physical resurrection comes to all through Christ. This seems to be an incidental reference to the wicked dead. The arguments that are advanced to make this refer to the righteous dead and not the wicked dead have merit. My main objection to that view is that it requires reading into the passage an idea that is not expressed, unless it be in the phrase "in Christ." I prefer to consider both clauses of verse 22 as instrumental, rather than locative. Thus the reading would be, "For as through Adam all die, even so through the instrumentality of Christ all shall be made alive."

Two reasons are advanced for this interpretation. First, the all who die in or through Adam should be comparable to all who are made alive in or through Christ. Since both saint and sinner die in or through Adam, then both saint and sinner are made alive in or through Christ; and it is easier to defend the "through Christ" than the locative or "in Christ" translation. The latter is defended by claiming that Christ is the federal head of the human race, hence all humanity is "in Christ" in this limited sense, but this meaning is extremely doubtful.

The second reason for preferring the rendering "through Christ," rather than "in Christ" is that it supports the idea of a general resurrection which I understand the Bible to teach. In this passage, as in I Thessalonians 4, Paul's thinking is centered on the Christians, rather than on the wicked or on both the righteous and the wicked. However, it strengthens the case for a general resurrection to find an incidental reference to the resurrection of the wicked within the framework of a discussion that does not directly refer to them.

Verses 23-26 are of sufficient importance to justify quoting them.

But every man in his own order: Christ the firstfruits; afterward they that are Christ's at his coming. Then cometh the end, when he shall have delivered up the kingdom to God, even the Father; when he shall have put down all rule and all authority and power. For he must reign till he hath put all enemies under his feet. The last enemy that shall be destroyed is death.

The order of the resurrection is given in verse 23. It is again stated that Christ is the firstfruits. Afterward, or at a later time, those who belong to Him are to be raised, resurrected, or made alive. The wicked are ignored at this point, but the idea of a general resurrection is not excluded by this fact. Paul is answering questions regarding Christians, and he addresses himself to those questions. He is not writing a systematic theology. For this reason some details are omitted. But surely Paul would have clarified the issue if the evil were to be resurrected at a time different to that of the righteous.

Paul only lists two resurrections in verse 23. Christ's resurrection constitutes the "firstfruits." That is the first of the harvesting. A single general harvest is then indicated by the words, "afterward they that are Christ's at his coming." The Greek term for the word "coming" is *parousia*. It has been shown that the term *parousia* always refers to the second coming of Christ. Thus the only future resurrection envisioned by Paul is at the second coming. But this is explained away by advocates of several resurrections.

Tan draws an unwarranted conclusion from this verse. He says, "Paul calls the resurrection of Christ 'the first fruits' (I Cor. 15:23), denoting a harvest scene of many 'fruits' (resurrections). The Scriptural concept of the resurrections can therefore admit the resurrection of saints at the rapture before the tribulation."[227] But the Greek text says Christ is the "first fruit" (singular) rather than plural. The argument by Tan is inaccurate. His conclusion is erroneous. Christ's resurrection and the general resurrection are the only two resurrections Paul mentions. There is only one future resurrection.

But Tan holds that the Church will be raptured away seven years prior to the *parousia* or true second coming. Paul's words do not admit of this interpretation. Tan bolsters his position with imported concepts from the Revelation which he in turn misinterprets. It is hermeneutically unsound to displace plain statements such as I Corinthians 15:23 with concepts formed from a book filled with symbols such as is true of the Revelation.

Scofield makes no reference to verse 23 in his notes, but in his note on verse 52 he does refer back to verse 23. In this note he envisions a resurrection of the righteous at the rapture, and a resurrection of those who became saved and died during the seven year interval he sees between the rapture and the true second coming. He combines these two separate resurrections into a single resurrection of two phases. Then he states there will be a

---

227 Tan, *op. cit.*, p. 343.

resurrection of the wicked dead at the time of the consummation. He says nothing about the resurrection of the nation of Jews who are supposed to be converted at the second coming, and others who just might become saved during the millennium. Tan's "many 'fruits' (resurrections)" is the logical end of these unscriptural concepts and projections.

Moving on to verse 24, Paul speaks with finality: "Then cometh the end." According to the order of events Paul has set forth in these verses, the next event of importance is the end of the age, of the world, and of Christ's reign, following the second coming of Christ. This is quite in accord with the teaching of those who say that the kingdom was established at the first coming; that Christ is now reigning on the throne of David, and that the consummation occurs at the second coming. But for those who say the kingdom is yet future, it plays havoc; for it completely omits their projected establishment of the kingdom at the second coming as they believe.

It is argued that the "then" of verse 23, and the "then" of verse 24 (from *epeita* and *eita*) do not prohibit a time element between the events. No objection is raised to these. These words simply establish the sequence of events. But if Paul believed in a millennial reign in which Christ was to reign over a kingdom yet to be established, it is inconceivable that he would omit the establishment of that kingdom in the order of events which he has given us. Thus we conclude that no such kingdom is to be established, and that the time of the end, and the time that Christ delivers the kingdom over to the Father are closely associated with His second coming, the *parousia*. Thus, the time that Christ ends His reign is in reality the time that most Premillennialists contend He will begin His reign.

The putting down of "all rule and all authority and power" (v. 24) is interpreted as referring to the dissolution of all temporal governments, and the complete suppression of all antagonistic spiritual powers. This is accomplished at the second coming along with the general resurrection and the end of the world. An earthly reign in which these powers remain to some extent, but are held in subjection by divine power is not required, nor is it the scriptural approach.

Verses 25-26 state that Christ is to reign until death is abolished. But when is death destroyed? Is it to be gradually eliminated on a piecemeal basis, or is it to be by a sudden stroke? Amillennialists and Postmillennialists contend it will come by a sudden stroke through a general resurrection at the second coming of Christ. Premillennialists in general and

Dispensationalists in particular hold that it will be a process which lasts for over 1,000 years.

Since death is destroyed for those who are resurrected, each resurrection indicates a partial destruction of death. At least it no longer holds sway over resurrected persons. The Premillennial doctrine demands at least two resurrections, and it is practically impossible to limit it to just two. It is not reasonable to assume that Christ's victory over death will be a lingering battle such as this would indicate. A single stroke coming suddenly is much more likely.

This idea of a lingering death posits resurrected beings living with and having communication with persons who are still in the flesh. A situation such as this is incongruous. It cannot be substantiated by biblical exegesis. It is only by importing ideas that are not clear-cut in themselves into other ideas that are not clearly defined that such a conclusion can be reached.

But does Paul indicate that death will be destroyed at the *parousia*? I believe he does. Premillennialists have been unable to prove a period of time between the *parousia* and the abolishment of death, therefore I contend that death is abolished at the *parousia* through a general resurrection of the dead. A later chapter on the resurrection will deal with this question more fully.

Verses 27-34 are interesting, but they are not important in relation to our subject. For this reason they are not discussed. Verses 35-38 discuss the mysterious way in which the resurrection will occur. The body that is buried and goes back to dust bears the same relation to the future body God will give each person as the seed that is planted bears to the plant that springs from that seed. There is a very real connection between the two, but they are not identical.

In verses 39-49 Paul explains the change from corruptible and mortal to incorruptible and immortal. From the terms he uses, there can be no question but that he is thinking primarily of Christians. He does not describe the "resurrection of damnation" (John 5:29) which will be the lot of wicked men. It is the glorious resurrection of life that he describes. Verse 49 is very pointed in this regard. It reads, "As we have borne the image of the earthy, we shall also bear the image of the heavenly."

Verse 50 points out the necessity of a change before we can "inherit the kingdom of God." Although Christians are now in the kingdom, and though they possess it in a measure, we do not fully inherit it while in the flesh. The heavenly phase is yet future. After this mortal has put on immortality, and this corruptible has put on incorruption, then, and only then, do we come into our full inheritance in heaven. This points to the time when Jesus will say, "Well done, good and faithful servant;...enter thou into the joy of thy Lord" (Matt. 25:23).

The idea that Paul envisioned an earthly physical kingdom of one thousand years has been refuted already, but a review at this point may be helpful. Paul preached a kingdom unacceptable to the Jews. Had he preached the kind of a Jewish kingdom now being proclaimed, no doubt they would have accepted his message (Acts 19:8-9). Paul established churches through preaching the kingdom (Acts 20:25). Paul continued to preach the kingdom of God while in prison at Rome (Acts 28:23, 31). Thus the church at Rome was a product of kingdom preaching. Preaching the kingdom as a future millennium would not produce churches. Thus Paul tied the kingdom and the Church together, whereas Dispensationalists and others separate them in time and in nature.

Paul taught the kingdom as a present reality. In Paul's earliest writing he wrote that God, "hath called you unto his kingdom and glory" (I Thess. 2:12). The Greek preposition translated "unto" is *eis*. Of the several translations consulted, over half of them translated it as "into." This is the correct translation of *eis*. So Paul wrote that God had called (is calling is better since he uses the present tense) you *into* His kingdom. These words would be inaccurate and incorrect unless the kingdom was established and people were entering it.

Equally impressive is Paul's later statement written while he was a prisoner at Rome. It reads, "Giving thanks unto the Father,...who hath delivered us from the power of darkness, and hath translated us into the kingdom of his dear Son" (Col. 1:13). The use of the aorist tense and the indicative mood places the transporting into the kingdom as having occurred prior to the time of writing. This is amply supported by the various translations. Paul and the Colossians had been transferred from the devil's territory into the kingdom. Any effort to twist Paul's meaning to the Premillennial view should be recognized as an effort to subvert Paul's true intent.

Of course, Paul recognized a future heavenly phase of the kingdom. In the chapter now being considered he speaks of inheriting the kingdom (I Cor. 15:50), even as he does in his other writings. But this expression refers to the time of the consummation. One inherits something already in existence. Assuming for the moment that a future millennial kingdom is to be established, the time of the inheriting would have to come after the establishing, otherwise it would not be inheriting. Inheriting and establishing cannot be synonymous.

Although death has been passed upon all men, Paul recognizes that those living at the time of the *parousia* will not die. Instead, their bodies will be changed from mortal to immortal in a moment of time. There are technical difficulties regarding the translation and interpretation of verses 51-52, but the apparent meaning is that those who sleep (die) will be resurrected, and those who are living at that time will undergo a change from corruptible to incorruptible. As in the rest of the chapter, Paul's attention is focused on the Christian believer. This is not to say that he did not recognize that the wicked dead would be raised and that the wicked living would be changed. Rather the meaning is that the wicked were largely outside his thinking as he wrote these words.

Verses 53-54 continue the discussion of the change from mortal and corruptible to immortal and incorruptible bodies which will be accomplished for the dead through a resurrection, and through a change of those living. In verse 54 Paul sounds the note of victory over death. He quotes from Isaiah 25:8, "Death is swallowed up in victory." In our study of verses 25-26 the question of whether or not death was destroyed at the *parousia* received some attention. We return to that subject in verse 54. Since Christ is to reign until the last enemy, death, is destroyed (I Cor. 15:25-26), the end of Christ's reign can be pinpointed if it can be determined when death is destroyed. And through this shout of victory Paul gives us the needed information.

The Greek word Paul uses for "swallowed up" is a form of *katapino*. The literal meaning of the term is to drink down. It is used both literally and symbolically. Peter uses it symbolically of the devil seeking whom he may devour (*katapino*—1 Pet. 5:8). The Hebrew writer uses it very literally of the drowning of the Egyptians in the Red Sea where the sea "drank down" the Egyptians. We take it that Paul uses it symbolically in this passage. Even so, the intent is of death ceasing to reign or possess power, for it is replaced by victory. The complete conquest of death is indicated. This points to the destruction of the last enemy to be destroyed, death.

And when is this destruction or swallowing up of death to occur? The first part of verse 54 contains the answer. It reads, "So when [*hotan*—at the time that, at the time when, or whenever] this corruptible shall have put on incorruption, and this mortal shall have put on immortality, then [*tote* - at that time or when the foregoing is accomplished] death will be swallowed up in victory." In our discussion of *eita* and *epeita* (vv. 23-24), it was admitted that Paul was simply giving the order of events and that the two *thens* of those verses did not preclude a period of time between one event and the next, although we argued that this did not prove that a period of time must intervene.

But in verse 54 Paul does not use *eita* or *epeita*. Instead, he uses *hotan* (a particle of time which connects two events in such a way that it is impossible to read a period of time between the two events) and *tote* (an adverb of time, which has practically the same meaning). Paul's use of these two Greek terms proves beyond a doubt Paul is saying that when the change from corruptible and mortal to incorruptible and immortal occurs (not one thousand years later nor one thousand and seven years later, but at that time or in connection with that event) death will be conquered by complete victory over it. It should be borne in mind that this is said primarily of the Christians or godly persons, rather than of evil men, but Paul's reference, as shown above, does include the wicked.

And when does this corruptible put on incorruption and this mortal put on immortality? According to the Premillennial view it is at the rapture; and that view holds that the rapture is at least one thousand years prior to the final subjugation of death and the end of all mortal life. Pretribulation rapturists make it one thousand and seven years between the time the righteous dead and living cease to be mortal and corruptible by being resurrected or changed to incorruptible and immortal beings. But Paul's statement in verse 54 allows no such period of time. At the time the change from mortal to immortal takes place, death is conquered, subdued, subjugated, destroyed, or "swallowed up." On the other hand, Paul's statement clearly implies the Amillennial position that there will be a general resurrection of all the dead, both good and evil, to be followed by a general judgment.

Premillennialists are sure to contend that chapter 20 of the Revelation places the disposal of death after the millennium (Rev. 20:14), but the Revelation, and chapter 20 in particular, is subject to a variety of interpretations because of the extensive use of figures and symbols, hence is not a suitable anchor for any doctrine. Certainly, it is not hermeneutically sound to give that highly controversial book preeminence over such plain passages as I Corinthians 15:54. The reader is asked to reserve judgment on this question until this question is considered a second time in the chapters on the Revelation.

In the remaining verses of chapter 15, Paul continues his cry of ultimate victory over death through Christ. The sting of death has been removed through salvation from sin. The law has no dominion over us for we live above the law. This points to the conquest of sin in this life, and ultimate victory over death at the *parousia*. He closes with an admonition to remain faithful since we know that ultimate victory is certain.

## II Corinthians 5

The very first verse of this chapter is fraught with difficulties. All will agree, it is a verse of hope, but a great deal of disagreement exists regarding some of the details. It reads: "For we know that if our earthly house of this tabernacle were dissolved, we have a building of God, an house not made with hands, eternal in the heavens." At least three views exist regarding the meaning of this verse:

1. That heaven is the house we occupy after death.

2. That Paul has our resurrection bodies in mind as the house we will occupy.

3. That an intermediate body will be given for us to use until the resurrection at which time the intermediate body will be dissolved, and our resurrection body will again become the habitation for the soul.

The first view is rejected because the house he is talking about is to be "eternal in the heavens." This phrase would hardly be appropriate if heaven itself were the house. The third view is that of Scofield (note on Heb. 9:27) and certain other Dispensationalists. Scofield's statement says in part, "At the believer's death, he is 'clothed upon' with a 'house from heaven' pending the resurrection of the 'earthly house' and is at once 'with the Lord.'" One of his references is II Corinthians 5:1-8. In the absence of supporting evidence of the giving of, and the dissolution of, an intermediate body, this view must likewise be rejected. The same phrase used against the first view also negates this view. A temporary body could not be considered "eternal in the heavens" or anywhere else. Therefore, we take it to refer to our resurrected or changed bodies.

In verses 2-4b Paul considers the disembodied state through the expressions "unclothed" and "naked." The idea of a disembodied state was not appealing to Paul. Apparently he preferred to be alive at the *parousia* in order that he would avoid this disembodied or unclothed state, although he was submissive to the will of God. Then in 4c, Paul again uses a form of *katapino* which we found in I Corinthians 15:54 in the expression, "Death is swallowed up in victory." In this verse it is "that mortality might be swallowed up of life." Both have the same significance. At the *parousia* death ceases to exist because mortality is swallowed up. When mortality no longer exists, death becomes an impossibility.

Verse 5 tells us that God saved us that we might enjoy this victory over sin, death, and mortality, and that He has given us the Holy Spirit as a guarantee that this will become a reality. Verses 6-9 inform us of Paul's willingness to become a disembodied spirit in order that he might be with Christ, even though he would prefer to avoid the disembodied state. His job is to be faithful to the task assigned to him and to leave the question of having a body or not having a body up to the Lord.

Verse 10 informs us that "we must all appear before the judgment seat [*bema*] of Christ." Scofield's note on this verse indicates that this judgment is of believers, only, and that it "occurs at the return of Christ." Through a study of other statements by this author, we understand him to mean at what he would term "the rapture." Tan places it "between the rapture of the church to heaven and Christ's return again to earth."[228] However, this conclusion does violence to the word of God. This judgment is of the deeds of men whether "good or bad." Making this a judgment different from the final one is not justified. The problem of one final judgment versus the several judgments which are a part of the Dispensational approach will be studied more fully in a later chapter.

## Concluding Remarks

Five points of disagreement have been considered in the study of the Corinthian correspondence. These are:

1. Will there be a millennial reign?
2. Will there be more than one resurrection?
3. When does death cease to reign?
4. Does the soul possess a body between death and the resurrection?
5. Who are judged at the *bema* judgment?

The question of a single judgment versus several could be considered as

---

228  *Ibid.*, p. 337.

a sixth point, but since the question is largely answered by number 5, it is considered as incorporated in that question.

The answers to these questions which have been given in this volume are:

1. There will be no millennial reign of Christ such as is envisioned by Premillennialists, or Postmillennialists.

2. There will be but one general resurrection of the dead which will include both the righteous and the unrighteous.

3. Death is vanquished at this general resurrection.

4. The soul exists without a body (unclothed) between death and the resurrection.

5. All men, the evil as well as the good, are judged at the *bema* judgment, hence there is but one judgment as there is but one resurrection. The writings of the early fathers of the Church largely endorse these views, at least the writings on the Corinthian letters of Paul.

Irenaeus was the only writer found who based a millennial reign on these letters, and this was more by inference than by definite statements. But Irenaeus is the one leader among the ante-Nicene fathers who was definitely a millennialist, hence this finding is not a surprise. He was also the only writer found who supported the idea of more than one resurrection from the Corinthian correspondence, and this is not a certainty. He wrote of the "resurrection of the just" but more than one conclusion can be reached from this reference.[229] A statement he makes regarding the destruction of death makes it difficult to know for certain just what he did believe about one or more resurrections.

After arguing that Adam was rightly related to God at the time of his death, Irenaeus wrote, "When therefore the Lord vivifies man, that is, Adam, death is at that time destroyed."[230] This seems to teach a general resurrection, after which death would cease. It is possible to conclude from this that Irenaeus did not anticipate a resurrection of anyone until after the millennium. We found no objection to a general resurrection, unless it be the one given above by Irenaeus.

All references to the time death would be destroyed were in agreement that it would be at the resurrection discussed in I Corinthians 15. Inasmuch

---

229 Irenaeus, *op. cit.,* vol. I, p. 567.
230 *Ibid.,* p. 457.

as it is generally conceded, even by millennialists, that Paul wrote mainly of the resurrection of the righteous in this chapter, it follows that the early Church believed that death would be destroyed when the righteous were resurrected, rather than 1,000 or 1,007 years later. Even Irenaeus is in agreement with this.

Tertullian wrote, "Death shall not continue. When and how shall it cease? In that moment, that twinkling of an eye, at the last trump, when the dead shall rise incorruptible."[231] That he is referring to the resurrection of I Corinthians 15:52 is too plain for questioning. But since that resurrection concerns the righteous, primarily, it follows that Tertullian did not believe that mortal life and death would continue beyond the resurrection of the righteous. This is in complete harmony with the view that both good and evil will be resurrected at a single resurrection at the second coming, but it strongly disagrees with the several resurrections currently taught by Dispensationalists and many other Premillennialists.

Hippolytus, who is often considered a Premillennialist because of his teaching of a future Antichrist, believed in a single resurrection. He wrote, "For concerning the general resurrection...at that time the trumpet shall sound, and awake those that sleep from the lowest parts of the earth, righteous and sinners alike."[232] Augustine held that the Church would be resurrected at the end of the world.[233] Chrysostom placed the second coming at the end of the world.[234] Thus, the early Church had little in common with present day Premillennialism.

No writer of the early Church was found who advocated a temporary body for those in paradise between death and the resurrection. This teaching which is largely confined to the Dispensationalists has nothing to commend it to the Church of today.

Nor was any writing on the Corinthian letters found to support a multiplicity of judgments such as advocated by Dispensationalists. Scofield's notes on I Corinthians 5:10, Matthew 25:32, and Revelation 20:12 refer those passages to a judgment of the works of Christians at the so-called

---

[231] Tertullian, *op. cit.*, vol. III, p. 584.
[232] Hippolytus, *op. cit.*, vol. V, p. 251.
[233] Augustine, *op. cit.*, vol. I, p. 304.
[234] Chrysostom, *op. cit.*, vol. XII, p. 329.

rapture, a judgment of nations seven years later at the second coming, and the judgment of the wicked. This order is generally accepted by Dispensationalists as well as many others. But this denies a general judgment, and posits in its stead no less than three separate judgments which differ in time as well as character. The early Church knew of no such teaching.

CHAPTER 18

# THE ESCHATOLOGY OF I AND II THESSALONIANS

These two letters are generally recognized as the first one's written by Paul, and among the earliest writings found in the New Testament. There is no valid reason for rejecting these conclusions, although the evidence for this may not be absolutely certain. Every effort will be made to distinguish between truth and surmise in this chapter, because a great deal of conjecture is being taught as fact. Those who contend that these letters prove that Paul taught a pretribulation rapture of the Church to be followed by an earthly millennium are gifted with, or plagued by, an uncontrolled imagination. Paul did not subscribe to these tenets, and they cannot be substantiated by legitimate exegesis of these letters.

There are grounds for believing that the Thessalonians had misunderstood his first letter, or they had received a forged letter which had created some problems. They may have labored under the belief that Christ was certain to appear very soon, and that this belief had resulted in them leaving their normal pursuits of life to await His coming. This also has a reasonable degree of support.

## I Thessalonians 1

Four things are evident from I Thessalonians 1:10 which reads, "And to wait for his Son from heaven, whom he raised from the dead, even Jesus, which delivered us from the wrath to come."

1. Christians are to "wait" with patience and fortitude for the return of Christ.

2. Christ's resurrection is affirmed as a historical event.

3. Christ's second coming is accepted as a future certainty.

4. A day of wrath is also a certainty, at least for the ungodly, but Christ has delivered His people from that calamity. It is not distinctly stated that the day of wrath and the second coming occur at the same time, or are

two phases of a single event, but the text itself does not suggest anything to the contrary.

It has already been shown that verse 12 of chapter 2 indicates that the kingdom of God was a reality in Paul's day, rather than a future millennium. The argument will not be repeated, except to say that this does stand opposed to the future establishment of the kingdom. A few verses further down Paul asks, "For what is our hope, or joy, or crown of rejoicing?" He answers his own question by adding, "Are not even ye in the presence of our Lord Jesus Christ at his coming?" (*parousia*) (I Thess. 2:19). Thus Christ's second coming is reaffirmed, and the Thessalonians were to be there.

In chapter 3 Paul states that the afflictions which had come to them was part of God's plan for their lives. Through the grace He imparted to them, God would be able to "stablish your hearts unblameable in holiness before God, even our Father, at the coming [*parousia*] of our Lord Jesus Christ with all his saints" (I Thess. 3:13). This verse was considered in the discussion of Christ coming "for His saints" versus "with His saints." Actually, He does both in a single event. He comes for the living saints, and for the bodies of the dead saints, but He also comes with the disembodied souls of deceased Christians, and with His holy angels who are also covered by the expression *hagioi* or holy things.

## I Thessalonians 4-5

One of the great eschatological sections of the New Testament begins with verse 13 of chapter 4. It is unfortunate that the chapter divisions make an artificial break in the continuity of thought which carries over into chapter 5. Among the things Paul had in mind in writing this section were the imparting of information (4:13-17), comforting them (4:18 and 5:11), reminding them of his previous preaching (5:1-2), and giving them certain warnings (5:3-10). Verses 13-17 of chapter 4 are quoted below. That those "which are asleep" refers to deceased Christians has been discussed adequately elsewhere. For most it will not create a problem.

But I would not have you to be ignorant, brethren, concerning them which are asleep, that ye sorrow not, even as others which have no hope. For if we believe that Jesus died and rose again, even so also them which sleep in Jesus will God bring with him. For this we say unto you by the word of the Lord, that we which are alive and remain unto the coming of the Lord shall not prevent them which are asleep. For the Lord himself shall descend from heaven with a shout, with the voice of the archangel, and with the trump of God: and the dead in Christ shall rise first: Then we which are alive and remain shall be caught up together with them in the clouds, to meet the Lord in the air: and so shall we ever be with the Lord (I Thess. 4:13-17).

In verse 13 Paul contrasts those who have hope with those who do not have any hope. The intent is to comfort those who had believing relatives who had died, but it strongly implies that those who die outside of Christ are beyond redemption. The idea of a second chance after death is not compatible with this verse. Paul's primary references in this section are to deceased Christians. What happens to non-Christians must be gleaned from other passages. We cannot be certain whether or not Paul is answering a question asked by the Church, and there is no point in conjecturing about it.

The first clause of verse 14 is a conditional clause. The use of "if" from the Greek *ei* makes this apparent. But some may not know that it is a first-class conditional clause which means that the writer, Paul, assumes the reality or factuality of the statement. For this reason, no violence is done to the intent of the sentence by translating this clause, "Since we believe that Jesus died and rose again," as certain translations do so render it. Thus it becomes an affirmation of the resurrection of Christ, rather than raising some doubt about its occurrence. Then, on the basis of the truth of the resurrection of Christ, Paul assures the Thessalonian brethren that, "Even so them also which sleep in Jesus will God bring with him."

This statement and others which follow destroy the soul-sleeping doctrine. The bodies of these deceased Christians lay in graves, yet these same people are to come with Christ at the *parousia*. This also militates against the two-phase second coming doctrine, for it pictures Christ coming with His saints and at the same time for His saints, rather than coming for His saints seven years before He comes with them. Although the term "saints" is not used here, the meaning is there. Thus this is dealing with the time Christ comes *with* His saints as well as *for* His saints.

The use of the word "God" (*Theos*) raises some problems. Since Christ is the second person of the Trinity, it is permissible to use this expression of Him, but in this sentence God is placed in contrast to, and is distinguished from, Jesus. However, "the Lord" in verses 15, 16, and 17 seems to be used of Christ rather than God the Father. Therefore, some other translation of verse 14 is required.

It is my opinion that the RSV gives Paul's intent. It reads, "For since we believe that Jesus died and rose again, even so, through Jesus, God will bring with him those who have fallen asleep." This makes God the Father the author of the event, but it is through Jesus as the effective means by which the event is accomplished that the Father functions. The key to this is the Greek *dia*. The idea of instrumentality is included in the scope of its meaning. This involves one being using another being or thing as the means by which the first one accomplishes an act. The Jews did not crucify Christ by nailing Him to the cross. They did it through the instrumentality of the Roman leaders and army.

Thayer lists this verse under this category. From these considerations I hold that verse 14 tells us that Jesus is the one who will come, and that He will bring the disembodied spirits or souls of all deceased Christians with Him when He comes; but in all of this He will be functioning as the agent or effective instrument by which God the Father accomplishes His divine purpose.

That this is the true second coming is further indicated by verse 15. In this verse Paul uses the term *parousia* when he mentions this coming of the Lord, and it has been shown already that this refers to the time of the consummation. This is in full agreement with I Corinthians 15 where Paul uses the same term of the final and general resurrection. In both, he affirms that some will be living when that event occurs. In the Corinthian passage he affirmed that the living would be changed, and that the dead would be raised incorruptible. In the passage now being considered, he points out that the living will not have any advantage over the dead in any sense of priority or special favor.

In the KJV, it reads that the living "shall not prevent them which are asleep." Because of the change that has come in the accepted meaning of the word "prevent," this translation conveys an erroneous impression to many. Paul assuredly meant that the living would not go ahead of, before, or precede those who were deceased, but he may have meant that they would have no kind of advantage over the dead. Dr. Summers stresses this latter meaning.[235]

Verses 16 and 17 establish a sequence of events, especially of those things which precede the resurrection, and the resurrection itself. It is to be a noisy affair. First, the Lord (Christ) gives a shout as He descends. This is followed by the voice of the archangel. Then there is the trump

---

235 Summers, *op. cit.,* p. 58.

of God. Paul does not give us the particulars of these three sounds, but the fact that three distinct noise producing activities are listed emphasizes the noisiness of the event. In order for this to be heard by people throughout the world, it would have to be of tremendous force. Possibly, a miracle of reinforcement would be involved.

Regarding this noisy return De Haan states, "None of the wicked dead will hear it. They shall remain in their graves. Nor will any of the unbelieving living hear that shout."[236] Does De Haan support this view by exegeting the passage? Not at all. Does he bring other texts to bear that might give some basis for his assertion? Not a single text or argument is presented. The reader is expected to accept this without any support, merely on the word of the author. Personally, I am unwilling to accept such unreasonable claims.

The truth is that Paul does not consider the wicked in this passage. He does not say what they will hear or not hear. Surely, if God was going to perform a miracle by temporarily deafening all the wicked, Paul would have said something about it. Paul's purpose is best served by focusing his attention on the righteous, as it was in I Corinthians 15, so there is no point in one saying what the wicked will do or not do from this passage. They are completely ignored. He deals with the wicked in his second letter to the church at Thessalonica, and there is no valid reason for believing these two passages refer to different occasions.

And now we come to that clause that is misinterpreted by almost all Premillennialists. It reads, "... and the dead in Christ shall rise first" (v. 16). A misinterpretation continues, not because it can be defended exegetically, but because it fits in with the Premillennial schedule of events. It has already been pointed out that Blackstone quoted this clause twice without quoting any of verse 17, with the apparent intention of leading his readers to infer that the wicked dead would be raised later. This is indefensible.

I have attempted to avoid lengthy quotations from other authors in support of my positions, but Summers deals with this passage in such a superb manner that I am constrained to pass his words on to you.

In this passage Paul did speak of two events as they were related to the Lord's return and as they were related to the problem immediately before him. Two groups of people were awaiting the Lord's return to the earth. One group was made up of the Christians who died before his return and the

---

236 De Haan, *The Second Coming of Jesus*, p. 30.

other group, of the Christians who will be still alive when he returns. Paul spoke of what will happen to them and the order in which it will happen. That is all he gave in this passage. There is an element of sequence expressed in the two words "first" and "then." Inversion of the words in the first clause will make the meaning clearer: "first the dead in Christ shall rise; then we who are alive who are left will be gathered with them, will be caught up in the clouds to welcome the Lord in the air, and thus we will always be with the Lord." Paul had this in mind when he said that living believers will have no advantage over believers who have died, because when the Lord returns he will first raise the dead and then catch up the living. There will be no longer two groups waiting for the Lord but one group eternally in his presence.[237]

The weakness of the Premillennial position is advertised by the fact that they so consistently misinterpret this passage despite the indefensibility of their position. When a misinterpreted text is a part of the basic framework of a doctrine, it not only is evidence of a weak position, but any who catch the misinterpretation will tend to reject other interpretations on the basis of one known misinterpretation.

Recognition of this, possibly combined with the need for intellectual honesty, is gradually forcing Premillennialists to abandon two positions previously taken on this passage. First, the contention that this is a secret event known only to Christians. This is the more apparent misinterpretation. The second is more subtle. It is the claim that Paul referred to the Christian dead as the first group, and the wicked dead as the second group, whereas the two groups are the Christian dead versus the living Christians. Although this is less apparent than the first fallacy mentioned, it is so indisputably in error that the position is basically untenable.

We conceive of Paul as thinking that if the living Christians and the dead Christians began to leave this earth at exactly the same moment, the result would be that the living Christians would come into the presence of the Lord slightly in advance of the dead Christians. But living Christians are not to precede the dead Christians, nor are they to have any other advantage or priority. Thus, Paul contends that the first to move will be the dead Christians. Only after they have come out of their tombs and places of burial, so that the living and those previously dead constitute a single body, rather than two bodies, would there be any upward movement of those who had not died. This would enable them to ascend as a single body, rather than as two separate groups.

---

237 Summers, *op. cit.*, pp. 59-60.

Thus, after the dead have risen and a single group is formed, then all "shall be caught up together" to "meet the Lord in the air." Two bodily resurrections cannot be claimed, legitimately, as the teaching of these verses. The wicked are ignored much like they are in I Corinthians 15. What happens to the wicked must be ascertained from other passages.

We now consider something that is implied but not stated. Verse 14 places the host of deceased righteous persons, i.e., the souls or spirits of these righteous dead, as descending with the glorified Christ. The bodies of these persons are placed with the ascending body of believers. A union or reuniting of souls and bodies is implied in this meeting without being explicitly stated. Therefore, we conceive of a fusion of resurrected bodies, newly immortal and incorruptible, with the disembodied souls or spirits which had inhabited those bodies during their life span here on earth; thus the entire group are whole persons, possessing both soul and body.

The concluding clause of verse 17, "and so shall we ever be with the Lord" is important. Paul uses the same *houtos* in this clause that he did in Romans 11:26. As in that passage, the meaning is after this manner, and it has reference to that which was said before. Two things stand out in the immediate context as the "manner" of our being with Christ. First, there was the change from mortal to immortal by all, and from disembodied to embodied by those who had died. The second point of importance is that of departure from the world. This at least implies that neither Christ nor the Church will return to the earth to engage in mundane affairs. So, this text not only says nothing about a return to earth, but strongly militates against it.

Had Paul believed in a two-phase second coming followed by an earthly millennium, it would have been most inappropriate for him to have written, "and so shall we ever be with the Lord." He could have said no more than that for seven years so we would be with the Lord. If Paul believed in the two-phase second coming and a millennium afterwards, he missed a golden opportunity to elaborate on it in this connection. We conclude that Paul did not believe these teachings, and that he was trying to say that when the Church is raptured away from this earth, time as we now know it ceases and eternity begins.

There is no break in the continuity of thought as one moves from chapter 4 into chapter 5. Evidently Paul had given them some information regarding the consummation (v. 1). Among other things they knew "perfectly that the day of the Lord cometh as a thief in the night" (v. 2). It is to come without signs or any kind of warning, for that is the way thieves come. They give no advance notice. But what is this "day of the Lord"? The simple explanation is that it includes the second coming of Christ, the general resurrection, the final judgment, the dispensing of awards and penalties, and the beginning of eternity; but many are unwilling to accept so simple an explanation. Because Dispensationalists and other Premillennialists have developed a very complicated order of events for the last days, some consideration must be given to their theories.

In line with the two-phase second coming concept, Scofield relates the "day of Christ" to the so-called rapture (see his note on I Cor. 1:8), whereas in the same note he relates the "day of the Lord" to a time of judgment. By this means he attempts to justify the two-phase second coming theory. He takes pains to point out that the AV incorrectly has "day of Christ" for "day of the Lord," but he fails to mention the fact that in the AV, for one of the passages he refers to, the day of Christ may have originally read "day of the Lord." In fact the evidence is overwhelming that the word "Jesus" was not a part of the original manuscript in I Corinthians 5:5. This makes this verse refer to the time of judgment, according to Scofield, rather than the time of the rapture where he prefers to place it.

But this makes untenable the contention that the "day of Christ" and the "day of the Lord" refer to two distinct periods of time. Scofield could not place I Corinthians 5:5 at the day of judgment, for he holds that Christians will not appear at that judgment. Therefore Scofield must hold that this man whom Paul desired to be saved, be saved "in the day of Christ," rather than "in the day of the Lord." But the best Greek texts make the verse refer to the "day of the Lord," rather than "the day of Christ." The only valid conclusion is that some will be saved in the "day of the Lord," and some will be damned in "the day of the Lord."

We conclude that the "day of Christ" and the "day of the Lord" refer to the same day, and that in that day some will be blessed and others cursed just as Matthew 25 indicates. We conclude further that Scofield and others who attempt to separate the "day of Christ" and the "day of the Lord" are mistaken. The judgment of unbelievers and the rewarding of the righteous are but two aspects of a single event.

Let us now return to the statement that "the day of the Lord so cometh as a thief in the night" (I Thess. 5:2). Can you imagine a thief posting a notice on the door of a home he intends to rob stating the date he expects to rob that home? Of course you can't. Thieves do not announce their plans. Similarly, the word of God says that the day of the Lord will not be preceded by signs or portents. He will come suddenly and without warning.

Scofield and Dispensationalism say otherwise. In his note on Revelation 19:19 Scofield lists seven signs which shall be indicators that the "day of the Lord" is near. Some of these might go unnoticed by sinners, but if there is to be a rapture of the Church seven years before "the day of the Lord," it would be an event of such magnitude and so disruptive of life on this earth that the news media would publicize this as no other event ever was or ever will be. I can imagine headlines such as *Christian community disappears! Thousands vanish! Wrecks! Crashes! Chaos! Apostate preacher explains!* This preacher would tell people that the rapture had occurred and that seven years from that date, Christ would come in glory and judge the wicked.

With this kind of information available, the "day of the Lord" simply could not come "as a thief in the night." People might ignore the information given them, but every one would have the necessary information to pinpoint the exact time of the "day of the Lord." Thus, the Bible nullifies the elaborate system of the Dispensationalists.

Verse 3 completes the annihilation of the schedule of events as set forth by Scofield. It reads, "For when they say, Peace and safety; then sudden destruction cometh upon them, as travail upon a woman with child; and they shall not escape." This verse indicates that conditions will be such that peace and safety, rather than destruction, might be expected. But Dispensationalists claim that the apocalyptic judgments of Revelation 11-18 are to be literally fulfilled as a time of great tribulation just prior to the "day of the Lord." Thus they misinterpreted these plagues either as to their time or their nature; and it is our opinion that they err in both the time and the nature.

Verses 4-6 are equally devastating to the Dispensational schedule. "That day" of verse 4 refers to "the day of the Lord" of verse 2. The Thessalonian church was instructed to watch, so that day would not take them unawares. But how could that day take them unaware when the Dispensational schedule calls for them to be in heaven when that day arrives. If the Church is raptured away to heaven for a seven year period immediately prior to the "day of the Lord," Paul's admonition should have been for them to watch for the rapture, rather than the "days of the Lord." Was Paul mistaken, or is the Dispensational schedule in error? Those who reverence the Bible as God's word should have no difficulty in deciding who is wrong. Surely Paul would not instruct persons who had already received their immortal bodies to watch for anything. Watching pertains to this mortal existence. Our days of watching will end when we receive our resurrection bodies.

Paul again uses the term *parousia* in verse 23. His prayer is that they "be preserved blameless unto the coming [*parousia*] of our Lord Jesus Christ." This applies to mortal existence, for preservation is guaranteed beyond the resurrection. With immortal bodies, there could be no need for concern about their preservation. Thus Paul links the resurrection of the righteous to the *parousia*. But, as has been shown already, the *parousia* does not refer to a secret coming to rapture the Church away. Rather it refers to the general resurrection and final judgment. Thus, Paul ties the resurrection of the righteous, the "day of the Lord," and the *parousia* together in such a manner as to identify these as a single event.

## II Thessalonians 1

It is generally accepted that Paul considered this second letter necessary because of incorrect conclusions the church had arrived at from his first letter, or else from some forged epistle which was attributed to him. We see no reason to dissent from this opinion. Following words of greeting such as Paul was wont to make in all of his letters, he leads up to a further discussion of the second coming by considering certain pressures they were then enduring. The extent and nature of these persecutions are not stated.

They were then suffering for the kingdom of God (v. 5). Premillennialists are unable to account for this suffering for the kingdom of God which they claim is yet to be established. How could they suffer for something that did not exist? Of course, they were already in the kingdom of God, and they were being persecuted because they were a part of it. Verse 6 encourages them in their suffering by telling them that God would "recompense tribulation to them that trouble you."

A portion of Scofield's introductory notes on this book reads, "The Thessalonian converts were 'shaken in mind' and 'troubled,' supposing…that the persecutions from which they were suffering were those of the 'great and terrible day of the Lord,' from which they had been taught to expect deliverance by 'the day of Christ, and our gathering together unto him' (2:1)." It has been shown already that the day of Christ and the day of the Lord are the same. Scofield and those who follow his reasoning assume too much on too little. It cannot be proved that the Thessalonians had been taught what Scofield claims they had been taught. And verses 7-10 substantiate this.

The Thessalonian brethren are promised rest (v. 7) when Christ is "revealed from heaven" (v. 7) at which time He will come "taking vengeance on them that know not God, and that obey not the gospel of our Lord Jesus Christ" (v. 8). According to most Premillennial teaching, Christians are to receive rest at the rapture seven years before the revelation (*apokalupsis*) of Christ. These attempt to make *parousia* refer to both the rapture and the revelation, but *apokalupsis* can apply only to the unveiling or revealing of Christ. This makes the pretribulation rapture doctrine untenable. And it tends to support the fact that the *apokalupsis* and the *parousia* refer to a single event.

The taking vengeance on the wicked (v. 8) cannot refer to the pretribulation rapture, for the wicked are said to remain unaware of what is taking place. Nor can it refer to the coming of Christ to set up His kingdom. Verse 9 makes it clear that this is the end of the age judgment, for the wicked are to be "punished with everlasting destruction from the presence of the Lord." Thus the rest the saints are to receive (v. 7), and the revelation of Christ (v. 7), and the vengeance of Christ (v. 8), and the eternal punishment of the wicked (v. 9), and the glorification which is involved (v. 10), are but different aspects of a single event. We conclude Paul taught a single second coming, a general resurrection of all men, a general judgment of all men both good and evil, and the assessment of penalties and the giving of rewards as occurring in relation to one another.

## II Thessalonians 2

Reference is made to the *parousia* in verse 1. We are to be gathered together unto Him at the coming or *parousia* of Christ. Pretribulation rapturists make this refer to the rapture, just as they do in I Thessalonians 4 and in I Corinthians 15, although they admit it refers to the true second coming elsewhere. But until they prove that *parousia* does indeed refer to two separate events, I must reject their claim. The *parousia* and a gathering of Christians to Him will be realized at the second coming, and not at a so-called rapture.

In verse 2 Paul admonishes them to "be not soon shaken in mind." This may refer to simple inner agitation over the issue, or it could mean serious mental depression and instability. If these had left the normal pursuits of life to watch for the second coming, as many believe, then he may have meant for them to quit acting like insane people. The basis on which Paul says this is a matter of controversy. Two problems are involved in the expression, "as that the day of Christ is at hand."

First, does Paul mean the day of Christ or the day of the Lord? For those who make no distinction between these two expressions, no problem exists; but since Scofield and others attempt to make them refer to different days and different times, some consideration must be given to it. Scofield is correct in his contention that this should read "day of the Lord," rather than "day of Christ"; but we deny the implication he draws from this. It has previously been shown that the expression in I Corinthians 5:5 should read "day of the Lord," but he classifies it as referring to the "day of Christ" by claiming that the expression "day of the Lord Jesus" is the equivalent of the "day of Christ." However, the word "Jesus" appears to have been added, making the original autograph read "day of the Lord."

The second problem is more complicated. The Greek term in question is *enhistimi*. Its etymological meaning is to stand in or upon. In usage it normally refers to an impending event or something that was in the process of occurring. Present day scholarship tends to translate this as meaning that the day of the Lord was present or had arrived. We admit that such a translation is possible, but we deny that conditions warrant it. We believe an analysis of the circumstances will bear this out.

Those who advocate the two-phase second coming usually explain verse 2 in the following manner. It is claimed the Thessalonians had been taught that at some unknown time but quite soon, the righteous would be raptured to heaven for a period of seven years. During this seven year period a time of great distress and tribulation would come upon the inhabitants of the world, especially Jews. Then at the end of this seven year period, the true second coming would occur and Christ would establish His earthly throne in Jerusalem (or elsewhere) and reign for 1,000 years. These also contend that the Thessalonians reasoned that the rapture had passed, and that for some reason they were not included in it.

First of all, it must be recognized that the above is surmise. Only in recent years has the two-phase second coming been taught as far as can be ascertained. This is an effort to read into a passage meanings not known prior to the nineteenth century. Historic Premillennialism knew nothing of the two-phase second coming. Now let us examine how well these surmises fit the conditions which obtained in Thessalonica at the time Paul wrote his two letters to that church.

From I Thessalonians we learn the following facts. Paul had established the church in Thessalonica (1:5-6; 2:1-16). Paul became concerned about the church enough to send Timothy to them while he remained at Athens. He had feared lest tribulation might have caused them to depart from the faith (3:1-5). Timothy had brought back a good report (3:6). Nothing is said about a "great tribulation." The afflictions and tribulations (3:3-4) are those common to all Christians. This is similar to Paul's statement to Timothy, "Yea, and all that will live godly in Christ Jesus shall suffer persecution" (II Tim. 3:12).

It is easy to say that the Thessalonians believed that the rapture had taken place and that they were among those who were left behind, but it is quite another matter to prove such an assertion. I have yet to read an attempted proof. Invariably, it has been built on assumptions which are short of real evidence. There is no real evidence that their persecutions had anything to do with their state of mind. The meager evidence we do have supports the idea of a concern for their deceased brethren, rather than any problem about themselves.

Allow me to reconstruct the conditions as I see them. This is not presented as proof. It is furnished solely to offset assumptions of others, and to show that these assumptions need not be true. The Thessalonians understood that Christ would come soon to judge the world and to usher in eternity. Their concern was that their dead brethren also participate in the glorification which they anticipated. Although Paul had taught them of the resurrection of the dead, this truth was not fully established in their minds.

Paul's first letter, especially in chapter four, dealt with their fears at this point. Then, either because they misunderstood his first letter, or because some forged letter disturbed them, they concluded that the second coming and the end of the world would occur in a matter of days. For this reason, they left the normal pursuits of life to await Christ's second advent. They may have even gone out on some hillside to be in a group at the expected coming. Paul heard of this foolish activity and wrote his second letter to correct their mistaken expectations.

A comparison with the two-phase second coming concepts will be helpful. If their persecutions had caused them to believe the rapture had occurred and the great tribulation was on them (these are teachings of the two-phase second coming which this author rejects), then the coming of Timothy (I Thess. 3:1-6) would of itself have laid their fears to rest. Surely, Timothy would have been raptured away had a rapture occurred! And what about Paul? Timothy had just come from Paul, so Paul had not been raptured away. There is no conceivable way to harmonize the two-phase second coming expectations with the conditions that actually existed in Thessalonica.

And if they believed in the "great tribulation" as a prelude to the second-second coming, they would have known it would last not less than three and one-half years. For this reason, if for no other, they would not have gone outside the city to await that coming. They would rather have settled down to endure the troubles that were besetting them until the allotted time had elapsed. In view of these considerations, we contend that the assumptions of two-phase second coming advocates are false assumptions and should be treated as such.

Verse 3 states that a "falling away" or an apostasy would occur before the "day of the Lord" would come. The time and duration of this apostasy are not given. The revelation given Paul was probably limited in scope, so that he was uninformed at these points. But we must not accept the idea of a future apostasy without first examining history. Has a great apostasy occurred in the past? Beyond question the answer is, yes. That period in history that is sometimes called the dark ages was beyond doubt a great apostasy. This does not preclude the possibility of this verse referring to a future apostasy, but this apostasy of the past must be ruled out before such an approach can be justified. That apostasy *could* be the one Paul intended.

An event connected with this falling away or apostasy was:

...that man of sin be revealed, the son of perdition; Who opposeth and exalteth himself above all that is called God, or that is worshipped; so that he as God sitteth in the temple of God, shewing himself that he is God (II Thess. 2:3-4).

Our first consideration is whether Paul wrote of a man of sin (Greek *harmartias*), or a man of lawlessness (Greek *anomias*). There is considerable support for both renderings. However, since *anomias* is used in verse 7 (translated "iniquity") it appears that lawlessness is probably correct in verse 3. This is the view taken by the editorial committee of the United Bible

Societies.[238] Although sinfulness and lawlessness are related, it is possible to be sinful without being lawless. It appears that the lawlessness of this one is emphasized, rather than the sinfulness which inevitably accompanies lawlessness.

Our next consideration involves the problem of whether Paul is referring to a certain individual, a human being, or to a composite personality as would be the case of those who hold a certain office, or of an organization which has a certain continuity, although in different periods it is composed of different persons. For example, could the Communist party or its leaders such as Lenin, Stalin, and others be spoken of in terms of a single human personality? None other than Paul himself furnishes us with a specific example of his thinking.

Paul refers to the Church as a man (Greek *anthropos*) (Eph. 2:15). After writing of how Jesus had broken down the middle wall of partition between the Jews and Gentiles, he indicates the purpose he had in mind was "for to make in himself of twain one new man, [*anthropos*] so making peace." Although he uses the term *anthropos* only of the Church, there is no escaping the fact that he also thought of the Jews as one man and the Gentiles as another man. These two are combined in Christ to make one man where two had formerly existed.

Scofield's note on this verse admits as much. It reads in part, "Here the 'new man' is not the individual believer but the Church, considered as the body of Christ." I am in agreement with this opinion. Of course, it will be contended that this is a figure of speech. That has merit, but can it be proved that Paul was not also using a figure of speech in II Thessalonians 2:3 when he spoke of the man of sin or lawlessness? It may just as well be a figure of speech as Ephesians 2:15.

Others hold that the use of the definite article "the man" makes it refer to a single person. But this need not be. Paul uses the definite article several times when he has no specific man in mind. Of the following examples of this, some English translations have the definite article and some do not, but in each case the Greek does have the definite article. "David also describeth the blessedness of the man, unto whom God imputeth righteousness without works, Saying, Blessed are they whose iniquities are forgiven, and whose sins are covered" ( Rom. 4:6-7). "... the law hath dominion over a

---

238   Bruce M. Metzger, *A Textual Commentary on the Greek New Testament*, p. 635.

man [Greek "the man"] as long as he liveth" (Rom. 7:1). "For Moses describeth the righteousness which is of the law, That the man which doeth those things shall live by them" (Rom. 10:5).

Additional passages include, "All things indeed are pure; but it is evil for that man [Greek "the man"] who eateth with offence" (Rom. 14:21). Also, "That the man of God may be perfect, throughly furnished unto all good works" (II Tim. 3:17). These passages show that Paul does use the definite article without meaning some specific man. Thus the contentions that "that man of sin" must refer to a single human personality are shown to fail of their objective.

Considering further the fact that Paul spoke of the true Church as one man (*anthropos*) formed of two men, Jews and Gentiles, there is no legitimate basis for rejecting the idea that he may also have referred to the nominal Church or its leadership through the same figure of speech. It cannot be denied that this was possible within those expressions of his which are known. For this reason, the fact that the sixteenth century reformers so interpreted Paul should be given greater consideration than they are receiving today. It is just possible that they were correct.

As late as the time of Bishop Newton, this opinion was widely held. In his discussion of the falling away or the apostasy, and of the man of sin, he gives several explanations that had been advanced, or which were being advanced at that time. Apparently some Papists were claiming that the Reformation itself was the apostasy Paul had in mind, but most of them had accepted the futuristic view which the Papists themselves had originated in an effort to combat the claim that the pope was the man of sin. Most Premillennialists of today have swallowed the bait Rome held out to them which is a most regrettable situation. The lengthy quotation which follows is part of the Bishop's elaboration on II Thessalonians 2.

The greater part of the Romish doctors, it must be confessed, give another interpretation, and acknowledge that the fathers and the best interpreters understand this unanimously of Antichrist, who will appear in the world before the great day of judgment, to combat religion and the saints. But then they conceive that Antichrist is not yet revealed, that he is only one man, and that he will continue only three years and a half. But we have shown before, that the man of sin is not a single man, any more than the whore of Babylon is a single woman. The one, as well as the other, is to be understood of a whole order and succession of persons. The mystery of iniquity was working, and preparing the way for the man of sin even in the apostles' days: and is it not very extraordinary that 1700 years should elapse, and that he should not be yet revealed? What withholdeth, they say, was the Roman empire; and the Roman empire might be powerful enough to hinder his appearance at that time, but how hath it withheld and hindered all this while? As this evil began in the apostles' days and was to continue in the world till the second coming of Christ in power and great glory; it necessarily follows that it was to be carried on, not by one man, but by a succession of men in several ages. It cannot be taking root and growing imperceptibly 1700 years and more, and yet flourish under its chief head only three years and a half. There needeth not surely so much preparation for so little effect. Neither are three years and a half, a period sufficient for Antichrist to act the parts and to fulfill the characters which are assigned him.[239]

It should be noted that apostasy was essential to the revealing of the "man of sin." If Paul referred to a single member of the human race who was supremely wicked, he could be revealed at any time, regardless of the condition of the Church. But the revealing Paul had in mind was to come through apostasy of the Church. Still, the emphasis which prevails in many minds today is that the Antichrist or "man of sin" produces the apostasy, rather than the apostasy producing the "man of sin." This teaching cannot be reconciled with Paul's words, but Paul's words fit the way the papacy came into being.

Although the expression "Antichrist" will be considered fully in a subsequent chapter, the fact that most equate the "man of sin" with the Antichrist makes a few words necessary at this juncture. John is the only writer who uses the expression "antichrist." He uses the plural as well as the singular form. The plural form categorically denies that he had a single person in mind. The contexts where the singular form appears indicate that he had no reference to a single individual. He writes, "Who is a liar but he that denieth that Jesus is the Christ. He is antichrist, that denieth the Father and the Son" (I John 2:22). Again he says, "Many deceivers are entered into the world, who confess not that Jesus Christ is come in the flesh. This is a deceiver and an antichrist" (II John 7). Note that others equate the supposed Antichrist with the man of sin, but I do not. The Bible knows nothing of the *antichrist*. Furthermore, I consider

---

[239] Thomas Newton, *Dissertations on the Prophecies*, p. 402.

"the man of sin" to be popery, rather than a person yet future.

It is also noteworthy that the definite article appears before Antichrist in both instances in the Greek. Those who make so much of the definite article in "the man of sin" should consider this. A literal translation would read, "This is the antichrist, the one denying the Father and Son" (1 John 2:22). Similarly, "This one is the deceiver and the antichrist" (II John 7). The definite article appears before both expressions; the deceiver and the Antichrist. This strongly supports our earlier contention that the definite article in the expression "the man of sin" does not require that it refer to a single human being.

In verse 4 Paul gives some of the distinguishing characteristics of this "man of sin." He is one, "Who opposeth and exalteth himself above all that is called God, or that is worshipped; so that he as God sitteth in the temple of God, shewing himself that he is God." Biederwolf lists 18 commentators who hold that the temple of God refers to the Church, and that other expressions of this verse refer to the "tyrannical power" the pope exercises over the Church.[240] Biederwolf's list is by no means complete, but we shall not attempt a series of quotations in support of this view. Rather, we shall confine our references mainly to statements as they appear in an authoritative Roman Catholic publication.[241] To avoid a series of footnotes, page numbers will be given following quoted material.

1. "The Pope possesses full and supreme power and jurisdiction over the whole Church, not merely in matters of faith and morals, but also in Church discipline and in the government of the Church" (p. 285). Other claims include the pope as "the supreme law giver of the Church" and "supreme judge of the Church" (p. 286). This claim of the supreme lawgiver identifies him as the "lawless" person of verses 3-8. He is lawless in the sense that he substitutes man made laws for God's laws. This also identifies him, the pope, with the little horn of Daniel 8 who thought to change laws in verse 25 of that chapter.

2. The above claim of power by the pope is based on Rome's contention that Christ appointed Peter "to he the visible Head of the whole Church" (p. 279.) It is further claimed that the "Primacy of Jurisdiction of the Pope" is "according to Christ's ordinance" in that "Peter is to have successors in his

---

240 Biederwolf, *op. cit.*, p. 493.
241 Ott, *op. cit.* (page numbers follow material cited).

Primacy over the whole Church and for all time" (p. 282). And further "the successors of Peter in the primacy are the bishops of Rome" (p. 282).

3. Such titles as Pontifex Maximus and Vicarius Filii Dei stem from the above claims. I do not find these titles in the book from which these quotations are taken, but it is stated that he is "the representative of Christ." The Latin term "Christi vicarius" does appear (p. 279).

4. "The Pope is infallible when he speaks ex cathedra" (p. 286.) This means that when he speaks from the chair of St. Peter as the supreme ruler of the Church, it is impossible for him to err. Since his pronouncements never state when he speaks "ex cathedra," there is no way of knowing which pronouncements are considered infallible. By this means all of his pronouncements carry this claim to some degree.

5. "The Faithful on earth can, by their good works performed in the state of grace, render atonement for one another" (p. 317.)

6. "It is permissible and profitable to venerate the relics of the Saints" (p. 319).

7. "It is permissible and profitable to venerate the images of the Saints" (p. 320).

8. "The living Faithful can come to the assistance of the Souls in Purgatory by their intercessions" (p. 321.)

9. A sacrament is defined as "a thing perceptible to the senses, which on the ground of Divine institution possesses the power both of effecting and signifying sanctity and righteousness." This is said to be the equivalent of "sanctifying grace." (p. 326).

10. The sacraments are said to "work ex opere operato." This phrase is said to mean that "the Sacraments operate by the power of the completed sacramental rite" (p. 329). An effort is made to deny that this means it works magically, but the argument is unsound. The source of the cleansing is not said to be through some activity of Christ or the Holy Spirit. The source is in the rite itself according to Roman Catholic theology.

11. It is claimed that since the gospel became effective that "Baptism by water…is,…necessary for all men without exception, for salvation" (p. 356).

12. It is claimed that "Baptism confers the grace of justification" (p. 354). Justification is said to include "remission of sin" and "sanctification and renewal of the inner man" (p. 354). A quotation taken from the actions

taken at the Council of Trent reads, "If any one denies that by the grace of our Lord Jesus Christ which is conferred in Baptism, the guilt of original sin is remitted; or even asserts that the whole of that which has the true and proper nature of sin is not taken away…let him be anathema" (p. 354).

13. The doctrine of transubstantiation is stated as follows: "Christ becomes present in the Sacrament of the Altar by the transformation of the whole substance of the bread into His Body and the whole substance of the wine into His Blood" (p. 379).

14. It is claimed that in taking communion, "The Body and the Blood of Christ together with His Soul and His Divinity and therefore the Whole Christ are truly present in the Eucharist" (p. 384).

15. This claim of the actual presence of Christ in the elements, or host as they would term it, is the basis for full adoration or worship of the consecrated elements. "The Worship of Adoration (latria) must be given to Christ present in the Eucharist" (p. 387). This is rank idolatry.

16. It is claimed that Christ is sacrificed or resacrificed each time the mass is performed. "The Holy Mass is a true and proper Sacrifice…The Eucharist is a Sacrifice in so far as in it Christ is partaken as nourishment for the soul; it is a sacrifice in so far as in it Christ is offered as a sacrificial gift to God" (p. 402). This is in direct opposition to Hebrews 9:26 which affirms a single sacrifice of Christ.

A brief analysis of the foregoing reveals that the pope is a dictator (no. 1), and that he has exalted himself as the head of the Church (no. 2), whereas the Bible makes Christ the head of the Church. In number 3 it is found that he, the pope, has assumed blasphemous titles. The claim of infallibility (no. 4) is blasphemous. Offering a means of human atonement (no. 5) minimizes the sacrifice of Jesus, and attempts to establish a doctrine of works. Worshiping relics and images (nos. 6-7) substitutes human laws for biblical laws. The doctrine of purgatory (no. 8) is a human invention that has no biblical support whatsoever.

The claims that the sacraments convey sanctifying grace of themselves (no. 9) is a perversion of the ordinances of the Church. The claim that these sacraments operate of themselves (no. 10) is sacrilegious. To say that baptism is essential to the removal of sin (no. 11), and that it does remove sin (no. 12) is in opposition to the Bible's teaching that sin is removed through faith in Christ. All of this is closely related to the extra-sacramental absolution granted by the parish priest (p. 441 of the work cited above). Even the Pharisees knew that only God could forgive sin (Mark 2:7).

The doctrine of transubstantiation (no. 13) is especially obnoxious, because it makes Christ obedient to the call of men, when men are required to be obedient to Christ. It is illogical and unscriptural to hold that Christ is present in body and soul in the eucharist (no. 14). To ingest the literal body and blood of Christ in communion (no. 15) would be cannibalism. And to worship the "host" (no. 16) is rank paganism.

Do these justify identifying popery and the Roman hierarchy as the man of sin? I contend they do. It has already been shown that the conditions of verse 3 are satisfied. First, a serious apostasy did occur before popery was fully revealed in all of its perfidious power. And secondly, it is legitimate to consider "the man of sin" to refer to a succession of men such as have held the office of pope and to the hierarchy that supports his claims (II Thess. 2:3).

During the peak of the popes' power, thousands of true Christians were slain because a pope desired it so. Seldom is this kind of opposition exhibited today. An insidious, covert, Judas type of opposition is now evident. In his role as defender of the faith, he has introduced damnable heresies which undermine and destroy true faith. He has substituted human dogma for the revealed word of God. His opposition and exaltation are very real (v. 4). And whether we consider the pope as occupying the "chair of St. Peter," or as the titular head of the entire Church, or as the accepted head of the Roman Catholic Church, he does sit in the temple of God as if he were God (v. 4).

One way of confirming that he does show himself as God is to use the same reasoning as the Jews did in condemning Jesus which is probably the way that Paul approached this matter. Jesus was condemned because he made Himself equal with God by forgiving sin. The pope claims he has the power to forgive sin. Jesus was condemned for making Himself equal with God by claiming to be the Son of God. The titles claimed by the pope (*Vicarius Filii Dei* and *Pontifex Maximus*) partake of this quality. An old ritual included the phrase *Domino Deus Nostre Papa* which means "Our Lord God, the Pope." Add to these his claim of infallibility which is an attribute of God, and one needs no more to recognize that he does sit in the temple of God from which he shows himself as being God.

Those who contend that the man of sin has not been revealed need to give more consideration to history. Alford, along with a number of others, contends that popery cannot be the "man of sin" because the day of the Lord and his destruction is to follow closely on his revealing. But this is unacceptable, for that day is to come as a thief in the night, unannounced, and if the man of sin is to be revealed immediately before the day of the Lord, his being revealed would constitute a sign or warning of the day of vengeance. For this reason the argument must be rejected.

As I personally observed Pope Paul (Paulus VI) carried into St. Peter's on the shoulders of men who are his subordinates where he was placed upon a throne which rested on a dais especially prepared for the occasion, I experienced no difficulty in relating him and his office with that one who was to show himself as if he were God. The adoration shown this member of the human family certainly had all of the appearances of worship. Jesus himself could hardly have been accorded any greater homage or reverence than was lavished on this man.

We now consider what it was that restrained or kept from developing this "man of sin." Dispensationalists hold that it is the Holy Spirit. They claim that the Holy Spirit will vacate the earth at the so-called rapture of the Church, and this will be the factor that enables the Antichrist to blossom out into his true character. Now, it is true that the Holy Spirit has the power to restrain certain developments here on earth, but this explanation which has so recently been introduced into Christian theology cannot be true.

First of all, the so-called rapture of the Church seven years before the second coming has not been proved. This doctrine is built on surmise, rather than exegesis. Nor has it been established that the Holy Spirit is the power Paul referred to as restraining the development of the "man of sin." Thirdly, although the restraining power is to be taken away, unless other texts can be produced which indicate that at some time the Holy Spirit will be withdrawn from the human scene, such a conclusion from this text alone is not justified. And lastly, the Holy Spirit is omnipresent, hence could restrain just as well from heaven as He can from the earth.

The relationship of the little horn of Daniel 7 and "the man of sin" in the chapter now being considered must not be overlooked. The little horn was to "wear out the saints of the most High, and to think to change times and laws" (Dan. 7:25). The things said of the "man of sin" harmonize with the description of the little horn. We claim, as a host of others have done, that the two refer to the same power. Although the Bible does not specify a single person or organization as the man of sin, popery comes closer to meeting the requirements for such a designation than any other person, organization, or power.

Verse 8 tells of the destruction of that "Wicked" power that is termed "the man of sin." It is said to occur at His "coming" (*parousia*). It has been shown already that when *parousia* is used of a future return of Christ, it refers to that visible return called the second coming. The force of *parousia* is strengthened by the use of *epiphaneia*. This is improperly translated "brightness" (KJV). No doubt His appearance will be bright, but the term itself implies no more than His actual presence, and the visibility of that presence. The term could not be used properly of the so-called secret coming of Christ to rapture the Church to heaven. It refers to the true, visible, second coming.

## Opinions of the Church Fathers on I and II Thessalonians

Although several of the ante-Nicene fathers left writings which included eschatological references from I Thessalonians only four are worthy of note. We had anticipated a large number of remarks on chapter 4, but only Origen left anything, at least as far as I was able to ascertain, which has much import regarding millennialism. He did accept the truth I have already emphasized that after we have been caught away to meet the Lord in the air (1 Thess. 4:17) our permanent residence will be established at a distance from this earth.[242]

Three statements from chapter 5 are worthy of note. Cyprian declared that the end of the world would come suddenly and without warning.[243] This does not agree with the Premillennial view that the rapture, the great tribulation, and the thousand year reign establish a time sequence which makes the time of the consummation 1,000 or 1,007 years after the rapture. Archelaus stresses the same idea.[244]

In the apocryphal *Revelation of John* a portion that deals with judgment (I Thess. 5:3) establishes an order of judgment quite different from that of any present day school of thought. According to the order given in this writing, the wicked will be judged first, the Israelites later, and the righteous

---

242 Origen, *op. cit.*, vol. IV, p. 299.
243 Cyprian, *op. cit.*, vol. V, p. 553.
244 Archelaus, *Ante-Nicene Fathers*, vol. VI, p. 212.

last of all.²⁴⁵ This is contrary to the views of most Premillennialists who say the righteous will be judged first (before the millennium), whereas the wicked are to be judged after the millennium. Amillennialists hold to a single judgment of all people.

Nothing important was found on chapter 1 of II Thessalonians. However, a number of significant references were found on chapter 2. Barnabas identified the little horn of Daniel 7 with the "man of sin" or the Antichrist.²⁴⁶ Justin Martyr said, "Two advents of Christ have been announced."²⁴⁷ These were His first advent as a babe, and His second advent when He will destroy the "man of apostasy." He knew nothing of a third advent which is commonly placed seven years before the second advent Justin Martyr recognized. Irenaeus held that the Antichrist would reign for three years and six months,²⁴⁸ and that he would be an individual.²⁴⁹ Tertullian considered the Antichrist to be Satan or an embodiment of Satan.²⁵⁰

Commodianus made a resurrected Nero the Antichrist. He expected a millennium quite different from that generally taught today. He believed that the wicked would be judged at the same time as the righteous, but that they would not be sent to *gehenna* until after the 1,000 years.²⁵¹ Hippolytus was not a millennialist, but he wrote a long treatise on the Antichrist. He believed that the Antichrist would be related to Satan somewhat as Christ is related to the Father. He envisioned only one return of Christ. He knew nothing of a so-called rapture. The Church would endure the persecution of Revelation 12 after which the second coming, the judgment of all men, and the end of the world would occur. He saw but one physical resurrection when "righteous and sinners alike" would be resurrected and judged.²⁵²

Only two references to a Jewish temple were found. Cyril of Jerusalem believed that the Antichrist would rebuild the Jewish temple.²⁵³ John of Damascus taught that the Antichrist would come to "the old Jewish

---

245 Archelaus, *Ante-Nicene Fathers*, vol. VII, pp. 583-585.
246 Barnabas, *op. cit.*, vol. I, p. 138.
247 Martyr, *op. cit.*, vol. I, p. 253.
248 Irenaeus, *op. cit.*, vol. I, p. 554.
249 *Ibid.*, p. 559.
250 Tertullian, *op. cit.*, vol. III, p. 234.
251 Commodianus, *Ante-Nicene Fathers*, vol. IV, pp. 210-212.
252 Hippolytus, *op. cit.*, pp. 190-251.
253 Cyril, *op. cit.*, vol. VII, p. 108.

temple."[254] He fails to explain how this could be since the old temple had been destroyed before his time. Nothing was found to even faintly resemble the current teaching that the Jews would rebuild the temple and that Christ would come to reign there seven years after the so-called rapture.

Of the later writers, Augustine confessed he did not know who or what Paul meant by the "man of sin," but conjectured he could have referred to the Roman empire or to Nero.[255] Chrysostom placed the Antichrist at the end of time.[256] Jerome equated the little horn of Daniel 7 with the Antichrist.[257] St. Hilary of Poitiers accepted a plurality of Antichrists, rather than a single person.[258]

There was general agreement that the restraining force was the Roman empire. Tertullian, in his *Apology*, makes the strongest statement on this subject that we found. It reads:

> There is also another and a greater necessity for our offering prayers in behalf of the emperors, nay, for the complete stability of the empire, and for Roman interests in general. For we know that a mighty shock is impending over the whole earth—in fact, the very end of all things threatening dreadful woes—is only retarded by the continued existence of the Roman empire. We have no desire, then, to be overtaken by those dire events; and in praying that their coming may be delayed, we are lending our aid to Rome's duration.[259]

Regarding the "falling away," Cyril of Jerusalem wrote that it was occurring at that time.[260] Basil was even more pointed saying, "Has the last hour come, and is the 'falling away' thus coming upon us, that the lawless one 'may be revealed' …?"[261]

Among the early writers, not one witness was found who taught that the Holy Spirit was the restrainer, and that He would be taken away at the so-called rapture. The nearest we found to this was a statement by

---

254 John of Damascus, *Nicene and Post-Nicene Fathers*, vol. IX, p. 99.
255 Augustine, *op. cit.*, vol. II, pp. 437-438.
256 Chrysostom, *op. cit.*, vol. X, p. 464.
257 Jerome, *Commentary on Daniel*, p. 77.
258 St. Hilary, *Nicene and Post-Nicene Fathers*, vol. IX, p. 113.
259 Tertullian, *op. cit.*, vol. III, pp. 42-43.
260 Cyril, *op. cit.*, vol. VII, p. 106.
261 Basil, *Nicene and Post-Nicene Fathers*, vol. VIII, p. 203.

Chrysostom: "Some indeed say, the grace of the Spirit, but others the Roman empire, to whom I most of all accede. Wherefore? Because if he meant to say the Spirit, he would not have spoken obscurely, but plainly."[262] Thus the present Premillennial teachings from the Thessalonian letters have little support from the Church fathers.

## Concluding Remarks

The Thessalonian letters say nothing about a millennium. The rapture of the Church is better equated with the consummation and the eternal state, than with a secret rapture seven years before the revelation of Christ. Paul could have referred to one man as the "man of sin," but he could have also referred to popery. I believe he does mean popery. Belief in a personal Antichrist is no evidence of one's belief about a millennium. Amillennialists such as Augustine and Jerome believed in one person as the Antichrist. The few Church fathers who believed in a millennium did not base their beliefs on Paul's letters to the Thessalonians.

---

262 Chrysostom, *op. cit.,* vol. XIII, p. 388.

CHAPTER 19

# THE ESCHATOLOGY OF THE REVELATION [263]

The book of Revelation is interesting, scintillating, powerful, dramatic, challenging. Some find it enigmatic, obscure, puzzling, frustrating. Others are certain that they understand the intricacies of the book so faultlessly that they approach the task of interpreting it with absolute assurance that their interpretation is right and anybody who disagrees is wrong. Many of these are so confident of the truth of their interpretation that they make the book the cornerstone of their eschatological system, rather than taking the plain texts of the Bible as the foundation, and interpreting the Revelation in harmony with the plain portions of the Bible.

Having ascertained that the rest of the Bible does not teach a millennial reign either before or after the second coming of Christ, that the "secret rapture" of the Church is a myth, that there is but one bodily resurrection of all men both good and evil, one final judgment, and after that eternity these plain teachings of Scripture are given priority over this book of symbols. This is the only sound hermeneutical principle available. Those who make this book the basis for their eschatological system violate this important rule of biblical interpretation. It is better to have a weaker superstructure and a strong base, than a weak foundation and a stronger superstructure. This is the only book on which Premillennialists have a reasonably strong case, but it is without solid foundation, hence must be rejected.

Before discussing the several chapters of the Revelation, it is necessary that consideration be given to the nature of the book. It is accepted as true prophecy for the book makes this claim in five verses (Rev. 1:3; 22:7, 10, 18, 19). However, it is not written in the factual style of history, but tells

---

263 The material on the Revelation has been reduced from two chapters to one chapter because of space limitations. Several important points had to be deleted. This necessary reduction is regretted. It is hoped that the reader will understand.

the story of future events (future at the time of writing) as well as current happenings (Rev. 1:19) through pictorial representations. This is part of the apocalyptic style of writing then in vogue. It is as though John saw a series of pantomime scenes with a narrator giving certain clues with sound effects and other visual manifestations.

Thus the very nature of the literary style calls attention to the fact that it contains many symbols. The text confirms this by presenting stars and candlesticks as factual presentations, then explaining what these symbolize (Rev. 1). Elsewhere the sea is presented visibly, but later the sea is said to symbolize people (17:15). A beast with seven heads and ten horns appears (chap. 12). Later the heads are said to be mountains (17:9) which in turn are said to symbolize kings or kingdoms. The horns also refer to kings or kingdoms (17:12). Therefore, this book cannot be taken literally in many instances. Those who insist on literalizing most of this book fail to give adequate consideration to these facts.

Albertus Pieters correctly states the hermeneutical principle which is in perfect agreement with that of Terry given previously. Pieters says:

Therefore, the ordinary rule of interpretation must be reversed in our study of it [the Revelation]. Ordinarily, the words of any passage of scripture must be understood in their plain and natural sense, unless there is reason to take them figuratively. The presumption is always in the literal sense: if any man takes it otherwise, he must show cause. This is not so in the Revelation. Here, the entire book being in the realm of the pictorial, i.e. symbolical presentation, we are to assume that any picture shown to us has a symbolic meaning; unless it is clear that the expression must be taken literally. Here the symbolical, not the literal, interpretation has the right of way.[264]

Interpreting symbols is not easy, yet it is necessary that we do so. Objects that are interpreted within the Revelation are accepted on the basis of the interpretation given to, and by, John. Thus, stars are symbols of ministers, the sea of people, candlesticks of churches, *horns as kingdoms or kings, and since the horns grow out of beasts, the beasts themselves, including the dragon of chapter 12, must refer to some type of political power.* Other objects must bear an analogous relationship to that which they represent. Thus the woman of chapter 12 must be Mary, if Christ is interpreted as the manchild. If the woman is Israel or the Church, then the manchild must also be a

---

264 Albertus Pieters, *Studies in the Revelation of St. John*, p. 67.

composite group, for a composite group giving birth to a single individual violates the rule of analogy.

Another hermeneutical rule which has been overlooked by most commentators is that beasts and inanimate objects usually refer to civil and political matters, whereas men, angels, and other important and consequential symbols refer to religious or ecclesiastical matters. Where these are combined in a single symbol, the inference is that a power that is both political and religious is intended.[265] Thus stars represent ministers of the gospel (Rev. 1:20) because of their brilliance. In the same verse the golden candlesticks symbolize churches because gold is important, and also because this kind of device was used in the temple worship of the Jews.

Symbols are combined in two ways to indicate a politico-religious entity or power. The ten horns of Daniel 7 are specifically identified as ten kings or kingdoms (v. 24). The eleventh horn of that same verse must also be a political power, but human capabilities (speaking) are attributed to this unique kingdom. This latter characteristic of this horn tells us that this eleventh horn was also a religious power. Similarly, the dragon of Revelation 12 is a political power based on it being a ferocious animal, but it is also a religious power because of the non-animal characteristic of being an accuser of those who opposed him (v. 10). The same rule applies to the two beasts of Revelation 13.

Another way of indicating a dual role is through the use of two symbols—one being a person and the other an animal. This is particularly true of Revelation 17. In this chapter the beast the woman rides has the same seven heads and ten horns as the dragon of chapter 12 and the first beast of chapter 13. There is a connection between these three which must not be overlooked. The dual nature of the first two is made known by giving the beasts human capabilities. In this last mentioned symbol, the animal represents the civil or political aspect of this power, whereas the harlot woman riding and controlling it depicts the religious character of the institution.

The Revelation is interpreted according to several schools of thought of which only two will be considered. These are the methods adopted by Dispensationalists and the method used in this chapter. A brief summary of each will be given. A Jesuit named Ribera invented the futuristic approach

---

265 For a fuller discussion of the nature of symbolic language see F. G. Smith's, *The Revelation Explained*, pp. 9-18.

in 1580. This was done to protect the Roman Catholic Church from the charge of being the beast of chapter 13. It received little attention from Protestants until it became the accepted interpretation of Dispensationalism.

According to this view chapter 1 is introductory. Chapters 2-3 are said to be symbols of seven periods of the Church, usually seven specific periods of time. The Church is said to be raptured to heaven at the beginning of chapter 4. The rest of chapter 4 through chapter 19 are said to cover the seven year period between the rapture of the Church and the second coming. Chapter 20 is said to refer to the millennium, followed by the judgment of the wicked, and the eternal state. The preferred interpretation is strictly literal and events follow in the order they are found in the book itself.

The view I hold may be classed as the resumptive method. Dean Alford suggests that certain series of the Revelation "are not continuous but resumptive:...each evolving something which was not in the former, and putting the course of God's Providence in a different light."[266] All recognize that Daniel is written like this, and all recognize certain similarities between Daniel and the Revelation. I maintain that the two books are also similar in that certain portions are parallel to certain other portions. Several reasons can be given for this conclusion, but only one will be discussed.

The fact that the final judgment is brought into focus several times in different portions of the Revelation leaves little room for doubt about the parallelism of the book. Efforts to make these judgment scenes apply to separate judgments held at different times fail of their objective. Portions of three of these scenes are quoted below. The first is from chapter 6 which is considered as a table of contents, summary, or brief outline of what is to follow. It ends with apocalyptic upheavals in nature which accompany pronouncements of judgments, then states that men

hid themselves in dens and in the rocks of the mountains; And said to the mountains and rocks, Fall on us, and hide us from the face of him that sitteth on the throne, and from the wrath of the Lamb: For the great day of his wrath is come; and who shall be able to stand ( Rev. 6:15-17)?

Note that the judge sits on a throne. We affirm this can be no other judgment than the great white throne judgment of Revelation 20. Also note that it refers to the "great day of his wrath." This can be nothing other than God's final judgment on evil doers at the end of the age. The next

---

266 Alford, *op. cit.*, p. 665.

## The Eschatology of the Revelation

passage affirms that both the righteous and the wicked will be judged at a single judgment.

And the nations were angry, and thy wrath is come, and the time of the dead, that they should be judged, and that thou shouldest give reward unto thy servants the prophets, and to the saints, and them that fear thy name, small and great; and shouldest destroy them which destroy the earth (Rev. 11:18).

Then at the close of one of the series of the Revelation is found another word picture of the final judgment. It is affirmed without fear of contradiction that this judgment scene is the same as that found in chapters 6 and 20. That the judgment in Revelation 20 is the final judgment is admitted by all. However, most Premillennialists deny that it includes the righteous. This denial cannot be supported exegetically. Parts of the text read:

And I saw a great white throne, and him that sat on it, from whose face the earth and the heaven fled away....And I saw the dead, small and great, stand before God; and the books were opened...and the dead were judged out of those things which were written in the books...and they were judged every man according to their works (Rev. 20:11-13).

Note that John does not say the wicked dead were judged to the exclusion of the righteous. Instead he simply states that the dead were judged. The expression refers to all the dead, both good and evil. The expression, "every man according to their works" is especially meaningful. Jesus said, "For the Son of man shall come in the glory of the Father with his angels; and then shall he reward every man according to his works" (Matt. 16:27). This refers to His second coming at which time all men, good and evil, will receive the reward or punishments they have merited by the way they lived.

Paul likewise adds that at the revelation (*apocalupseos*) "of the righteous judgment of God; Who will render to every man according to his deeds" (Rom. 2:5-6). Verses 7-10 then make it abundantly clear that this involves both the good and the evil. Note the reading.

To them who by patient continuance in well doing seek for glory and honor and immortality, eternal life: But unto them that are contentious, and do not obey the truth, but obey unrighteousness, indignation and wrath, Tribulation and anguish, upon every soul of man that doeth evil, of the Jew first, and also of the Gentile; But glory, honour and peace to every man that worketh good" (Rom. 2:7-10).

Both shall receive their rewards at the revelation (singular—not plural) of the righteous judgment of God. Surely, if a thousand year period was to come between the judging of the righteous and that of the wicked, Paul would have used the plural form or otherwise have stated that a long interval existed between the judgments. Our conclusion is that there is but one revelation and but one final judgment.

Another aspect of the controversy is whether chapters 4-19 relate to the Church. Dispensationalists hold that these chapters cover the seven year period of the Antichrist which they claim will begin at the rapture of the Church to heaven, and which will end when Christ returns to establish an earthly reign on earth. Others contend that these chapters are concerned with the Church and those forces which have opposed her. Before locating the Church in chapters 4-19, let us consider the stratagem by which Dispensationalists claim the Church is removed to heaven in Revelation 4. This chapter begins with a statement about John:

After this I looked, and behold, a door was opened in heaven: and the first voice which I heard was, as it were a trumpet talking with me; which said, Come up hither, and I will shew thee things which must he hereafter. And immediately I was in the spirit: and, behold, a throne was set in heaven, and one sat on the throne (Rev. 4:1-2).

From these verses we learn that John entered into the presence of God in heaven. Whether he was transported or raptured there in his spirit while his body remained on the isle of Patmos, or whether both soul and body left the earth is not clearly stated. Even if his body was taken to heaven, it was John alone, and not the Church, who was involved. However, J. A. Seiss, possibly the ablest exponent of the theory being considered, claims it refers to the Church and is yet future. In his comments on Revelation 21 he states:

In Revelation 4:1-2 we read that the Church is caught away from the earth, and she does not appear again in the book of Revelation until she is seen in this passage immediately before the description of our Lord's glorious return.[267]

Such statements as this one show to what extremes Dispensationalists are forced to go in order to have their teachings accepted. It would have been legitimate for Seiss to say that he considered John's rapture a symbol of the

---

267  J. A. Seiss, *Lectures on the Apocalypse*, vol. III, p. 229.

future rapture of the Church, but that is not what he says. He claims we read about the rapture of the Church in Revelation 4:1-2. This is not an accurate statement. We read only of John's rapture. Scofield's note on Revelation 4:1 teaches the same theory as Seiss, but it is less objectionable. It reads, "This call seems clearly to indicate the fulfillment of I Thessalonians 4:14-17. The word 'church' does not again occur in the Revelation till all is finished."

It is granted that the word "church" does not appear in chapters 4-19, but that does not mean that the Church is not indicated symbolically. Just as the Church is represented in Revelation 21:1 as the city, the new Jerusalem, and in that verse and verse 10 as the bride of Christ, so is she symbolized in the chapters which are said to cover the time the Church is in heaven.

I hold that the white horse and rider of Revelation 6:2 is a symbol of the Church. Seiss admits it refers to converted people, but he contends it refers to people who are saved after the Church is raptured to heaven.[268] Even so, if they are born again believers in Jesus Christ, they will be a part of the Church, even if the major body had been raptured to heaven. It is our contention that when the Church is raptured to heaven the world will come to an end, hence there will be no salvation work accomplished after that event. But if time is to continue, as many claim, and if people will continue to be saved after the rapture, those who are saved will be just as much a part of the body of Christ—the Church as those who participated in the rapture. Not one text can be advanced to indicate otherwise.

The Church is symbolized by the temple in Revelation 11:1-2. Seiss[269] and Tan[270] hold that this refers to a literal temple yet to be built in Palestine, but this makes the passage absurd. Assuming that the temple described in Ezekiel 40-42 is yet to be built, and further assuming as they do that this future temple is the one John the Revelator was told to measure, one wonders what was the need or purpose for such a measurement. Ezekiel gives the dimensions of his temple. If Ezekiel's temple refers to a future literal temple, it certainly will be built according to the dimensions Ezekiel gives in great detail. If there was any need for measuring the temple, it would not be apparent. All one would need to do would be to refer back to Ezekiel.

---

268  *Ibid.*, vol. I, pp. 310-318.
269  *Ibid.*, vol. II. pp. 158-161.
270  Tan, *op. cit.*, p. 320

But when the temple is considered a symbol of the Church, the passage becomes meaningful. Bear in mind that in less figurative letters, Paul said, "Know ye not that ye are the temple of God?" (I Cor. 3:16). Also, "For ye are the temple of the living God" (II Cor. 6:16). The true believers, the Church, are represented in Revelation 11:1 by the temple itself. Unsaved persons who have attached themselves to the Church are symbolized by the "court which is without the temple" (Rev. 11:2). The measuring reed is the word of God, the Bible. When it is preached today, those who do not measure up to its demands are excluded. Only the true believers are included in the temple.

The Church also appears as the woman clothed with the sun in Revelation 12. More commentators accept this view than any other, although there are a variety of opinions regarding the identity of the woman. Our reasons for believing she is a symbol of the Church will be given later in this chapter. The Church appears in other places in the Revelation, but these are enough to prove the Dispensational view untrue.

## Revelation 1-4

It is my belief that most of the Revelation has been fulfilled in the past. For this reason only a small portion of the book is considered eschatological in nature. However, because of the futuristic emphasis of our day, a brief statement will be made regarding the contents of the more important portions of the book.

The risen glorified Christ is introduced in chapter 1. His second coming is emphatically foretold in verse 7. Note that "every eye shall see him" when He does come. No secret coming of the Lord is indicated. If such a coming was to be expected, why was it not mentioned in this connection? The fact that the book would be full of symbols is indicated by the seven stars and seven candlesticks being interpreted as meaning messengers (angels) and churches.

Chapters 2-3 contain letters to seven churches located in Asia Minor. These seven churches are to be the recipients of the entire book (Rev. 1:11), although only a few verses are addressed to the angel of the each church. Scofield considers these a "foreview" of the history of the Church from John's day to the end. These letters, he contends, give this history in the "precise order" in which they appear (note 3 on Rev. 1:20). But if this be true, the whole gospel era of over 1900 years is covered by two chapters, whereas the seven year period of the Antichrist, according to Scofield and other Dispensational writers, requires sixteen chapters although the length of time involved is but seven years. No satisfactory explanation can be given for such a disproportionate division of the book.

In chapter 4 Christ is shown seated on His mediatorial throne—the throne of David, if you please. Nothing pertaining to last things is found in this chapter. The claim of Dispensationalists that verse 2 depicts the rapture of the Church has been refuted already.

## Revelation 5

The book or scroll sealed with seven seals is the principal object of chapter 5. That this book was a symbol of things accomplished through the atonement is evident from the fact that Christ is represented as a "Lamb as it had been slain" (v. 6). Verse 10 makes it clear that at the time of the writing the kingdom of God had been established already, provided an accurate translation is used. This should read "kingdom" instead of "kings." The RSV reads, "and hast made them a kingdom." Phillips reads, "Thou hast made them a kingdom." The RV reads, "and he made us to be a kingdom." This does not refer to some future period for the kingdom was already established.

After discussing the proper translation of verse 10, Pieters adds, "There are some Bible students who are not willing to admit that Jesus is king of the church, or, indeed, a king at all, as yet."[271] In a similar vein Lenski observes, "Chiliasts point to the future tense, and date this reigning in their future millennium. But here we read, 'he made them a kingdom,' not, 'he shall make them.' "[272]

## Revelation 6

Chapter six begins with the militant picture of the Church, and ends with the second coming of Christ in judgment. Certain graphic presentations of the Church are made in this chapter. These serve as a synopsis or table of contents. Futurists place this chapter between the time they say the rapture will occur, and the second-second coming of Christ. This "Johnny-come-lately" doctrine was not the teaching of the early Church. The reference is to the white horse and its rider (Rev. 6:2).

---

271 Pieters, *op. cit.,* p. 83.
272 R. C. H. Lenski. *The Interpretation of St. John's Revelation,* p. 208.

The other three horsemen are considered as the successive opponents of the Church. The current one was paganism. The blackness of apostasy followed this. Then came the half-Christian half-pagan horse of a sickly pale-green hue. The use of "the beasts of the earth" as an instrument of death points to the inquisition and other uses of political power to accomplish their desires.

The fifth seal takes us from the earthly scene where the Church faced great persecution to paradise where the martyrs are portrayed. This picture was designed to strengthen the Church through whatever periods of persecution she had to face. Verse 11 indicates that the time of this scene is prior to the end of Christians suffering martyrdom. Since Christians are being slain even today in some areas, and since more severe persecution may develop in the future, the complete fulfillment of this part of the prophecy is probably in the future.

The fact that the sixth seal takes us to the disturbances which culminate in the final judgment has been discussed already. It is not considered necessary to repeat that material.

## Revelation 7

Chapter 7 moves beyond the judgment scene of chapter 6 to the time when "God shall wipe away all tears from their eyes" (Rev. 7:17). The actual sealing has been in progress throughout the gospel age, but the picture takes us to the time of our ultimate reward. But who are the 144,000? Most Premillennialists say that they are men of the Jewish race. Futurists contend that this represents Jews who will be saved during the "great tribulation" which they expect. But all Christians are to suffer persecution. There is no necessity for verse 14 to be interpreted as some special time of persecution.

It has been shown already that the true Jews are the Christians. The terms Israelites and Jews are repeatedly used of the Church. In this case the twelve tribes symbolize the Church. The sealing of 12,000 from each tribe should not be taken literally. First, it is not reasonable that any exact number would be saved from each tribe. Nor is it reasonable to assume that the same exact number would be saved out of one of the larger tribes as out of the smallest tribe. Nor is it reasonable to assume that the tribe of Dan should have no one saved from that tribe. In most listings the tribe of Levi does not appear. In this listing it does. In other listings the tribe of Dan appears, but in this one it does not.

I am aware that many expect the Antichrist to come from the tribe of Dan, but until evidence is presented that this means that the tribe of Dan is to be disinherited, this cannot serve as an explanation of the omission. And unless the omission is fully explained, along with answers to the other questions raised in the preceding paragraph, the literalness of the numbers must be rejected, as well as the claim that Gentiles are excluded from the 144,000.

An even more cogent reason for rejecting a futuristic interpretation is that this 144,000 are said to be "firstfruits unto God and to the Lamb" (Rev. 14:4). If this 144,000 are indeed physical Jews, they refer to men like Peter and Paul who were saved during the first Christian century. The expression "firstfruits" cannot be applied, legitimately, to persons of some future age.

Those who insist that this refers to fleshly descendents of Jacob should consider the fact that the gates to heaven are named after the twelve tribes of Israel (Rev. 21:12-13). Does this mean that only physical Jews are to enter that haven of rest? No, for "the children of promise are counted for the seed" (Rom. 9:8): "Now, we, brethren, as Isaac was, are the children of promise" (Gal. 4:28).

## Revelation 9

The scene which follows the sounding of the sixth trumpet (Rev. 9:13-21) is interpreted by many able Bible scholars as a symbol of the Turkish conquests during the mid-centuries. I agree. Most futurists consider it as a symbol of demons working out God's will during what they call the "great tribulation." However, extreme literalists, like Lindsey, apply this to an army of men. This is discussed more fully in the chapter on the Battle of Armageddon, but for the present let us consider the impossibility of a literal meaning.

The number of horsemen alone—not the total army—is two hundred million. Mechanized units have almost eliminated the cavalry division of the army. But with that many horsemen, one would expect several times as many foot soldiers, enough at least to bring the number up to one billion or more. And with an active army of one billion, there would have to be four or five times that many taking care of logistics, repairs, care of the horses, etc. This would make this army exceed the present population of the earth. A literal interpretation is ridiculous.

## Identifying the Dragon and The Woman of Revelation 12

That the woman is a symbol should be apparent from the impossibility of a woman being as tall as this woman is said to be. Nor could a literal woman wear literal stars as a crown. For it to represent Mary would conflict with Jesus' refusal to accord Mary any special honor because of her selection as the mother of Jesus. Certainly, it is not national Israel, for national Israel was unworthy of being represented by such an exalted symbol. If it symbolizes the remnant, then it also refers to the Church, for the remnant became the Church.

The only option left is that the woman is a figure of the Church. She is clothed with the light of Christian truth and stands on the next major source of light for mankind. The twelve stars are symbols of the twelve apostles. This is in accord with the interpretation of stars as ministers in chapter 1. The war she is engaged in is pictured as being started in the astral heavens where the sun, moon, and stars have their orbits, but this is considered a symbol of the religious world here on earth, inasmuch as we do sit in "heavenly places," while in these mortal bodies. The conflict is pictured on the earth (vv. 9-17). So the Church *is* found in the Revelation, and she is still on the earth in Revelation 12, Dispensational arguments notwithstanding.

The opponent of the Church in chapter 12 is given four descriptive titles or names. These are "red dragon," "old serpent," "Devil," and "Satan." These designations have caused many to jump to the conclusion that this red dragon is none other than that spirit being who is the head of the nether regions. Although three of these terms are used of that being, they are also used of other entities. Egypt is called a dragon (Isa. 51:9-10). Ahaz is called a serpent (Isa. 14:28-29), as is Dan (Gen. 49:17). The Hebrew term *satan* and its Greek equivalent *satan* or *satanas* mean opponent, adversary, or opposer. It is used a number of times of anyone who was considered an opposer of another person. The Philistines considered David a *satan* (adversary in the KJV) to them. In the Hebrew text Rezon is called a *satan* (adversary in the KJV) in I Kings 11:23 and again in verse 25. The psalmist uses the plural form of his adversaries in Psalm 109:29.

Possibly the most significant use of the term *satan* in the Old Testament is in Numbers 22:22. The story of Balaam and how God talked to him through the animal he was riding is familiar to all Bible students. What is not so well known is the fact that the angel of Jehovah, thought by many to be preincarnate appearances of Christ, is called a *satan* to Balaam (adversary in the KJV). Since men, and even the angel of Jehovah, are called satans, we must not take it for granted that the use of the term of the dragon in Revelation 12 must refer to the ruler of the underworld.

In the New Testament, two of the accounts tell of Christ calling Peter *satana* or *satan* (Matt. 16:23; Mark 8:33). Jesus did not curse Peter as one man might call another a devil. He simply used the word in its basic meaning of opposer. It was as if He had said, "Peter, you are my opponent or adversary in what you suggest." Thus both of the Testaments testify to the use of the appellation *satan* to others than the chief opposer, the ruler of the lower division of *hades*.

What is true of the term *satan* is also true of the Greek term *diabolos* (devil) at least as far as the New Testament is concerned. There is no Hebrew equivalent. The plural form, devils, does appear four times in the KJV, but later translations correctly use other terms in these verses. But let us note that Christ called Judas a devil (*diabolos*). Some of the meanings of the term are: slanderer, traitor, deceiver. Probably the idea of Judas being a traitor was uppermost in the mind of Jesus as these words were uttered.

Paul uses the plural form of certain people. In writing of the great apostasy which he knew would come, he listed some as being *diaboloi* (plural of *diabolos*). The KJV translates this as "false accusers" (II Tim. 3:3). This is an acceptable translation, but other possibilities cannot be ruled out. Then in Titus 2:3 we again have "false accusers" as the translation of the plural form in the admonition Paul gives to the aged women.

It would not be grammatically incorrect to translate these expressions of Paul with the term "devils," nor would it be grammatically incorrect to translate Jesus' expression of Judas as "traitor" instead of "devil." Other considerations must decide, rather than an appeal to rules of syntax—all of which proves that the various designations of the dragon in the Revelation are capable of other translations. Instead of being called the Devil and Satan, he could as correctly be termed the false accuser and adversary. It is our opinion that this is not only grammatically correct, but that it conveys the meaning of the book better than the present translation.

There are other reasons for contending that the dragon of Revelation 12 is not that spirit being called the Devil. This dragon had seven heads and ten horns just as the first beast of chapter 13 had seven heads and ten horns. And the first beast of chapter 13 is well nigh universally accepted as a political power. The dragon of chapter 12 must therefore be a political power. To make it anything else is to violate the rules of analogy.

The horns on the first beast of chapter 13 are universally recognized as lesser political divisions which grew out of, or shall grow out of, the Roman empire. That being the case the laws of analogy require that the same horns on the dragon also be those same political divisions. And since the horns grow out of a dragon or a beast, the animal out of which they grow can be nothing other than the larger political division out of which the lesser ones grow. Thus, the dragon represents some phase of the Roman empire.

Another indication that the dragon is not the ruler of the nether regions is found in Revelation 13:2. In this verse we are told that the dragon gave the first beast his own power, and his own seat (throne is better) and great authority. Now the Devil has been known to give power and authority to his agents, but he has never resigned his throne to another, and his nature is such that he never will. But if the dragon is interpreted as a political empire, then it is easy to find in this imagery the passing of one political power and the rising of another which receives authority, power, and the throne from the government that fades out of the picture.

Having proved the dragon to be a political power, it is now necessary to identify that power. The red horse and rider of chapter 6 is identified as paganism, the first opponent of the Church. In chapter 12 the color of the dragon is red. This serves to indicate the two symbols are to be interpreted as identical. It said that the dragon was "the accuser of our brethren" (Rev. 12:10). It is recorded of the second beast of Revelation 13 that he "spake as a dragon." From these texts we know that the dragon did speak. These human capabilities in a beast indicate an entity that is both religious and political. Thus we identify the dragon as the Roman empire while pagan.

It is not an easy task to identify the seven heads for they are first identified as mountains (Rev. 17:9), and then as kings or authorities (Rev. 17:10). The former could point to the seven hills on which Rome is built, but apparently the second identification is of seven different forms of government or authority by which Rome was governed. Bishop Newton lists these as the kingly or regal, consuls, dictators, decemvirs, and military tribunes as the first five.[273] He refers to the great Roman historians Livy and Tacitus as

---

273 Newton, *op. cit.,* pp. 539, 573ff.

his sources of information. The sixth which then existed was the imperial. This was the head wounded unto death, but which was later revived under Charlemagne and Otto the Great as the Holy Roman empire.

The sixth head we identify as either the exarch of Ravenna or the Patrician form under Pepin which lasted only 26 years. I tend to prefer the latter for under the exarch of Ravenna, Rome did not govern herself so much as she was governed from without. The eighth head which is said to be of the seven was a restoration of the imperial form which had been wounded unto death in the fall of Rome in A.D. 476. The crowns being on the heads of the dragon means that authority was still vested in the head then existing, i.e., the imperial. The ten minor kingdoms had not yet arisen.

Since stars were interpreted as ministers, the stars that were cast down by the dragon represent the thousands of ministers of the gospel which were slain by pagan Rome (Rev. 12:4). The flight of the woman into the wilderness (v. 14) for a time, and times, and half a time represents the period known as the dark ages when the Church was driven underground. This verse takes us beyond the time when the crowns were on the heads, to the time when the crowns were on the horns (Rev. 13:1), and even to the time the imperial head was wounded unto death (Rev. 13:3) and was healed or restored to power in the Holy Roman empire which is symbolized by the harlot and beast (Rev. 17). When properly interpreted, the time sequence of chapters 12-17 is very plain.

Identifying the dragon has been eschatologically important, for it is the dragon that is bound 1,000 years in Revelation 20. It is interesting to note that this dragon which has been identified as paganism is introduced without the definite article. The Greeks did not have an indefinite article (a or an), only the definite article which is the equivalent to our "the." It is called a dragon (Rev. 12:3) by the absence of the definite article. But in each subsequent appearance, the definite article appears. These are correctly translated "the dragon." The verses where this occurs are Revelation 12:4, 7, 9, 13, 16, 17; 13:2, 4, 11; 16:3; 20:2. If the explanation that the dragon in chapter 12 refers to paganism can be accepted, then it is paganism that is bound in chapter 20, rather than the prince of the nether regions.

## Revelation 14

This chapter is known to close another series for it again describes the final judgment. Verses 14-20 tell of a time of reaping. This is the reaping at the end of the age. Jesus plainly told the disciples that the harvest was at the end of the world (Matt. 13:39). Thus, the reaping or harvesting done in these verses again brings us to the end of time. When Revelation 19:15 is compared with verse 20 of this section, it is quite evident that they refer to the same reaping; and chapter 19 definitely refers to the second coming of Christ. We read in Revelation 19:15, "And he treadeth the winepress of the fierceness and wrath of Almighty God." And from verses 19-20 of this section we read, "And the angel…gathered the vine of the earth, and cast it into the great winepress of the wrath of God. And the winepress was trodden without the city." The two are so similar in meaning that they unquestionably refer to the same event.

Even so, Dispensationalists contend that Revelation 14:14-20 is a vision of the battle of Armageddon, but not the battle itself. Scofield lists chapter 14 as parenthetical, rather than real. The real battle is to be fought, so they say, in chapter 19; but what is said in Revelation 14:20 will literally occur at that time. Since the battle of Armageddon will be considered in a later chapter of this volume, further discussion of that battle will be deferred until later, except to discuss the latter part of Revelation 14:20.

Verse 20 reads, "And the winepress was trodden without the city, and blood came out of the winepress, even unto the horse bridles, by the space of a thousand and six hundred furlongs." In spite of the strong evidence that this verse is figurative or hyperbolic, many insist on taking parts of it as literal. The winepress is taken by these to be symbolic, and the "vine of the earth" thrown into the winepress they understand to be symbolic, but the 1,600 furlongs, or approximately 200 miles, is taken by some as literal.

## Revelation 16

It is said that the sixth angel "poured out his vial upon the great river Euphrates; and the water thereof was dried up, that the way of the kings of the east might be prepared" (Rev. 16:12). The first event that happened was the drying up of the Euphrates river. This seems a rather mild event to constitute a "plague," if it be interpreted literally; but since the other bowls were figurative, this one is no doubt figurative, also. Since the river is specifically named, it focuses our attention on Old Testament events that might serve as the basis of an analogy.

The city of Babylon depended on the Euphrates for its water supply. The river ran through the walled city. Daniel tells of the capture of the city by the Medes and Persians, but he gives none of the details. From secular historians we learn that Cyrus had a new channel dug for the Euphrates. By diverting the water into this new channel, he dried up the river enough to march his troops into the heart of the city along the old river bed. We conclude that the drying up of the Euphrates river is analogous to that event.

The major event that resulted from the drying up of the Euphrates by Cyrus was the fall of Babylon. Therefore, the sixth plague is a plague against spiritual Babylon which is analogous to the literal desolation that came to the earthly city named Babylon. And as the Medes and Persians of that day came from the East, the forces that are to produce the downfall of spiritual Babylon are depicted as the "kings of the east." Therefore, the sixth plague is against spiritual Babylon.

The fall of Babylon was announced back in Revelation 14:8. That series ended with the final judgment in the latter part of chapter 14. The fall depicted by the drying up of the river Euphrates is not a different fall. Rather it is the same fall. Just the symbolism is different. A fuller description of that fall is given in Revelation 17-18

The Bible contains the word "Armageddon" only in a single verse. A great deal has been written and preached about the battle of Armageddon. The biblical basis for all of this is found in the words, "And he gathered them together into a place called in the Hebrew tongue Armageddon" (Rev. 16:16). Various other passages are said to be of that battle, but this depends on interpretation, not on exegesis. In this passage the battle is definitely a spiritual battle. If other passages apply to it, they, too, must be spiritual.

The basis for contending the battle of Armageddon will be, or is, a spiritual battle depends on many things beyond the bounds of Revelation 16:12-16, but one of the main reasons is in these verses. Inspiration has given the key which must not be ignored. The dual nature of certain symbols in the Revelation has been discussed already. But if a symbol is both religious or spiritual as well as civil or political, it could be difficult to separate the two areas under certain circumstances. This would be particularly true of a battle or war. For example, if the beast was shown to be at war with some nation, it might be confusing to know whether it was a war of armies or a war of theology or both. Verse 13 clears up any speculation about the battle of Armageddon.

Verse 13 reads, "And I saw three unclean spirits like frogs come out of the mouth of the dragon, and out of the mouth of the beast, and out of the mouth of the false prophet." The false prophet is identified by most commentators as the second beast of Revelation 13. I have further identified this second beast as that part of Protestantism where the church is supported and controlled to some degree by the state. But these beasts were not the combatants. Instead, unclean spirits came out of the mouths of the dragon, the beast, and the false prophet. As I have interpreted this, it means that some type of confederation would develop between paganism, papalism, and that part of Protestantism that has become apostate. This confederation would be the opponent of the Church in this battle.

Thus the battle of Armageddon is a spiritual battle. Instead of the clashing of armies of up to 200,000,000 men, as is so glibly pictured by many writers, the true interpretation is that the battle is between spiritual forces. It is the last stages of the battle between good and evil, right and wrong, the Church and all opposing forces. It is possible that persecution and violence may be used against the Church in this great battle, but the battle is between truth and error; not between opposing armies armed with carnal weapons. Our warfare is not with guns and planes. Our weapons are spiritual in nature, and it is spiritual foes we must fight against.

The seventh angel poured his bowl into the air. This points to worldwide convulsions which shall end with the second coming of Christ, and the end of the world. The natural phenomena which are listed in verse 18 point to the political unrest of our day, the moral decay which is so evident, the increase in crime, the rebellion against legitimate authority, the use of force to subject other people, the atheistic philosophies of our day which may well grow worse, and the materialism that accepts God's bounty but which leaves no place for Him in the living.

## Revelation 17

Although the preceding chapter takes us to the last time, this chapter picks up a portion of the preceding series. The resumptive nature of this chapter is evidenced by the fact that one of the seven angels pictured as pouring out their bowls, is now the one speaking to John. Since the subject is the fall of Babylon, it is reasonable to believe that this was the sixth angel, for the sixth angel is the one who dried up the Euphrates; and this was interpreted as God's judgments on Babylon.

The picture John saw was that of an impure woman who rode on a scarlet colored beast that had seven heads and ten horns (v. 3). The woman has written upon her forehead the name Babylon, and the fact that she was the mother of harlots. John marvelled at what he saw, but the angel promised to explain the significance of what he saw. In another section the explanation given and our interpretation of it is found, but stating it again may be helpful. The five kings or authorities that had already fallen (v. 10) were forms of Roman authority: kings, consuls, dictators, decemvirs, and military tribunes. The sixth which existed in John's day was the imperial. Another, the patrician, was future in John's time, but it would not endure for long.

The beast on which the woman rode was said to exist, yet not to exist (vv. 8, 11) is said to be one of the seven, although it is also said to be the eighth. In Revelation 13:3 the first beast of that chapter had one of its seven heads wounded unto death, but the wound was then said to be healed. In this chapter an eighth head is presented which is of the seven. Thus two pictures of the same thing are given. Both refer to the dissolution of the Roman empire and its later restoration as the Carolingian empire under Charlemagne and still later as the Holy Roman empire under Otto the Great. These facts of history fit the conditions set forth in the prophecy. Instead of the revival of the Roman empire being future, as Dispensationalists and other futurists claim, it can be read about in any history of Europe.

It was the forces represented by the harlot riding the scarlet colored beast that Martin Luther faced after his 95 theses were nailed to the door of the Wittenberg church. The impure woman is a figure of Pope Leo X, Tetzel, Eck, Alexander, and the Roman Catholic hierarchy in general. The scarlet colored beast is a figure of the Holy (?) Roman empire whose emperor at that time was Charles V of Spain. The woman (the Roman Catholic hierarchy) told the beast (Charles V) what to do. He attempted to carry out the orders given him, but he was thwarted in his efforts by friends of Luther in Germany.

The three pictures we have of the seven-headed ten-horned beast are as follows: (1) The dragon or paganism with the crowns still on the heads (Rev. 12). (2) The first beast of Revelation 13 which is papalism with the crowns on the horns which indicates a time after A.D. 476. (3) The scarlet colored beast ridden by the impure woman which is a figure of the restored empire under Charlemagne and Otto the Great and their successors. Thus the fulfillment of this prophecy is found in history—not in some future restoration of the Roman empire.

## Revelation 18

This chapter is a continuation of the discourse on the fall of spiritual Babylon. Verses 2-3 tell how spiritually corrupt she becomes. Then in verses 4-5 there is given the clarion call for the children of God who remain in her to come out. This refers to any Christians who remain in the Roman Church or in apostate Protestant churches. The remaining verses of the chapter picture the sad state into which Babylon has fallen, much of which is pictured in terms of buying and selling.

Of special note is verse 23 which reads, "And the light of a candle shall shine no more at all in thee; and the voice of the bridegroom and of the bride shall be heard no more at all in thee ..." The dearth of spiritual light is indicated by there being no candle light available. The voice of the bridegroom (Christ) or of the bride (the Church) is heard no more in her. Institutions may remain as they had been, externally, but internally they will have lost all spiritual life. Probably this condition is yet future, but some churches are so destitute of spiritual vitality today that the condition may be applicable already to some institutions.

## Revelation 19

The first six verses of this chapter show the saints rejoicing at the judgments meted out to the great whore. Verses 7-10 mention the coming marriage of the Lamb to His bride, the Church. There is a sense in which the Church is already the bride of Christ, but in another sense the marriage is yet future. In verse 7 she is referred to as the wife of the Lamb even though the marriage is yet future. The Church is called the bride and the wife of the Lamb in Revelation 21:9.

The verse referred to above is an important factor in proving that chapters 20-22 are resumptive rather than continuous historical. One thing that indicates this is that Christ's marriage is mentioned in chapter 21 after being indicated in chapter 19. In addition to this, he was shown the Lamb's wife by one of the angels who poured out the bowls of wrath. The connection should be evident. Thus, what was shown in Revelation 19:7-10 is enlarged upon in Revelation 21:9-27. In our study of chapter 20, these proofs that chapters 20-22 are resumptive in nature will play an important role in our interpretation.

Verses 11-16 depict the second coming of Christ. Riding a white horse is symbolic of His victories, and the sword proceeding from His mouth rather than being carried in His hand indicates the power of His word. He is called "Faithful and True" in verse 11, and "King of Kings and Lord of Lords" in verse 16. Although the horse and the sword are symbolic, there can be no escaping the fact that the person is none other than our risen Lord, Jesus Christ.

Sifting out the symbolic from the literal in the remaining verses of this chapter is not easy. However, by carefully observing the rules of analogy, it can be done. Since the sword in the mouth of Jesus is definitely a symbol, the destruction wrought by Christ must also be symbolic. The fowls eating flesh (vv. 18, 21) is symbolic, for the sword out of the mouth of Jesus does not destroy physical life. Making "war against him that sat on the horse, and against his army" (v. 19) is symbolical of a spiritual warfare. Those who claim this is a literal carnal war discredit Christ and the New Testament.

Jesus said to Pilate, "My kingdom is not of this world: if my kingdom were of this world, then would my servant fight, that I should not be delivered to the Jews" (John 18:36). Such a reversal of policy on the part of Jesus and the Church is a central aspect of the teaching that this is a physical combat. It must be rejected in no uncertain terms. Should Christ wish to destroy the armies of the world, He has the Power to do so by simply speaking the word. He would not have to have help from the puny arm of men to do this. The whole idea is abhorrent to us who know we are to love our enemies.

A further indication that chapters 20-22 are resumptive, rather than continuous historical, is the fact that the battle of chapter 19 says nothing of the dragon or the unclean spirit which came from him. In the only battle named Armageddon (Rev. 16:13-14), three opponents of Christ are named. These are the unclean spirits that came out of the mouths of the dragon, the beast, and the false prophet. A battle that does not include these three cannot be called, legitimately, the battle of Armageddon. Chapter 19 standing alone does not qualify.

Now this battle that is recorded in Revelation 19:17-21 is often called the battle of Armageddon, and I am not inclined to contest this, but it is important for it to be noted that only two of the contestants which the Bible indicates are involved in that battle (Rev. 16:13-16) are involved in the battle in Revelation 19:17-21. The dragon is not so much as mentioned in the latter verses. He is not involved in the fighting, nor is he disposed of. The opponents of Christ are the beast and the false prophet. Note the reading:

"And the beast was taken, and with him the false prophet...These both were cast alive into a lake of fire burning with brimstone" (Rev. 19:20).

Now this forces us to conclude that what is given in Revelation 19:17-21 is either a different battle than the battle of Armageddon (Rev. 16:13-16), or it is only part of it. I consider the latter to be the more logical. Therefore, I hold that chapter 20 is resumptive. It begins by giving an account of the battle from the standpoint of the dragon. According to this viewpoint, chapter 19 gives the story of Christ's victory over the beast and the false prophet, or papalism and apostate Protestantism; whereas Revelation 20:1-9 recounts that battle only in part—that part which pertains to the dragon or paganism. Thus the latter part of chapter 19 and the early part of chapter 20 account for separate parts of the battle of Armageddon.

## Revelation 20

One could easily write a book on this one chapter. But brevity is necessary in this instance. The angel of verse 1 cannot be Christ. Christ as our redeemer may be symbolized by a Lamb, but otherwise He appears in person. The angel has the key to the abyss, and a chain to use to bind a certain entity described in verse 2. We read, "And he laid hold on the dragon ..." (Rev. 20:2).

I cut the verse short for a reason. This is the same dragon that had seven heads and ten horns which was first introduced in Revelation 12:3. In that verse he is introduced as "a dragon." He appears eleven other times in the Revelation, and in each instance he is designated "the dragon." This is true in this verse. *The* dragon is bound—not just a dragon. But who or what is "the dragon"? In discussing chapter 12 the dragon was shown to be paganism. Among the reasons given for that interpretation are: (1) The terms devil and satan are used of humans and other adversaries, hence need not refer to that spirit being often intended by these appellations. (2) Horns refer to rulers or governments in both Daniel and the Revelation, hence a dragon that has horns must refer to a political power. (3) To make the dragon with seven heads and ten horns refer to a spirit being, and to interpret the beast with the same seven heads and ten horns as a political entity, is to be inconsistent. Such interpretations violate the rules of analogy.

Quotations from other authors in support of the above are not given because of space limitations, but for those who wish to read further in this area, the following are recommended. *Studies in the Revelation of St. John* by Albertus Pieters; *The Apocalypse of St. John* by Henry Barclay Swete; *The Revelation Explained* by F. G. Smith.

The length of the binding is said to be one thousand years. The figure could be taken literally or figuratively. My personal preference is figurative. One thousand is ten to the third power. Now both ten and three are numbers indicating completeness. Therefore I believe this number to represent the complete time, regardless of its actual years of duration.

The time of the binding or the beginning and ending dates of that binding are difficult to establish beyond controversy, if the literal interpretation of the period is insisted upon. If it is considered as figurative for the period, it would be from the time of Constantine to whatever date one might hold that paganism was no longer bound. Since all plausible dates extend beyond 1,000 years, the figurative is preferable. But it is possible to make out a case for a literal 1,000 years. Although Constantine made Christianity the state religion, he did not persecute pagans. Paganism became less desirable, but it continued to function far beyond the time of Constantine. The pagan, Julian, was elected emperor in A.D. 361. An influx of barbarians which eventuated in the dissolution of the Roman empire in A.D. 476 added new strength to the pagan influence.

But these were gradually persuaded to become Christians as far as profession was concerned, so paganism had to retreat a second time. Control of paganism by force began under the Frankish ruler, Charles Martel. He gained victories over the heathen to the north and the Saracens to the south. His son, Pepin, conquered much of the Lombard territory which he gave to the pope. Pepin's son, Charlemagne, conquered what remained. Thus was uprooted one of the three horns Daniel had prophesied would be displaced by the eleventh horn, the papacy (Dan. 7:8). The seventh head of the Roman empire, the patrician, was formed through the collaboration of these rulers with the pope.

Gibbon, in writing of the three Frankish rulers mentioned in the preceding paragraph said, "But the most essential gifts of the popes to the Carolingian race were the dignities of king of France and of patrician of Rome."[274] Again he says, "... the decrees of the senate and people successively

---

[274] Edward Gibbon, *The Decline and Fall of the Roman Empire*, vol. II, chap. XLIX, pp. 598-599.

invested Charles Martel and his posterity with the honors of patrician of Rome."[275] That this resulted in a practical restoration of the empire under a seventh head is also indicated by this notable historian. After listing the powers exercised by Charlemagne under this patrician form, he adds, "Except an original and self-inherent claim of sovereignty, there was not any prerogative remaining which the title of emperor could add to the patrician of Rome."[276] The patrician form was replaced by the restoration of the sixth head, or eighth which was of the seven, when Charlemagne was crowned as emperor in A.D. 800.

Thus, the binding of the dragon, paganism, did not come until the patrician form of government prevailed, according to this mode of reckoning. One thousand years from that time would take us to the time of the pouring out of the first vial of wrath (Rev. 16:2) which was interpreted as the atheism, licentiousness, and infidelity that led to the French Revolution in A.D. 1789. Thus the dragon, paganism, was forcefully bound from the time of the patrician form of government under Charles Martel, Pepin, and Charlemagne to the development of pagan philosophies which led to the French Revolution.

Premillennialists have no adequate answer for the question, why would God bind Satan for 1,000 years and then turn him loose? But if the dragon is recognized as paganism, the binding and loosing take on a historical significance that does not exist in the literal application. It is forces at work in this world of humanity that are responsible for the binding of the dragon, paganism, and it is the failure of these forces to continue to hold paganism in check that releases the dragon. So the binding could be from A.D. 730 to 789 and the loosing from A.D. 1730 to 1789, the latter date being the year of the French Revolution.

Verse 4 of this chapter pictures a heavenly reign by certain disembodied spirits or souls. It reads in part, "… and I saw the souls of them that were beheaded for the witness of Jesus…and they lived and reigned with Christ [in heaven or paradise] a thousand years" (Rev. 20:4). That this scene is not of an earthly reign is evident from the fact that they were disembodied spirits or souls. Any effort to make this apply to persons with resurrected bodies is futile. It is true that the Hebrew *nephish* and the Greek *psuche* are sometimes applied to living human beings, but never in this manner.

---

275  Ibid., p. 601.
276  Ibid.

## The Eschatology of the Revelation

In Exodus 1:5 certain souls (*nephish*) are said to have come from the loins of Jacob. Also, there were a certain number of souls (*psuche*) on the ship with Paul (Acts 27:37), but in no place does it say souls of certain persons were seen except in the Revelation. In this passage John saw the souls of certain persons, namely those who had been martyred. The soul is thereby distinguished from the total person. He saw souls or disembodied spirits of certain people, rather than resurrected persons. A fair exegesis of this verse can produce no other conclusion.

The text does not say whether the 1,000 years the dragon is bound is the same 1,000 years these disembodied spirits reign in heaven. It is impossible to prove that they cover the same period of time. Even if they begin and end at the same time, they are not identical. The binding of the dragon, paganism, takes place here on earth. The 1,000 years mentioned in verses 4-6 has its setting in heaven or paradise.

Verse 5 reads, "But the rest of the dead lived not *again* until the thousand years were finished. This is the first resurrection." The word "again" is written in italics because it does not appear in the Greek text. This verse does not speak of the rest of the dead living a second time. The absence of the word "again" indicates this. Some argue that the phrase, "until the thousand years were finished," does indicate they lived again at a later time. But this is not a necessary conclusion, as I have shown in another connection. The Greek *archri* makes no statement as to conditions beyond its limits. Paul wrote in Romans 5:13, "For until the law sin was in the word ...," but he certainly did not mean that sin ceased to exist after the law was given. On the contrary, sin was even greater after the law. (See also Acts 7:15.)

But it will still be argued that the expression, "This is the first resurrection," implies that the rest of the dead will be resurrected at a later time. This is a cogent argument, but it misses the point. Those who reigned with Christ in verse 4 had been beheaded for their witness of Jesus. They had not worshipped the beast nor his image. Thus, although their reign is pictured in heaven, it began on earth. They were victorious over all the attacks against their faith. This victory came while living on earth. So the first resurrection is not a bodily resurrection. It is a spiritual resurrection from a dead state of sinfulness.

Those who have attained the first resurrection are made blessed and holy by that act as the next verse indicates: "Blessed and holy is he that hath part in the first resurrection." Jesus said those who believed on Him had "passed from death unto life" (John 5:24). No one can deny that this involves a resurrection. The next verse supports the idea of the dead being made alive, spiritually. Paul wrote that even though we were dead in our sins, we have been quickened together with Christ (Eph. 2:5; Col. 2:13). These verses indicate that we are no longer dead. We have been made alive together with Christ. The complex Greek term used by Paul means just that.

This spiritual resurrection from the dead state of being in sin is the only resurrection this verse can refer to, for no physical resurrection is mentioned in the preceding verses. Only by forced exegesis can a physical resurrection be established in verse 4. The persons involved were not complete. They had not been physically resurrected. Only the souls in the disembodied state are presented. Their bodies still rested in their respective graves. The resurrection they had experienced was from spiritual deadness to spiritual life.

This makes the first portion of verse 5 understandable. It reads, "But the rest of the dead lived not again until the thousand years were finished." The "rest of the dead" must refer to those who did not participate in the spiritual resurrection or the "first resurrection." We again call attention to the fact that the word "again" is not in the Greek text, and that *achri* (until) does not speak of conditions beyond, but only of conditions up to. In this case the rest of the dead are said to not live during the 1,000 year period regardless of what may happen after the period is over.

On the basis of other texts, we know that the wicked will one day live in the sense of a bodily resurrection, but they will never possess the kind of life that makes them "blessed and holy" as those who participated in the first resurrection—that resurrection from a state of sin and death to one of righteousness and life eternal.

Verse 7 tells us that Satan is to be loosed after the 1,000 years are ended. Since it was the dragon that was bound, it is the dragon that is loosed. It is true that the dragon, paganism, is called Satan in this passage; but Satan was used of the angel of Jehovah (Num. 22:22), and of Peter (Matt. 16:23). It may refer to any opposer or opponent. So Satan or paganism was to be loosed at the end of the 1,000 years. Has this been fulfilled? Very definitely so. Prior to the French Revolution, paganism was definitely on a rampage. Pagan spiritualism is rampant in our day. There are thousands of women who openly claim to be witches. Devil worshipers have their dens of iniquity in many of our major cities. New religions that are pagan as well as older ones are flourishing in the United States as well as elsewhere. Zen Buddhism in the form of transcendental meditation is prospering in this country. Yes, paganism has been released.

Verse 8 tells of the battle involving Gog and Magog. This will be considered more adequately in a later chapter on the battle of Armageddon. At this point we simply affirm that this refers to the present spiritual battle between truth and error. It is not fought with carnal weapons such as guns and bombs.

The encompassing of the camp of the saints is now in progress (v. 9). The Church has its back to a wall. Atheism, scoffers at religion, religious leaders who deny the inspiration of the Bible and other cardinal principles of Christianity, materialistic philosophies, and countless other opponents of the Church are making things difficult even in this country. Where Communism rules, conditions are even worse. The second coming of Christ brings defeat to these opposers of God and the gospel.

Verse 10 tells of how the devil, paganism, is cast into the lake of fire where the beast and the false prophet were. Just why two of the enemies of the Church are disposed of before the third can only be conjectured. One possible inference is that Roman Catholicism, the beast, and the apostate part of the Protestantism which is the false prophet, may not be involved as much as the dragon or paganism in the final attack on the Church. If this be true, then Communism may be the major enemy of the Church in the last days.

The remainder of the chapter deals with the final judgment. It is often called the "great white throne" judgment from these words in verse 11. Dispensationalists and many Premillennialists contend that this involves the wicked, only. But several times in these verses the dead are referred to as though they were all of the dead. I accept these words as having just that meaning. When John writes, "And the dead were judged...according to their works" (Rev. 20:12), he can mean nothing but all the dead. This matter will be pursued further in the chapter which deals with the problems of a single judgment versus several judgments.

## Concluding Comments

Although the early writings of the Church include many references to the Revelation, few references were found on the prominent issues of today. This makes a digest rather difficult for these chapters. It has already been pointed out that the early writers considered the woman of Revelation 12 to be the Church. No dissenting voice was found. The man child she gave birth to was either converts or Christ. The dragon is considered to be the devil or the Antichrist. Hippolytus, who is classified by some as a millennialist but improperly so, interpreted the dragon as the Antichrist. Inasmuch as the dragon persecuted the woman (the Church), Hippolytus definitely did not believe the Church would be raptured to heaven prior to the great tribulation.[277]

Those who interpreted the first beast of Revelation 13 considered it to be the Antichrist. I found nothing of worth regarding the two-horned beast of chapter 13. No references to the battle of Armageddon were found. Babylon was considered a reference to Rome, and chapter 19 refers to the final judgment.

The dragon of Revelation 20 was considered the ruler of the nether regions. Augustine held that the binding took place at Christ's first advent.[278] Others projected it into the future. Lactantius allowed for two physical resurrections, but failed to give an adequate exposition of his beliefs.[279] Hippolytus taught a single physical resurrection. Apparently, he considered the first resurrection to be a spiritual resurrection, just as Augustine did.[280] Commodianus made the first resurrection a bodily resurrection, but he included in it those who died under the Antichrist, hence he did not believe in the rapture of the Church prior to the great tribulation.[281]

Regarding the belief in a millennial reign on earth, some were for it and some against it. There were variations in the belief at this point. In a later chapter, a full discussion of this will be given. Also, there was no unanimity of opinion regarding whether chapters 21-22 were to be taken literally or symbolically.

---

[277] Hippolytus, *op. cit.*, p. 217.
[278] Augustine, *op. cit.*, vol. II, p. 426.
[279] Lactantius, *op. cit.*, vol. VII, pp. 216ff.
[280] Hippolytus, *op. cit.*, vol. V, p. 222.
[281] Commodianus, *op. cit.*, vol. IV, p. 212.

— PART FOUR —

# BEFORE AND AFTER THE SECOND COMING

CHAPTER 20

# THE EVENTS PRECEDING THE RAPTURE

In answer to the question, could Christ come at any moment?, I said it was God's intent that every generation live in anticipation and expectation of the second coming of Christ occurring during their lifetime. Both Paul (I Thess. 5:2) and Peter (II Pet. 3:10) testified that the day of the Lord would come suddenly and without warning, even as "a thief in the night." Even in the Olivet discourse from which many commentators claim they find specific signs of the second coming, Jesus said, "watch therefore: for ye know not what hour your Lord doth come" (Matt. 24:42). This was spoken to the apostles. It has equal importance to the Church today.

To emphasize this fact, he added, "Therefore be ye also ready: for in such an hour as ye think not the Son of man cometh" (Matt. 24:44). These and several other similar statements indicate that the apostles were not given means by which they could know when the second coming would take place, and since the information we have is the same as that which they had, we conclude that those who have established time tables of events leading up to the second coming are misinterpreting God's word. The Church is to look for Christ every day. In this sense He will not come unexpectedly, but Jesus affirms that He will not come at the time we expect Him to come. Rather it will be at such a time as we "think not."

Although it is felt that all of the several eschatological systems other than Amillennialism are guilty at this point, the Premillennial system and specifically the Dispensational system are the worst offenders, hence our attention is directed to them. All Premillennialists establish a seven year reign of their expected Antichrist which includes a time of great tribulation immediately before the second coming, regardless of their position on the rapture. According to all of these all one has to do to determine the date of the second coming is to count seven years from the date the Antichrist begins this reign or three and one-half years from the time the great tribulation he institutes is begun. Since Dispensationalism includes doctrines that are especially reprehensible, it is considered first.

The Dispensational system is strongly Judaistic. It is built on Old Testament promises to Israel. Dispensationalists say these promises have not been fulfilled; hence there must be a future fulfillment. Therefore the regathering of the Jews to Palestine is possibly the keystone of their system. The establishment of the nation of Israel, and the subsequent occupation of the old city of Jerusalem in recent years is considered by them to be positive proof of their entire system. However, they assume too much from too little. But rather than discussing this point here, let us consider this teaching regarding a regathering of the Jews more fully.

The principal basis for contending that the Jews are to be regathered to Palestine is the Abrahamic covenant. Dispensationalists hold that these promises made by God to Abraham were not fulfilled in the past, hence must be fulfilled in the future. I hold that the Abrahamic covenant had two distinct aspects:

1. Those made to Abraham's physical posterity which could be, and which actually were, revoked, and,

2. Those pertaining to Christ which could not be revoked. In support of this we offered a portion of the 89th Psalm which reads, "Thou hast made void the covenant of thy servant" (Ps. 89:39).

The context indicates that it was the promises to the physical descendants of Abraham and David that were abrogated or annulled. It is common for the first 37 verses of this Psalm to be quoted in support of a regathering of the Jews to Palestine, but I have yet to read of an adequate answer to verses 38-45. The inspired writer emphatically asserts that the promises made to David and his heirs were made void. Those promises were forfeited. Only the spiritual heritage that all Christians have through Christ remains. That the Abrahamic promises to physical Israel were conditional was proved in the first chapters of Part Two of this volume.

## The Modern Nation of Israel

The Jewish nation of Israel was established in 1948. Some say this is merely a political phenomenon. Others say it is a fulfillment of prophecy. The interpretation of Ezekiel 37 is the focal point of contention. In that chapter Ezekiel sees a valley filled with dry bones. These bones are said to be "the whole house of Israel" (v. 11). Dispensationalists, and many other

Premillennialists, refer this to political or national Israel. Others contend Israel is used here as a symbol of the Church. These hold that this prophecy was fulfilled in the coming of the Holy Spirit on the day of Pentecost.

Dispensationalists do admit that Israel is sometimes used as a symbol of the Church. For example, Tan quotes Charles C. Ryrie as follows:

"It is one thing to say that Israel *typifies* the Church, as premillennialists rightly do; it is quite another thing to say that Israel is the Church, as amillennialists wrongly teach."[282]

Of course, Amillennialists do not say that Israel is the Church. The accusation in the above quotation is based on the fact that Amillennialists insist that the expression "Israel" in some places does refer to the Church, rather than national Israel, on the basis of typology. And Ezekiel 37 is one of those places.

That Ezekiel 37 contains figures of speech is admitted by all. Even Scofield claims that the graves of verses 12-13 are to be taken symbolically rather than literally. (See his note on Ezek. 37:1.) But if the graves are symbolic, why not the entire story? If graves really do not mean graves but nations, as Scofield claims in the note mentioned above, he has no basis for criticizing us who hold that the bones that were very dry represent national Israel, whereas in the giving of life to them Israel is used as a type of the New Testament Church. The life thus refers to eternal life which we have through Christ and the Holy Spirit.

Therefore, we deny that the giving of life to the dry bones was a prophecy of national Israel being restored in 1948. Rather it was the giving of life to spiritual Israel, the Church. Possibly neither interpretation can be proved to the satisfaction of all concerned, but there are additional reasons for rejecting the literal interpretation that most Premillennialists insist upon. These are found in the chapters which follow chapter 37. If chapter 37 is considered literal, the remaining chapters must also be so interpreted. But to do so leads into impossible conditions.

That the battle depicted in chapters 38-39 is symbolic of the battle between truth and error, right and wrong should be evident through the expressions found in these chapters. Some of these are, "and the mountains shall be thrown down" (Ezek. 38:20); and "everyman's sword shall be against his brother" (Ezek. 38:21); and "I will smite thy bow out of thy left hand, and

---

[282] Tan. *op. cit.*, pp. 169-170.

will cause thine arrows to fall out of thy right hand" (Ezek 39:3); seven years are required to burn the bows and arrows and other wooden weapons (Ezek. 39:9) which is completely at odds with modern weapons which are mostly metal; and seven months being allocated to bury the dead (Ezek. 39:12-14) is evidently to be understood as a metaphor, rather than as a literal period.

The latter chapters of Ezekiel cannot be interpreted literally as of a future period without serious disagreement and open conflict with some very plain and important teachings of the New Testament. Since these matters have been discussed already in the chapter on Ezekiel, only a digest of them will be given here. If these chapters refer to a future time and are to be taken literally, rather than symbolically of the Church, then the Mosaic law is to be restored, Sabbath keeping and fleshly circumcision will again be enforced, the Levitical priesthood will again function as it did before Christ's atoning work abolished that priesthood, and animal sacrifices will again be offered as they were under the law. The teaching of such is rank heresy.

Many texts of Scripture refute this teaching of Dispensationalism, but Hebrews 7:11-28 should be sufficient. The Levitical priesthood was abolished, and Christ became our high priest (vv. 11, 12, 26). The Mosaic law was changed or abolished (v. 12). Since the law was set aside, the requirements of the law, such as Sabbath keeping and circumcision were necessarily also set aside. Animal sacrifices were eliminated in Christ, for His sacrifice makes other sacrifices unnecessary (v. 27).

The Dispensational interpretation of these chapters from Ezekiel denies several aspects of the work of Christ. The restoration of the Levitical priesthood denies the eternal and solitary priesthood of Christ. It restores the middle wall of partition which Christ eliminated in His own body on the tree. The claim that these animal sacrifices will be memorial in nature (Scofield's note on Ezek. 43:19) is unacceptable for Ezekiel 43:27 implies that God will accept the person because the several sacrifices conciliate Him. In Ezekiel 45:15, 17 the sacrifices produce "reconciliation" or atonement. Thus Ezekiel destroys the contention that he was writing about memorial sacrifices. The sacrifices he wrote about were for reconciliation and atonement. The only suitable interpretation is that they are types of Christ's sacrifice, just as the other Old Testament sacrifices were.

In view of these facts which cannot be denied, we conclude that the latter chapters of Ezekiel are to be interpreted as symbolic of spiritual truths, since they cannot be interpreted as literally applicable to a future period without nullifying the work of Christ. It is also the only way of harmonizing Ezekiel with New Testament doctrines that are related to that book.

## The Regathering of the Jews

Old Testament prophecies that are interpreted as referring to a regathering of the Jews in the latter days were considered in Part Two of this volume. These were interpreted as having been fulfilled in the literal returns found in Ezra and Nehemiah, or else they were prophecies of the Church couched in symbols. A second study of those passages is not justified at this juncture. Instead, the problem will be discussed from a different point of view.

Scofield's note on Revelation 7:14 attempts to make the tribulation mentioned in verse 14 refer to what is often called "Jacob's trouble" or "the great tribulation." Premillennialists claim this time of severe harassment will come after the so-called secret rapture and immediately preceding the second coming of Christ. He adds, "It involves the people of God" (and by this he means physical descendents of Jacob) "who will have returned to Palestine in unbelief." Now it is only by a considerable stretch of the imagination that people who are unbelievers can be thought of as the people of God. Unbelievers are the children of the devil—not the people of God. Jesus told the unbelieving Jews of His day, "Ye are of your father the devil" (John 8:44). Unbelieving Jews are not the people of God. But Scofield and other Dispensationalists contend that the Jews are still the people of God, even though God has rejected them as a people.

Scofield also recognizes a righteous remnant (see his note on Rom. 11:5). Now if it were claimed that this righteous remnant would be regathered to Jerusalem, the teaching would have a greater claim of validity; but that a group of unbelieving Jews who return to Palestine is a beginning of the reestablishment of an Israelitish nation under God is absolutely unacceptable. That the present inhabitants of Israel are unbelievers in the true sense of the term can hardly he doubted. The Zionist movement which is mainly responsible for Jews immigrating to Israel is motivated politically rather than religiously. Through personal investigation in Jerusalem, I have found that no temple is now being built, and that the story about this stemmed from a cartoon which was intended to be sarcastic or ironical rather than factual.

And now we come to the question, Are the Jews being regathered to Palestine? Although there has been an increase in the number of Jews residing in Palestine during the 20th century, the migration to that area is now being counterbalanced by emigration from Israel. Writers who contend a return in our day was prophesied usually give figures on the number of Jews living in Israel for certain years. These usually ignore the fact that in 1976 only about one fifth of all Jews lived in Palestine, and that since 1974 more Jews are immigrating from Israel than are immigrating into the country.

Facts that require evaluation in this connection disprove any claims that have been made. Approximately twice as many Jews live in the United States as live in Israel. More than half the Jews who obtain visas from Russia to Israel change their minds and their destinations when they get to Vienna.[283] And the United States is the number one country of those who change. It could be held that this constitutes a gathering to the United States instead of Israel.

Although it is impossible to know how many Jews who leave Israel leave for good, the statistics prove more are leaving than are entering. In 1974 those leaving Israel were about 33,000. This was slightly more than those who entered Israel. Then in 1975, 64,000 left (almost twice the number of 1974), whereas only 20,000 entered.[284] This constitutes an exodus from Israel, rather than a return. Another problem that worries the Jews is the fact that the Arab population in Israel increased 3.5 per cent "this year" whereas the Jewish population increased only 2 per cent.[285] (Whether this refers to 1975 or 1976 or part of each year is not clear.) Does this mean we have an Arab return? It is not a Jewish return.

The figures cited above have the Israelis worried. They constitute a valid basis for denying that the country of Israel is a fulfillment of prophecy. It is time for those who have so confidently made such a claim to reexamine the foundations of their doctrine.

### The Great Apostasy

Paul indicated that a great apostasy by the Church would occur prior to the second coming. He said in part, "... the day of Christ is at hand...for that day shall not come, except there come a falling away first" (II Thess. 2:2-3). The time of this falling away or apostasy is not stated. It cannot be

---

283  *Houston Chronicle,* issue of Dec. 13, 1976
284  *Ibid.,* issues of Oct. 10, 1976 and Sept. 24, 1976.
285  *Ibid.,* issues of Sept. 24, 1976.

determined exegetically, for Paul does not tell us when it is to be. However, he does relate it to certain other events. Out of this apostasy "that man of sin" (v. 3) is to be revealed. From verse 7 we learn that some person or force hindered the development of what is termed "that man of sin" in verse 3.

This passage has already been interpreted in the chapter on the Thessalonian letters, but under the above caption, additional consideration must be given to it. Without going into great detail, two major interpretations will be given. Dispensationalists and many other Premillennialists place the great apostasy as yet future and closely associated with the second coming. The man of sin is said to be a certain person whom they call *the* Antichrist. The restraining force is the Holy Spirit, they say, who will be taken away when the Church is raptured to heaven. With the Holy Spirit removed, the Antichrist will gain power and after three and one-half years he will display his true nature.

The other interpretation is that the great apostasy came during that period of history when Roman Catholicism perverted the truth and controlled the minds of men almost completely. Some have termed those years "the dark ages." A study of the perversions of truth, of immortality, deceit, murder, oppression, disregard of human rights, and debauchery unequaled in the annuls of history, make the designation "the dark ages" appropriate. The Church did apostatize in a fashion and to an extent that makes the appellation "the great apostasy" fitting.

The man of sin is understood to be the system of popery. The continuance of the power of the Roman emperor is what held the development of this monster in check. It was taken out of the way when Rome fell in A.D. 476. It stirs my righteous indignation for folks to talk about the Holy Spirit being taken out of the way so long as unsaved people live upon earth. The Holy Spirit is the one who convicts of sin. Salvation would become an impossibility if He were taken out of the way. The claim that He would continue to operate from heaven in soul saving is proved contradictory to the other side of the issue. If He could function from heaven in soul saving, He could function from heaven in restraining the development of the man of sin. The Dispensational teaching is inconsistent.

It is recognized that the spiritual condition of the Church today is not above criticism. Its stand on premarital sex, abortion, drink, divorce and remarriage, homosexuality, and many other issues is not as strong and as universal as it ought to be. But there is still a strong evangelical witness within the Church. As long as that exists, it cannot be said that a "great apostasy" has occurred. Be that as it may, I see no reason to look for another "great apostasy." And if such should come. I would see no reason to consider it a fulfillment of prophecy. That prophecy has been fulfilled in the past.

## A Revived Roman Empire

Properly understood, no Bible prophecy tells of a restored Roman empire at some future date. I do believe the Revelation foretold a demise and a later revival of the Roman empire, but there is ample evidence that this has been fulfilled already. It is not future; it is already history. The claim that we can expect a Roman empire to again be established is built on certain interpretations of Daniel chapters 2 and 7 with some assistance from chapter 9, and on related interpretations of portions of Revelation chapters 12, 13, and 17. The disagreement is over whether or not this has already been fulfilled or is it yet future.

The events of this century that are claimed to be the beginning of this revival are connected with the formation of the European common market. For example, Lindsey quotes from a former president of the European economic community as follows: "At about 1980 we may fully expect the great fusion of all economic, military, and political communities together into the United States of Europe."[286] Lindsey not only accepted 1980 as the probable date but added that "the timetable may be accelerating." Here, Lindsey shows himself to be a false prophet. We are nearing 1980 and the European common market is in trouble.

One of Lindsey's arguments that the common market will develop into a United States of Europe is the threat of Communism. But acceptance of Communism is also a possibility. The Communist Party has won places in the government of Italy. If the Socialists and Communists of France can heal the breach that now separates them, a similar situation in that country is foreseen. Could NATO and the common market survive this? But apart from the Communist aspect, the European common market has failed to live up to the expectations of those earlier days. The three stronger powers, England, France, and Germany, have irritated one another repeatedly. It appeared for a time that England might withdraw. The organization is still quite shaky. There is no real indication that it will ever firm up into a United States of Europe. National interests keep intruding into the conferences.

---

286 Lindsey, *op. cit.*, p. 96.

## The Events Preceding the Rapture

These debates show how tenuous are the ties that now bind them together.

In the chapters on Daniel and the Revelation, full consideration was given to the arguments for a future Roman empire. Only a short review of the arguments can be given here. The argument from Daniel 2 is particularly strained and hermeneutically unsound. The vision of this chapter is of four empires as symbolized by four metals. These are correctly interpreted as the Babylonian, the Medo-Persian, the Grecian, and the Roman. Daniel declared that during the days of these kings the God of heaven would establish His eternal kingdom. The Roman empire ceased to exist in A. D. 476. Daniel's prophecy does not properly reach beyond that date. This chapter is positive proof that the kingdom of God was established at Christ's first advent while the Roman empire still existed.

Daniel chapter 2 says nothing of the Roman empire ceasing to exist, after which it is to be revived in the form of a ten nation confederation. This is imported into chapter 2 without adequate support. Daniel fails to give the toes any significance. He does not even say how many toes the image has. Does Daniel have the toes disconnected from the feet? Not at all. For the toes to represent a future confederation and fit in with the vision of Daniel 2, the toes would have to be separated from the feet by at least 1500 years. But no such separation is found in Daniel 2. Daniel 2 does not teach a revived Roman empire. Those who claim it does are guilty of eisegesis.

Ten minor kingdoms are depicted in Daniel 7, but they do not constitute a revival of the Roman empire. Rather they are separate nations or governments that followed the dissolution of the Roman empire in A.D. 476. Although the number has not constantly remained at ten, various historians have at sundry times recognized that ten kingdoms did exist. As far as Daniel 7 is concerned these ten nations are separate and distinct. Nothing is indicated of the formation of an empire out of them. From the Revelation we have further information in this connection, but not in Daniel 7. In interpreting Daniel 7, one must consider these as separate nations—not as an empire.

Now Daniel 7 tells of an eleventh horn which was to subdue three of the original ten horns. Premillennialists tend to interpret the eleventh horn as a person, rather than a kingdom. This person is said to be the future Antichrist which they expect. Lindsey states it in these words, "In other words, when this Roman dictator comes, he is going to take over the ten-nation confederacy." (It should be borne in mind that Daniel does not even say there is a confederacy, much less that the eleventh horn is going to head up a confederacy.) "Seven of the kings or leaders will willingly give him their allegiance, but three of them will not. So he will overthrow these three."[287]

This illustrates very well the reason that so much Premillennial literature must be read so carefully. Daniel says nothing about a confederation. He says nothing about the eleventh horn uniting seven horns under his dominion. This is pure surmise. A careful reading of Daniel chapter 7 would seem to indicate that there were then eight horns instead of ten or eleven. By subduing three horns, the eleventh horn would possibly be stronger than any of the others, but Daniel does not give the least intimation that he will assume the leadership of the total group.

The explanation that I have given is that the original ten horns are the ten kingdoms that arose out of the Roman empire which was dissolved in A.D. 476. The eleventh horn represents the papacy. It is said to have the ability to speak (Dan. 7:9, 20) which I take to signify that it is a religious power as well as a political power. This horn did subdue three of the original horns, and it would have subdued the others had it been powerful enough to do so. Thus it is contended that Daniel 7 does not point to a future Antichrist. Instead, it is a prophecy that has been fulfilled in the past.

Premillennial interpretations of Daniel 9 do not deal directly with the subject of a revived Roman empire. It is only through the medium of the Antichrist that this is involved. Daniel 9:27 is interpreted by them to refer to the Antichrist and his activities, rather than to Christ and His activities. A similar situation exists regarding the last ten verses of Daniel 11.

According to my understanding of the Revelation, it does teach that the Roman empire would cease to exist, and that at a later time it would be reestablished. The major difference between my interpretation and that of many Premillennialists is that I place the reestablishment in the past, whereas they place it in the future. Inasmuch as a long chapter has been given to the discussion of the Revelation, only the strands of thought that deal with the restored Roman empire will receive consideration in this chapter.

Premillennialists usually interpret the dragon (Rev. 12 and elsewhere) as Satan. I have rejected that position because in symbolic and apocalyptic writings, a ferocious wild beast is used as a symbol of an oppressive

---

287  *Ibid.*, p. 105.

government. Thus, while a dragon could symbolize Satan in more general literature, in the Revelation it refers to pagan Rome. It is impossible for me to conceive of Satan having the same seven heads and ten horns as the beast of chapter 13.

It is also important to note that the horns grow out of the animal, whether it be the dragon or the beast. It is admitted by all that the horns are symbols of governments. Now if the same meanings are given to the heads and horns of the dragon that are given to the heads and horns of the beast, it can be seen that both the dragon and the beast represent certain aspects of Rome as a power. I hold that the dragon represents pagan Rome, whereas the beast represents papal Rome. In support of this, consider the fact that the crowns are on the heads of the dragon (Rev. 12), whereas the crowns are on the horns in the next chapter. This clearly portrays the transference of power from the empire to the ten divisions into which it divided.

This transfer of power from the heads to the horns is made possible by the wounding of the head which then existed which was the imperial. The Revelator phrases it, "And I saw one of his heads as it were wounded unto death; and his deadly wound was healed" (Rev. 13:3). Scofield's note on this verse correctly says, "It was the imperial form of government which ceased; the one head wounded to death." But I consider his claim that this restoration is yet future to be ill-founded. At least two revivals are worthy of note.

On Christmas day A.D. 800, Pope Leo III crowned Charlemagne emperor of a revived Roman empire. The Carolingian empire did not last for a full century, and there is little evidence that it constitutes the healing of the wound or the restoration of the Roman empire. However, under Otto the Great a revival of the empire occurred and it lasted for more than 800 years. The original empire did not last so long. It began under Augustus in 31 B.C. and ceased in A.D. 476. The years of its existence thus were slightly more than 500. The Holy Roman empire officially began in 962 when Pope John XII crowned Otto the Great emperor. The empire was officially dissolved in 1806 under tremendous pressure from Napoleon Bonaparte.

It is contended that the Holy Roman empire is symbolized in Revelation 17. The picture John gives us is of an impure woman riding on a scarlet colored beast having seven heads and ten horns. The color of this beast being scarlet is a strong basis for relating this beast to the great red dragon first introduced in chapter 12. And the seven heads and ten horns are even stronger evidence that this beast is related to the dragon, and also to the beast of chapter 13, both of which had seven heads and ten horns. The dragon was interpreted as pagan Rome; the first beast of chapter 13 as papal Rome; and now this beast can be identified as the Holy Roman empire.

In his note on Revelation 18:2, Scofield correctly identifies the great whore as "Ecclesiastical Babylon." He further identifies ecclesiastical Babylon as "apostate Christendom, headed up under the Papacy." I am prepared to accept this for Revelation 18, but in chapter 17 the wording points directly to papal Rome. The impure woman is not only designated as Babylon, but she is termed "THE MOTHER OF HARLOTS AND ABOMINATIONS OF THE EARTH" (Rev. 17:5). This seems to distinguish the mother from the daughters. Thus we interpret this as the Roman Church using the Holy Roman empire as the means of accomplishing her desires, just as a person uses a horse to transport him from one place to another.

But is this a picture of the past or of the future? Shall Roman Catholicism once again become the dominant persecuting power she was during the dark ages? Chapter 17 negates the idea. At one time the ten horns would support the beast (v. 13) and by inference its rider, papal Rome; whereas at a later time (v. 16) the ten horns would hate the whore and make her desolate and naked. The ten horns have already taken away most of her power and glory. Only the few acres of Vatican City remain of her once vast domain. In 1870 Garibaldi united Italy thus freeing that nation from the pope's control. Germany, France, and England had long since ceased to be puppets of Rome. Thus the picture was future when written, but it has been fulfilled, already.

The symbol of the great whore, Roman Catholicism, riding the scarlet colored beast with seven heads and ten horns, the Holy Roman empire, very accurately describes the relationship that existed between those two bodies for centuries. It is particularly accurate from the time of Pope Innocent III and the early part of the 13th century to the close of the 16th century. The Inquisition, later designated as the Holy Office, was the instrument by which the church eliminated dissenters. Secret trials were held. Tortures became commonplace. Those convicted of heresy were not killed by the church. Instead, they were turned over to the authorities, that is representatives of the Holy Roman empire, to be burned at the stake.

This is the opposition Luther faced at Worms. I envision Eck, the archbishop of Trier as the prosecuting attorney. Charles V as emperor of the Holy Roman empire was the judge. The jury was composed of the electors present. Luther's strongest defenders were absent when the final decision was made. Luther, who was on trial for heresy, served as his own defense attorney. Charles V, obedient to the power that held the reins by which he was guided, continued the trial until he knew a majority of the electors were in favor of a conviction. And Luther would have shared the same fate as Huss and Savonarola had it not been that friends hid him from the papal wrath.

Since the head that was wounded (the imperial) was restored as the eighth head, which was of the seven in the form of the Holy Roman empire, there is no legitimate basis for expecting a future fulfillment of this prophecy. It has been adequately fulfilled in the past. Prophecy does not require a future United States of Europe. This is being taught today as though a future Roman empire is demanded by prophecy, but this is not true. The eighth head reigned over thousands of martyrs as it obeyed the wishes of the harlot who held the reins in her hands.

## Concluding Remarks

There are other things that some claim must appear before the rapture occurs, but for one reason or another it appears unnecessary to do more than mention them. Some claim that the old enemies of Israel will again exist. With present day Israel surrounded by hostile forces, it should be no problem to envision them as already existing. However, prophecy does not require that this occur.

According to most Premillennial teaching, the man who is to be the Antichrist must have appeared prior to the rapture. However, it is generally held that he will not assume power until after the rapture has occurred. A special chapter will discuss the matter of a future Antichrist. Further discussion of this teaching will be considered in it.

Inevitably there will arise questions regarding the signs of Jesus' coming. This was discussed in the chapters on the Olivet discourse. I contend that those who take statements from that talk as giving signs of the second coming misinterpret those passages. We insist that the second coming could not be unexpected if definite signs of its approach are given. Therefore, another explanation of those so-called signs is given. They are either not signs at all, or else they are signs of the destruction of Jerusalem. Natural events such as famines, earthquakes, wars, and the like are not signs at all. They have occurred from time immemorial. Every century has had its share of them.

The early Church knew absolutely nothing about the present day teaching of the Church being caught away to heaven seven years prior to the second coming, hence most of what is discussed in this chapter has little or no relevance to the teaching of those days. No regathering of the Jews was expected, for the early Church held that the Church had inherited the promises made to Abraham. Any talk of a restored Judaism would have been met by an immediate and forceful denial. The literal interpretation of the latter chapters of Ezekiel would have been classed as rank heresy in those early days.

CHAPTER 21

# THE RAPTURE

Three views of the rapture of the Church are worthy of note. Dispensationalists and other pretribulation rapturists claim that the Church will be raptured to heaven prior to the great tribulation they expect to follow. For seven years, the Church will have a marriage festival in heaven after which the saints will return to earth as part of the group accompanying Christ to establish His millennial kingdom. The rapture is generally held by these to be a secret event in which the righteous dead will be resurrected, and the righteous who are alive will be changed, and all will depart this world without sinners having any awareness of what was happening.

Posttribulation rapturists believe in pretty much the same order of events for the seven year period as far as the earth is concerned, but they say the Church will remain on earth during the great tribulation. At the end of the seven year period, these expect the Church to be raptured into the upper atmosphere, but not into heaven. A glorious meeting with Christ is envisioned as He enters the atmosphere of the earth. The Church serves as a welcoming committee, according to this view. Having met Christ, the Church then is supposed to turn about face, and it is to return to earth with Christ to establish His millennial kingdom.

The third view is the one held by this writer. This view is that held by Postmillennialists and Amillennialists. According to this view, the rapture will take place at the second coming. All the dead, both good and evil, will be resurrected. All those living, both good and bad, will be changed from mortal to immortal. A judgment of all men will follow, after which the righteous will be taken to heaven, and the wicked will be consigned to the lake of fire.

Theologically speaking, the doctrine of a pretribulation rapture of the Church is a "Johnny-come-lately." It was completely unknown to the Church until about one-third of the 19th century had passed. It is associated particularly with such names as Darby, Kelly, Gaebelein, Scofield, Ironside, and

Blackstone. A number of influential men were at one time supporters of this doctrine, but they later repudiated it. W. J. Erdman and W. G. Moorehead, two of the consulting editors of the Scofield Reference Bible, were two of these. Others include G. Campbell Morgan, Philip Mauro, R. V. Bingham, Oswald J. Smith, and H. J. Ockenga. Some of these became Amillennialists; others remained in the Premillennial ranks, but gave up Darbyism, as it was called originally. Dispensationalism is the term now used.

Dispensationalism has been given that title because it emphasizes seven dispensations in the plan of God. But that is not the important innovation these people have implanted within the Christian community. The teaching to which I refer is called the pretribulation rapture of the Church. It is a special branch of Premillennialism. It requires two second comings, or what is often termed a two-phase second coming. It has transferred the "blessed hope" of the Church from the true second coming to a so-called secret coming seven years prior to the true second coming. The term "rapture" is applied to the Greek *arpagesometha* (caught up). Scofield's note on I Thessalonians 4:17 says of this rapture, "It is peculiarly the 'blessed hope' of the Church." But Paul says this "blessed hope" is connected with the "glorious appearing of the great God and our Saviour Jesus Christ" (Titus 2:13) This can have no other meaning than the true second coming.

No text of Scripture can be cited that teaches the Church will be raptured to heaven seven years prior to the true second coming. The doctrine depends on interpretations of certain passages which in turn depend on interpretations of other passages. So much is pure assumption, rather than proof, that it amazes me that it has come to be so widely accepted. Tan, one of the more recent defenders of this doctrine, lists seven reasons for believing the Church will be raptured seven years prior to the second coming. Space will not permit a full quotation of Tan's seven points, but every effort will be made to present his ideas as clearly as possible.

His first point is that, "the nature of the tribulation demands that the church be kept from it."[288] This statement is meaningless apart from the Premillennial interpretation of texts which deal with times of tribulation. Being one of those who believe the tribulation of the Olivet discourse was fulfilled in the destruction of Jerusalem in A.D. 70, the above statement has no vestige of validity. His major effort at proof is a simple analogy. Now

---

288  Tan, *op. cit.*, p. 338.

anyone who has studied logic knows very well that an analogy proves nothing, hence Tan's first point is rejected as meaningless.

His second point reads in part, "while signs of the second coming of Christ are given to the nation Israel (Matt. 24-25), the church is given no signs in passages on the resurrection of the dead in Christ and the translation of believers (cf. John 14:1-3; I Thess. 4:13-18; I Cor. 15:51-58)."[289] Few, except "dyed in the wool" Dispensationalists, will be able to accept the idea that Matthew 24-25 is not written to the Church. For these the problem is whether the so-called signs of Matthew 24 are truly of the second coming. In the chapters on the Olivet discourse, this author has expressed the view that most of these are not signs at all. Rather they were events Jesus knew would occur, but which had no bearing on the second coming. Other signs were of the impending destruction of Jerusalem or apocalyptic expressions, rather than signs of the second coming.

From this very questionable foundation, Tan reaches a momentous conclusion. He writes, "The implication is clear: the church, which will not go through the tribulation, needs no intervening signs."[290] This illustrates the way Dispensationalists support their views by interpretations which rest upon other interpretations. If any single interpretation is incorrect, the entire structure falls. If their theory of Matthew writing to the Jews is correct, and if their belief regarding the great tribulation is correct, and if their interpretation of the way God will protect the Church from the great tribulation is correct; then this proves that the Church will be raptured to heaven before the great tribulation begins.

Tan contends that this interpretation is necessary so that the imminence of Christ's return may be maintained. He writes, "The coming of the Lord for the church is always imminent."[291] I agree with this statement, but not with Tan's interpretation of that statement. Tan, along with most Dispensationalists, contends that no intervening event that demands fulfillment can come between any point of time and the return of Christ. They insist that the two-phase second coming is the only means by which the true imminence of Christ's return can be maintained. There are two fatal weaknesses to this claim.

---

289  *Ibid.*
290  *Ibid.*
291  *Ibid.*

First, the claim that the rapture of the Church seven years before the true second coming is that "blessed hope" cannot be sustained. The second coming cannot be a two-phase event. It was a one-phase event in Christ's departure (Acts 1:10-11), and these verses demand that His return be "in like manner." Christ's return will be a single event. It cannot be two separate comings separated by a span of seven years. No single text of Scripture establishes two future returns, and Acts 1:11 clearly indicates it will not be. The Bible supports the idea of a single return, rather than two returns.

The second problem with Tan's argument is that he teaches a type of imminence that is unbiblical. The biblical view does permit the intervention of certain events. Jesus foretold a number of things that would occur before His return. The destruction of the temple was one of these. These were not signs of His coming, but they were to occur before His second coming. Paul indicated that an apostasy would occur before the second coming (II Thess. 2:3). This was not a sign of Christ's return, but it would occur before His return.

Certain other prophecies, especially from the Revelation, tell of various events that would transpire before the return of Christ, but these were couched in terms that were sufficiently vague to enable each generation to anticipate the second coming during its existence. According to my interpretation, the apostasy that Paul mentioned in II Thessalonians 2 was to last for 1260 years (Rev. 11:3; 12:14); but this could only be known after the period was finished. Paul did not say how long it would last. And the Revelator couched the time in such terms as 1260 days and a time, and times, and a dividing of time. Only after the 16th century Reformation was it possible to properly assess these time elements of the Revelation.

From this it can be seen that the Bible teaching on imminence does not preclude the possibility of certain intervening events. It does preclude two things, however. First, the intervening events must not be worded in such a way as to enable any generation to know that the second coming could not occur during its lifetime. The other thing it must not do is establish a specific time when the Lord will return. Jesus said He would return at such a time as we think not. Therefore, any system of eschatology that establishes the time of Christ's return through a time schedule is definitely erroneous.

Note that Dispensationalists and most Premillennialists do teach that certain things must be fulfilled before the rapture can occur. The Roman empire must be reestablished for the Antichrist to rule over before the rapture. According to many of these, the European common market is the beginning. According to the time schedule these accept, the Antichrist will be ready to take over as soon as a European confederation firms up. Also, the nation of Israel had to become a reality before the rapture could occur. Therefore the imminence they teach for the rapture is denied by their time schedule of events. They should admit that prophecies must be fulfilled between this date and the rapture, or they should eliminate their teaching regarding a revived Roman empire and a restored Israel. The two are contraries which cannot be reconciled.

Tan's third point is a defense of pretribulationism against posttribulationism.[292] It involves the question of propagation of children during the tribulation period, and certain technical matters of millennial interpretation. Inasmuch as I find no basis in the Bible for a millennial kingdom, the arguments he presents in this division have no bearing on my position.

Tan's fourth point is also an attack on posttribulationism or a defense of pretribulationism.[293] The point here is that posttribulationists do allow a short interval between the supposed meeting with Christ in the air at the rapture, and the return to earth. He contends that even a short period of time makes a seven year period possible. This point is not really a point, for the time element the posttribulationists envision is after the great tribulation, as they see it, whereas the time the pretribulationists envision is during the great tribulation as they see it. Like point three, this point has no bearing on this refutation, for I reject a separate rapture of the Church. I believe the Bible teaches that Christ's second coming and the consummation cannot be separated in time.

Tan's fifth point involves a discussion of II Thessalonians 2:1-2.[294] Tan repeats what many Dispensational writers have said, "Someone in Thessalonica had taught the believers that the great tribulation was already present and that they had therefore been left behind (II Thess. 2:1-2)."[295] This is a blatant effort to read modern thinking into the eschatology of the first Christian century. The early Church knew nothing of a secret rapture of the Church separate from the true second coming. Nor does the context

---

292  Ibid., p. 339.
293  Ibid., p. 340.
294  Ibid., pp. 340ff.
295  Ibid., p. 340.

demand this assumption, although Tan attempts to prove otherwise. His attempt to make "a falling away" from the Greek *apostasia* refer to the rapture is a misguided effort on his part. He has taken an indefensible position. He writes,

> The Greek word for "falling away," taken by itself, does not mean religious apostasy or defection...The best translation of the word is "to depart." The apostle Paul refers here to a definite event which he calls "the departure," and which will occur just before the start of the tribulation. This is the rapture of the church.

Then in an added footnote, we find,

> The apostle Paul uses this word in I Timothy 4:1, "Some shall *depart* from the faith." The necessity for qualifying the word with the phrase "from the faith" shows that the word taken by itself has no such connotation.[296]

The term in question is *apostasia*. It is a member of a family of Greek words based on the joining of the Greek *apo* which means "from" to the Greek term *histemi* which means "to stand." Thus, the basic meaning of these words is "to stand from." This family of words includes *aph-histemi*, *apostasia*, and *apostasion*. Tan is mistaken where he says Paul uses the same word in I Timothy 4:1 as he did in II Thessalonians 2:3. The two words are from the same family, but they are not used in the same identical manner.

*Apostasion* is used exclusively of divorce in the New Testament. *Apostasia* is used exclusively for religious defection in the New Testament. *Aph-histemi* is used of various kinds of departures. Now it was this last word that Paul used in I Timothy 4:1. And since he was led to use this more general term, he was also led to add the qualifying phrase "from the faith." Had he used *apostasia*, the phrase would not have been needed. This single meaning of *apostasia* is sufficiently confirmed by the Septuagint version of the Old Testament that Thayer says "in the Bible" its meaning is to defect "from the true religion."

Tan insists that this departure would "occur just before the start of the tribulation." But Paul does not say so. Paul does not say how long this departure will come before any event. He simply indicated that this apostasy would occur before the second coming of Christ. It is my contention that this apostasy began in the third Christian century and ended with the

---

296  *Ibid.*, p. 341.

Lutheran Reformation. If Paul had said that the apostasy would occur "just before the start of the tribulation." I would have to revise my theology. But it was not Paul who said that. It was Tan's assertion.

Tan's sixth point is that the 24 elders which appear in Revelation 4 "represent the saints who are raptured before the tribulation."[297] His argument is based on the claim that Revelation 2-3 gives a summary of the conditions the Church will exemplify during its existence. Tan believes that the history of the Church ends with Revelation 3. Chapter four is considered a picture of the raptured saints in heaven, or at least the 24 elders represent them. And all of this is literal interpretation, according to Tan.

First of all, the letters to the seven churches of Asia (Rev. 2-3) are not said to be symbols of the vicissitudes of the Church. I am the literalist at this point. I contend these letters are what they appear to be. So-called literalists depart from their literalism in saying they represent seven stages in the life of the Church.

They further depart from their claim of literalism by claiming that the command to John, "Come up here" (Rev. 4:1) is a symbol of the rapture of the Church. Again. I am the literalist. I believe this meant no more than that John needed to go up higher in order to see the things God desired to show him.

My interpretation of the 24 elders is closer to the literal than Tan's claim that they symbolize the raptured Church. In the New Testament, the term *presbuteroi* (elders) is reserved for two classes of people: aged people and those gifted persons who exercised leadership roles in the Church. Since the term *presbuteroi* is applied to these beings several times, it is nearer the literal to say they are representatives of the ministers of the Church, rather than the entire Church.

Tan failed to discuss the four beasts (living creatures is better) of chapter 4, but I wish to use them to further refute his position. When Israel encamped in the wilderness, three tribes camped to the east, three to the south, three to the west, and three to the north. The leaders of the three groups were Judah, Reuben, Ephraim, and Dan. Now the ensigns of these four tribes were the same as the objects the four living creatures resembled. Thus we have a symbolism based on Israel in encampment. The 24 elders are comparable to the Levites, who camped in a separate group.

---

297  *Ibid.*, p. 342.

Now I believe that the 24 elders and the four living creatures do symbolize the Church. However, the picture is of paradise, before the resurrection, rather than afterwards. And Tan, as well as other Dispensationalists, holds that the 24 elders symbolize the Church, in spite of his claim to interpret the Bible literally. This has the effect of forcing him to find what the four living creatures signify. Ironside interprets them as referring to the "attributes of God."[298] This is absurd, as if the attributes of God could be separated from His person. This is completely arbitrary. Nothing supports this view.

However, the fact that the four living creatures resemble the ensigns or standards of the leading tribes of Israel when they were encamped is strong reason to interpret the four living creatures as Israel. If the picture does refer to Israel, it may be interpreted in two ways. Literal Israel can be taken as a symbol of spiritual Israel, as I have done; or it could mean literal Israel. But Tan would be unwilling to admit that Israel is used as a type of the Church, so he would have to say that if the four living creatures do constitute a symbol of Israel, it must be literal Israel that is meant.

But this would involve him in a contradiction, for he places Israel on earth making a covenant with the Antichrist at the time the raptured Church is in heaven. Later, according to Dispensationalism, these same Jews are to suffer severe persecutions at the hands of the Antichrist. Therefore, it would be devastating to admit that Israel was in heaven during the seven year period. But the four living creatures do symbolize Israel as encamped in the wilderness. But neither Tan nor Ironside will admit this. We trust that these men will see the error of their position, just as various others have.

Tan's seventh point is that the Bible teaches several bodily resurrections, hence teaching one additional bodily resurrection is compatible with other texts of Scripture.[299] But the claim that there will be several future bodily resurrections is not taught by the Bible. A refutation of this claim is reserved for a future chapter in this volume.

## Texts and Arguments Regarding a Pretribulation Rapture

Matthew 24:36-42 is part of the Olivet discourse that is often said to refer to the rapture of the Church. The specific verses (40-41) tell us that some will be taken and others left at the "coming [*parousia*] of the Son of man."

---

298 Ironside, *op. cit.*, p. 85.
299 Tan, *op. cit.*, pp. 341-342.

However, in the two parables that speak of this separation (the net and the tares), the wicked are the ones taken, and the righteous are left. This does not fit in with these verses referring to a rapture of the Church. Another meaning must be found. Also the two parables teach that the separation will be at the end of the world—not 1,007 years before the end.

It is also interesting to note the things that will be accomplished at the second coming (*parousia*) of our Lord. Christians will be established in holiness (I Thess. 3:13) at the coming (*parousia*) of Christ "with all his saints." If He comes "for" His saints at the rapture, and comes "with" His saints seven years later, as Dispensationalists teach, then Christians will be fully established after they have spent seven years in heaven, rather than at the time they are taken to heaven. This is not a reasonable conclusion.

Paul informs us further that "our gathering together unto him" will be at the *parousia* (II Thess. 2:1). It is most interesting to note that Paul goes on to say that "the man of sin" will be destroyed at the *parousia* (II Thess. 2:8). Thus the occasion of our being gathered together unto Christ will also involve the destruction of "the man of sin." But Dispensationalism says we will be gathered unto Jesus seven years before the Antichrist is destroyed. This effectively refutes the two-phase second coming.

In spite of the fact that most Dispensationalists admit that Luke 21:20 refers to the destruction of Jerusalem in A.D. 70, they also contend that Luke 21:36 refers to the great tribulation and that this indicates that the Church will escape that time of persecution. But it has previously been shown that verse 36 refers to escaping the trials of the siege of Jerusalem, rather than some future tribulation. It is a fact of history that the Church did escape the privations and tyranny of that disaster.

The last enemy to be destroyed is death (1 Cor. 15:26). But when will death be destroyed? The answer to this question very naturally is at the resurrection. But since Dispensationalism teaches several resurrections, the question remains unresolved unless the particular resurrection that eliminates death can be determined. Paul indicates this will be "… at the last trump: for the trumpet shall sound, and the dead [all of the dead both good and evil] shall be raised incorruptible" (and at this time) "Death is swallowed up in victory" (I Cor. 15:52-54). The Greek expression "swallowed up" is literally translated as "drunk down." The word is used symbolically or metaphorically to indicate destruction or annihilation. The several Greek lexicons I have consulted all agree that it does have that meaning, and some of them give this verse as an example of that meaning.

Now all agree that in I Corinthians 15 Paul has the resurrection of the righteous uppermost in his thinking. Thus, he contends that death is to be destroyed at the time the righteous are resurrected. This means that if the righteous are resurrected and raptured to heaven seven years before the true second coming, then death will not exist during those seven years, even here on earth. But Dispensationalists contend that people will continue to die, not only through the seven year period, but also during the millennial kingdom. But this contradicts Paul who says death is destroyed at the resurrection of the righteous.

Pretribulation rapturists point to I Thessalonians 4:13-18 as a key text. It is admitted that this passage refers to the resurrection and rapture of the Church, but one searches in vain for any indication that it is at a time other than that of the general resurrection. The ungodly are ignored in this passage just as they are in I Corinthians 15. Two resurrections are not set forth in either of these passages. The claim to the contrary has been refuted over and over again, but that does not stop the flood of literature defending two resurrections. The order of events is not the resurrection of the righteous and later the resurrection of the wicked, for the wicked are not mentioned. The first event is the resurrection of the righteous, and the second, the changing of the living righteous. Assuredly, the righteous are both first and second. The righteous dead come first; then the righteous living. And the closing phrase of verse 17 should clinch the matter. It reads, "And so shall we ever be with the Lord." This indicates that we will go to heaven, not for seven years, but forever.

Other passages such as I Thessalonians 5:9 and Revelation 3:10 are often interpreted as meaning the Church will be raptured before the great tribulation. But these verses say nothing of the rapture. The first of these indicates God's wrath will not fall upon the Church, but it does not say that the wrath of men will not affect the Church. The long list of martyrs proves that God has in the past allowed His children to suffer from the wrath of men. In Revelation 3:10, only the church at Philadelphia was promised this protection, and this need not mean that they were translated to heaven. God is able to protect us while we live in this world, when He so desires.

Since no text of Scripture clearly says the Church will be raptured to heaven seven years before the true second coming, it is well that we consider the way pretribulation rapturists interpret the main eschatological passages. Matthew 24 does not mention the rapture of the Church, but pretribulation rapturists contend that the rapture must occur before the abomination of desolation (Matt. 24:15). But they have to admit that they do not find this in Matthew 24. Surely Christ would have said something about the rapture if it was a separate event from the final consummation.

The next great eschatological passage is I Corinthians 15. This chapter does deal with the rapture of the Church, but it does not speak of it as a separate event seven years before the true second coming. To make up for this deficiency, Scofield twice refers the reader to I Thessalonians 4:14-17 (See his note on I Cor. 15:24 and his insertion between vv. 50 and 51 of I Cor. 15.) Of course when I Thessalonians 4:14-17 is consulted, it isn't mentioned there either. And the fact that death is to he destroyed at the resurrection of the righteous (1 Cor. 15:54) makes the claim of a secret rapture seven years before the true second coming completely untenable.

The effort to twist what Paul says in I Thessalonians 4 to make it say the righteous are to be resurrected 1,007 years before the resurrection of the wicked is still continuing. Since this passage is one of their stronger supports, pretribulation rapturists can hardly yield at this point even though it is evident to all true exegetes that they are guilty of reading foreign material into the passage when they so interpret it. Actually, this demonstrates the weakness of their position. The tragic aspect is that they are able to fool many by this twisting of Scripture.

In II Thessalonians the effort to establish the rapture prior to the true second coming of Christ centers around the terms "day of Christ" and "day of the Lord." These terms have the same significance. The claim that the day of Christ refers to the rapture, and the day of the Lord to the true second coming is not confirmed by sound exegesis. This teaching has been refuted earlier. And in this chapter it has been shown that "our gathering together unto him" (II Thess. 2:1), and the destruction of "the man of sin," both occur at the *parousia* of the Lord. The *parousia* cannot be stretched to include two future comings, which would be necessary for this book to agree with pretribulationism.

Pretribulation rapturists depend a great deal on their interpretation of the Revelation for much of their eschatology. A great deal of emphasis is placed on the idea that all of the Revelation beyond chapter 3 is yet future. Chapter 4 is said to teach the rapture of the Church and from there on is thought to teach of the seven year period during which the Antichrist is to reign. The weakest link in all of this is the pretribulation rapture. Revelation 4 says absolutely nothing about the rapture of the Church.

But since this interpretation is almost essential to their entire schedule, they are forced to read the rapture into it even though it is not there. They are forced out of their so-called literalism in accomplishing their objective. In Revelation 4:1 we read, "Come up hither, and I will shew you things which must be hereafter." This message was directed to John. I take it literally as referring only to John. Scofield comments on this clause, "This call seems clearly to indicate the fulfilment of I Thess. 4:14-17." So the literalist sacrifices his literalism in order to make people believe that the Church is symbolized by the apostle John. Since consistency is said to be a jewel, this stratagem is a lack-luster imitation.

## Posttribulationism

Posttribulationism is much less offensive than pretribulationism. It does partake of some of the same errors of interpretation found in pretribulationism. The major difference is that pretribulationism involves a two-phase second coming, whereas the teaching now being considered expects a single second coming. Both hold that following the second coming at the close of the great tribulation, Christ will return to set up his millennial kingdom. At Christ's return, Antichrist will be destroyed, the wicked will be slain, and all the world will yield to the sovereignty of Christ. Other than whether there will be one or two second comings, the major point of distinction between pretribulationism and posttribulationism is that the former is very strongly Judaistic, whereas the latter is not.

The weakness of posttribulationism is illustrated by its interpretation of I Thessalonians 4. George E. Ladd is one of the ablest defenders of posttribulationism. He points out that the word used for the meeting of the righteous with the Lord in the air (I Thess. 4:17) is the same word that is used of the five virgins who met the bridegroom with lamps trimmed and burning (Matt. 25:6). He says, "It is just possible, and, as we shall show later on, even suggested by the word used for the meeting, that after this meeting, Jesus continues His descent to the earth, but now accompanied by His saints."[300]

---

300  George E. Ladd, *The Blessed Hope*, p. 78.

# THE RAPTURE

The Greek word used here makes no such suggestion. It means no more than "to meet." What follows must be supplied by the context. It is used three times for sure, and possibly a fourth time. The text in doubt is Matthew 25:1, but since the word is used in verse 6 of this chapter, the problem is of minor consequence. Of the three occurrences in the New Testament, the only one that involved a going out to meet someone, then followed by a return to the starting point was where the brethren at Rome went to meet Paul (Acts 28:15). These brethren did return to Rome with Paul, but we know this from the context, not from *apantesis* the word that is used.

The example that Ladd gives does not involve returning to the place where the virgins were waiting, but to the place prepared for the wedding. If this place has any meaning in the parable, it would refer to heaven—not to the earth. And in I Thessalonians 4:17, the destination is heaven. This is shown by the expression, "… and so shall we ever be with the Lord." We have previously shown that this means "after this manner" we shall ever be with the Lord. And the manner involved was a togetherness away from the earth—not on it.

The above is fairly conclusive that the Greek term does not of itself imply a return, but when the Septuagint version is considered the evidence is complete to the point of certainty. Thayer states that *apantesis*, the Greek word being considered, is often the equivalent of the Hebrew *liqerath*. Davidson gives one meaning of *liqerath* as of hostile meetings. Three citations from the Septuagint version are given to prove the accuracy of these statements.

"Now Israel went out against the Philistines to battle, and pitched beside Ebenezer" (I Sam. 4:1). The Septuagint version has "to meet" instead of "against" and is a translation of *apantesis* which in turn is a translation of *liqerath*. A similar condition is found in the meeting of Jehu and Joram (II Kings 9:21). The same words are in the Hebrew and Greek as in the above, and the context shows it was not a peaceful meeting. It ended in the assassination of Jehoram (Joram) by Jehu (v. 24). And when Josiah "went against" Pharaoh-necho of Egypt (II Kings 23:29), the same words are used. There can be no doubt of Josiah's intent. However, he was the one who was slain.

Since *apantesis* is used of such a variety of meetings, it is inaccurate to draw any implications from the word itself. All it says is that two persons or groups meet. What happens after that is entirely dependent on the context for meaning. Jehoram did not return with Jehu (II Kings 9:24) for Jehu killed him. Only one instance can be found in the New Testament where those who went out to meet a man returned with him. Ladd has made an assertion which cannot be accepted because it is false. When the Church meets the Lord in the air, Christ will take us on to that heavenly home He has gone to prepare for us; and it will be forever—not for just seven years.

## The Rapture as Part of the Consummation

Amillennialists and Postmillennialists expect the Church to be raptured to heaven, all right, but they understand it to be a part of the final consummation. When Christ returns, He will raise the dead, change the living from mortal to immortal, judge all men, destroy the world, and assess to each man the penalty or reward he deserves. Eternity is ushered in and time as we know it ceases. In this chapter the idea of a separate rapture of the Church, separated from the final consummation by 1,000 years or by 1,007 years has been disproved. The only option left is to believe it to be a part of the final consummation. However, a short review may be necessary.

In the Olivet discourse, Jesus does speak of some being taken and others left, but from the parables of the tares and the net, we know that it is the wicked that will be taken, leaving the righteous. Therefore, Christ Himself had earlier made it clear that the wicked would be taken out from among the righteous, rather than the righteous being taken out from among the wicked, as Premillennialists say it will be. Jesus did not teach a separate rapture of the Church.

Nor did Paul teach it. In that great resurrection chapter (I Cor. 15), Paul indicated that at the time they, the Church, were resurrected or changed, death would be annihilated (I Cor. 15:54). Premillennialists hold that death will continue to reign over those who are not raptured, and over those who are born after the rapture. This passage from Paul does not teach a separate rapture of the Church.

And only by the twisting of Scripture can I Thessalonians 4 be made to teach a separate rapture. The wicked are ignored in this passage as they are in I Corinthians 15. It is true that Paul says the righteous dead will be resurrected first, but to make this mean the wicked dead are to be resurrected at a later time is to misinterpret Paul. What Paul really says is that the living righteous will not be taken to heaven ahead of the righteous dead, and to this end the righteous dead are to be resurrected first, so that all can proceed to heaven in a single group. Paul does not say when the wicked will be resurrected in this chapter. And verse 17 implies we go to heaven forever at that time.

The effort to make the Revelation teach a separate rapture of the Church is equally indefensible. In Part One of this volume, the myth of a single hermeneutic was exploded. Those who claim to interpret the Bible literally cannot make the Revelation teach a separate rapture of the Church without departing from their literalism. They make the letters to the seven churches represent seven epochs in the life of the Church. This is without adequate justification. Even more bizarre is their claim that John's experience of being carried to heaven actually refers to the rapture of the Church. Thus, while claiming to be literalists, they feel perfectly free to depart from that position whenever such a departure seems to strengthen their position. What is does do is demonstrate their inconsistency.

## Concluding Remarks

The teaching that the Church would he raptured to heaven just prior to a time called the great tribulation was not known prior to the 1800's. It is inconceivable that the Church could have endured through the centuries without some voice being raised in support of this doctrine, if it does have any validity. Since no voice spoke out in favor of this doctrine, the only conclusion possible is that the Church did not teach this in the beginning, and that it should not be teaching it now. It is rank heresy.

The teaching of the resurrection of the dead was ably defended by many early writers, but the order of events is seldom given in an orderly manner. Therefore, it is difficult to know for certain just what some did believe would be the order of events. I found nothing in the writings of the early Church that spoke of a separate rapture of the Church. Lactantius, one of the ante-Nicene fathers, does allow for two physical resurrections, but he does not speak specifically of a rapture.[301] Commodianus believed in two bodily resurrections,[302] but I found nothing about a separate rapture in his writings. No positive testimony for a separate rapture was found in any of my research.

The evidence in opposition to a separate rapture of the Church is largely that for a single bodily resurrection, for without two or more resurrections

---

301 Lactantius, *op. cit.*, vol. VII, pp. 216ff.
302 Commodianus, *op. cit.*, vol. IV, p. 212.

of bodies, there can be no separate rapture. Justin Martyr believed in a "general resurrection at which time the judgment of all men would likewise take place."[303] Hippolytus believed in a single physical resurrection.[304] Victorinus said, "There are two resurrections, But the first resurrection is now of the souls that are by faith."[305] From Augustine onward, the evidence is almost unanimous in favor of a single resurrection. The statement quoted above from Victorinus came to be the accepted view.

---

303  Justin Martyr, *op. cit.*, vol. I, p. 240.
304  Hippolytus, *op. cit.*, vol. V, p. 222.
305  Victorinus, *op. cit.*, vol. VII, p. 359.

CHAPTER 22

# ANTICHRIST & THE GREAT TRIBULATION

Because it is impossible to discuss the Antichrist without also discussing the great tribulation, these two important matters are considered in a single chapter. Both of these subjects have been considered previously. It has already been shown that the Bible says not a word about a personal Antichrist. John is the only writer who uses the term, and he uses it in the plural as of many. It has been shown, also, that the great tribulation occurred during the siege of Jerusalem in A.D. 70. A fuller consideration of these matters is the intent of this chapter.

## The Antichrist

There are so many variant teachings regarding the Antichrist that it will be impossible to consider all of them fully. Some hold that he will have a similar relation to the devil that Christ had to the Father. These anticipate a conception similar to that by Mary, except that the impregnating source is from Satan rather than God. Some believe he will be a Jew. Most of these contend that he will be from the tribe of Dan. Bases for this are that Dan apostatized, and that as Christ is called the lion of the tribe of Judah, so Dan is called a lion's whelp. All of this is pure surmise, of course.

Instead of giving the teachings of the Church fathers last, as has been done heretofore, they will be given first in this study. What may be the most ancient witness in this connection is Polycarp. He followed the teaching of John very closely. He indicated that "whosoever [i.e., anyone who] perverts the oracles of the Lord to his own lusts…he is the first-born of Satan."[306] This expression became quite common very early in the life of the Church. It is considered the equivalent of the Antichrist. Barnabas, writing about the same time as Polycarp, favored a personal Antichrist. He expected this "final

---

306  Polycarp, *op. cit.*, vol. I, p. 34.

stumbling block" to arise rather quickly.³⁰⁷ The 11th horn of Daniel 7 was interpreted as the Antichrist.

The next one to write on this subject, at least as far as I was able to find, was Commodianus. He wrote, "Nero shall be raised from hell."³⁰⁸ He expected Nero, as the Antichrist, to reign for the latter half of a seven year period. Origen apparently expected an Antichrist,³⁰⁹ but he did not elaborate on it. Cyprian also expected an Antichrist, but apparently he expected God to curtail his activities. He wrote, "Antichrist is coming, but above him comes Christ also."³¹⁰

Hippolytus wrote most extensively of the Antichrist. Some writers classify him as a millennialist, but failed to find anything to substantiate the claim. He certainly was not in agreement with the Judaistic millennium so many advocate today. Also, he interpreted the woman of Revelation 12 as the Church. This is contradictory to the present explanation of the Revelation by Dispensationalists. However, much of the present teaching on Antichrist is based on his writings.

He expected the Antichrist to be a future king. He was to come from the tribe of Dan. The little horn of Daniel 7 is the Antichrist. The final week of Daniel 9 is to be at the end of the world. (This follows the parenthesis theory, but it contradicts the millennium which so many envision after that final week.) Since he interpreted the woman of Revelation 12 as the Church, he believed that the Church would endure the tribulation. The woman being driven into the wilderness is his basis for believing this.³¹¹

Four other ante-Nicene writers expected an Antichrist. These are Irenaeus,³¹² Cyprian,³¹³ Lactantius,³¹⁴ and Victorinus.³¹⁵ The absence of any polemic over this question prior to the Council of Nicea may mean

---

307 Barnabas, *op. cit.,* vol. I, p. 38.
308 Commodianus, *op. cit.,* vol. IV, p. 211.
309 Origen, *op. cit.,* vol. IV, p. 594.
310 Cyprian, *op. cit.,* vol. V, p. 346.
311 Hippolytus, *op. cit.,* vol. V, pp. 204-219, 246.
312 Irenaeus, *op. cit.,* vol. I, p. 560.
313 Cyprian, *loc. cit.*
314 Lactantius, *op. cit.,* vol. VII. pp. 212-215.
315 Victorinus, *op. cit.,* vol. VII, pp. 354-355.

that most expected an Antichrist, or that it was not considered of sufficient import to warrant a refutation. I believe it was the latter. Controversy did develop in the course of time.

Augustine took a firm stand against the teaching of a personal Antichrist. Except for one debatable quotation,[316] he was uniformly opposed to this teaching. Of his various comments, the following is an example: "And each person ought to question his own conscience whether he be an antichrist."[317] Here, as in several places, any person who opposed Christ was an Antichrist. He followed John's teaching at this point. Chrysostom held that the Antichrist teaching denied the imminence of Christ's return. He wrote, "If Antichrist comes, and Elias comes, how is it 'when they say Peace and safety,' that then a sudden destruction comes upon them? For these things do not permit the day to come upon them unawares."[318] Few references to a personal Antichrist were found among the later Christian writers.

The evidence from the early Church fathers is inconclusive. It is evident a number of the early writers did believe in a coming Antichrist. Just how prevalent this was cannot be determined. And since this was yet future in their time, it would not be surprising for an erroneous view to become the accepted interpretation. Prior to the revealing of "the man of sin," an exegete might well take this to be an oppressive ruler. There is nothing in the prophecy to forbid this interpretation. Only as popery developed and devoured three of the ten horns was real evidence available to show that "the man of sin" referred to a politico-religious system, rather than a single ruler.

In refuting the teaching of a coming Antichrist, I am faced with a similar situation to that of a so-called prophet I heard recently. He prophesied that President Ford would not finish the year 1976 as president, and that Rockefeller would become president for a short time. I could not disprove this claim at that time, but now that Ford has served his term out, it is evident to all that this statement was untrue. Neither can I now prove that a world ruler will not arise. All I can do is point out that prophecy does not require that such an event occur. If it does occur, it will be an event outside the prophetic vision.

---

316  Augustine, *op. cit.,* vol. II, pp. 393-394.
317  *Ibid.,* vol. VII, p. 476.
318  Chrysostom, *op. cit.,* vol. XIII, p. 362.

Although the several portions of the Bible which are used to support the doctrine of a future Antichrist have been interpreted in previous chapters, these must now he drawn together to focus on the doctrine now being considered. The reader is urged to review the chapters in which the several texts are discussed, if the present discussion is less than convincing.

Much of the present day teaching on the Antichrist is built on the interpretations of Hippolytus who wrote during parts of the second and third Christian centuries. Hippolytus held that Isaiah 14:12-14 referred to the Antichrist.[319] The present day teaching is that this passage refers to Satan after a manner of speaking, but that it moves beyond that to mean the Antichrist (see Scofield's note on Ezek. 28:12). This is without a shade of justification. Isaiah affirms that he refers to the king of Babylon (Isa. 14:4). A literal interpretation requires that it refers to the king of Babylon. So-called literalists forsake their literalism in making this apply first to Satan and secondarily to the Antichrist.

Hippolytus held that Ezekiel 28:2-19 referred to the Antichrist.[320] Scofield's note on Ezekiel 28:12, "the prince of Tyrus foreshadows the Beast," is another instance of literalism giving way to an unsubstantiated hypothesis. Ezekiel asserts that he is speaking about the "king of Tyrus" (v. 12), but Scofield and others say he really means the Beast who in turn is said to mean the Antichrist. I accept Ezekiel's statement. Apparently, followers of Scofield do not. They feel constrained to interpret it to fit their schedule.

Hippolytus believed that Daniel 7:8, 24 refer to the Antichrist when reference is made to the "little horn" that came up among the ten. Scofield identifies this little horn as the "prince that shall come" from Daniel 9:26, as well as "the man of sin" from II Thessalonians 2:4-8. These in turn are identified as the Antichrist. But it has been proved before that this little horn refers to the Roman Catholic church and the papacy. It has already been fulfilled. The ten kingdoms did form after Rome was defeated in A.D. 476. The papacy seemed small, but it did displace three of the established countries. That it has spoken blasphemously against God in arrogating to itself the power to forgive sin, and to enact laws that were considered binding on the consciences of men is hardly subject to refutation.

---

319 Hippolytus, *op. cit.,* vol. V, p. 207.
320 *Ibid.,* p. 208.

Although additional points of agreement exist between the views of Hippolytus and present day Premillennialism, some of their views clash as contradictory positions. Since the next text considered has in it a contradictory element, this is a convenient place to say why these references to Hippolytus have been made. To show that their views go back as far as the fourth Christian century would seemingly strengthen a view. But this would only be true if the major emphasis were acceptable to both. In this case, Hippolytus agrees on minor issues, but on the really important issue, he is in total disagreement.

The principal issue in eschatology is the millennium. The matter of an Antichrist is secondary. Some men of every millennial persuasion have accepted the idea of a future Antichrist. But Hippolytus was not a millenarian. This will be brought out as consideration is given to chapter 9 of the book of Daniel. Three points of controversy stem from Daniel 9:24-27. First, are the periods consecutive? Secondly, is the prince of verse 26 Titus and his legions, or is it the Antichrist? The third point is whether or not a millennium is to follow. Hippolytus deals with the last week of seven years in a separate manner that leaves room for it to be separated from the other 69 weeks, but he does not actually say so. He expects Enoch and Elias to occupy the first half of this period, and the Antichrist the latter half.[321] From this it appears that he considered the Antichrist to be the destructive prince of verse 26. But he did not expect a millennium to follow. His words are, "By one week, therefore, he meant the last week which is to be at the end of the world."[322]

It can be seen from this that Hippolytus was not a millennialist. Instead of expecting the establishment of a millennial kingdom at the close of the seventieth week, he foresaw the consummation. It can be said further that he did not disagree with Premillennialists on a minor matter like the Antichrist, but on the major issue of a millennium, he was definitely at odds with them. Hippolytus also said nothing about a secret rapture. Further, he believed the Church would endure the great tribulation,[323] and his dissertation against the Jews is definite evidence that he would be opposed to the Judaistic emphasis which is so prevalent in Premillennial circles.

---

321 *Ibid.*, p. 213.
322 *Ibid.*
323 *Ibid.*, pp. 217-218.

The idea that the seventy weeks of Daniel 9 are not consecutive would be ludicrous except for the fact that many intelligent people believe this figment of the imagination. A fourth area of controversy not mentioned in the above is whether the covenant of verse 27 is a future covenant Antichrist will make with the Jews, or whether it is the new covenant Christ instituted through His death. This is discussed in the chapter on Daniel.

Daniel 11 is another controversial passage. All admit that the first part of the chapter refers to Antiochus Epiphanes, but many contend that at some point in the chapter the text switches from a discussion of Antiochus Epiphanes, who is considered a type of the future Antichrist, to the Antichrist himself. The fact that at least three different points for marking this change exist among its advocates is evidence that this approach is very tenuous. No solid basis exists for this interpretation of Daniel 11.

Dispensationalists have a great deal of trouble with the Olivet discourse, for it makes no mention of the Antichrist. They are also forced to violate the hermeneutical principle regarding parallel passages by making Luke's account refer to A.D. 70, and Matthew and Mark refer to a future event. But apparently rules are made to be broken, so they break this one. The point in question has to do with Christ's statement about the abomination of desolation as used by Matthew and Mark, whereas Luke refers the same event to the Roman armies surrounding Jerusalem.

Now the rules require that all three accounts have the same meaning. Since Luke's account cannot speak of anything except the siege of Jerusalem by Titus, the abomination of desolation found in Matthew and Mark must also refer to that time. But not so, according to these interpreters. They say this refers to the time of the Antichrist. Also, this abomination of desolation is, according to these teachers, accomplished by the so-called Antichrist of the future. But strangely enough, Jesus says not a word about an Antichrist. Therefore, it is necessary for them to read into the accounts by Matthew and Mark the restoration of the Roman empire in a ten nation confederation, and the rise of the Antichrist to rule over it. This is a very arbitrary way of handling God's word.

The claim that the man of sin (I Thess. 2:3) refers to a future Antichrist is more reasonable than many of their explanations. Prior to the full development of popery, it would be a very natural way to interpret the passage. But since the apostasy did come, and since the power that developed through it was the Roman Catholic hierarchy, and since that power did displace three of the ten nations (horns of Dan. 7), there is no legitimate basis for rejecting this as the fulfillment of several of the prophecies which many refer to a future Antichrist.

Thus, those who advocate a future Antichrist must reject a clear fulfillment of these prophecies, as well as establish a series of events that are not set forth in the Bible. I refer specifically to the development of a ten nation confederation within the confines of the territory of the ancient Roman empire, and an Antichrist ruler who will make a covenant with the Jews and then break it. He is then said to institute the great tribulation. All of this without the term Antichrist being used anywhere in the New Testament of a single person. John is the only writer to use the term. He does recognize that his readers had "heard that antichrist shall come" (I John 2:18), but he hastens to explode the idea of one certain Antichrist by adding "there are many antichrists." (No definite article precedes "antichrist" in the better Greek manuscripts, or in most translations.) But a future ruler who is *the* Antichrist is still being taught.

Advocates of a future Antichrist think he is often portrayed in the Revelation. They place everything beyond chapter 3 in the future. This futuristic approach was first invented by a Catholic priest. He developed it as a means of minimizing the claim that the Roman Church was the Antichrist or man of sin. Dispensationalism adopted this unusual interpretation and expanded it. For obvious reasons it is suspect from its source, even until today. Although Hippolytus was not a futurist in the present day sense of that term, some of his interpretations are incorporated into the Dispensational schedule.

Hippolytus believed that the final seven years of time would be divided into two halves. From Revelation 11, he held that the two witnesses were the "prophets Enoch and Elias," and that they would occupy the first half of that week. The Antichrist was to occupy the second half.[324] This has been somewhat modified by Dispensationalists, but the core of his thought is retained. The beast coming up out of the earth (Rev. 13:1-3) was interpreted as the Antichrist.[325] This has been retained by Dispensationalists.

---

324  *Ibid.*, p. 213.
325  *Ibid.*, p. 214.

But all of this has been fulfilled in the past. It was shown that the seven heads and ten horns of the dragon and of the beast are identical, except as to the location of the crowns. Hence there must be a continuity of relationship between the dragon and the beast. We identified the dragon as pagan Rome. With the crowns moving from the heads (forms of government) to the horns (the ten nations which grew out of imperial Rome), the transfer of authority from the emperor to the several kings is indicated. The beast, however, had human capabilities such as that of speech. For this reason, the beast was identified as that politico-religious power that developed. This power was nothing other than papal Rome. Thus, the beast is a symbol of the papacy, and the papacy is certainly an Antichrist—one among many.

Satisfactory interpretations are available without a personal Antichrist. Many Antichrists existed in John's time, and many more have arisen since. The "man of sin" and "the beast" have been shown to refer to the Roman Catholic hierarchy or popery. This powerful organization that has been, and to some extent still is, a political organization as well as a religious body, is the subject of prophecy, but it is not called the Antichrist; for the Bible knows of a plurality of Antichrists, but not a single Antichrist as is often taught.

### The Great Tribulation

The great tribulation has been connected so closely with the expected Antichrist of the future that proving there will be no future Antichrist disproves, for all practical purposes, a future tribulation period such as many envision. However, for the sake of completeness, the subject of the great tribulation will be considered independent of whether or not there will be a future Antichrist. The first passage considered is from Jeremiah 30:7. In this verse it is termed "the time of Jacob's trouble." Although the expression "great tribulation" is not found in this text, it is said to be the same thing as the great tribulation.

Chapter 30 of Jeremiah should not be considered independent of chapter 31 for the latter chapter throws light on chapter 30. Both of these chapters deal with matters which were fulfilled during the first Christian century. The deliverance (Jer. 30:9) is the deliverance Christ gives to those who come to Him for deliverance. Instead, they "serve the Lord their God, and David their king" (Jer. 30:9). David here refers to the Son of David, Jesus Christ, who is now sitting on the throne of David in heaven. The time of Jacob's trouble is the destruction of Jerusalem in A.D. 70. Josephus recounts some of the most horrible stories of that time to the point that there should be no difficulty in recognizing it as the time of Jacob's trouble.

In an efforts to refute this interpretation, it is claimed that Jacob was not delivered out of that ordeal. Thousands were slain or died from famine and other causes. This is true of the physical descendents of Jacob, but the remnant, the spiritual descendents of Jacob were spared this calamity. They fled to Pella where they were free from the tragedies of the siege.

Chapter 31 reaffirms the time of these things. Through Jeremiah, God promised a new covenant (Jer. 31:31). This covenant was to be with the house of Israel (Jer. 31:31, 33) which I interpret as with spiritual Israel—not national Israel. The fact that Christ did institute a new covenant through His death on the cross is abundantly testified in that portion of the Bible which we call the New Testament. The Greek terms make "New Covenant" the true meaning of the expression. Is the New Testament really the new covenant? Who can deny this? Yet, Dispensationalists contend that Jeremiah referred to a yet future covenant God will make with national Israel.

That Jeremiah referred to the gospel era is proved by verse 33 which reads in part, "I will put my law in their inward parts, and write it in their hearts." This indicates the change in man's nature that is accomplished through the power of God in the regeneration and sanctification that He gives to His children. This takes place now under the new covenant which is now in operation, and which has been functioning ever since Calvary.

Chapters 11-12 of Daniel are parts of a single prophecy. Hence, chapter 12 is but a continuation of chapter 11. The interpretation of chapter 12 will depend a great deal on the interpretation of chapter 11, especially the latter portion. Antiochus Epiphanes is universally recognized as the ruler being described from Daniel 11:21, but many hold that somewhere between that verse and the close of the chapter, the description switches to the Antichrist. Those who follow this interpretation, make Daniel 12:1 refer to the great tribulation they expect to come at a future time. I see no sound basis for this change in chapter 11, so I refer Daniel 12:1 to the time of Antiochus Epiphanes.

The statement that is said to refer to a future time of tribulation reads, "And there shall be a time of trouble, such as never was since there was a nation even to that same time" (Dan. 12:1). Note that it does not add "or ever shall be." That was said of the destruction of Jerusalem. But this refers to the persecutions by Antiochus Epiphanes during the Maccabean period (c. 171-165 B.C.) This prophecy was fulfilled over 2,000 years ago. Antiochus Epiphanes was a despot, and he oppressed the Jews without mercy. This was a time of tribulation for the Jews, but it does not refer to a future period. The tribulations of the Jews under Antiochus Epiphanes were the greatest up to that time, but those of A.D. 70 were greater.

Another expression found in Daniel figures in any discussion of future time of great tribulation. Three times Daniel mentions abominations and desolations. The first occasion (Dan. 9:27) apparently indicates that one who makes desolate will follow closely after abominations have become widespread. Two other places (Dan. 11:31; 12:11), are usually translated in such a way as to indicate an "abomination of desolation" would be set up. The matter is complicated by the fact that Christ referred to "the abomination of desolation" in the Olivet discourse.

The statement in Daniel 11:31 is generally recognized as applying to the desecration of the altar by Antiochus Epiphanes (I Macc. 1:20-59). But the controversy continues without abatement regarding the other two references. These two references are to "the 'Beast,' 'man of sin'; (II Thess. 2:3-4), and is identical with Matthew 24:15," according to Scofield's note on Daniel 9:27. Inasmuch as the passages involved have been fully interpreted elsewhere, only a short discussion will be given at this point.

Reasons why Daniel 9:27 cannot refer to a future time of great tribulation are several:

1. It requires that a block of time which involves seventy sevens (490 years) be split near the end so that the last seven years have a parenthesis of some 2,000 years or more between them and the first 483 years. This cannot be justified exegetically or otherwise.

2. This places the sacrificial death of Christ on the cross in the parenthesis, rather than within the seventy sevens, whereas verse 24 highlights the redemptive work of Christ as being within the 490 year period.

3. It denies that the destruction of Jerusalem in A.D. 70 is foretold in verse 26.

4. It makes the new covenant which is mentioned in verse 27 a future covenant between the Antichrist and the Jews.

The proper interpretation of this passage makes the work of Christ the focal point of the prophecy (Dan. 9:24-27). The 490 years must be

## ANTICHRIST & THE GREAT TRIBULATION 409

considered as consecutive years. The prince that was to come and "destroy the city and the sanctuary" has reference to the destruction of Jerusalem in A.D. 70—not to some supposed future disaster. The covenant of verse 27 can be none other than the new covenant. By His sacrifice, Jesus caused the need for further animal sacrifices to end, as he was crucified in the midst of the 70th week (v. 27). This prophecy was fulfilled over 1900 years ago. It does not refer to a future time of great tribulation. Tribulations may come in the future, but this prophecy does not so indicate.

To make the "abomination of desolation" (Dan. 12:11) refer to a future time of great tribulation requires that a shift be made in chapter 11 from Antiochus Epiphanes to a so-called Antichrist. Three different points have been advocated as the place this supposed shift occurs. This shows the tenuous grounds on which this teaching is founded. The abomination of desolation in chapter 12 is nothing other than a second look at the abomination of desolation mentioned in Daniel 11:31. All are agreed that this was by Antiochus Epiphanes. Daniel 12:11 refers to the same actions by the same ruler.

Inasmuch as the abominations mentioned in chapters 11 and 12 of Daniel refer to actions which took place before Christ's first advent, the only abomination of desolation Christ could have meant as future is the one in Daniel 9:27. We have shown already that this referred to the destruction of Jerusalem in A.D. 70. It was future when Christ foretold this event, but it was fulfilled in the lifetime of many who heard him utter this prophecy.

The juggling of Scripture in an effort to make Christ in the Olivet discourse refer to some yet future time of tribulation shows an utter disregard for the principles of hermeneutics. I have reference to the claim that Matthew and Mark wrote of a future time of tribulation, but that Luke wrote of the tribulation of A.D. 70. Two rules are violated by this subterfuge. The first is that parallel passages must be interpreted with the same significance. The second is that the clear passages explain the obscure.

That the three accounts of the Olivet discourse are parallel is exegetically certain. All three say that it came from an observation of the temple buildings (Matt. 24:1; Mark 13:1; Luke 5:5). All three report that Jesus said that a time would come when, "There shall not be left here one stone upon another that shall not be thrown down" (Matt. 24:2; Mark 13:2, Luke 21:6). All three ask, "... when shall these things be?" (Matt. 24:3; Mark 13:4; Luke 21:7). Luke adds the question of signs when this would be done, and

Matthew adds questions regarding signs of the second coming and the end of the world. All of these additions are accepted as part of what was said.

In the next several verses this parallel continues. Matthew omits some things which are included in the accounts of Mark and Luke, and he also adds a few things they do not include; but the fact that the accounts are fully parallel cannot be denied (Matt. 24:4-14; Mark 13:5-13; Luke 21:8-19). But Dispensationalists contend that the parallelism stops at this point. Scofield's note on Luke 21:20 reads in part, "Two sieges of Jerusalem are in view in that discourse. Luke 21:20-24 refers to the siege by Titus, A.D. 70....The references in Mt. 24:15-28, Mk. 13:14-26 are to the final tribulation siege; Lk. 21:20-24 to the destruction of Jerusalem by Titus." This idea comes from a fertile imagination—not from God's word.

The particular verses in question are Matthew 24:15, Mark 13:14, and Luke 21:20. The principal point of difference is that Matthew and Mark refer to the "abomination of desolation spoken of by Daniel the prophet," whereas Luke says "when ye shall see Jerusalem compassed with armies." Just what is the "abomination of desolation" that Daniel spoke of is a matter of interpretation. Since it is subject to more than one interpretation, it is to some degree obscure. But seeing Jerusalem "compassed with armies" is not obscure. It is very plain. Therefore, we hold that the "abomination of desolation" mentioned by Matthew and Mark is fully explained by Luke. All three refer to the same event—the destruction of Jerusalem in A.D. 70.

Now let us see if the parallelism that was fully established up to these key verses continues after them. When this event occurs, all three say, "Then let them which be in Judaea flee into the mountains" (Matt. 24:16; Mark 13:14; Luke 21:21). That doesn't sound like two separate events. It sounds like what happened when the Church fled to Pella prior to the destruction of Jerusalem in A. D. 70. At any rate the parallelism continues.

Then we find that all three mention a woe on those that are pregnant, or which have children that still nurse (Matt. 24:19; Mark 13:17; Luke 21:23). Thus the parallelism continues after the key verses as well as before them. In other words, Matthew Mark, and Luke all refer to the single event—the destruction of Jerusalem in A.D. 70. Every effort to read two sieges into these accounts is a perversion of scriptural truth. We should accept Luke's plain statement which indicates that the "abomination of desolation spoken by Daniel the prophet" was nothing other than the Roman legions which destroyed Jerusalem in A.D. 70.

# ANTICHRIST & THE GREAT TRIBULATION    411

It is also worthy of note that conditions as they are pictured at the expected battle at the close of the so-called great tribulation are not suited to the instructions given in all three accounts. With 200,000,000 Chinese soldiers involved,[326] and an innumerable army from Russia, Europe, Africa, and elsewhere, the idea of anyone fleeing from Jerusalem to the mountains has no meaning. Army units would be everywhere. Those fleeing would get caught in a cross-fire. And since a miraculous deliverance is expected, the admonition we would expect under such circumstances would be to stay close in Jerusalem and wait for this expected miraculous deliverance. But Jesus said to flee to the mountains. The Christians did that in A.D. 70.

The futuristic interpretation of the Revelation, in spite of the fact that it is suspect from the very start, is freely used to bolster the argument for a great tribulation period. Just which chapters of the Revelation refer to which parts of the great tribulation is a matter of dispute among those who advocate this theory. Scofield was of the opinion chapters 11-18 describe the great tribulation (see his note on Rev. 7:14). Tan holds that the first half of the tribulation is covered by chapters 6-11, and the second half by chapters 12-18.[327] But in both cases chapter seven proves a problem, for in that chapter John sees those who "came out of great tribulation" (Rev. 7:14).

Much is made of the fact that the Greek has the definite article before tribulation. This emphasizes a specific tribulation more so than it would without the article. But if chapter seven is in the first half of the tribulation, according to Tan, or if it occurs before the tribulation period begins, according to Scofield—how is it that John sees them at the time he does? The appropriate time would be at the close of the tribulation period, if indeed the Revelation tells of a period of tribulation that is yet future.

The claim that the middle chapters of the Revelation tell of a future period of great tribulation is a matter of interpretation. And since the Revelation is written in symbolic terms instead of terms which are more easily understood, a variety of interpretations are available. One can take his pick. I have given an interpretation that makes most of the Revelation fulfilled in times past, but I recognize it to be an interpretation. It goes beyond exegesis. My interpretation is satisfactory to me. I present it to you hoping it will also be satisfactory to you. But most of those who believe the Revelation tells

---

326  Lindsey, *op. cit.,* p. 162.
327  Tan, *op. cit.,* p. 348.

of a future time of great tribulation present their views as if there could be no other acceptable interpretation. The reader should not be fooled by this *seeming* certitude on their part.

## Concluding Remarks

There was some teaching of a great tribulation among the ante-Nicene fathers, but where such was found, the Church was to endure it. No evidence of a rapture of the Church prior to the tribulation was found among the ante-Nicene fathers. Tan attempts to establish such a teaching from Irenaeus and the *Shepherd of Hermas,* but neither instance is convincing. In the *Shepherd* (or *Pastor*) *of Hermas* the story is of an escape from a large wild beast because of his faith in God. The heavenly visitor then explains to the shepherd that the "beast is a type of the great tribulation that is coming."[328] Tan goes far beyond the interpretation given in claiming that the escape is a type of the pretribulation rapture of the Church.

His words are, "The heavenly interpreter explains to the shepherd that his escape from the beast means that the elect of God will escape the Great Tribulation."[329] But this is not what the angel told him. All he said was that the beast was a type of the tribulation which was to come. Nothing was said about the Church escaping it. And a further analysis indicates that the great tribulation really referred to God's judgments on the wicked, rather than by Antichrist. For a few lines farther on, the shepherd says one escapes by repenting and spending one's life in blameless service to God.[330]

Tan's other effort to prove a pretribulation rapture has as its foundation this statement of Irenaeus: "And therefore, when in the end the Church shall be suddenly caught up from this, it is said, 'There shall be tribulation such as has not been since the beginning; neither shall be.' "[331] But Tan takes this out of context and makes it mean something other than Irenaeus had in mind. The chapter preceding the above quotation (chap. 28) shows Irenaeus believed the Church had to go through a tribulation experience. He writes, "And for this cause tribulation is necessary for those who are saved, that...

---

328 The Pastor of Hermas, *Ante-Nicene Fathers,* vol. II, p. 18.
329 Tan, *op. cit.,* p. 71.
330 The Pastor of Hermas, loc. Cit.
331 Irenaeus, *op. cit.,* p. 558.

they may be fitted for the royal banquet."[332] From this we must interpret Irenaeus as referring to martyrs being caught away when their lives are taken. Thus Tan has read his thinking into this statement by Irenaeus, rather than allowing Irenaeus to speak for himself.

At least one other of the ante-Nicene fathers believed in a great tribulation. I refer to Hippolytus who wrote extensively on the Antichrist. But he, also, expected the Church to endure the tribulation. Prior to quoting extensively from Revelation 12 he wrote, "Now concerning the tribulation of the persecution which is to fall upon the Church from the adversary, John also speaks thus: …" He interpreted the woman of Revelation 12 as the Church, and the woman being driven into the wilderness as the great persecution.[333]

From this it can be concluded that there was considerable belief among the ante-Nicene fathers of a coming Antichrist and a period of great tribulation. But the idea of a two-phase second coming, and a pretribulation rapture of the Church, was not present. The pretribulation rapture of the Church is a product of 19th century thinking. It cannot be adequately supported from the early Church fathers. It is a new idea. Nor can it be adequately supported from the Bible.

---

332  *Ibid.*, p. 557.
333  Hippolytus, *op. cit.*, vol. V, p. 217.

CHAPTER 23

# THE BATTLE OF ARMAGEDDON

The term *Armageddon* appears but once in the Bible. According to the best Greek manuscripts, it should be aspirated so that it becomes Harmageddon. The latter part of the word comes from the Hebrew *Megiddo* or *Megiddon* which has been brought over into the English vocabulary without change. Its meaning is uncertain. It may mean the place of troops or of slaughter. To this should be added "city" if unaspirated, or "hill" if aspirated. Our problem is complicated by the fact that nowhere in the Old Testament is mention made of either a hill or a city of Megiddo.

Mention is made of "the waters of Megiddo" (Judg. 5:19), and the "valley of Megiddo" (Zech. 12:11). But nothing is said of a city or hill of Megiddo. This makes it impossible to determine just where a literal place called Armageddon might be. Without knowing whether to look for a city, a hill, or a valley, it is not likely that any consensus of opinion can be reached as to the location of Armageddon. Yet, there stands today in the ancient valley or plain of Esdraelon, a large sign which states that the final battle of history would be fought in that particular area. Where is the hill or city?

The indefiniteness of the term Armageddon has caused some to assert that it does not refer to a particular place. Instead it is to be thought of as a word that will characterize the final battle between good and evil—right and wrong. The general area of Megiddo was the scene of several battles. Joshua defeated the Canaanites there (Josh. 12:21). Barak overcame Sisera there (Judg. 4:4-24). King Josiah in a fatal encounter with Pharaoh-necho of Egypt contributes to the historical importance of the place. But is Armageddon to be equated with Megiddo and Megiddon? It is impossible to know for sure.

Since Armageddon cannot be located as a place, and since even the plain of Megiddo is much too small to contain the vast armies which literalists claim will one day battle there, it is deemed most fitting to consider the term as having a derived meaning, rather than referring to a particular spot. An analogy will explain my meaning. Today, people symbolically "cross the Rubicon," or meet their "Waterloo." Those who are knowledgeable regarding history and literature have no difficulty in grasping the significance of these statements. It is in such a derived meaning that Armageddon is used, at least as I see it.

If this be true, the victories of Joshua and Barak would be the historical background of importance: for in the battle of Armageddon, the forces of right prevail. As we proceed, further areas of symbolism will be noted.

With but one text containing the word "Armageddon," it might seem that little could be said about it. But a number of Scriptures in both the Old and the New Testaments are interpreted as referring to that battle, hence the task of one analyzing the teaching on this subject is not a simple one. Portions of the Bible which others see as having no connection with the battle of Armageddon are interpreted as referring to it, even though no mention is made of the battle involved. Some of these are quite tenuous. In other cases the connection is not discernible. Of this last mentioned variety is Isaiah 10:28-32.

Isaiah 10 contains a prophecy against Assyria (Isa. 10:5). No change of meaning is indicated by Isaiah through the remainder of this chapter. But Scofield contends that the expression "that day" (Isa. 10:20) jumps from "historic and fulfilled judgments upon Assyria to the final destruction of all Gentile world-power at the return of the Lord in glory" (note on Isa. 10:20). Having made this tremendous jump without adequate justification, he inserts the following statements between verses 27-28: "The approach of the Gentile hosts to the battle of Armageddon." The reader should read these final verses of chapter 10 and note that nothing even faintly refers to the battle of Armageddon. This is forced exegesis.

Scofield has a similar explanation of Isaiah 29:3. In this prophecy he says "the near and far horizons blend." The near view, according to Scofield, is the destruction of Sennacherib's army, whereas the distant view is of "the final gathering of the Gentile hosts against Jerusalem." It is not apparent by what means two separate ideas are involved in a single statement. The idea of a distant view is untenable.

## Ezekiel 38-39

An extensive prophecy that is frequently interpreted as referring to the battle of Armageddon is Ezekiel chapters 38-39. The following is gleaned from Scofield's note on Ezekiel 38:2. The major attacking nation is Russia.

"Meshech" is taken to mean "Moscow" for no better reason than that there is a certain similarity in spelling. "The whole prophecy belongs to the yet future 'day of Jehovah'...and to the battle of Armageddon...but includes also the final revolt of the nations at the close of the kingdom-age." Premillennialists in general and Dispensationalists in particular foresee the battle of Armageddon as a battle between earthly armies just before the millennium. Then, after the 1,000 years, they envision a revolt of nations just before God's judgments are poured out on the wicked.

The above quotation from Scofield shows how unsound they are in their interpretations. Surely, if chapters 38-39 do tell of two battles with 1,000 years between, inspiration would have seen to it that these facts were stated in the prophecy. But they are not so stated, therefore, Scofield's views must be accepted as human efforts to make the Bible fit his scheme of interpretation. The time of fulfillment is not given in chapters 38-39. The only basis on which this is given eschatological import is the interpretation given chapter 37, which is considered erroneous. Nor can it be proved that the two chapters now being considered have a time relationship to chapter 37.

In chapter 38 we read of an attack by Gog and Magog upon the land of Israel (vv. 14-18). The remainder of the chapter tells of God's power being used against the attacking forces. Thus far no particular problems have arisen regarding the literal interpretation often given to this. However, several unanswerable problems appear in the chapter that follows. The first of these is found in verse 3 which reads as follows: "And I will smite thy bow out of thy left hand, and will cause thine arrows to fall out of thy right hand" (Ezek. 39:3).

The interpreter has several options in interpreting this verse. He may insist that this refers to a time when bows and arrows were used in warfare. He may say that a cataclysm will occur that will cause bows and arrows to be used in this future war. He may take the position that bows and arrows are symbols of tanks, guns, and bombs. Or he may go so far as to say the entire battle is symbolic of the battle between right and wrong, good and evil, God and Satan. There are advocates of all these positions. Since one has different presuppositions to another, advocates of these several interpretations are likely to continue.

The literalist who is also a futurist is bound up to the second option. Because he is a literalist, he must maintain that bows and arrows will be used in the battle Ezekiel describes. And since he is also a futurist, he must hold that bows and arrows will be the major weapons used in this battle. Only a cataclysmic disruption of modern technology could make this possible. Therefore, these insert such an event in their prognosis. But bear in mind that Ezekiel says nothing of this. Interpreters insert this, unjustifiably, into the account.

I am unable to find fulfillment of these chapters in the past, hence it does not refer to a literal battle of the past. This forces me to accept this as symbolic to some degree. If other texts strongly indicated that this was a picture of a battle between armies of men attempting to kill one another, I could accept the explanation that bows and arrows were symbols of guns, bombs, and tanks. But I fail to find justification for this in this passage or elsewhere, so I hold that Ezekiel is describing the battle between good and evil in terms of earthly warfare. Others have come up with different answers, but this one appeals to me as the one having the least difficulties.

Verse 9 continues the problem of verse 3 with an added complication. It reads in part, "And they…shall set on fire and burn the weapons, both the shields and the bucklers, the bows and the arrows, and the handstaves, and the spears, and they shall burn them with fire seven years." In addition to bows and arrows, other older forms of armament and weapons are listed here. Are the shields and bucklers, spears and handstaves to be taken literally? If so, how are we to account for them? Was this fulfilled hundreds of years ago? Will armies revert to this kind of weapons? Or is it symbolic?

The new element in this verse is the seven years burning that is to follow this battle. It continues over into verse 10 where the Israelites are pictured as a culture that heats and cooks through the burning of wood. For seven years they cook and heat by burning the wooden weapons used by the invading forces. Is this to be taken as literal? Even if all the gas, oil, and coal are used up, other sources of heat will be found other than wood. Solar, wind, atomic, and other forms of energy will make it most unlikely that Israel will be a wood burning culture at any time in the future. This is strong reasoning for a symbolic interpretation.

The time element, seven years, is conclusive. Most Premillennialists place this battle as coming near the close of the seven year reign of the Antichrist, and in progress at the time of Christ's return in glory, and, as they say, to set up His millennial kingdom. But this seven year period is not broken by Christ's return, according to Ezekiel. If verses 9-10 speak of the victory over the Gog forces through Christ's return, how is it that no mention is made of it here? Surely that would be the all important element. It is impossible for this writer to reconcile these elements with the Premillennial interpretation of these chapters as referring to a literal battle between immense armies as the battle of Armageddon.

Then what is the answer? The valley of dry bones (Ezek. 37) refers to national Israel as a type of the Church. The coming to life is accomplished through the new life that Christ brought to mankind. As the Church is spoken of as the Israel of God (Gal. 6:15-16), so Israel in chapter 37 typifies the Church. This coming to life points to the first Christian century—not to 1948 when national Israel became a nation once more.

In line with this, chapters 38-39 tell of the warfare that was to be between the Church and the forces of evil. Chapter 39 tells of the victory of the Church over evil in figurative terms. The ultimate triumph of right is the lesson we should draw from these chapters. The terms by which this victory is presented are not intended to be taken literally, any more so than the heavenly gates being of literal pearl and the streets paved with gold.

## Zechariah and the Battle of Armageddon

The prophecies considered thus far are timeless. By this I mean that the times of fulfillment is not stated in the prophecies. Any time one assigns to them is done on the basis of secondary considerations, rather than on direct testimony within the prophecy. However, Zechariah 12-14 is less vague regarding time than those already considered. But before dealing with that point, it is needful to consider the explanations given by others.

According to Scofield, chapter 12 begins with the siege of Jerusalem at the start of the battle of Armageddon. Then comes the battle itself. Verse 10 is said to be a future pouring out of the Spirit on the Jewish remnant, after which the remnant repents. In chapter 13 it is said the remnant is pointed to Christ (v. 1), after which evidences of repentance are mentioned (vv. 2-5). Israel becomes an evangelist, says Dr. Scofield, in verses 6-7. The result of the Gentile invasion is said to be found in verses 8-9. Chapter 14 is said to be "a recapitulation of the whole matter." (See Scofield's notes and inserts on these three chapters.)

The major basis for giving these chapters an eschatological significance is the use of the expression "in that day." Scofield's note on Isaiah 10:20 declares that this term is "often the equivalent of 'the day of the Lord.'" By the use of the word "often," he is able to apply it so when he desires to do so, and avoid doing so when he prefers that procedure. Actually, the expression is used of the days of the kings of Israel (I Sam. 8:18), and of the gospel era (Isa. 29:18), and of the judgment day (Matt. 7:21-23). From this we learn that the specific day cannot be determined unless the context describes conditions sufficiently for identification, or unless a New Testament text refers to it in such a manner as to assure proper identification.

An example of how the tendency of Premillennialists to interpret most of the expressions "in that day" eschatologically forces them to twist the Scriptures is Amos 9:11. Amos declares, "In that day will I raise up the tabernacle of David that is fallen down." James declares that the conversion of Gentiles under the preaching of Paul and others fulfilled this prophecy (Acts 15:13-18). But because they feel Amos referred to conditions toward the end of the age, they refuse to accept James' interpretation of the prophecy. The same situation exists in their interpretation of Zechariah. The only difference is that Zechariah himself denies their claims.

Zechariah's use of the designation of *branch* for Christ indicates he is writing of Christ's first advent. When He comes a second time, He will come as deity—not as a man. The word "Branch" is appropriate for His first advent, but it has no place in His second advent. At that time He will come as King of kings and Lord of lords.

The *branch* was to "build the temple of the Lord" (Zech. 6:12-13). Premillennialists claim the Jews will build the new temple in Palestine—not the Christ. Hence, even according to their own doctrine, this must refer to Christ building the New Testament Church (II Cor. 6:16). So the "in that day" (Zech. 3:8-10) which involves the work of the branch, Jesus Christ in His first advent, cannot refer to a time yet future, howbeit there be those who attempt to explain it in that fashion.

Another interesting prophecy of Christ is found in Zechariah 9:9. The reference is to Christ's triumphal entry into Jerusalem "riding upon an ass, and upon a colt the foal of an ass." Scofield has to recognize this for what it is, but between this verse and the next he inserts the caption, "The future deliverance of Judah and Ephraim, and the world-wide kingdom." This jump of some 2,000 years or more is not indicated by Zechariah. The saving "in that day" of verse 16, refers to people becoming saved today—not some future bodily salvation.

Scofield is again forced to recognize that "in that day" refers to the time of the first advent (Zech 11:11) for in the next verse the price Judas received for betraying Christ ("thirty pieces of silver") is foretold. But he ends the chapter with a reference to the judgment of God on the Beast, which elsewhere he places as a part of the battle of Armageddon. Then he places all of the next three chapters as connected with the battle of Armageddon. But the fact that prophecies of the first advent and the gospel age are sprinkled in these chapters makes his deductions untenable.

Scofield has a special caption for Zechariah 11:10. It reads, "The Spirit poured out: the pierced One revealed to the delivered remnant." By this means he tries to make this verse refer to a yet future time. But John refutes this. The phrase in question is, "And they shall look on me whom they have pierced" (Zech. 12:10). But John testifies, "For these things were done, that the scripture should be fulfilled, A bone of him shall not be broken. And again another scripture saith, They shall look on him whom they pierced" (John 19:36-37). Note that the word "fulfilled" means just that. Zechariah 12:10 was fulfilled at the crucifixion. It does not refer to a future time.

Scofield's caption for the remainder of chapter 12 reads, "The repentance of the remnant." By this he means the Jewish remnant. But it is impossible to have an unbelieving remnant. The very reason for designating some as "a remnant" is that they have faith, whereas the main body of Jews are recognized as unbelievers. And if they are people of true faith, they will be believers in Christ before His return.

Also, the idea of people being converted at the second coming is incompatible with the Scripture. For when Christ returns, He will come "In flaming fire taking vengeance on them that know not God, and that obey not the gospel of our Lord Jesus Christ" (II Thess. 1:8). And it must be borne in mind that God is no respecter of persons. Unbelieving Jews will get the same treatment as unbelieving Gentiles. The teaching that a generation of Jews will be converted at Christ's return is heresy. When Christ leaves His mediatorial throne to come back to earth, the possibility of anyone being converted from that time onward is foreign to the intent of the Bible.

That these chapters refer to the first advent is made clear by verse 1 of chapter 13. It reads, "In that day there shall be a fountain opened to the house of David and to the inhabitants of Jerusalem for sin and uncleanness." That this fountain was opened at Calvary cannot be successfully denied. Jews have had access to this fountain for more than 1900 years. We regret that so few have availed themselves of its cleansing power. But Scofield makes this refer to the second coming. His caption for this verse reads, "The repentant remnant pointed to the cross." But this verse speaks of the opening of the fountain through the shedding of Christ's blood—not to some imagined situation at the second coming.

That these chapters refer to the first advent is further clarified by the words, "Awake, O sword, against my shepherd,...smite the shepherd, and the sheep shall be scattered." Both Matthew and Mark quote Jesus as saying that this referred to events connected with Christ's passion (Matt. 26:31; Mk. 14:27). Scofield admits as much in his center column references, but in his heading for verses 6-7 we find, "The preaching to Israel after the return of the Lord." This kind of double talk is not worthy of an exponent of the Bible.

With chapters 11-13 all referring to the first advent, it is to be assumed that chapter 14 will also, although it is recognized that a move to later things is a possibility. Taken alone, the first seven verses of chapter 14 could well have eschatological significance, but verse 8 makes it clear that he refers to the gospel as living water. This verse reads, "And it shall be in that day, that living waters shall go out from Jerusalem; half of them toward the former sea, and half of them toward the hinder sea."

That this is a figure of speech cannot be denied, since it is a physical impossibility for waters to flow in two directions from the point of origin. The natural lay of the land would cause waters from Jerusalem to flow eastward to the Salt Sea, as Ezekiel has it. But in this place, as well as in Ezekiel, the waters refer to the water of life—not to literal water. The same figure of speech is used of Jesus: "Jesus stood and cried, saying, If any man thirst let him come to me and drink. He that believeth on me, as the scripture hath said, out of his belly shall flow rivers of living water" (John 7:37-38).

Literalists are hard put to explain this as rivers of ordinary water, for it is not ordinary water. It is living water. Jeremiah spoke of people forsaking the fountain of "living waters" (Jer. 2:13; 17:13). These waters flowing to the east and to the west from Jerusalem point to the universality of the gospel message. It is for all men—not for the Jews only.

Since chapter 14 also refers to the first advent and the gospel age, we must interpret the verses that preceded verse 8 in like manner. This is done by recognizing that the battle mentioned is of the battle between good and evil, expressed in apocalyptic terms. The splitting of the Mount of Olives is a figurative method of expressing the division that occurred at Christ's first coming, and which persists unto this day. Some have accepted Him: some have not accepted Him. If Christ is to again stand upon the Mount of Olives, this would be abundantly confirmed by the New Testament, but no such confirmation is given, hence the entire passage must refer to the first advent.

From this discussion it can be seen that the Old Testament says absolutely nothing about the battle of Armageddon. The several passages that are interpreted as referring to it have no reference to a future conflict between earthly armies. Were it not for a single reference in the New Testament's last book, the whole doctrine would fall of its own weight; but no doctrine should he based on that book which is universally known to be a book written in symbolic form. Since the plain portions of the Bible fail to establish a literal battle of Armageddon, it should be rejected.

## The New Testament and Armageddon

Advocates of a literal battle of Armageddon are embarrassed by a dearth of New Testament references to such a battle other than the Revelation. This makes it necessary for them to insert this expected event into some of the accounts of events connected with the consummation, or at least interpreted as relating to the consummation. A prime example of this is in the Olivet discourse. Premillennialists consistently interpret the earlier portions as found in Matthew and Mark as eschatological, in spite of Jesus' statement that everything down to verse 34 would be fulfilled while the generation then living was still living.

But these verses say absolutely nothing about an Antichrist or the battle of Armageddon. If their interpretations of other texts are accurate, one would expect Christ to mention these in any major discourse on last things. The fact that He omits any reference to these things places the entire doctrine in a questionable status. The truth of the matter is that their interpretation of the battle of Armageddon, plus their interpretation of the Olivet discourse, are in error.

## The Revelation and Armageddon

Four passages in the Revelation are often interpreted as referring to a literal battle between armies of men just prior to the second coming of the Lord, although only one of them uses the designation Armageddon. This very important verse tells of the gathering of certain forces of whatever nature they be to Armageddon. The verse reads, "And he gathered them together into a place called in the Hebrew tongue Armageddon"

(Rev. 16:16). But who or what are to be gathered together at Armageddon. The verses that follow say absolutely nothing about great armies, or armies of any kind.

The context speaks of spiritual forces—not literal armies. The leaders are not men but spirits. John saw "three unclean spirits" emerge from the mouths of the dragon, the beast, and the false prophet (v. 13). These are said to be "the spirits of devils [demons], working miracles, which go forth unto the kings of the earth and the whole world, to gather them to the battle of that great day of God Almighty" (v. 14). Nothing is said of armies. God fights spiritual battles—not carnal battles: and this is the battle that involves Almighty God. Of course humans are involved in this battle, but even so, it is not to be fought with carnal weapons.

Those who teach a literal battle of Armageddon should reread Paul's listing of our armor and the kind of enemies we fight (Eph. 6:11-17). This battle of Armageddon is but the climax of the warfare that Christians have been fighting throughout the centuries.

One passage in chapter 14 is commonly applied to a literal Armageddon. Verses 14-18 speak of angels with sickles reaping the "clusters of the vine of the earth" (v. 18). Even literalists must accept this as a figure of speech. But who is to interpret this figure of speech? Do the clusters refer to human armies fighting, as most who teach a literal Armageddon hold? Or do the clusters have the same significance as the tares and wheat of Matthew 13:24-30; 36-43? Angels do the reaping in both cases. The logical conclusion is that both passages speak of the time of the consummation—not of physical warfare.

Then in verse 20 we read, "And the winepress was trodden without the city, and blood came out of the winepress, even unto the horse bridles, by the space of a thousand and six hundred furlongs." How anyone can interpret this literally is beyond my ken. Blood coagulates quickly when exposed to the air. It soon becomes hardened sufficiently that it will not flow. Horses could not move within a mass of such high viscosity. Add to this the fact that the ground, the clothing of the dead, and other materials present would soak up so much of the blood that it constitutes a physical impossibility for enough men to be killed to create a stream of the proportions given above (between 175 and 200 miles in length).

Even literalists must admit that the winepress is a figure of speech. They admit it does not refer to a press that is used to obtain the juice from grapes.

They must also admit that the "clusters of the vine" refer to people rather than grapes. Having admitted this much, the logical thing to do would be to admit that the blood is also a figure of speech. But this does not fit their preconceived ideas of the intent of this passage, hence they fall back on their literalism. But they cannot explain how a symbolic winepress, filled with symbolic grapes, can produce human blood that does not react like human blood normally reacts. The case they make is very, very weak.

Since only one of the passages in the Revelation which are said to refer to the battle of Armageddon mentions great armies, or small ones for that matter, literalists are hard put to establish the tremendous armies they envision participating in the battle. Scofield and many others do this by using obscure Old Testament references which have nothing to do with eschatological events. Some of these they admit have reference to current happenings of that day (see Scofield's note on Micah 1:6). Then, without adequate grounds for doing so, it is said that these events are to have a second fulfillment toward the end of time or the last days.

Others, however, find their base in the Revelation itself. Lindsey finds his answer in Revelation 9:16. In our study on the Revelation, it was shown that this chapter refers to the Moslem invasions, first by the Saracens and later by the Turks. He makes no effort to show how chapter 9 is related to chapters 14, 16, and 19. He simply lifts a few verses out of chapter 9 and superimposes them on these other chapters. His main verse reads, "And the number of the army of the horsemen were two hundred thousand" (Rev. 9:16). He contends that this army of two hundred million horsemen is from China and that it will destroy a third of the earth's population.[334]

Lindsey makes this apply to the total army, but the verse speaks of 200,000,000 horsemen. It says nothing of infantry and other combat units. It says nothing of the supportive men who care for the horses, drive the supply trains of food and ammunition, and sustain the fighting units in many ways. Let us estimate some of these units. An army of 200,000,000 horsemen might have four times as many infantrymen. This would make one billion fighting men. Then assuming that it takes five men back of the lines for each fighting man, we have an army that totals six billion men. The reader is asked to compare that figure with the present estimate of the world's population and to draw his own conclusions.

---

334 Lindsey, *op. cit.*, p. 82.

Lest some readers be unfamiliar with Lindsey's writings, I hasten to point out that Lindsey claims this will happen by 1988 or shortly thereafter. His words are, "If this is a correct deduction, then within forty years or so of 1948, all these things could take place."[335] He was discussing Matthew 24 at this point, but the things he expected to occur around 1988 include the battle of Armageddon. Only time can fully reveal whether Lindsey is a true or false prophet, but the population explosion in China will have to reach atomic proportions for some of his predictions to become reality.

The chapter in Revelation that speaks of armies and which is also generally recognized as referring to the battle of Armageddon is chapter 19. In verse 11 one called "Faithful and True" appears on a white horse. This can be none other than the glorified Christ. He is further identified as "KING OF KINGS AND LORD OF LORDS" (v. 16). An invitation to fowls to come and feast upon human flesh is given (vv. 17-18). Then we read, "And I saw the beast and the kings of the earth, and their armies, gathered together to make war against him that sat on the horse, and against his army" (Rev. 19:19).

The opponents in this battle are identified as "the beast" and his allies against "him that sat on the horse, and against his army." Scofield, Lindsey, and most Premillennialists contend that these armies will be besieging Jerusalem at this time. They say that the second coming of Christ "will deliver the Jewish remnant besieged by the Gentile world-powers" (Scofield's note on Rev. 19:17). But these verses say nothing like this.

Revelation 19:17-21 has nothing to say about Jerusalem being besieged. Jerusalem, or Israel for that matter, is not mentioned at all. These verses do not tell us where this battle is fought. We do know that Christ and His armies fight against the beast and his armies (v. 19). Now Christ has no army such as nations have. He never has had that kind of an army and He never will. Jesus testified before Pilate, "My kingdom is not of this world: if my kingdom were of this world, then would my servants fight, that I should not be delivered to the Jews: but now is my kingdom not from hence" (John 18:36).

But in Revelation 19:19 Christ is leading an armed force against the armies of the beast. This cannot be a literal battle fought with the usual weapons of war. Christ's army is nothing less than the Church. It is composed of all

---

335  *Ibid.*, p. 54.

born again Christians. Shall we who have been taught to love our enemies, and to turn the other cheek, suddenly become the takers of human life: and under the banner of Christ at that? Christ would no longer be Christ, and the Church would no longer be the Church, should such as is envisioned here by many become a reality.

Since the Church is fighting a spiritual warfare using spiritual weapons, this battle must be recognized as a spiritual battle. It is now in progress. It may well be in its closing phase. The conquest of Christ over the beast and the false prophet (chap. 19), and over the dragon (chap. 20), are parts of this great titanic struggle. When God destroys these evil forces, it will be through His divine power—not through the Church taking up carnal weapons by which they kill other men.

And the idea that certain unbelieving Jews, improperly called the remnant, will be converted at Christ's return is completely foreign to the Scripture. All unconverted people will receive the same kind of treatment when He returns. He will come in flaming fire taking vengeance on all unbelievers, Gentiles and Jews alike. Only believing Jews can be considered a part of "the remnant," and if they are believing Jews, then they are a part of the Church.

## Concluding Remarks

The importance of the battle of Armageddon to different schools of thought is a variable. Since Postmillennialists hold that the second coming of Christ is to be preceded by 1,000 years of peace, the teaching of such a battle must be firmly rejected as incompatible with the schedule of events as they see them. Premillennialists have made this such an important part of their teaching that their entire program would be seriously threatened were it to be taken out. Its importance to the Amillennial system is negligible. It can be included or excluded without serious implications to the system itself.

However, I have chosen to oppose the idea of a literal, bloody battle for reasons other than of protecting the system. My major basis for rejecting such a battle is that it reverses the role of the Church at the close of the age. I know some will say that the Church will not be directly involved, but at least one of the major texts used to support the teaching (Rev. 19:17-21) definitely involves both Christ and His army (the Church) in the struggle. But it is unthinkable that we who now love our enemies are to undergo a reversal of our natures and start killing our enemies. The only alternative that I have been able to accept is that the writer is using symbols to describe the spiritual warfare between right and wrong, good and evil.

In support of this view is the fact that problems are insuperable regarding the literal interpretation of Ezekiel 38-39 and Revelation 14:19-20. In the former case the battle is to be fought with bows and arrows, handstaves and spears. What kind of circumstances could lead to this type of regression is too much for my imagination. Similarly, the stream of blood mentioned in Revelation 14:20 is an impossibility apart from a miracle. I could believe literal streams of milk and honey would flow in Palestine some day more readily than I can accept a literal stream of blood such as the Revelator describes.

The battle of Armageddon apparently did not concern the early Church. I found no reference to it in my notes on the early Church writings, so I reviewed each index of the 38 volume sets and failed to find a single reference to this subject. Some of them who expected the Antichrist to come may have associated him with the battle of Armageddon, but if so, I have not been able to substantiate it.

CHAPTER 24

# THE MILLENNIUM

A variety of issues make the study of eschatology a complex matter. Some of these are the Jews and the Abrahamic covenant, the rapture of the Church, the two-phase second coming, the number of resurrections, the number of judgments, and renewal or dissolution; but the two major problems are the kingdom of God and the millennium. If these two questions can be settled, the other issues will fall into place. In Part One of this volume, it was shown that the kingdom of God was never intended to be an earthly reign of Christ. It was established at Christ's first advent, and the only future aspect to it is the heavenly aspect which will follow the general resurrection and general judgment. We now address the problem of a millennial reign.

The teaching of the three major schools of thought regarding the kingdom of God and the millennium follows by way of review. Postmillennialists hold that the kingdom was established at Christ's first advent. They believe that the gospel will eventually win most of the world to Christ. Following this, a long period of peace and prosperity is envisioned. Some say a change in carnivorous animals and the productivity of the soil will occur. Their millennium is not an earthly reign of Christ. Instead, it is the triumph of the gospel. After the millennium, the second coming of Christ will be followed by the general resurrection, general judgment, and dissolution of all the earth.

Premillennialists deny that the kingdom was established at the first advent. The kingdom is to be an earthly kingdom yet to be established. At Christ's glorious appearing, it is claimed, He will begin a reign in Jerusalem which will last for 1,000 years. The righteous are to be raised at that time or seven years before, depending on certain other interpretations. This reign will involve a mixture of resurrected beings and mortal men. It usually is said to involve a change in carnivorous animals and the productivity of the land. At the end of 1,000 years, the wicked will be raised and eternity will begin.

Amillennialists are in agreement with Postmillennialists regarding the establishment of the kingdom of God at the first advent. Both contend that it was. Both teach a single future resurrection of the dead followed by a general judgment. Dissolution is expected by most of both schools of thought. The single area of difference between Postmillennialists and Amillennialists is about the millennium. Amillennialists deny the 1,000 years of peace and prosperity of the land. Rather they agree with Premillennialists that things will be worst, rather than better, toward the end of time.

Amillennialists recognize that Revelation 20 does speak of a reign of 1,000 years, but since that book is largely a book of symbols, they interpret this period symbolically. The majority tend to follow Augustine in interpreting it as the total gospel era. Others, of which I am one, interpret this chapter as a reign of martyrs in paradise to indicate victory even while the Church flees to the wilderness. This second discussion is necessary for completeness.

The belief in a millennium was strongly entrenched among the Jews prior to Christ's first advent. It was largely wishful thinking, being based on analogy and noncanonical writings, rather than Scripture. Some of this was imported into the Church by one means or another.

## Errors of Premillennialism

### I. It Perpetuates a Jewish Fable

The millennium originated in Jewish thought. Such a period is not once mentioned in the Old Testament. It is largely based on an analogy drawn with the day of rest following the six days of creation, with each day of creation being a symbol of one thousand years. Similarly, the day of rest was said to represent 1,000 years of peace and prosperity. But an analogy proves nothing. The details of this reign are found in Jewish apocalyptic writings which are noncanonical. Therefore, it is not incorrect to speak of this doctrine as a Jewish fable that has from time to time received some recognition by Christian leaders.

Just as the Jews were mistaken in their expectations of the Messiah, so were they mistaken in their millennial expectations. And just as their erroneous concepts caused them to reject their Messiah, so they are now causing some to reject Him today. It is most unfortunate that many

Christian leaders are encouraging this rejection by teaching that all Jews who are living at the time of Christ's glorious appearing will be converted. No doubt these men are honest in their convictions, but they are working at cross-purposes to the true plan of God.

### 2. It Denies the True Nature of the Kingdom of God

Jesus held that His kingdom was not of this world (John 18:36). Paul also affirms that the kingdom of God is not mundane in nature: rather it is "righteousness, and peace, and joy in the Holy Ghost" (Rom. 14:17). In contrast to this, Premillennialism teaches a worldly kingdom with Christ as the chief civil ruler over all the nations of the world. The true nature of the kingdom is spiritual: Premillennialism makes it secular and worldly.

### 3. It Denies the Method of Establishing the Kingdom

Jesus said the "kingdom of God cometh not with observation" (Luke 17:20). Thayer says the Greek term translated observation means "in a visible manner." Since the kingdom is to come in a nonvisible manner, he adds that it will come in a manner such as cannot be observed or "watched with the eyes." To the contrary, Premillennialism says that the kingdom will come through His glorious appearing, when every eye shall see Him. It further contends that Christ will place His feet on the Mount of Olives (Zech. 14:4) in plain view of the immense armies they say will be attacking Jerusalem. The kingdom of God comes through spiritual processes—not through visible means.

Dispensationalists and many other Premillennialists further deny the true mode by which the kingdom will be established by saying it will be "established by power, not persuasion" (Scofield's note "e" on Zech. 12:1). Not only is this contrary to the nature of Christ, the Prince of Peace, but it is contrary to the nature of God's dealings with man. When God made man, He gave to him the power of choice. He holds men responsible for their choices, and He will punish them for wrong decisions.

### 4. It Denies the True Purpose of the Incarnation

Dispensationalists and many other Premillennialists claim that Jesus came to establish an earthly kingdom rather than to die for the sins of mankind. The very first prophecy concerning Christ which was made in connection with the fall of mankinds at the sacrificial death of Christ. All of the Old Testament animal sacrifices, and especially the lamb slain for the passover meal, all point to Christ's redemptive act. Isaiah 53 tells of Christ's sacrificial death some 700 years before it occurred.

Since Christ is deity, all who truly believe that to be true are obligated to believe that He accomplished the will of the Father by and through His first advent. If He came to die for our sins, He did not come to establish an earthly kingdom over which He was to rule. The two are incompatible. They are contradictory. He could not come to do both. That He did die for our sins is beyond dispute. Therefore He did not come to establish an earthly kingdom, as Premillennialists contend. He came to die for our sins which He did.

Of course, He did come to establish a kingdom; but it was not an earthly kingdom. He came to establish a kingdom that was compatible with His death on the cross. This was a spiritual kingdom. He did establish that kingdom as the New Testament testifies to over and over again. It is not erroneous to hold that He came to establish a kingdom, as well as to die on the cross, but it is a tremendous error to hold that He came to establish an earthly kingdom, a kind of kingdom that is incompatible with His redemptive sacrifice.

### 5. It Denies Jesus Established His Kingdom

In Part One of this volume, a large number of Scriptures were given which showed that the kingdom was established at the first advent. Jesus Himself said, "Verily I say unto you, That there be some of them that stand here, which shall not taste of death, till they have seen the kingdom of God come with power" ( Mark 9:1). Was Christ mistaken? Never! However, those who teach that the kingdom of God is yet future are guilty at this point. Thus Premillennialism reflects on the deity of Christ by implying that He was mistaken at this point.

It also reflects on Christ's deity by contending that He came to establish an earthly kingdom but was unable to do so because of the rejection by the Jews. However, Christ Himself testified that He could ask the Father for "twelve legions of angels" (72,000) and they would be sent to Him promptly by the Father. In other words, He had the resources available to have forced the Jews to accept His kingship. The reason He did not do this is that it was not part of the plan. That it was not part of the plan is testified to abundantly by Old Testament references to Christ's passion. Jesus testified to this Himself when He refused to call 72,000 angels to rescue Him. He said, "But how then shall the scriptures be fulfilled?" (Matt. 26:54). Jesus testifies here that He came to die for our sins—not to establish an earthly kingdom.

However, He did establish the kind of kingdom He came to establish—a spiritual kingdom which was compatible with His death on the cross. He established it in spite of the rejection of most of the Jews. Thank God, when we were translated out of the kingdom of darkness through our conversion, we were translated into the kingdom Jesus came to establish, and which He did establish, at His first advent.

It should be borne in mind that if Jesus did come to establish an earthly kingdom at His first advent, and He failed to do so because the Jews rejected Him, then we have no assurance that He will be able to do later that which He was unable to do the first time. I do not understand how God fearing men can support a doctrine that reflects on the deity of our Lord at this teaching does.

### 6. It Misinterprets Prophecies about the Throne of David

All admit that prophecies regarding the throne of David are to some degree figurative. No one expects the physical substances which composed the throne on which David sat to be reconstituted and that literal throne to again become a reality. It is generally accepted that the phrase "on the throne of David" refers to Christ and to the power and authority He is now exercising or which He will one day exercise. The question simmers down to the extent of the symbolism. I am thankful that we do not have to depend on our own imagination or mental processes for the answer. Through inspiration, God has given us the answer. Peter is God's spokesman, and Luke is the inspired writer who recorded it for posterity. The occasion is the day of Pentecost when the Holy Spirit was first imparted to men.

Peter's words are recorded in Acts 2. Peter discusses the relation of Jesus' resurrection to the prophecies of the Old Testament (Acts 2:25-31). In verse 30, Peter points out that David, being a prophet, foresaw that God would raise up Christ to sit on his throne. Biederwolf makes a great deal over the fact that the expression "raise up" may be a gloss,[336] however, he fails to discuss the fact that verses 31 and 32 definitely tie all of this in with the resurrection of Christ.

The phrase "by the right hand of God exalted" (v. 33) may also be translated "to the right hand of God exalted." The latter is to be preferred for it

---

336 Biederwolf, *op. cit.*, p. 407.

harmonizes with the quotation from the Psalms of Christ sitting at the right hand of the Father (vv. 34-35). This leaves little room for doubt that Christ is now sharing the throne with the Father. Verse 36 speaks of Christ thus being "made...both Lord and Christ." That all of this is a fulfillment of the prophecies regarding the throne of David should be apparent to any who permit the Bible to speak for itself.

Scofield uses a different method of evading the force of this passage. He argues that "the throne of David" cannot refer to the present rule of Christ over the Church. Back in Isaiah 9:6-7 we have a prophecy of the incarnation. The child which was to be born was given titles such as "The everlasting Father, the Prince of Peace." In verse 7 this child is to rule from "the throne of David." Scofield's note on verse 7 reads in part, "The 'throne of David' is a phrase as definite, historically, as 'throne of the Caesars,' and as little admits of 'spiritualizing.' "

However strongly Scofield may contend that the throne of David cannot be spiritualized, the inspired word does indicate that Christ is now reigning on the throne of David. If that be spiritualizing, it is the Bible that does it—not I. Then in an effort to cover up the fact that Christ is now on David's throne and that the Old Testament prophecies regarding the throne of David are now being fulfilled through the Church which is spiritual Israel, he attempts to say that Acts 2:25-32 points to a future fulfillment in a literal fashion. A reading of these verses rather indicates that Peter understood they were being fulfilled at that time, and, of course, would continue to be fulfilled throughout the gospel age.

### 7. It Reduces God's Everlasting Kingdom to a Millennium

Daniel prophesied that "in the days of these kings shall the God of heaven set up a kingdom, which shall never be destroyed,...and it shall stand forever" (Dan. 2:44). Only four kingdoms are mentioned, and these are most frequently recognized as the Babylonian, the Medo-Persian, the Grecian, and the Roman. Not one word is said about a later division of the Roman empire into ten major divisions. This is imported into this chapter from chapter seven. The application is made by which the ten toes (if he indeed had ten toes—Daniel doesn't say he did) are said to be identical with the ten horns of chapter 7.

In order to make the picture from Daniel fit in with their idea, Premillennialists have to envision a revived Roman empire, yet not really an empire, but a confederation of ten separate states. All of this is added material. Daniel only mentions four empires. Scofield contends that the necessary conditions for the fulfillment of the prophecy regarding God setting up an everlasting kingdom (note on Dan. 2:44) did not exist at Christ's first advent, and could not exist until after the dissolution of the Roman empire and its reestablishment. Scofield's efforts to make Daniel 2 refer to a revived Roman empire with ten divisions is an extreme case of eisegesis. Daniel 2 says not one word about ten kings. Of the four mentioned, the fourth then existed.

However, the point we are trying to make is that this kingdom they say will be set up at the return of Christ is, according to the schedule they insist upon, not an eternal kingdom as the text says. It is to last no more nor less than 1,000 years. By no stretch of the imagination can 1,000 years be made to mean forever. Daniel said very pointedly that the kingdom God would set up "in the days of these kings" would "stand forever." Therefore, the kingdom that Daniel prophesied in chapter 2 was not the so-called millennial kingdom of Premillennialism.

Then what was it? It was the kingdom Christ established at His first advent. It was established during the time that the four kings or kingdoms that Daniel mentioned were still in existence. The last of these kingdoms was the Roman kingdom, and it was exerting a tremendous influence over the Mediterranean area when Christ was born. Christ's kingdom is spiritual in nature through which He rules over those subjects who voluntarily accept His authority. It is not of this world, even as Christ stated. Its nature will not change following the resurrection and judgment. The major change will be that it will no longer operate in the worldly sphere. Its citizens will be in heaven forever and forever. We are already citizens of that kingdom (Eph. 2:19). There will be no change of citizenship when we arrive in heaven. That has been our home all the time, anyway.

But the millennial kingdom envisioned by Premillennialists is not identical to the eternal kingdom. The millennial kingdom, according to most Premillennialists, will contain people who have not voluntarily submitted to God. They will submit under duress. These and possibly others are expected to rebel against God at the end of the millennial reign. This, they say, will result in another terrible battle similar to the battle of Armageddon which they teach. So the eternal kingdom is different from the millennial kingdom. Therefore, according to the teaching of Premillennialists, the eternal kingdom will be established at the end of the millennium, rather than at the beginning.

But how can it be "in the days of these kings" when there are to be no kingdoms other than the millennial kingdom during the one thousand year reign, according to their teaching? The inconsistency of their interpretation should be evident to all. The only possible interpretation of Daniel 2:44 is that the kingdom of God was established in the days of the four kingdoms mentioned. It came with Christ's first advent during the days of the fourth kingdom, the Roman empire.

### 8. It Exalts the Old Testament Above the New Testament

That Premillennialism depends too much on the Old Testament is recognized by most. But this is the reverse of what is proper and correct. The New Testament is a fuller, more complete revelation than the Old. The New explains the Old. The Old is full of types and shadows (Heb. 8:5), whereas the New contains the realities. If Old Testament prophecies are explained in the New Testament, the explanation given in the New Testament takes precedence over any interpretation one might consider or give to the Old Testament record. But Premillennialists often refuse to accept New Testament interpretations. They continue to insist that their interpretation of Old Testament prophecy is correct, even when the New Testament says otherwise.

The following are but a few of the many examples which could be cited in this connection. Amos prophesied that at some future time the "tabernacle of David" would be raised up (Amos 9:11-12). James clearly interprets this as applying to the Gentile converts which were accepting Christ through the labors of Paul and others (Acts 15:13-18). But Premillennialists refuse to accept this plain statement by James, placed in the Bible by inspiration. By one means or another, it is claimed that it applies to a future age.

Dispensationalists and many other Premillennialists refuse to accept the New Testament teaching that the Abrahamic covenant has its fulfillment in Christ, rather than through those who are racial descendents of Abraham and Jacob. Paul contends, "Now to Abraham and his seed were the promises made. He saith not, And to seeds, as of many; but as of one, And to thy seed, which is Christ" (Gal. 3:16). According to this inspired statement, individual descendents of Abraham have no promise based solely on their descent from Abraham. The promise is to Christ. Thus, only as one believes into Christ does the promise take him in. Unbelieving Jews have no promise.

Premillennialists are likely to be literalists, but the Bible itself, and the New Testament in particular, spiritualizes the Abrahamic covenant. Paul argues that there is no longer "Jew nor Greek,...And if ye be Christ's, then are ye Abraham's seed, and heirs according to the promise" (Gal. 3:28-29). Those who attempt to maintain the Old Testament distinction between Jews and Gentiles do so at the expense of denying or twisting the intent of New Testament inspiration. A Gentile Christian is just as much a descendent of Abraham, insofar as God is concerned, as those who are genetically descended from Abraham.

This leads to the further conclusion that the Church is the Israel of the New Testament. Most Premillennialists deny this. One is a true Jew by the circumcision of the heart—not by genetic descent or physical circumcision (Rom. 2:28-29). Paul argued further that "they are not all Israel [i.e., part of the true N T Israel], which are of Israel" (i.e., lineal descendants of Jacob, Rom. 9:6). In the next verse he points out that not all of Abraham's descendents participated in the promise, but Isaac only. Elsewhere Paul writes, "Now we brethren [i.e., believers in Christ], as Isaac was, are the children of promise" (Gal. 4:28). It follows that Christians of all races constitute the true Israel of God.

Similarly, Peter contends that what happened on the day of Pentecost was the fulfillment of a prophecy from Joel. Peter quoted Joel 2:28-31 and part of verse 32, stating very clearly that what was occurring was what Joel had prophesied would happen. His words are, "But this is that which was spoken by the prophet Joel." From this unequivocal statement, he proceeded to quote the verses from Joel. Now if this was indeed that, as Peter declared, then Joel's prophecy was fulfilled at that time. But Premillennialists tend to ignore this, or attempt to twist its meaning. Scofield admits a partial fulfillment during the gospel age, but he contends that "the greater fulfillment awaits the 'last days' as applied to Israel" (note on Joel 2:28).

### 9. It Attacks Some of Christ's Redemptive Work

One of the notable achievements of Christ's redemptive work was to break down the middle wall of partition between the Jews and Gentiles (Eph. 2:14). Judaistic Premillennialists attempt to prove that this wall will again be raised. By perpetuating the distinction between Jews and Gentiles, they deny this accomplishment of Christ either completely or as being temporary in nature. It is well nigh incredible that Christians do this, but the facts cannot be denied.

The work of Christ also abolished the law. In order for Christ to become our high priest, the Mosaic law had to be set aside. The main reason for this is that the law confined this office to descendents of Levi and Aaron, whereas Christ was from Judah (Heb. 7:11-14). A restoration of the law of Moses and its animal sacrifices, as many Premillennialists teach, is another very serious attack on the redemptive work of Christ, and His continuing high priesthood.

### 10. It Makes the New Covenant Future with the Jews

The eternal priesthood of Christ and our salvation are closely related to the new covenant. Dispensationalists and many other Premillennialists deny that Christ established the new covenant of Jeremiah 31 at His first advent. But the law of Moses was set aside in order for Christ to become our high priest. And the law of Moses is the heart of the old covenant. This means that the old covenant was abolished. Then either the new covenant was established at Christ's first advent, or we Christians are operating without a covenant.

Tan, Scofield, Walvoord and many others place the new covenant in the future, but the Hebrew writer places it as being operative at the time that book was written. In chapter 8 we find a lengthy quotation from Jeremiah 31 in which a new covenant was promised. In chapter 9 certain ordinances of the "first covenant" are discussed. These were "a figure for the time then present" (i.e., while the temple continued to stand and the priests functioned therein, v. 9). Following some discussion of Christ's sacrifice, he adds, "And for this cause he is the mediator of the new testament" (Gr. *diatheke*, v. 16). The present tense "he is the mediator of the new covenant" indicates the new covenant was presently operative. It reads "is" (Gr. *estin*), the mediator—not "shall become the mediator."

In most instances where the Greek *diatheke* is used it should be translated "covenant," but in verses 16-22 the idea of a last will or testament is the meaning. In these verses the inspired writer contends that the new covenant, the same one found in chapter 8 and in Jeremiah 31, became operative with the death of Christ the testator. In Hebrews 10:9 we read, "He taketh away the first, that he may establish the second." That He did establish the second is verified in verse 10 which indicates its present effectiveness by sanctifying us through the redemptive work of Jesus Christ. And that he is still referring to the covenant of Jeremiah 31 is proved by a quotation from verse 33 of that chapter (Heb. 10:16).

It is considered necessary to relate chapter 10 of the Hebrew epistle with chapter 8 of that letter, because Dispensationalists usually confine their discussion to chapter 8. For example, Tan states, "The context of Hebrews 8 does not contain any statement affirming that Jeremiah 31 has been (spiritually) fulfilled."[337] This statement is inaccurate. The context of chapter 8 includes chapters 9 and 10. The writer continues his discussion of the new covenant in these chapters, and does affirm that the new covenant is now operative through the sanctifying grace of God to believers.

Of course, Tan and others claim that Romans 11:27-28 places the fulfillment of the new covenant in the future, but I have proved that this is not true. The passage from Romans is controversial at the best, and since Hebrews 8-9-10 place the operation of the Jeremiah covenant in the present tense, the Romans passage must be interpreted in harmony with the very plain statements of the Hebrews epistle.

### 11. It Reflects on the Importance of the Church

Dispensationalists contend that the Church is an after-thought of God. They say that no Old Testament prophecy foretold of the Church, and that God instituted it because Christ was unable to establish an earthly kingdom during His first advent. This makes the Church a substitute for what God really wanted. Other Premillennialists may not reflect on the Church quite to this degree, but there is a tendency to exalt the millennium age above the Church age. To show that the Old Testament does speak of the Church, two passages which have been discussed in this chapter are again mentioned.

Chapters 8-9-10 of the Hebrews epistle definitely state that the new covenant of Jeremiah 31 was functioning at the time that letter was written. It was Christian believers who were receiving the sanctifying grace made possible by the redemptive work of Jesus Christ. This does indeed speak of the Church. Therefore, when Jeremiah prophesied of the new covenant, he was prophesying of the Church. The prophecy of Amos regarding the raising up of the tabernacle of David (Amos 9:11) does refer to the activity of the Church according to the New Testament (Acts 15:13-17).

In the New Testament, the fact that Jesus died for the Church (Acts 20:28;

---

337 Tan, *op. cit.*, p. 196.

Eph. 5:25-27) is some indication of its importance to God and Christ. Christ died for no other institution. For this reason no other institution can have the meaning to God that the Church does. But all Premillennialism causes the Church to stand in the shadow of the so-called millennium. This is not the way it should be. Any doctrine that reflects on the Church is reflecting on Christ's prized possession—His bride.

### 12. It Relies Unduly on a Single Obscure Passage

In this connection there are two types of Premillennialists. Dispensationalists are representative of one group. These make the Abrahamic covenant, and other Old Testament prophecies, the main foundation for their doctrine; and they rely on Revelation 20 for New Testament support for their teaching. The other group makes Revelation 20 the major support for its doctrine, but relies heavily on Old Testament prophecies to support its position. I have read many books from both viewpoints, and I find that both groups depend a great deal on this single chapter in the Revelation.

But why has Revelation 20 been classified as obscure? This is a legitimate question which requires an adequate answer. First of all, it is written in apocalyptic style which all admit involves many figures of speech. Some of these figures are interpreted; others are not. No single hermeneutic exists for this book. Dispensationalists and many other Premillennialists consider chapters 2-3 as symbolic. I consider them as having no significance beyond the matters stated in the letters to the seven churches. On the other hand, I consider Revelation 20:1-10 as largely symbolic, whereas Premillennialists generally consider it largely literal.

Since it is impossible to prove or disprove either position, it is fitting that the passage be considered obscure. Any doctrine that depends a great deal on an obscure passage is suspect, for our theology should be established on clear passages. After this has been done, if seeming conflict exists between the plain passages and the obscure passages, the obscure passages should be interpreted in harmony with the plain passages. Premillennialism has reversed this principle of hermeneutics.

But there are other reasons for considering this passage obscure. First of all, it is impossible to ascertain with absolute certainty whether Revelation 20 is a continuation of chapter 19, or resumptive, or an entirely new period, or a summing up of all the previous visions. Advocates of all of these positions could be quoted. Until this matter is settled, any interpretation given the passage lacks sufficient support to justify building a doctrine on it. Why this is true will become evident in the discussion that follows.

Just when do the events of Revelation 20:1-6 occur? On the assumption that Revelation 20 is a continuation of Revelation 19, most Premillennialists say the events of Revelation 20:1-6 occur after the battle of Armageddon (Rev. 19:17-19). But why was not the dragon involved in that battle? If chapter 19 is accepted as final on that battle, the dragon was sidelined for some reason; for only the beast and false prophet are engaged in that battle, unless chapter 20 depicts the same struggle. Because it is illogical that the dragon not be in the final battle, the claim that chapter 20 describes things after that battle is subject to serious questioning.

E. D. Allen concludes that chapter 20 is a "summing up of what has already been revealed in former visions."[338] By this means he says the gathering of armies (Rev. 20:8) is before the battle of Armageddon, rather than after it. Albertus Pieters, along with many others, believes chapter 20 is resumptive or else a new series. He holds, as I do, that the thing that is bound in chapter 20 is paganism. He quotes extensively from a commentary by Dr. S. Greijdanus in support of this position.[339]

Strong support for chapter 20 being resumptive is evident when the Premillennial interpretation of the latter chapters of Ezekiel is compared to their interpretation of Revelation 20. They interpret Ezekiel 38-39 as foretelling of a final physical struggle often called the battle of Armageddon. The chapters that follow are said to speak of the millennium which they say will follow this terrible battle.

Premillennialists usually interpret Revelation 19:17-21 as referring to this physical battle of Armageddon, although the term is not used except in Revelation 16:16. On the assumption that chapter 20 is a continuation of chapter 19, chronologically, they place the millennium as following the battle of Armageddon. Thus far, their interpretation of the latter chapters of Ezekiel harmonizes with their interpretation of Revelation 19-20. But they overlook one very important aspect of these prophecies.

I refer to the fact that the Revelator makes no mention of the Gog-Magog forces in the battle of chapter 19, but he does make them the key forces in the battle following the millennium. This is not in accord with their

---

338 E. D. Allen, *Armageddon (Studies in the Revelation of St. John)*, pp. 89-90.
339 Pieters, *op. cit.*, pp. 305-309.

interpretation of Ezekiel 38-39 in which the Gog-Magog forces are destroyed in the battle prior to the millennium. If the literal interpretation of these battles is insisted upon, no method of harmonizing these two accounts is available. But when these battles are considered as spiritual battles, instead of physical confrontations, and when chapter 20 is interpreted as resumptive, a beautiful harmony prevails. According to this approach, the battles of Ezekiel 38-39, Revelation 19:17-21, and Revelation 20:7-9 all refer to aspects of the eternal battle between truth and error and right and wrong.

Also, as Boettner points out,[340] Revelation 20 speaks of two millenniums. The one in verses 4-6 is a millennial reign of martyrs (disembodied spirits—not resurrected beings) which is in paradise. These martyrs are souls in a disembodied state. The millennium of verses 1-3 refers to a time when nations exist as such here on earth. But Premillennialism generally claims that during the millennium they envision, all government will be under the immediate control of Christ, and nations as we now have them will not exist. It is not stated that these two millenniums run concurrently. This is added reason for calling this passage obscure.

Although Premillennialists claim that this passage speaks very plainly of two physical resurrections, one of the righteous and a later one of the wicked, the fact of the matter is that this is as obscure as the other details of this prophecy. It should be noted that those who "lived and reigned with Christ a thousand years" (Rev. 20:4) is limited to martyrs who had been beheaded. This is not referring to a resurrection of all the righteous dead, nor is any mention made of the righteous living who are to be changed into immortal beings at the second coming. This reign is confined to a special few.

And these are "souls," not men with bodies. I am aware that an effort to prove that souls (from the Greek *psuche*) may mean people with bodies, but this argument is not valid. It is one thing to say, "And we were in all in the ship two hundred threescore and sixteen souls" (Acts 27:37), and to say, "I saw the souls of them that were beheaded for the witness of Jesus" (Rev. 20:4). These were disembodied spirits, just as those were in Revelation 6:9.

And just who are the "rest of the dead" (Rev. 20:5)? The group that reigned with Christ, according to verse 4, is limited to persons who "were beheaded for the witness of Jesus and for the word of God, and which had not worshipped the beast, neither his image, neither had received his

---

340 Boettner, *op. cit.*, p. 66.

mark upon their foreheads, or in their hands" (v. 4). Any effort to enlarge this group to include all the righteous must go beyond the limitations the inspired writer gives. If expositors are going to be literalists, then let's be literalists. This does not refer to a physical or bodily resurrection of all the righteous.

Taken literally, the "rest of the dead" would include martyrs by stoning, as in the case of Stephen, and those burned at the stake. It would include all righteous people who died natural deaths. Any effort to make the term apply to all the wicked and to them alone, requires some spiritualizing. Thus literalists violate their own rules.

The problem of the "first resurrection" (v. 5) is further complicated by the fact that it can refer to the spiritual resurrection which comes through conversion. John's terms almost demand some refinement or symbolic explanation. This being the case, there should be no reason for Premillennialists to object to our holding the first resurrection to be the resurrection from a dead state in sin to a living state in Christ. Many expositors understand it that way.

Now that it has been shown how obscure this passage is, a list of reasons why Premillennialists should avoid using it as prime source material in defending their position should be helpful:

1. It is found in a book containing many, many symbols.

2. The style of the book is apocalyptic rather than plain statements.

3. It is impossible to prove what time sequence is involved as one moves from chapter 19 to chapter 20.

4. The 1,000 years reign is not an earthly reign, but a heavenly one.

5. The 1,000 years reign is of disembodied spirits—not of resurrected beings.

6. That reign is confined to martyrs who were slain by decapitation.

7. The 1,000 year reign occurs while nations still exist, rather than when all government is supposed to stem from Jerusalem.

8. The millennium of verses 1-3 is not identical to the one in verses 4-6 and it cannot be proved from the text that they cover the same period of time.

9. The "rest of the dead" (v. 5) must include all infants and righteous people who were not decapitated, rather than just wicked people only.

10. The "first resurrection" in point of time must come before one's physical resurrection if he is to participate in the bodily resurrection of the righteous. Otherwise he will have a resurrection of damnation.

11. The "first resurrection" makes one "blessed and holy" (v. 6). This reinforces the idea that the first resurrection is a spiritual resurrection from a dead state of sin to a live state in Christ.

12. It brings a contradiction between Ezekiel and the Revelation over when the Gog-Magog forces are conquered.

Dispensationalists and other Premillennialists teach a number of events related to the second coming that are not stated in the Revelation, and especially in chapters 19-20 where you would expect to find them if their teaching is correct. A few are given below.

1. The Revelation says nothing of the Jews returning to Palestine.

2. The Revelation says nothing of Jerusalem becoming the capital of the world.

3. The Revelation says nothing of an earthly throne at Jerusalem.

4. The Revelation says nothing about converted Jews doing extensive evangelistic work during the reign of Antichrist.

5. The Revelation says nothing of increased longevity of life.

6. The Revelation says nothing of carnivorous animals becoming docile nonmeat-eaters.

7. The Revelation says nothing of a restoration of the law of Moses.

8. The Revelation says nothing of animal sacrifices being reinstituted.

9. The Revelation says nothing of a generation of Jews being converted at Christ's glorious appearing.

10. The Revelation says nothing of nations ceasing to exist.

11. The Revelation says nothing of increased productivity of the earth.

12. The Revelation says nothing of an earthly reign by anybody.

If most of the Revelation does tell of the future reign of Antichrist and the millennium, as Dispensationalists and others claim, it is strange indeed that so many of their claims for that period are not even mentioned in the

Revelation. These omissions constitute another strong reason for Premillennialists to depend less on the Revelation and chapter 20 in particular.

## Errors of Postmillennialism

Although this writer contends that Postmillennialism is not correct in its teachings, its errors are less offensive than those of Premillennialism and Dispensationalism. Therefore, partly to conserve space, the discussion of these errors is omitted.

## Affirmations Regarding the Millennium

Two different millenniums are taught in Revelation 20. The first refers to the binding of the dragon, who is appropriately termed Devil and Satan. These terms mean adversary (Satan) or opposer, and deceiver, accuser, or slanderer (Devil). These terms are appropriate to paganism which was the chief opposer and accuser of Christians during the first Christian centuries. I hold that Revelation 20:1-3 refers to the binding of paganism as a persecuting power, and also as a deceiving power. It is true that the nominal church which ruled during the middle ages had many pagan practices and teachings, but it was all done in the name of Christianity.

The millennium of Revelation 20:4-6 is about a reign of disembodied martyrs whose bodies lay in graves here on earth. Although separate from the first millennium, and of a different nature, it is assumed they cover a similar period of time, not necessarily identical as to beginning and ending dates, but still very closely related. Thus the one in Revelation 20:1-3 refers to what happens on earth, whereas the one in Revelation 20:4-6 refers to things that will occur in heaven or paradise.

The beginning date for the first millennium (Rev. 20:1-3) is during the time of Constantine when Christianity superseded paganism as the state religion, or when paganism ceased to seriously oppress the Church. The ending date was when paganism again began to deceive the people as it has since the time of the French Revolution, or it is yet future when the true Christian will again find himself persecuted physically by pagans. This is already occurring in Communist countries, so the end may have come already.

The beginning date for the second millennium (Rev. 20:4-6) is set during the age of martyrs, and ended with the cessation of killing people because of the religious beliefs. This is based mainly on the belief that the martyrs of Revelation 6 and of Revelation 20 are the same. In Revelation 6:10, they asked how long they would go unavenged. They were told to "rest yet for a little season, until their fellowservants also and their brethren, that should be killed as they were, should be fulfilled" (Rev. 6:10). If this has been fulfilled already, then the period of their reign, as emphasized in the Revelation, has ended. This should not be taken to mean they have ceased to reign in other senses. It is recognized that Revelation 6:10 could refer to a future time of persecution. If so, the reign continues in paradise.

Thus, no earthly reign is involved. While it is true that the true Christians reign here upon earth through the power of God, it is also true that Revelation 20 says nothing about this. The Devil (paganism) is bound for 1,000 years (Rev. 20:1-3), and the disembodied souls of certain martyrs reign for 1,000 years in paradise or heaven. They are with Christ now—not shall be with Him upon earth at some future time.

When all of the Bible is properly understood, it will be found that there is no time for a millennial reign on earth; there will be no earth for the reign to exist upon; and there is no need for such a reign. It is a strange figment of the imagination that has been fostered on an unsuspecting group of Christians.

## Concluding Remarks

Although the amount of millennialism which existed in the early Church has been discussed already, this chapter would not be complete without some word about this matter. The one writer known to be of the first Christian century was Clement of Rome. In chapters XI and XII of his first letter to the Corinthians, he deals with the resurrection, but he gives no hint of a millennium or several resurrections and judgments. He is judged to be Amillennial in his teaching.

Barnabas was written near the end of the first century or very early in the second century. He was not a Premillennialist. His millennialism must be classed as Postmillennialism for no resurrection or judgment is indicated by him prior to the millennium which he based on the familiar analogy of the days of creation and the day of rest, each depicting 1,000 years.[341] Ignatius, who wrote very soon after the turn of the century gives no evidence of millennial views.

Three writers appeared about the middle of the second Christian century. These are Polycarp, Papias, and Justin Martyr. Polycarp gives no evidence of

---

341 Barnabas, *op. cit.,* p. 146.

millennialistic views. Justin Martyr was a Postmillennialist.[342] He did two things that many Premillennialists of today refuse to do or do very grudgingly. Both are based on his statement, "I signified to you that many who belong to the pure and pious faith and are true Christians, think otherwise" about a millennium.[343] First, he said that many true Christians of his day were not millennialists. Many Premillennialists of today deny this. Second, he accepted these Amillennialists as true Christians in spite of their belief, something many Premillennialists find it difficult to do today.

The third man who wrote around A.D. 150 was Papias. He was a Premillennialist. He made statements which were quite erroneous which Eusebius refuted many years later, but not in time to keep Irenaeus from being led astray.[344] Only a few fragments remain of his writings, but unfortunately those were the ones that spelled out his millennial beliefs. He cited apocryphal writings as gospel truth. It is impossible to judge his motives in doing this or if some one deceived him.

Five writers of note appear during the last half of the second century. The *Shepherd* (or *Pastor*) *of Hermas* is dated about A. D. 160. It is claimed by some that he is a millennialist, but I have studied this work quite closely, and the nearest he comes to it is mentioning his belief in a coming time of tribulation.[345] But this is inadequate to place him in the ranks of Premillennialists. Although most Amillennialists do not teach a special time of tribulation toward the end of time, some do; and it is just as compatible with Amillennialism as it is with Premillennialism.

Three writers gave no indication of a belief in a millennium. These are Tatian, Athenagoras, and Clement of Alexandria. The last began writing during the second century, but continued over into the third Christian century. The fifth writer, Irenaeus, was a Premillennialist. He accepted the writings of Papias as authoritative. No doubt this influenced him greatly. Irenaeus must be considered the victim of a misplaced faith. Possibly he would have taught differently had he known all the facts of the case.

---

342  Justin Martyr, *op. cit.*, pp. 239-240.
343  *Ibid.*, p. 239.
344  Eusebius, Series II of *Nicene and Post-Nicene Fathers*, vol. I, pp. 170-173, 308-309.
345  Hermas, *Shepherd of Hernias, Ante-Nicene Fathers*, vol. II, pp. 17-18.

Several writers of the first half of the third Christian century must be considered. Of these, Tertullian is the most controversial. He has been quoted already as spiritualizing the peace and absence of war in Isaiah 2:2-4. The reign of the future king (Isa. 9:6-9) was also identified with the gospel age. But the wolf and the lamb (Isa. 11:1-12) was spiritualized in one place and literalized in another. This seemed to indicate a change in belief. No other reason can be found. The question is which position did he hold first, and why did he change?

It is a well-known fact that Tertullian became a Montanist in his later years. In fact, he became a leader of this heretical body. Since it is impossible to date all of his writings, it is not possible to prove when certain portions were written. But since Montanists taught a millennium, his change from Amillennialism to millennialism must have been related to this defection. Even so, I found but one place where he definitely referred to a millennium, 346 and it is insufficient to classify him as a Premillennialist.

Other writers of the period A.D. 200-250 were Minucius Felix, Origen, Hippolytus, Commodianus (a millennialist) 347 and Hippolytus who is often claimed by Premillennialists, although he never declares himself to believe in such a period of time. On the contrary, his belief in an Antichrist and a time of great tribulation cannot be reconciled with Postmillennialism, and his belief in but one bodily resurrection followed by a general judgment cannot be harmonized with Premillennialism's multiplicity of resurrections and judgments. He was an Amillennialist.

No millennial writers were found between A.D. 250-300. The main writers of this period besides some who began writing in the first half of the century were Novatian and Methodius.

Of the great host of writers who wrote during the fourth Christian century, only two were found to be millennialists. These are Lactantius[346] and Victorinus.[347] The fact that Victorinus taught that the first resurrection of Revelation 20 was from sin, rather than a bodily resurrection,[348] indicates that he was at odds with present day Premillennialism.

---

346 Lactantius, *op. cit.*, vol. IV, pp. 218, 254.
347 Victorinus, *Ante-Nicene Fathers*, vol. VII, pp. 358-359.
348 *Ibid.*

Although every effort has been made to fairly review the teachings of the early Church writers, it should not be assumed that this is our basis for holding the Amillennial position. The only proper basis for maintaining any doctrine is that of its agreement with the New Testament writings. This, of course, includes the analogy of faith. This means, very simply, that a single passage of Scripture, which seems to contradict an established doctrine of the Bible, must be interpreted in harmony with the established doctrine.

On this basis, Revelation 20, which is the only chapter in the Bible that says anything of 1,000 years of some kind of reigning, must be interpreted in such a way as to avoid contradicting the fully established concepts that the Church fulfills the promises made to Abraham, and that the kingdom of God was established at Christ's first advent.

CHAPTER 25

# THE RESURRECTION OR RESURRECTIONS

The future resurrection of the body is one of the Bible doctrines that has abundant testimony to support it, especially the resurrection of righteous people. Less is said about the resurrection of the wicked, but even so, this is definitely taught in the New Testament and by no less authority than Jesus Christ Himself. In spite of these numerous references to the resurrection of the dead, considerable controversy exists regarding this doctrine, especially regarding whether there shall be one final, general resurrection, or if there be a plurality of resurrections.

The problem is complicated by the fact that the New Testament does not clearly distinguish between restorations to physical life, such as Lazarus being raised from the dead, and the resurrection that imparts an immortal body to the one raised. Lazarus, and others who were resuscitated to physical life, died again at a later date. But Jesus was raised completely victorious over death, never to die again. Death no longer had dominion over Him. It is to this latter kind of resurrection that we now address ourselves.

Several Greek words must be considered in this study, although only two families of words are involved. These are *histemi* and *egeiro*. These words are not used exclusively of a resurrection from the dead. This makes for some difficulty, but it is not insuperable. Of these Greek terms, the one most frequently translated "resurrection" is *anastasis*. Literally, it means to stand again. It is used of the resurrection of Christ nine times, and 27 times of the future resurrection of the dead. Its uses otherwise are quite limited. Jesus said, "I am the resurrection [*anastasis*] and the life." Luke used it once of the vicissitudes of life (Luke 2:34), and it is used once in the Hebrew epistle of people being restored to physical life or resuscitated (Heb. 11:35). Then in Revelation 20 it is used twice of what is called "the first resurrection." Different schools of thought explain this in different ways.

Closely related to *anastasis* is *exanastasis*. It is used but once (Phil. 3:11), and it refers to the future resurrection of the dead. The verb from which the above words are derived is *histemi*. It is never translated "resurrection" in the KJ V, and it is not used of the future resurrection except in an indirect manner. For example Jude says that God "is able to keep you from falling, and to present (*histemi*) you faultless before the presence of his glory with exceeding joy" (Jude 24). This presentation involves a resurrection, but it is indirect in its expression.

The Greek term *egeiro* means to raise in almost any sense. To rise from sleep, from a chair, to incite or stir up, and even of causing a building to rise. Included in the meaning is to raise one from the dead. When *egeiro* is used in this latter sense, additional words are added so that it is known to mean a resurrection from a state of being dead to a state of being alive. Whether it refers to a resuscitation back to physical life or to that resurrection which changes us to beings with immortal bodies can be determined only from the context. The kindred term *egersis* is used but once. It is not clear whether this was a resuscitation or if they received immortal bodies (Matt. 27:53). Whatever happened, it is too obscure to build a doctrine on it.

Not only does the Bible speak of the physical dead being restored to physical life, and of the dead being raised with immortal bodies, but it tells of persons being resurrected from a dead state in sin to a live state in Christ. Several passages point to the fact that those who live in sin are dead (Eph. 2:1; Col. 2:13; I Tim. 5:6). Christians have "passed from death unto life" (I John 3:14). This involves a resurrection, even though the terms used for bodily resurrections are not used. Jesus referred to this spiritual change or resurrection when He said that those dead in sin would hear His voice, and those who heard or responded favorably would live (John 5:24-25).

However, we do find *egeiro* in Ephesians 2, where it is combined with the preposition *sun* which means "with." In verse 5 it states that we are quickened together (Gr. made alive together), then in verse 6 he has "raised us up together" (Gr. *sun* plus an aorist form of *egeiro*.) So this is indeed a resurrection from spiritual death to spiritual life. It is not claimed that this proves the first resurrection of Revelation 20 is a spiritual resurrection, but it cannot be denied that the spiritual resurrection is first in time; for if one is not spiritually resurrected while yet living, he cannot reign anywhere any time with Christ.

# THE RESURRECTION OR RESURRECTIONS

In Jesus' day, the Sadducees denied a future resurrection. This is true of some today, but the issue confronting us is how many resurrections are taught in the Bible. In this connection it is interesting to note that the future resurrection is always referred to in the singular—never in the plural. I am aware that an effort is made to justify a plurality of resurrections from such passages as I Corinthians 15, but if Paul and the other writers were thinking in terms of more than one general resurrection of all people, it is very strange that they never expressed this through the use of the plural.

## Jesus Taught But One General Resurrection

One of the ways Jesus taught a single general resurrection was by the use of the definite article in connection with the resurrection. "The resurrection" is more definite and limiting than "a resurrection." Jesus used this form in answering the question put to Him by the Sadducees. Not even the words "of the dead" are added in most places. All three Synoptic writers express it this way. In Matthew it reads, "Therefore in the resurrection whose wife shall she be of the seven?" (Matt. 22:28). Jesus explains some things in connection with "the resurrection" in verse 30.

If the Dispensational teaching is true, Jesus failed to make this plain. Why didn't Jesus say that some of the husbands might be resurrected at the rapture, others at the beginning of the millennium, and still others at the end of the millennium—that if the woman was wicked she would not be resurrected until long after some of her husbands were resurrected? But Jesus did not say there would be these several resurrections. The question was asked in accordance with the idea of a single resurrection, by people who denied any resurrection. Jesus answered them using the same words. In *the* resurrection (singular) there would be no marriage.

Jesus taught two resurrections all right, but only one was a bodily resurrection. The first was spiritual in nature and referred to the transformation that takes place when one is born again. He exclaimed, "The hour is coming and now is, when the dead [those spiritually dead in trespasses and in sins] "shall hear the voice of the Son of God: and they that hear shall live" (John 5:25). He then tells of the future resurrection of the bodies of all men.

Marvel not at this: for the hour is coming, in which all that are in the graves shall hear his voice, And shall come forth; they that have done good, unto the resurrection of life; and they that have done evil, unto the resurrection of damnation (John 5:28-29).

Scofield, and many others, ignore the spiritual resurrection mentioned in verse 25, and concentrate on trying to prove two bodily resurrections in verses 29-30. The text, however, speaks of two kinds of resurrection which shall be given, rather than two resurrections which occur at different times. The omission of the definite article in the Greek text confirms this. Some will come forth to "a life kind of resurrection," and those who have done wickedly will come forth to "a damnation kind of resurrection." But the time of their coming forth is at that time when Christ speaks to the dead to come forth. And when He so speaks, *all* the dead will come forth immediately in response to that clarion call.

Others who teach two bodily resurrections deal more fairly with these verses. In reference to Daniel 12:2 and John 5:28-29, Tan admits that these "two texts of Scripture place the resurrections of saints and sinners side by side." He then adds, "However, when the parallel passage in Revelation 20 is consulted, it becomes apparent that when Christ comes, the righteous shall be resurrected and shall reign with Christ a thousand years (v. 4), whereas 'the rest of the dead live not again until the thousand years were finished' (v. 5)."[349] Now Tan is of that school which depends on the Abrahamic covenant and other Old Testament passages for their foundation, but in the New Testament shows dependence on an obscure passage in the Revelation by taking the obscure passage as a basis for setting aside the plain words of Jesus Himself.

And by what grounds does Tan declare that John 5:28-29 is parallel to Revelation 20:4-5? Why did not he include John 5:25 where Jesus discusses the first resurrection? If these two passages are to be considered parallels, John 5:25 must be included. In that verse Jesus declares that He has come to resurrect from spiritual death those who are spiritually dead. This is the first resurrection. Thus the first resurrection of Revelation 20:5, if it is interpreted in conformity with John 5:25-29, would be a spiritual resurrection, rather than a bodily resurrection.

Jesus did speak of "the resurrection of the just" (Luke 14:14), but it will take a great deal more than this to prove that the wicked are not resurrected at the same time. All that can be said for this is that it would not disagree with the doctrine of the two or more resurrections. It proves nothing either way.

---

349 Tan, *op. cit.*, p. 94.

# THE RESURRECTION OR RESURRECTIONS 455

But in John 6 we find four statements of Jesus that do prove something. These four statements state that the just will be resurrected (*raised up*, in most translations, but the word is *anasteso*, the future of the verb *anhistemi* of the same family as *anastasis* which is a noun). Regardless of the translation, the references are to the future resurrection of the righteous, and these place the resurrection of the righteous "at the last day." Let us note them.

"... that of all which he hath given me I should lose nothing, but should raise it up again at the last day" (John 6:39).

"... that every one which seeth the Son, and believeth on him, may have everlasting life: and I will raise him up at the last day" (John 6:40).

"No man can come to me, except the Father which hath sent me draw him: and I will raise him up at the last day" (John 6:44).

"Whoso eateth my flesh and drinketh my blood, hath eternal life; and I will raise him up at the last day" (John 6:54).

In these four verses we have a statement repeated four times. Evidently, Jesus did this for emphasis. And what was He emphasizing? He stressed the fact that the righteous would be resurrected on that day when time as we know it shall be replaced by eternity. Premillennialists teach that the wicked shall he resurrected at the last day, as do Amillennialists and Postmillennialists, but Premillennialists insist that the righteous are resurrected 1,000 or 1,007 years before the last day. Premillennialists who are also literalists are forced to spiritualize this passage by one means or another to make it consistent with their other teaching. Even so, their argument is very weak.

When read just as one would read any other book, these words mean that the sun will cease to rise every 24 hours after the just are resurrected. That is what I believe Jesus was saying, and that He said it four times to make sure we did not miss His meaning. Biederwolf argues that because one day with the Lord may be as a thousand years (II Pet. 3:8) that it does not follow that there shall be no more days after the resurrection of the just.[350] But this has the appearance of attempting to escape the force of these four expressions, rather than accepting them as Jesus meant them to be accepted.

The talk between Jesus and Martha after her brother's death has certain aspects that are similar to those of chapter 6, but it also has aspects that

---

350 Biederwolf, *op. cit.,* p. 394.

differ. Jesus said, "Thy brother shall rise again" (*anastesetai* from *anhistemi*) (John 11:23). This could just as well be translated "shall be resurrected." But was Jesus meaning that Lazarus would be resuscitated, or did He mean that he would participate in the general resurrection at the end of time? We cannot know for certain, for it could be either.

However, Martha took Him to mean the latter, for she said, "I know that he shall rise again in the resurrection at the last day" (v. 24). This indicates that Martha was familiar with the teaching of Jesus on this subject as is found in John 6. If Jesus did mean that He would resuscitate Lazarus, Martha was not able to accept this. But she did have faith for Lazarus' resurrection at the last day of time as we know it.

An effort to weaken the teaching of Jesus about the just being resurrected at the last day, rather than 1,000 years or more before the last day, is based on the claim that "the last day" in Jewish thinking referred to the last day or the closing day of the Jewish dispensation preparatory to the beginning of the Messianic kingdom. This was a Jewish misconception. It could be that this was what Martha had in mind, but it certainly does not prove that Jesus meant that. Jesus definitely did not go along with the Jewish idea of only pious Jews being involved in this resurrection. Jesus taught that all men would be resurrected at one time. And it has been shown in Part One that Jesus did not accept their idea of the Messianic kingdom. For these reasons we conclude that Jesus meant something quite different to the Jewish belief by "the last day."

That repentant people and unrepentant people will be resurrected at the same time is further indicated by the remarks of Jesus regarding that generation and the Ninevites. Jesus said, "The men of Nineveh shall rise [*anastesontai*] in judgment with this generation, and shall condemn it: because they repented at the preaching of Jonas; and, behold, a greater than Jonas is here" (Matt. 12:41). The term translated "shall rise" is from *anhistemi* and may be translated "resurrected" without violating the rules of Greek syntax. This indicates that all will be resurrected at the same time, and also judged at the time of their resurrection.

## Paul Taught But One General Resurrection

Luke records Paul as crying out, "But this I confess unto thee, that after the way which they call heresy, so worship I the God of my fathers… And have hope toward God, which they themselves also allow, that there shall be a resurrection of the dead, both of the just and unjust" (Acts 24:14-15). This is one of the instances where the Greek text does not have the definite article. Hence, it is translated "a resurrection" rather than "the resurrection." However, the use of the singular makes this almost as favorable to but one general resurrection as those passages which have the definite article. Paul here speaks of a single resurrection in which both the just and the unjust will participate.

Paul's statement cannot be twisted enough to make it fit the Dispensationalist view of several resurrections. They claim that "the harvest" resurrection occurs at the rapture of the Church. Seven years later, at His glorious appearing, they teach that a "gleanings" resurrection will occur. And if saved people die during the millennial reign which they envision, a third resurrection of the just is posited in addition to a resurrection of the wicked. This multiplicity of resurrections is not in agreement with Paul's use of the singular rather than the plural in this connection.

For Paul's statement to include these several resurrections, he would have had to use the plural form of resurrection for the just, and the singular form of the unjust. It would have to read something like the following: There shall be several resurrections of the dead; three or four for the just and a separate one for the unjust. But Paul does not do this. He speaks of a single resurrection or a general resurrection for both the just and the unjust. The Greek word used in this passage for resurrection is *anastasin*.

In Paul's famous resurrection chapter (I Cor. 15), he uses *anastasis* only four times, whereas he uses some form of *egeiro* 18 times. However, this should create no problem for the latter term is used several times of Christ's resurrection, hence does mean more than a mere resuscitation. The reason for Paul's preference for *egeiro* over *anastasis* is not known. For whatever reason it may have been, it has no affect on his teaching.

In an effort to make this chapter refer to a group of resurrections, Tan says that "Paul calls the resurrection of Christ 'the first fruits' (I Cor. 15:23), denoting a harvest scene of many 'fruits' (resurrections)."[351] Apparently, the Greek text was not consulted by Tan. The Greek term is *aparche*. It is singular—not plural. Paul uses it a number of times, always in the singular. Correctly translated, Paul speaks of Christ being a singular "firstfruit," rather than a plural "firstfruits."

---

351 Tan, *op. cit.*, p. 343.

The particular passage Tan refers to gives substantial evidence of a single resurrection with no millennial reign. Paul gives the simple order that has already occurred, and which will occur in the future. Of Christ's resurrection he says, "Christ the firstfruit(s); afterward they that are Christ's at his coming" (*parousia*). It has previously been shown that *parousia* refers to the second coming of Christ. The phrase, *"he deutera parousia"* which is translated "the second coming" was used a great deal by the early Church. This indicates that the *parousia* does indeed refer to His second coming.

And what follows the *parousia*? "Then cometh the end" (I Cor. 15:23-24). That which follows proves he means the end of the age. No millennial reign is even intimated in these verses. Surely Paul would not have omitted this period, if he anticipated such a period. Since he was writing to Christians, he does not mention the wicked; but we do know he believed they would be resurrected and that they would be resurrected at the same time as the Christians from Acts 24:15 which was discussed earlier. It is futile to try to make Paul teach several future bodily resurrections.

And it is just as futile to claim I Thessalonians 4:13-18 indicates more than one future bodily resurrection. As in I Corinthians 15, Paul ignores the wicked. He sees two groups of just people. Some are living and some are dead. The dead Christians are to rise first, then the group of living Christians will combine with the resurrected group and all will ascend together. Efforts to make this text say that the wicked will be resurrected later is either the result of ignorance or is prompted by a desire to deceive. Neither should be connected with biblical exegesis.

## Revelation 20 Does Not Teach Several Resurrections

Because this passage is obscure, it should not be made the basis or foundation for any doctrine. However, it is the only text in all of the Bible that speaks of a thousand year reign any time any place, therefore millennialists are forced to make it the capstone of their teaching. Without it, millennialism would never have gained the following it now boasts. But just as the text is obscure regarding the millennium, so it is obscure regarding any bodily resurrection. If it refers to a bodily resurrection at all, it is sufficiently obscure to make the question a debatable one.

The crux of our exegetical problem lies in the word *ezesan*, an aorist form of the word *zao*. Now, *zao* is used in a number of ways. It is used of God who is "the living God." It is used of Christians who "live by faith."

The "bread of life" and "water of life" are expressed by the noun form *zoe*. Over and over it is used of life without it meaning either a bodily resurrection or a spiritual resurrection.

For it to mean a bodily resurrection, two additional things would be necessary. First, the term would need to be *anazao* to convey the idea of living again. *Zao* simply means to live, whereas *anazao* refers to living again. It is unfortunate that the word "again" appears in the KJV in verse 5, something the Greek text does not justify. Also, something to indicate this living was the result of a bodily resurrection rather than a spiritual resurrection would be needed. Such an indication is lacking.

It is true that the expression "first resurrection" is used in Revelation 20:4, but we have shown that John makes the first resurrection a spiritual resurrection in John 5:25-29. Therefore, nothing is found in Revelation 20:4-6 which necessitates a bodily resurrection. In spite of the many voices which support such a claim, the claim is based on interpretation rather than true exegesis. Since the plain passages teach a single resurrection of the physically dead, it is best to interpret Revelation 20 in harmony with the plain passages.

## *Ek Ton Nekron* or "from the Dead"

This phrase has been considered already, but for the sake of completeness, a second consideration is necessary. Biblical writers used three expressions to convey the idea of a resurrection from the dead. A number of times no preposition is used. When this is done, it is always controlled by the genitive case. The normal translation in these instances would be the resurrection or the raising up "of the dead." When a preposition is used, it is either *apo* or *ek* with the latter being most frequently used. That there is no distinction in meaning between these two prepositions as they are employed in reference to a resurrection from the dead is proved by the fact that Luke uses both of them in a single passage.

In the conversation between the rich man and Abraham (Luke 16:24-31), the rich man contended that if some one from (*apo*) the dead would go to his brothers, they would repent (v. 30). Abraham contended that even if one rose from (*ek*) the dead, they would not hear. Now *apo* is normally translated "from," but *ek* is not always so translated. Since the argument stems around *ek*, further consideration of this term should be helpful.

*Ek* is normally translated "out" or "out of." It most often refers to coming out of some place, although it may refer to coming out of other things. For example, when Jesus was baptized, Matthew records that Jesus came up "out of" (from *apo* which literally is "from") the water: whereas Mark records that He came up "out of" (from *ek* which literally means "out of" the water. Many other examples of "from the dead" and "out of the dead" could be shown to have the same meaning.

Three major possibilities regarding the meaning of *ek ton nekron* must be considered. It could mean arising from the place of the dead. i.e., from the grave. It could also mean a change from the state or condition of being dead to the state or condition of being alive. A third possibility is that of arising from among the dead. This third possibility is the one that Premillennialists insist is the true meaning of the expression. Christ rose from "among the dead" it is true. But it is also true that He arose from the grave (the place of the dead), and from the state of the dead. Which was meant cannot be determined for certain. Similarly, it is impossible to determine the meaning of *ek ton nekron* when used of our future resurrection. It cannot be proved that it means "from among the dead." It may just as well have one of the other meanings.

Before leaving *ek ton nekron*, I wish to point out that this phrase is involved in two passages that show that Jesus' resurrection and our future resurrection are considered as distinct from resuscitations. In arguing for several resurrections, Scofield points to resurrections (resuscitations) of the Old Testament and also those who were resuscitated by Jesus. However, Jesus is said to be the "firstborn" (Col. 1:18) and the "first begotten" (Rev. 1:5) of or from the dead (*ek ton nekron*). He was the first of this kind.

## Concluding Remarks

The writers of the early Church wrote extensively on the future resurrection of the body. But any reference to two or more resurrections is very difficult to find. The fact that it would be most difficult to write on the resurrection without bringing in the number of resurrections expected, if one believed in more than one resurrection, forces us to conclude that most of the early churchmen did not believe in a number of resurrections. They believed in a general resurrection at the end of the gospel age, and only in this single resurrection. Of the few who were millennialists, Barnabas and Justin Martyr believed in but one general resurrection after the millennium was past. Thus they were Postmillennialists, rather than Premillennialists.

The twentieth century Church would do well to follow the lead of the early Church and discard the teaching of a number of different resurrections in point of time. Certainly, people will not have the same kind of resurrection, but this does not militate against the fact that all are resurrected at one time. Several resurrections cannot be adequately supported by plain texts of the Bible. Only by giving slanted interpretations to various passages, and by splicing these interpretations into a whole can the doctrine of several resurrections at different times be maintained.

CHAPTER 26

# A FINAL JUDGMENT OR A SERIES OF JUDGMENTS

Dispensationalists stress seven different judgments. Five of these have eschatological significance. These are the judgment of the works of believers, sometimes called the *bema* judgment, which is said to occur at the rapture. Seven years later they envision a judgment of nations and a judgment of the Jews at the glorious appearing of our Lord. After the thousand years, they see a judgment of angels and the judgment of the wicked. The latter is often referred to as "the great white throne judgment" (see Scofield's note on Rev. 20:12). Many Premillennialists do not accept all of these judgments. Amillennialists and Postmillennialists contend for a single final judgment of all men.

## The Judge's Identity

God is recognized as the Judge of all men (Heb. 12:23). This is further emphasized in Paul's letter to the Romans (Rom. 2:2, 3, 5). If one stopped at this point, his conclusion likely would be that God the Father would do the judging. But Paul explains his meaning further on in the chapter just cited. He adds that certain things would be true, "In the day when God shall judge the secrets of men by Jesus Christ according to my gospel" (Rom. 2:16). From this we know that God the Father is the author of the judgment, and in that sense He is the judge; but He judges mediately, rather than directly, through His Son Jesus Christ. Trinitarians should recognize that it is still God who will judge, for Christ is deity expressed in the Son.

That Christ will be the actual judge is reinforced by the declaration of Jesus: "For the Father judgeth no man, but hath committed all judgment unto the Son" (John 5:22). For these reasons, we must interpret passages which indicate God as the judge as meaning God the Son, rather than God the Father, as the presiding authority in the actual judgment.

Two passages require consideration in this connection. The better manuscripts read, "For we all shall stand before the judgment seat (*bema*) of God" (Rom. 14:10), rather than of Christ as in the KJV. In spite of this difference between Romans 14:10 where God (*Theos*) is used, and II Cor. 5:10 where *Christos* is used, we conclude that these refer to the same judgment, and that Christ is the presiding judge. The other is Revelation 20:12. The KJV has the dead standing before God. The better manuscripts indicate this should be "before the throne," rather than "before God." So the great white throne judgment is equivalent to the judgment seat of Christ.

It is sometimes claimed that some or all of God's people will participate in the judging procedures over angels and over the Israelites. The former stems from a misinterpretation of I Corinthians 6:3, which reads, "Know ye not that we shall judge angels?" Back in verse 2 Paul had indicated that "the saints shall judge the world." This certainly cannot mean that we determine the destiny of the wicked. All it means is that by living holy lives, we do by that means reflect on those people which sinned. It is in this same manner that we will judge or censure the angels that sinned.

The other text is a recording of the words of Jesus who said, "Ye which have followed me in the regeneration when the Son of man shall sit in the throne of his glory, ye also shall sit upon twelve thrones, judging the twelve tribes of Israel" (Matt. 19:28). Scofield's note on this verse places this in the so-called millennial kingdom, but no earthly throne could by any means refer to "the throne of his glory." This refers to the heavenly situation—not to any earthly reign. And it is questionable whether it should be interpreted literally or symbolically. If it is taken literally, the time element is still too obscure to build a doctrine on it.

## Who Will Be Judged?

In three separate texts we are told that the judgment will be of both the "living and the dead" (Acts 10:42; II Tim. 4:1; I Pet. 4:5). The apparent intent is to say that all men will participate in the judgment. Regardless of whether living or dead, and regardless of the kind of life one has lived, he will be judged at the final judgment. There is absolutely nothing in these texts to justify the idea of separate judgments for the righteous and the wicked.

After writing certain things regarding both Jews and Gentiles, Paul adds that "God shall judge the secrets of men by Jesus Christ" (Rom. 2:16). The implication is that all men will be judged whether Jew or Gentile, whether

# A FINAL JUDGMENT OR A SERIES OF JUDGMENTS 465

good or evil. In the next chapter he states that God would "judge the world" (Rom. 3:6). Although *kosmos* may be limited in its application in certain instances, there is no reason for so limiting it here. Just as God loved the world (*kosmos*), i.e., all the people of the world, so he will judge all the people of the world.

The Revelator tells us that the dead will be judged (Rev. 11:18). According to Dispensationalists, chapter 11 of the Revelation will be fulfilled during the first half of the seven year reign of Antichrist. But they also teach that the wicked dead will not be judged until after the millennium or more than 1,000 years later than the time they give for the fulfillment of chapter 11. This placing of the judgment of the dead, all of the dead insofar as exegesis can determine, right in the middle of the reign of Antichrist poses a tremendous problem for them. Accepted at face value, it throws their entire schedule and system of interpretation into a tailspin.

Dispensationalists, as well as many other Premillennialists, attempt to make chapter 11 agree with their interpretation of chapter 20 by claiming that the judging of the dead is stated proleptically rather than actually, and that the judging doesn't really occur until Revelation 20:11, and that it is for the wicked only. But this is not reading chapter 11 literally, as they repeatedly insist the Bible is to be read. Rather than attempting to twist this text by such means, I prefer to accept it as referring to the judgment of the dead, just as it claims to foretell.

But how can chapters 11 and 20 both tell of the same judgment? It has been shown elsewhere that just as Daniel was written in divisions that were parallel, so also is the Revelation. On this basis we claim that chapter 11 does bring us to the end of the age, and that chapter 20 also tells of the same time. Considering certain sections as parallel or resumptive affords a better explanation of the book than does the continuous historical. Having told of the end of time in chapter 11, John drops back to the struggle between the early Church and paganism (the woman versus the dragon) in chapter 12. Chapter 19 also brings us to the second coming of Christ and the end of the age, and likewise chapter 20 reverts back to the struggle with paganism (the dragon that was bound). This enables us to place the millennium of chapter 20 in the past instead of the future.

But many contend that the righteous will not he judged. This contention is largely based on the words of Jesus that believers "shall not come into condemnation [or judgment as most modern speech translations render it]; but is passed from death unto life" (John 5:24). Really, the KJV gives the correct meaning. Jesus means that no believer will receive an adverse judgment; such will not be accounted worthy of punishment. No sentence of death is to be passed upon them for they possess eternal life.

Peter informs us that "judgment must begin at the house of God" (I Pet. 4:17). That he refers to the righteous is plainly indicated by the use of "us" in verse 17, and the use of "the righteous" in verse 18. This, of course, refers to a judgment that is made day by day as one lives. Paul admits that "he that judgeth me is the Lord" (I Cor. 4:4). In this verse Paul adds the preposition *ana* (again) to the verb *krino*. It means to rejudge or to judge again if taken literally. It was usually used of reaching a decision after making a thorough investigation. So Paul recognized he was subject to investigation and judgment.

Paul goes even further in the previous chapter. Every man's work is to be tried by fire (I Cor. 3:13-15). That this refers to that final judgment when awards and penalties are meted out to all is clearly indicated by the expressions "the fire shall try every man's work," and of persons being saved "as by fire" (vv. 13, 15). The explanation Dispensationalists usually give of this judgment is patently false for it omits the fire. Scofield has no note on this passage, probably because the "fire" is a problem to him.

Scofield places his note on II Corinthians 5:10 which indicates that all must "appear before the judgment seat of Christ." His explanation that it is the believer's works that are being tried fails to recognize that the believer himself will be on trial. Since men are held responsible for their works, any trial of a man's works is a trial of the man. It is quite inconsistent to say Christians will not come into judgment, and at the same time admit that their works will be judged. It should be observed in passing that the trial of sinners is also based on their "works" (Rom. 2:5-11 and I Pet. 1:17). The Christian is just as much on trial when his "works" are tried as the sinner is when his works are tried.

Scofield in his note on II Corinthians 5:10 refers to the trial of the believer's works in I Corinthians 3:11-15. This enables him to ignore the fire that is so prominent in the latter passage. Pretribulation rapturists fail to explain this absence of fire in their teaching at this point. At the so-called rapture, no fire is evident. Lindsey writes, "However, in the Rapture, only the Christians see Him—it's a mystery, a secret. When the living believers are taken out,

# A FINAL JUDGMENT OR A SERIES OF JUDGMENTS

the world is going to be mystified."³⁵² No fire there. Lindsey does not deal with the trial which is supposed to take place in heaven, but Tan does. Tan also fails to mention the word "fire" or even hint at it in his discussion.³⁵³ And certainly the Bible does not indicate a separate trial of the righteous or of their works. This so-called trial of the works of the righteous separate from the trial of the wicked must be classified as a fabrication of men, rather than a teaching of the Scriptures.

Possibly the strongest argument against the righteous being judged is based on logic rather than the word of God. The argument is that it is illogical for persons like Paul who have been with Christ for centuries in the disembodied state to have to stand trial. But God's reasoning does not always follow human patterns. Doctrine must be based on the Bible—not on what we consider appropriate. Furthermore, it is no more illogical for sinners who have endured a period of torment to later stand trial, than would be true of those who are righteous.

Even more illogical, according to man's reasoning, would be the judgment of the evil angels. Premillennialists freely admit that these will be judged. But their destiny is sealed (Matt. 8:29). No plan of redemption is available for them. Yet, they are to be judged at "the judgment of the great day" (Jude 6). Peter also tells us that God has reserved them "unto judgment." This may appear illogical, but on closer examination it cannot be so classified.

Although some references speak of the final judgment as if it were a trial, other considerations indicate it will be more a time of meting out awards and penalties, more so than a trial to determine the destiny of each individual. If the judgment which is passed on each person at death is considered a preliminary judgment, to be superseded by a final decree at the final judgment, then it would not be illogical, even from human reasoning, for both saints and sinners to appear before Christ at His second coming. At this final judgment, the purpose may be to make known the degree of each one's guilt or faithfulness, and to mete out punishments and awards; instead of determining whether one is a saint or sinner.

## The Time of the Judgment

The time of the judgment can be established only in its relation to other events, for only God knows the date according to our manner of dating

---

352 Lindsey, *op. cit.,* p. 143
353 Tan, *op. cit.,* p. 143.

events. Paul informs us that God has "appointed a day in which he will judge the world in righteousness" (Acts 17:31), but Jesus informs us that the time of the second coming is known only by the Father (Matt. 24:36). And since Jesus placed the judgment as immediately following the second coming (Matt. 25), the time of the judgment as far as year and day is concerned is hidden from us.

That the judgment of Matthew 25 is the final judgment, rather than a judgment of nations as held by Dispensationalists, has been considered already. However, a review may be helpful. First of all, Christ will be judging from "the throne of his glory" (Matt. 25:31). This is the same as the great white throne from which the dead are judged (Rev. 20:11). Second, although they are gathered as nations, they are judged as individually. Third, it is the final judgment of the wicked, for they are consigned to "everlasting fire, prepared for the devil and his angels" (Matt. 25:41). Fourth, the righteous receive their eternal reward (Matt. 25:34). Fifth, an eternal separation is made. Matthew quotes Jesus as saying, "And these [the wicked who were on His left hand] shall go away into everlasting punishment: but the righteous into life eternal" (Matt. 25:46).

In his note on Matthew 25:32, Scofield distinguishes between this judgment and the great white throne judgment of Revelation 20 on three counts. His first objection is that no resurrection is indicated in Matthew's account. In answer, we say that it is implied. The fact that the righteous receive their eternal reward, and the wicked are consigned to eternal punishment, implies a resurrection. That this is the end of the age cannot be denied. If there is to be a resurrection of the dead, and I contend there will be, then it must be implicit in Christ's words, even though it is not explicit.

Scofield further contends that the scene is on earth. This is not true for Christ is sitting on "the throne of his glory" (Matt. 25:31). This is the same throne as we find in Revelation 20. No earthly throne could possibly be "the throne of his glory."

Scofield also objects on the grounds that this judgment occurs at the second coming. We concur in this. However, this fits in with what we expect at the second coming. It is our contention that the final judgment will take place at the second coming. Therefore, until it is proved that this is not the final judgment, Scofield's objection is worthless. That this is the final judgment has been proved in the preceding paragraphs. The dispensing of final awards and punishments is conclusive at this point.

# A FINAL JUDGMENT OR A SERIES OF JUDGMENTS

The final judgment will be closely connected with the resurrection. This is indicated in a statement which strongly condemned the generation of Jews then living. Matthew and Luke record the words of Jesus to the effect that "the queen of the south," i.e., the queen of Sheba, and the "men of Nineveh" would rise up, be raised up, or resurrected "in the judgment with this generation, and shall condemn it" (Matt. 12:41-42; Luke 11:31-32). Both writers in both references use the definite article with the term judgment (*krisei* in the Greek). It does not say, in one of several judgments. Rather, it refers to a singular event: "the judgment." And both the repentant Ninevites and the unrepentant Jews would participate in that one resurrection and that one judgment.

Both writers use a form of the verb *anhistemi* (resurrected) in referring to the Ninevites, and a form of *egeiro* (raised up) in referring to the queen of the south. The two terms are used interchangeably in this passage. But regardless of the term used, these verses indicate a single resurrection which involves all the dead whether good or evil, to be followed by a single judgment which includes all men.

Dispensationalists not only teach separate judgments for the just from the unjust separated by 1,000 years or more, but they also teach separate judgments for the Gentile nations as distinct from that of Jews, in addition to the judgment of the wicked which they believe to be the final judgment. All have been considered previously, except that of a separate judgment of the Jews. Some of the texts already used disprove this teaching.

Scofield's note on Revelation 20:12 has item 5 of the second paragraph which reads, "the judgment of Israel at the return of Christ" (Matt. 25:32, note). The time he sets for this judgment is correct, but there is no adequate reason for separating it from the general judgment which will occur at the second coming of Christ. The Bible indicates that Jews and Gentiles will be judged together.

Three paragraphs back it was pointed out that the queen of the south, the men of Nineveh, and the Jews would all be judged at the same time. In that paragraph the point was that the judgment of Matthew 25 did involve a resurrection, even though it was not stated in so many words. But the same verses show that Jews and Gentiles would be judged at the same time. This effectively eliminates the idea of several future judgments.

## Concluding Remarks

The doctrine of several judgments stems from a preconceived plan of eschatology, rather than exegesis of the texts dealing with the final judgment. The Bible passages that speak of people being judged regarding their total lives tell of a universal judgment—not of a piecemeal judgment such as Premillennialists envision. It has been shown that the judgment of Matthew 25 is an end of the age judgment. It has also been shown that it is identical to the great white throne judgment of Revelation 20. And it has been shown that the *bema* judgment, or the one at the judgment seat of Christ, is also an end of the age judgment, hence identical to the two mentioned above. The idea of a judgment of Christians separate from other judgments, and of nations at the second coming, and of sinners after the millennium, cannot be proved from Scripture. Devious wanderings are necessary to make such at all reasonable. Only one final judgment is needed or justified.

The early Church taught a single eschatological judgment. Few exceptions to this were found. Only one writer was found who taught a judgment of nations, and he taught that it would follow the millennium,[354] rather than precede it as Scofield and other Dispensationalists teach. Also, Lactantius had a different idea of the judgment. He held that only the righteous would be judged. According to his view, the wicked will have been judged at death, hence they will not be judged again. He based his opinion in part on the Septuagint version of Psalm 1:5 which indicates the wicked shall not rise in the judgment.[355] The KJV has "stand" instead of "rise."

It is doubtful that this verse applies to the final judgment. However, if it does, the interpretation given by Lactantius is to be preferred to that given by Premillennialists for these speak of the wicked rising in a separate judgment. This verse says nothing of a plurality of judgments. Rather than twisting this to make it say what they want it to say, it should be recognized that this verse has no eschatological significance.

We conclude that neither from the Scripture nor from the teachings of the early Church is there sufficient evidence to support the view that nations will be judged as such in the last days, nor that the righteous will he judged separately from the wicked. The teaching of the Scriptures and of the early Church agree on a single judgment of all men at the second coming of Jesus Christ.

---

354 Lactantius, *op. cit.*, vol. VII, p. 218.
355 *Ibid.*, p. 216.

# About the Author

Everett Carver held three academic degrees including a Master of Divinity from Southwestern Baptist Theological Seminary and a Master of Arts from the University of Houston. He was ordained to the ministry in 1936 and held pastorates in Arkansas, Louisiana and Texas.

From 1955 until his retirement in 1974, Reverend Carver was employed by Gulf-Coast Bible College. There he served as director of counseling and testing, as well as instructor in Bible, theology, and psychology. He retired with the title of Professor Emeritus.

Reverend Carver is the author of two other books plus several articles, tracts and booklets. His most recent ministry was serving two semesters as visiting instructor at a ministerial training institute in the Philippines.

## THE MISSION OF GREAT CHRISTIAN BOOKS

The ministry of Great Christian Books was established to glorify The Lord Jesus Christ and to be used by Him to expand and edify the kingdom of God while we occupy and anticipate Christ's glorious return. Great Christian Books will seek to accomplish this mission by publishing Gospel literature which is biblically faithful, relevant, and practically applicable to many of the serious spiritual needs of mankind upon the beginning of this new millennium. To do so we will always seek to boldly incorporate the truths of Scripture, especially those which were largely articulated as a body of theology during the Protestant Reformation of the sixteenth century and ensuing years. We gladly join our voice in the proclamations of— Scripture Alone, Faith Alone, Grace Alone, Christ Alone, and God's Glory Alone!

Our ministry seeks the blessing of our God as we seek His face to both confirm and support our labors for Him. Our prayers for this work can be summarized by two verses from the Book of Psalms:

*"...let the beauty of the LORD our God be upon us, And establish the work of our hands for us; Yes, establish the work of our hands."* —Psalm 90:17

*"Not unto us, O LORD, not unto us, but to your name give glory."* —Psalm 115:1

Great Christian Books appreciates the financial support of anyone who shares our burden and vision for publishing literature which combines sound Bible doctrine and practical exhortation in an age when too few so-called "Christian" publications do the same. We thank you in advance for any assistance you can give us in our labors to fulfill this important mission.

May God bless you.

For a catalog of other great
Christian books including
additional titles on
Eschatology
contact us in
any of the following ways:

write us at:
Great Christian Books
160 37th Street
Lindenhurst, NY 11757

call us at:
631. 956. 0998

find us online:
www.greatchristianbooks.com

email us at:
mail@greatchristianbooks.com